Skye and the Hebrides

Rock and Ice Climbs

Volume 1

The Isle of Skye

John R. MacKenzie and Noel Williams

Series Editor: Roger Everett

SCOTTISH MOUNTAINEERING CLUB
CLIMBERS' GUIDE

Published in Great Britain by the Scottish Mountaineering Trust, 1996

British Library Cataloguing in Publication Data
ISBN 0-907521-48-7

A catalogue record of this book is available from
the British Library

Diagrams by John R. MacKenzie, Mark Hudson and Noel Williams.
Maps by Jim Renny
Production by Scottish Mountaineering Trust (Publications) Ltd
Typeset by Elliot Robertson, Westec, North Connel
Printed by St Edmundsbury Press, Bury St Edmunds
and GNP-Booth, Clydebank
Bound by Hunter and Foulis, Edinburgh

Distributed by Cordee, 3a DeMontfort Street, Leicester LE1 7HD

Contents

Skye Outwith The Cuillin

List of Illustrations

x

List of Diagrams and Maps

The Climber and the Mountain Environment

With increasing numbers of walkers and climbers going to the Scottish hills, it is important that all of us who do so should recognise our responsibilities to the mountain environment in which we find our pleasure and recreation, to our fellow climbers, and to those who live and work on the land.

The Scottish Mountaineering Club and Trust, who jointly produce this and other guidebooks, wish to point out to all who avail themselves of the information in these books that it is in everyone's interest that good relations are maintained between visitors and landowners, particularly when there might be conflicts of interest, for example during the stalking season. The description of a climbing, walking or skiing route in any of these books does not imply that a right of way exists, and it is the responsibility of all climbers to ascertain the position before setting out. In cases of doubt it is best to enquire locally.

During stalking and shooting seasons in particular, much harm can be done in deer forests and on grouse moors by people walking through them. Normally the deer stalking season is from 1st July to 20th October, when stag shooting ends. Hinds may continue to be culled until 15th February. The grouse shooting season is from 12th August until 10th December. These activities are important for the economy of many Highland estates. Therefore, during these seasons consideration should be given to consulting the local landowner, factor or keeper before taking to the hills.

Climbers and hill walkers are recommended to consult the book HEADING FOR THE SCOTTISH HILLS, published by the Scottish Mountaineering Trust on behalf of the Mountaineering Council of Scotland and the Scottish Landowners Federation, which gives the names and addresses of factors and keepers who may be contacted for information regarding access to the hills.

It is important not to disturb sheep, particularly during the lambing season between March and May. Dogs should not be taken onto the hills at this time, and should always be kept under close control.

Always try to follow a path or track through cultivated land and forests, and avoid causing damage to fences, dykes and gates by climbing over them carelessly. Do not leave litter anywhere, but take it down from the hill in your rucksack. The number of walkers and climbers on the hills is leading to increased, and in some cases very unsightly erosion of footpaths and hillsides. Some of the revenue from the sale of this and other SMC guidebooks is used by the Trust to assist financially the work being carried out to repair and maintain hill paths in Scotland. It is important for all of us to recognise our responsibility to minimise the erosive effect of our passage over the hills so that the enjoyment of future climbers shall not be spoiled. As a general rule, where a path exists walkers should follow it and even where it is wet and muddy should avoid walking along its edges, the effect of which is to extend erosion sideways. Do not take short-cuts at the corners of zigzag paths. The worst effects of erosion are likely to be caused during or soon after prolonged wet weather when the ground is soft and waterlogged. A route on stony or rocky hillside is likely to cause less erosion than on a grassy one at such times.

Although the use of bicycles can often be very helpful for reaching remote crags and hills, the erosion damage that can be caused by them when used 'off road' on soft footpaths and open hillsides is such that their use on such terrain must cause concern. It is the editorial policy of the Scottish Mountaineering Club that the use of bicycles in hill country may be recommended on hard tracks such as forest roads or private roads following rights of way, but it is not recommended on footpaths or open hillsides where the environmental damage that they cause may be considerable. Readers are asked to bear these points in mind, particularly when the ground is wet and soft after rain.

The proliferation of cairns on hills detracts from the feeling of wildness, and may be confusing rather than helpful as regards route-finding. The indiscriminate building of cairns on the hills is therefore to be discouraged.

Climbers are reminded that they should not drive along private estate roads without permission, and when parking their cars should avoid blocking access to private roads and land, and should avoid causing any hazard to other road users.

Finally, the Scottish Mountaineering Club and the Scottish Mountaineering Trust can accept no liability for damage to property nor for personal injury resulting from the use of their publications.

The Mountaineering Council of Scotland is the representative body for climbers and walkers in Scotland. One of its primary concerns is the continued free access to the hills and crags that we now enjoy. Information about bird restrictions, stalking and general access issues can be obtained from the Access and Conservation Officer of the MCofS. Should any climber or walker encounter problems regarding access, they should contact him at the MCofS office, 4a St Catherine's Road, Perth PH1 5SE (Tel: 01738 638 227).

Acknowledgements

THE CUILLIN

Obviously this volume of the Skye and the Hebrides guide has depended to a significant extent on the previous guide book writers, who happen to include myself; this was the biggest spur to get it better this time. The guide has taken its time to gestate. Arduous checking, arguing, confusion and sometimes enlightenment has been encountered over the last few years and it soon became apparent that one person could not check the entire Cuillin range. Many climbers were press-ganged into helping check crags and one, Colin Moody, reclimbed all the routes on Sgurr Sgumain's north face, a fine crag that most visitors are abysmally unaware of. Such dedication in the face of inclement weather and doubtful rock shows the pull that the Cuillin exert.

I would also like to thank the following for invaluable help in the face of overwhelming odds:

Rab Anderson, Bob Brown, Ken Crocket, Graham Cullen, Dave Cuthbertson, Bob Duncan, Roger Everett, Mick Fowler, John Harwood, Roger High, Steve Hill, Kevin Howett, Mark Hudson, Pete Hunter, Mike Lates, Richard McLaughlin, Colin Moody, Andrew Nisbet, Paul Nunn, Clive Rowlands, Phil Thomas, Colin Threlfall.

For photographic help and advice I would also like to thank the following:

Mick Fowler, John Harwood, Roger High, Steve Hill, Gordon Stainforth, Phil Thomas, Colin Threlfall.

John R Mackenzie

SKYE OUTWITH THE CUILLIN

Only a handful of the routes outwith the Cuillin have appeared in previous SMC guides to Skye, so I am greatly indebted to numerous climbers for giving me their help and advice in compiling the information in this section. Firstly though, I would like to acknowledge the part played by the late Mike Geddes in arousing my interest in the dolerite sills of Skye.

Willie Jeffrey deserves a special mention for making countless trips from Edinburgh over the last fifteen years to help me explore the far corners of the island, at no small cost to his vehicles and my nerves. I also thank the following for their help and company on climbs: Stevie Abbott, Campbell Clark, Peter Duggan, Ed Grindley, Andrew Holden, Mark Hudson, Pete Hunter, Bruce Kerr, Gunars Libeks, Linda Taylor, Andrew Wielochowski and Carolyn Williams.

I received considerable help from certain climbers with particular areas. Neil Smith, Steve Hill, Rob MacDonald, Dominic Partridge and Andy Tibbs helped with Suidhe Biorach. Mark Hudson, Roger Brown, Andrew Holden and their team left no stone unturned at Carn Liath. Ed Grindley gathered most of the information on Staffin Slip South. George Szuca was enthusiastic in singing the praises of the upper crag at Neist. Bill Birkett, Dougie Dinwoodie, and Colin Moody gave me lots of help in several areas. Rab Anderson, Dave Cuthbertson, Kev Howett, Steve Kennedy, Ron Kenyon, Alan Kimber, Dave Leaver, John Mackenzie and Peter Thomas also gave me incidental help. I am also very grateful to Mark Hudson for producing his excellent crag diagrams and for his hospitality at Grealin.

Noel Williams

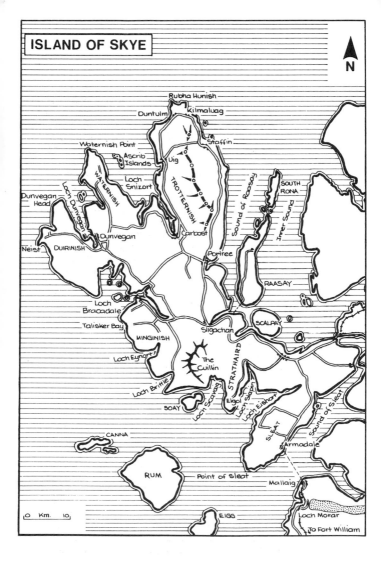

Introduction

If you love mountains then you will almost certainly love the Cuillin. A marriage between rock, water and sky, these are mountains unique in their ambience and configuration. A classic and near perfect horse-shoe provides the finest ridge traverse in Britain, whose flanks give a host of climbs on some of the finest rock imaginable. These are real mountains but on a human scale, and they present incomparable views across the western ocean to the dotted Hebrides and the mainland. Few places have such dramatic and sudden mist effects, vapour wraiths that form and dissipate making the ridge traverse anything but a static experience. Often, cloud inversions create a gloomy and damp mood down in Glen Brittle but up on the ridge blue skies and warm sun with views over peak-pierced cloud seas reign. The trick, of course, is to know when such conditions prevail and to recognise the more common frontal cloud that brings rain and midges – the so-called 'normal' weather expected in Skye. Spring and autumn are generally drier than mid-summer, but this is not invariably so. Look out for settled anticyclonic conditions and go!

The gabbro, a massive and crystalline plutonic rock, varies in colour from brown to orange, appearing almost black in certain lights. Coming in several varieties, it is mostly magnificent to climb on, giving routes that are sometimes harder than they appear, although this may also have something to do with the traditional Cuillin grades designed to suit the phlegmatic Harris-tweeded gentlemen and women who explored these mountains so ardently in bygone years. Some Cuillin traditionalists will have to stomach the fact that some, but not all, of these older routes have been upgraded to pander to the more sensitive and delicate modern climber. Modern gear has made the routes more protectable and it is rare that pegs need be carried. However, some of the bigger routes might still require them for belays and this is sometimes, but not invariably, mentioned in this guide.

Though most of the best lines have been climbed in summer, there is still an enormous wealth of virgin rock, particularly within the Coir'-uisg basin. Not all of these lines will be on perfect rock or with perfect gear, but it is inconceivable that there are not classics awaiting to be discovered. Although ideally climbed from the bottom up, a more circumspect abseil clean first may pay dividends, especially in areas that have been ignored in the past. In winter, much remains to be done and although a traverse of the ridge has to be the single best outing, there are major unclimbed lines on the crags. Winter conditions are more fickle than on the mainland, but it will not take too much imagination to see where some of these lines are.

Although most of the Cuillin visitors are anxious to complete a handful of classic climbs, well documented in books and history, remember that many others are as good, not as polished and less crowded. The star system that rates for quality should help to indicate the best of these climbs, but they may be found to be delightfully eccentric at times.

Take these mountains in the right spirit, bend with them and not against them and you will discover a freedom and joy that few, if any, other mountains can give. However, the mists of obscurity should never be allowed to finally clear from the Cuillin and with this philosophy in mind, there should still be plenty within to obfuscate and generally confuse those who believe guidebooks are all about clear directions and infallible grades. It is hoped that within those swirling mists there will still be some people who are happily climbing on a different crag from the one they thought themselves to be on, making the rock features fit the guidebook description and joyfully arguing about the grade for weeks to come. In many ways that is the essence of Cuillin climbing, you have to lose yourself to find yourself; the Cuillin are not just about individual routes or even individual mountains, but about a fragile symbiosis between ourselves, our aspirations and a unique mountain ridge, the sum of which vastly exceeds its individual parts.

SKYE OUTWITH THE CUILLIN

At one time there was little for the climber to do on Skye when the weather was bad in the Cuillin. This is no longer the case. In some of the most delightful corners of the island, which usually experience better weather than the mountains, there are now some very fine climbs. Although there is excellent climbing on quartz sandstone near Elgol, most of the better routes are on sills of dolerite. Some of the best jamming pitches in the country are to be found where the dolerite displays columnar jointing, such as at Kilt Rock. However, not all the climbing is as thuggish as this, and the lower grade climber can sample equally enjoyable routes at Flodigarry for example. Numerous sea stacks around the coast also offer adventurous outings.

Access to the island has improved now that the bridge is open. Regular visitors can benefit by buying books of ten tickets which halve the cost of the toll. Sea-cliff climbers still find Sligachan a reasonably convenient base. Discreet wild camping is possible at Neist, Kilt and Flodigarry, but fresh water can be surprisingly difficult to come by.

There is a campsite at Staffin, as well as Portree, and a youth hostel at Uig. Self catering flats can be rented in the lighthouse at Neist (now automated), and B&B is also available there by arrangement. It is possible to rent rooms in the former coastguard cottages at Duntulm, which are handy for Rubha Hunish.

There is a shop and tearoom in Glendale on the way to Neist, as well as a good cafe in Portree. The hotel at Flodigarry serves tasty bar meals, and of course there is a convivial atmosphere in the bar at Sligachan. What more could you want - apart from fewer midges?

Geology

Approximately 50 to 60 million years ago the area covered by Skye and the Inner Hebrides was essentially one of low relief. The rocks were of Pre-Cambrian gneiss and schists with areas of overlying Torridonian Sandstone. Overlying these basement rocks are younger Pre-Cambrian and Ordovician limestones (the Cambrian Blue series) and quartzites, whilst later still in the Jurassic period more limestone beds were laid down, together with shales.

This, together with sandstones, was the Skye landscape and it remained so until the edge of the tectonic plate which this area overlays was affected by volcanic activity at the start of the Tertiary Period. This outpouring of lavas was widespread, covering the Hebrides, Greenland, Spitzbergen and Iceland. Much of the lava was extrusive and took the form of the so-called Plateau basalts, together with slower cooling columnar dolerites. A thickness in excess of 800m of basalts accumulated in Skye, which in the later stages came from a few enormous volcanoes. Deep beneath this area a plutonic mass of molten rock eventually rose to form a dome that pierced the basalts, and although chemically similar to these quick-cooling, finely crystallised rocks, it was subject to a slower cooling regime in which the constituent minerals had time to form into a rock generically known as gabbro. Gabbro is a mixture of calcic plagioclase, pyroxene and usually olivine. It comes in several different varieties, although the only noticeable one is peridotite, an olivine-rich variety which is also the roughest and spongiest. It is found running in a wide arc from An Garbh-choire, across Sgurr Dubh an Da Bheinn and down the west side of Sgurr Coir' an Lochain, whilst an outlier occurs on Bealach Buttress.

The intrusion of the Cuillin pluton was accompanied by cone sheets and vertical dykes of basalt, injected through weaknesses in the gabbro. These basalts are fine-grained and markedly softer than the gabbros. The characteristic shape of the Cuillin today is largely due to the weathering of these injected rocks, which have formed preferentially into chimneys and gullies. Though most of the gabbro is sound, some areas of looseness occur when it is closely associated with basalt. All the basalt should be treated with suspicion because although it is superficially tough, it is very brittle and prone to failure.

The Red Cuillin are different, being formed after the intrusion of the Cuillin pluton. They are composed of granite and felsite of a finer crystal size, rough to the touch. The felsite of Marsco is very sound on the whole and it is free of the basalt sills and dykes, a point in its favour.

History

THE CUILLIN

Unlike many other Scottish ranges, the climbing history of the Cuillin is both well documented and heavily biased towards the exploratory (some would say predatory) urges of the English, often in the form of the Alpine Club. The geologist MacCulloch was the first to realise the difference between the hills of the mainland and the Cuillin and made seven partially horse-assisted but abortive attempts to reach summits. It was not until Professor Forbes scaled Sgurr nan Gillean in 1836 and Bruach na Frithe in 1847 that the vogue on the Cuillin began. Bla Bheinn was climbed in 1857 by Nicol and Swinborne, as was a new way up Sgurr nan Gillean by Inglis, the first guideless ascent, proving that motivation and initiative were not a recipe for sudden death. Despite local protestations, the Cuillin mirrored the birth of guideless climbing in the Alps and received similar mixed reactions.

Fortunately it was a local Skye man, Alexander Nicolson, who made the biggest impact on exploration, making the first ascent of the eponymous Sgurr Alasdair. Perhaps his greatest effort was the ascent of Sgurr Dubh in 1874 together with the first professional guide, John MacKenzie, a Sconser man, who was involved in practically every important ascent over a 50-year period. This particular epic involved the pair setting off up An Garbh-choire in September at 4pm and reaching the summit at 7pm. This entailed a descent in total darkness, using a plaid as a makeshift rope and finally reaching Coruisk by moonlight. It is unlikely that this feat has ever been emulated.

The Alpine Club arrived in earnest in 1880 in the form of the Pilkington brothers who climbed the Inaccessible Pinnacle by its East Ridge, the shorter West Ridge falling to Stocker and Parker in 1886. The long North Ridge of Sgurr Thearlaich was climbed by Charles Pilkington and John MacKenzie a year later. The unique practice (in Scotland) of calling a peak after its first ascensionist showed just how uncharted the individual peaks were; neither height nor accurate positioning was known, something unheard of in the Alps at that time. Sgurr Alasdair and the surrounding peaks of Sgurrs Thearlaich, Mhic Choinnich and Sgumain were all under the local generic name of Sgurr Biorach. MacKenzie was of course present when he climbed his eponymous peak in 1887, Sgurr Mhic Choinnich.

The first article on the Cuillin was published in the *Alpine Journal* in 1888, with the not inconsiderable exploit of an ascent of the Bhasteir Gorge by Clinton Dent: "I can recall no other recorded occasion on which any party ascended a mountain by water, since the days of Noah". Winter ascents were also recorded by Parker and Tatham in 1889, pioneers who realised the potential of such peaks under snow.

One of the greatest Cuillin teams, John MacKenzie and Professor Norman Collie, were active over the turn of the century, producing large numbers of routes including the discovery and ascent of The Cioch in 1906 as well as realising the magnitude of Sron na Ciche which effectively opened the way to its exploration and the swing in emphasis from Sligachan to Glen Brittle. An SMC member, the geologist Sir Archibald Geikie, appointed Dr Alfred Harker to draw up the first accurate map of the Cuillin and this encouraged other club members to to become more active. The English, however, were still to the fore with ascents of the redoubtable Waterpipe Gully direct in 1895, climbed by J.Kelsall and A.W.Hallitt. The less difficult Cioch Direct was climbed in 1907 by Harland and Abraham. This was the first open face climb in the Cuillin of importance and the scene of the memorably described first ascent and near fatal rock fall. Although classified as 'Exceptionally Severe' and now a more humble Severe, it is satisfying to record that this climb still sees the most awful thrutches and struggles in less than perfect conditions. These early activities were immortalised by Abraham's classic photograph.

A forceful approach to Deep Gash Gully (now HVS) in 1898 by Naismith and Gibbs, a Scottish pair and SMC members, saw partial success with the second pitch later 'nearly' falling to Shadbolt. Abraham's book *Rock Climbing in Skye* led to extensive pioneering by names known the Cuillin over; Steeple, Barlow, Buckle and Doughty. In fact Buckle and Barlow made an independent discovery of The Cioch, unaware of Collie and MacKenzie's earlier ascent. They made an unsuccessful attempt on the Crack of Doom in 1909, but a successful 600m girdle of Sron na Ciche. Together with MacRobert they produced the first guide, promptly doing a new route as soon as it was published, now a time-honoured custom. 1909 also saw the establishment of the Cuillin's most serious route for its grade by E.W.Steeple and H.E.Bowron, the classic Median on Sron na Ciche's Western Buttress.

1911 was an important year. Leslie Shadbolt and A. MacLaren succeeded on the Main Ridge Traverse, taking sixteen hours and forty-five minutes from Glen Brittle to Sligachan, including two and a half hours for rests; a good time by today's standards. Apart from this important event, the arrival of Archer Thomson and H.O.Jones, together with W.Wallwork and H.M.Kelly, saw such classics as Archer Thomson's Route and the undergraded Difficult of Wallwork's Route.

One of Skye's hardest climbs of the time was done without fuss in 1912 by C.O'Brien and E.L.Julian. North-East Gully is still graded Mild VS 4b and it represents a considerable achievement on a remote crag. Not many would lead it in nailed boots and a hemp rope today. Easier and a great deal more popular today is the classic Direct Route on Eastern Buttress, climbed by Steeple, Barlow and Doughty in 1912. A somewhat harder face climb, Trap Face Route, was climbed in 1914 by J.B.Burrell and C.N.Cross. Unlike many of the more modern (and often accidental) variations, the pioneers managed to find the easiest line. Mallory (of Everest) together with D.R.Pye and L.G.Shadbolt managed the more pleasant Mallory's Slab and Groove in 1918, and two years later Steeple and Barlow opened up the South Crag of Sron na Ciche with a number of good routes, of which the classic was and still is White Slab. Cioch West, an excellent and very popular Severe, was a product of C.F.Holland, H.R.C.Carr and Miss D.E.Pilley in 1919; it must have been a daunting lead at the time on a buttress that gave few clues away from below. The first solo of the Main Ridge was achieved in 1920 by T.H.Somervell in fourteen and a half hours who afterwards added "that with a water bottle and a pound of raisins he could better the time by an hour". Steeple and Barlow produced the Final Tower Direct on the edge of Sgurr Sgumain's North Face in 1920. Then graded Very Difficult, it is Hard Severe 4a by today's softer standards. After the publication of the next SMC guide to the Cuillin, another difficult route appeared, Amphitheatre Wall by Horne and Hughes, the same pair also climbing the long and easier Engineer's Slant.

The Greater Traverse was done in 1939 by Charleson and Forde in twenty hours from the summit of Gars-bheinn, a time cut by an hour by Bill Murray and R.G.Donaldson in the same year, inspired by the Wayfarers Club members ascending all the Munros in a single day.

Unlike the first World War, the second brought allied troops to train in the Cuillin under the leadership of E.A.M.Wedderburn and others. A particularly notable exploit by I.Allen in 1944 was Arrow Route on the seemingly smooth Cioch Slab, which despite appearances fell at Very Difficult, much to the amazement of his contemporaries who were convinced that the slab was a slick and holdless affair. Despite modern protection, it is still a fairly bold lead today. Active exploration reached a quality high point with the classic Integrity climbed by Haworth and Hughes in 1949 as well as Crack of Double Doom two years earlier by the same pair. The lesser known but good Rib of Doom was also climbed in 1949 by C.M.G.Smith and A.Cleland. A particularly strenuous venture was the first complete ascent of Deep Gash Gully in Coir' a' Mhadaidh in the same year by H.G.Nicol and A.S.Parker, now graded HVS and in some ways comparable to the better known Raven's Gully in Glen Coe.

The 1950s saw a general rise in standards and a move away from the 'gentleman climber' of the pre-war years. The Creag Dhu made their mark with Pat Walsh's mild extreme of Trophy Crack on the Cioch Upper Buttress, together with John Cunningham's Bastinado, which is distinctly harder. Climbed on the same day, they were the Cuillin's first Extremes. Cioch Grooves, an equally good but slightly easier route on Cioch Buttress, was climbed in 1957 by I.G.McNaught-Davis and G.H.Francis and freed of its aid point some years later to produce one of the most popular climbs in the Cuillin. Crembo Cracks, now free at HVS, was a bold lead by D.Gregory and R.Hutchison in 1958, despite the aid point on the superbly positioned top wall; it is still a bold lead today. Hamish MacInnes, Ian Clough and friends began an extensive exploration throughout the Cuillin, routes falling fast although not always without some assistance from the 'wee iron men'. Classics of that era are Creag Dhu Grooves, Strappado, Snake, Vulcan Wall (all on Eastern Buttress) and Shangri-La, an excellent VS on the West Face of Eastern Buttress. Clough and friends also extended J.D.Foster and B.C.Blake's good Sunset Slab of 1951 on the West Buttress of Sgurr Sgumain to create the excellent Yellow Groove Continuation. Sron na Ciche's Western Buttress received possibly its best route in 1957 with D.Leaver and J.Gott's superb Central Route, a climb making the most of its 300m length at a reasonable Hard Severe grade.

Sgurr Sgumain's rather forbidding north face attracted a few curious climbers who wished to know what lay either side of the original line of Wood-Johnson's route of 1932. The so-called Direct Route, which gives good but indirect climbing, gave a bold VS to D.D.Stewart, A.Colquhoun and P.V.Vaughan in 1957. This was subsequently straightened out by the better line of Frostbite in 1968 by M.J.Guillard and J.R.Irwin, and its even better companion, Purple Haze, the same year. MacInnes, earlier attracted to the cliff in 1957, climbed the splendid Prokroustes and the less good Prometheus, then hammered his way up the crux of Penitentiary Grooves a year later, fortunately freed by D.Dinwoodie and B.Lawrie in 1971.

The 1950s also saw the rediscovery of the Coireachan Ruadha face of Sgurr Mhic Choinnich by Bill Brooker, C.M.Dixon and R.W.P.Barclay. Dawn Grooves (1958), Crack of Dawn (1951) and Fluted Buttress

(1950) are three excellent lines, Crack of Dawn having the most serious climbing in Skye for its day, although not quite up to the other two for quality. Somewhat more friendly are the nearby Bealach Buttress routes, most of which were the product of the early 1950s, with Tom Patey, Bill Brooker, C.M.Dixon, R.Cra'ster and J.E.Monk featuring prominently.

More accessible places such as the Alasdair-Thearlaich crags were popular, with a good assortment of steep lines such as Commando Crack, Grand Diedre and its direct start being added to a cliff which had been neglected for thirty years. In 1921 Central Route had been climbed by the ever-active pair of Steeple and Barlow, a climb still graded Severe, and a follow-on from their earlier foray up West Gully in 1912.

Another classic is the Hard Severe Aesculapius (1958) by MacInnes and friends on the North-West Buttress of Sgurr Dearg, together with its equally worthy companion, Toolie Grooves, by Jimmy Marshall, C.L.Donaldson and G.Hood in 1953. A particularly bold ascent for its day was the HVS of Central Route on the South Buttress of Sgurr Dearg, climbed in 1950 by D.D.Stewart and D.N.Mill, possibly Skye's first 5a. Robin Smith also made his inimitable mark by adding to the remote crags of Sgurr nan Eag with the pleasant VS of Ladders in 1957, which he soloed, and the very serious Left Edge in 1957, now graded E1.

The 1960s was a period of extended exploration all over the Cuillin. The usual names of MacInnes and Clough crop up, as do those of John Harwood and Roger High, Robin Smith, Tom Patey, C.Boulton nad A.C.Cain. One of the Cuillin's best easier routes, Whispering Wall in Coir' a' Mhadaidh by Patey and Bonington, opened the sixties up. Thunder Rib, a loose and serious E1, was climbed by Robin Smith and G.Milnes in 1960. Particularly remarkable was the ascent of Thor in 1967 by Boulton and Cain, the island's second E2 and a big, bold route which sees very few ascents today. Other lines nearby that stand out are Harwood and H.Small's tricky Gail on the South-West Buttress of Sgurr Thuilm, a line that benefited from a thorough clean in 1992; Harwood, High, Evans and Small's exploration of the fine but neglected North-West Face of Sgurr a' Ghreadaidh, and the long and intriguing Goliath Buttress in Coir' a' Mhadaidh by Harwood and D.W.Robbins.

Elsewhere, exploration of the known crags produced Trojan and Spartan Groove by I.Heys, J.Firth and K.Roberts on the West Face of Eastern Buttress in 1965, thereby confirming the quality of rock on Eastern Buttress, with the latter climb still foiling many. The Alasdair-Thearlaich crags produced John McLean's Asp at E2, the Cuillin's first of that grade though a lesser proposition than Thor, and the easier but excellent Con's Cleft also by John McLean and friends, both being climbed in 1965.

In the Coruisk basin the exploratory urge was less intense, as ever. John Harwood and Roger High's Leviathan produced serious climbing on the crags of Sgurr nan Eag, whilst more pleasant climbing on the Mad Burn Buttress was found in two good Severes produced by Malcolm Slesser and Ken Bryan. The best find however was reserved for the forbidding Coireachan Ruadha face of Sgurr Mhic Choinnich when Bonington and Patey climbed the excellent and well protected E1 of King Cobra in 1960, a classic which is relatively popular despite the arduous approach. J.Barraclough and J.B.Cooper's Cocoa Cracks on the same crag was only marred by the almost permanent wet seep at the crux which forced the use of two aid nuts, now freed at E2 5c on one of the rare dry occasions. On Bealach Buttress, Barraclough and Cooper also climbed the steep and very fine Tinn Lamh Crack at E1, using a solitary nut for aid at the top; this was freed by John Harwood later. This is definitely a climb that deserves more popularity. Lesser known but on a good-looking crag, lie the routes on Coir'-uisg Buttress. Apart from the adventurous Original Route by C.M.G.Smith and R.C.Putman in 1949, the crag had to wait until 1966 for D.Chapman, J.R.Sutcliffe and P.L.Jackson to fill in the obvious gaps on excellent rock.

The Cuillin outliers also saw their maturity in the 1960s. The fine granophyre of Marsco had been neglected apart from Odell's eponymous route of 1943 and the equally pleasant Central Buttress by E.A.Wrangham in 1953. John Harwood and Roger High then climbed the best lines in 1968 with The Boojum and the impeccable Snark, one of the Island's great VSs.

Bla Bheinn's South Buttress became popular with MacInnes, Clough and friends, producing several good lines, notably the superb Very Difficult of The Outsider and the equally good VS of The Hem. The jutting Great Prow off the north-east wall of Bla Bheinn's East Ridge produced the superb-looking but rather over-rated VS of the Great Prow to a St Andrews University party of W.Tauber, T.W.Band, P.W.F.Gibbon and N.S.Ross in 1968. Despite any criticism of the quality of the climbing, the line is superb and it remains one of Skye's great and popular routes. The nearby and better Jib was climbed by Ian Clough and Hamish MacInnes, and again by Martin Boysen and Dave Alcock, in separate sorties in 1969. They used different starts over the worrying crux band and the climb still sees far fewer ascents than its more famous neighbour.

Higher up the East Ridge lies the rarely visited Main Wall which contains one particularly good line, the HVS of Ecstasis, climbed by C.Boulton, Paul Nunn and R.Toogood. This line has been compared to a harder but equally good version of Scafell's Botterill's Slab by those wise enough to have pushed past the crowds on the Great Prow. Over on Clach Glas, Ian Clough and party found the fine line of Sickle in 1968, on the north wall of Pinnacle Buttress. Not often ascended, it has been spoken of highly and probably deserves greater attention.

The 1970s saw a big breakthrough of technical climbs, particularly on the crack lines, due to better protection techniques. Eastern Buttress became and remains the Cuillin's most popular technical crag on excellent rock. Three routes stand out of that era, Mick Fowler and P.Thomas's Dilemma at E3, the free version of Creag Dhu Grooves at the same grade by Richard McHardy and G.Reagan, and Enigma also at E3 by Murray Hamilton and Dougie Mullin. The technical climbing here was matched by the E3 of Quark, the second great route of the trilogy on the North-West Face of Coir' a' Mhadaidh by C.Boulton and Paul Nunn in 1976, climbed with a single point of aid (freed by Tom Prentice and Calum Fraser in 1984). However the best and easiest of the trilogy was Megaton, climbed by a combination of Boulton, Nunn, Toogood, Boysen, and Braithwaite in 1972 and 1974. At E1 it was both long and not too hard with a point of aid. Unfortunately the crux ramp collapsed and although subsequent parties have freed the aid move at 6a, the remains of the ramp have deterred further progress. It is hoped that what was the Cuillin's finest Mild Extreme can be made climbable again either by natural stabilisation or by heroic cleaning after abseiling down the acres of rock to reach the loose section; any volunteers?

Wilf Tauber and J.S.Shade produced the oddly named Grannie Clark's Wynd on the North Face of Sgurr Sgumain in 1971, a fine climb only marred by a loose exit. On the Cioch Upper Buttress a fine if harder companion to Integrity, Atropos, was created from the remains of an earlier version by MacInnes and Clough, this time by Mick Fowler and P.Thomas in 1978. The original line was partially aided and also suffered a massive rockfall; now it gives solid and excellent climbing at E1. A significant pointer to the future was the free ascent of Overhanging Crack on The Cioch at E2 5c by Geoff Cohen and Murray Hamilton. Over on the Coireachan Ruadha face of Sgurr Mhic Choinnich, the usually wet but stunningly obvious line of Mongoose Direct also went at E1 to a combination of J.Lamb and Pete Whillance and Mick Fowler and P.Thomas in 1974 and 1977, when the direct linking pitch was dry enough to climb.

The seventies climaxed with Mick Fowler and P.Thomas's tremendous Stairway to Heaven, a mean E5 that climbs the impressively steep left wall of The Prow on Bla Bheinn. Despite being extremely well known due to exposure in various 'glossies', it is unlikely that it will attract the crowds in the same way as the neighbouring Great Prow. It seemed a high point in gabbro climbing, taking a big line on a big wall and in many ways it still represents the pinnacle of exploratory climbing in the Cuillin.

However, the 1980s continued the technical drive of the 1970s, together with an increase in exploration of entirely new areas that had until then been overlooked. Clive and Steph Rowland, Ken Hopper, A.Livesay and Paul Nunn continued the development of a large and seemingly obvious south-west facing crag to the left of Waterpipe Gully on Sgurr an Fheadain. On the accessible but practically unknown crag of Craig Druim Eadar Da Choire, Clive and his friends Ken Hopper, Ginger Cain, J.Smith and Paul Nunn produced about a dozen lines, of which the best, Cuckoo Waltz, produced in 1980 was probably only repeated in 1990 when all the lines were checked. Elsewhere, the Eastern Buttress of Sron na Ciche continued to produce superb lines such as the bold Spock by Pete Hunter and C.Lees at E3, a grade the crag seems to lend itself to, as well as the harder Confession at E4 5c. This was the Cuillin's boldest route at the time, produced in 1982 by Dave Cuthbertson and Garry Latter and a precursor to the island's second E5, Zephyr, which boldly follows the arete right of Creag Dhu Grooves, climbed by Dave Cuthbertson and Duncan McCallum also in 1982.

1983 saw the strong team of Pete Whillance, Murray Hamilton and Rab Anderson ascend the E3 6a of Lightfoot on Bealach Buttress, a fine line adjacent to Tinn Lamh Crack.

Another hard but well protected climb was produced by Cuthbertson and Latter on an area of rock near the toe of Eastern Buttress. Magic gives a superb crack climb at E4 whilst its companion crack to the right gave Rab Anderson and Murray Hamilton another excellent E3 called The Conjuror in 1983. Much more remote, but glaringly obvious for years, was the unclimbed crack line left of Naismith's Route on the Bhasteir Tooth. This gave a fine E3 to Steve Hill and T.Dickson in 1989, a reminder that those supposedly secret lines were no longer so and that complacency was no substitute for action. 1983 also saw the ascent of the small but difficult Erotica at E3 6b by Dinwoodie and G.Livingston, the first 6b in Skye and a logical continuation of the short but hard climbs increasingly in vogue in Britain. The obvious but unaccountably neglected line of what was to be called The Klondyker on the Western Buttress of Sgurr Sgumain produced pure gold for Andy Tibbs and D.Bearhop at an amenable HVS 5a and proved the rule that the glaringly obvious was usually the last to be climbed, especially in the Cuillin.

The opening years of the 1990s saw different faces but fewer major new crags being developed, apart from Sgurr Hain where a combination of T.Walkington, A.Cunningham and M.Smith began the development of this low level and reasonably accessible crag. Another obvious line, Hearthammer, by Grahame Nicoll, K.Noble and A.Chamings on Sgurr an Fheadain's South-West Face at E3 showed the quality climbing at a reasonable grade to be found on accessible big crags. The continued development of The Cioch by G.Farquhar and G.Latter resulted in the Cuillin's first E6 6b, the arete of The Highlander, a thoroughly modern route. On a more exploratory approach, Sgurr Sgumain's North Face provided a good HVS to Colin Moody and M.McLeod in 1994. In fact Colin and friends explored the North Face, repeating all the existing lines in the process of checking the guide, probably the only person to have an intimate knowledge of a major Cuillin crag. Eastern Buttress, now undoubtedly the best high standard crag in the Cuillin, saw the superb Uhuru at E3 5c, by Kevin Howett and Tom Prentice in 1990 and the equally good Pocks at E2 5c by George Suzca and Colin Moody in 1988; the second pitch was added by Moody and N.Smith in 1992. To the right on the West Wall, the aptly named Helen (sandwiched between Trojan and Spartan Grooves) gave Steve Hill and Colin Moody an apparently excellent E3 6a.

1990 also saw the culmination of exploratory climbing on Druim Eadar Da Choire by John Mackenzie and Graham Cullen, who repeated the existing routes and added some others, of which Rites of Passage at E1 5b gives the best climbing on the crag while Black Magic at E2 5c is the hardest so far. The latter had been attempted by others earlier on sight, which resulted in a bad fall from the main pitch; it was more cautiously pre-cleaned by Mackenzie before its ascent in 1990. On the same crag and on the same day, a bold direct start to the superb Cuckoo Waltz at E2 5b was added by M.Haltree, M.Frew and S.Price.

Much remains to be done in summer in the Cuillin, the weather and the lack of exploratory urges remaining the biggest drawbacks to this. A few hot summers and a few bold spirits would see routes of all grades blossom.

On a bizarre note, the most unusual event of 1992, and one which posterity should record, is the following: (10/6/92). "The phantom of Sir Hugh T.Munro, in the form of a full size effigy, completed his posthumous traverse of all the Tops today by ascending the Inaccessible Pinnacle of Sgurr Dearg. He was accompanied to Sgurr Dearg summit by R.N.Campbell (who else!) and H.E.Ross. A passing Yorkshire climber, J.Kenyon, joined forces with Campbell to help convey Sir Hugh to the Inaccessible's summit, whilst Ross remained below to record the occasion on film. After abseiling onto Sgurr Dearg, all four enjoyed a celebratory bottle of champagne before returning to Glen Brittle. Sir Hugh's round of the 538 Tops of his 1891 Tables was begun in 1870 with an ascent of Ben Lawers; his compleation span of 122 years is most unlikely to be bettered."

In winter, the Cuillin provide something quite different from other hills in Scotland; the easy ways off are often not so and the time involved on short days requires early starts. However, this did not deter the pioneers who ascended all the peaks. The first known winter climb, and one that has never received the recognition that it deserves, was the ascent at Easter 1915 of The Chasm of Sgurr nan Eag by G.Barlow and E.W.Steeple. (Their first summer ascent of the same route was done four years later).

The greatest of all Cuillin prizes, The Main Ridge Traverse under true winter conditions, had to wait until 1965 when Patey, Robertson, MacInnes and Crabbe delivered the goods under full conditions.

Other ascents multiplied over the following winters, and it would seem that most winters have a period of stable cold conditions, even if short, whereby a traverse is possible. A degree of chance and luck with the weather and being at the right place at the right time helps. Winter ascents of the numerous faces and gullies in which the Cuillin abound were only achieved sporadically. Pinnacle Ridge on Sgurr nan Gillean gave W.L.Wood and party a tremendous outing at Grade III in 1947 and has continued to give such outings ever since. Skye's first Grade V, an ascent of Frankland's Gully by Clive Rowland, P.Cairns and B.Ledingham in 1981, was a significant and technical outing, possibly unrepeated and not given the credit that it richly deserved.

Other easier and earlier winter ascents include Abraham's Climb on Sgurr Alasdair at Grade III/IV by C.M.Dixon and J.W.Morgan in 1952 and Collie's Climb at Grade IV by Rowland and friends. Both of these give excellent climbing to the highest peak in Skye. The fine and accessible Little Gully gave a short but concentrated Grade III/IV to Roger O'Donovan and M.Chalwin in 1970, whilst the prominent North-East Gully of An Diallaid gave D.Rogerson and Martin Eastwood a fine Grade III in 1978. The most obviously challenging of all the Cuillin gullies, Waterpipe Gully, was eventually ascended in 1986 by B.S.Findlay and Greg Strange on 24th Febuary and a complete ascent was made by Colin Downer and Doug Scott on the 28th February. Expecting the chance of a lifetime, the pioneers were a bit disappointed in that the pitches were separated by walkable snow and the whole climb was, overall, Grade IV. However, this is not to say that leaner conditions might not produce an altogether harder and better climb. It was the ubiquitous Mick Fowler who left the greatest mark on classic Cuillin ice. His ascent with T.Saunders in 1986 of the classic South Gully in Coir' a' Mhadaidh gave a good Grade III/IV, although again this was largely banked out and leaner conditions would give something different. The same year saw the same team ascend the formidable and superb Icicle Factory at Grade V in Coir' a' Mhadaidh, the Grade V being a rather traditional grade in keeping with certain other Cuillin routes in summer.

An earlier icefall climbed nearby by J.Duff and D.Scott in 1979 gave the Smear at Grade V whilst in the South Branch of Coire a' Ghreadaidh, White Wedding at Grade IV gave Fowler, Saunders, and C.Watts a fine outing in 1986. However the Cuillin gully that gave 'the mostest' was undoubtedly Deep Gash Gully in Coir' a' Mhadaidh. Climbed by two parties on the 2nd and 14th February 1991, the ascent was considered Grade VI and was both 'formidable and atmospheric'. Needless to say Fowler and J.Lincoln were there on the 2nd and the local team of Martin Moran and M.Welch there on the 14th, not knowing of Fowler's successful raid.

Much more reasonable and just as good was the ascent of the prominent B Gully on Clach Glas which gave a fine Grade IV to S.Kennedy and D.Ritchie in 1991, and even the relatively low-lying Druim Eadar Da Choire gave a good ice climb up Seilg Gully at Grade III/IV to R.MacDonald, S.Hill, D.Benn and M.Francis.

SKYE OUTWITH THE CUILLIN

Given the attractions of the Cuillin, it is perhaps not surprising that climbing interest in the rest of the island was slow to develop. Early ascents were concentrated on pinnacles and stacks. Harold Raeburn climbed a minor pinnacle at Storr in 1898. "We will not venture to assert that the Old Man will never be ascended, but we were quite content to look at him without making an attempt." It was left to Don Whillans to show the way in 1955. His remarkable ascent continues to impress modern climbers. Ian Clough and John McLean climbed the largest of Macleod's Maidens in 1959. Over the next two years Tom Patey teamed up first with Chris Bonington to climb The Cathedral, then with Fred

Harper to climb The Green Lady - the latter being the first route on dolerite at Neist. Ascents of Stac an Fhucadair and The Needle followed.

It was some time before Patey's enthusiastic comments about Neist were acted upon. Mike Geddes paid a visit in December 1977, and together with Noel Williams put up Two Step and Side Step near An t-Aigeach. This aroused Williams' interest in the line of Supercharger. However, it took a further ten visits, some lengthy cleaning sessions, and the services of a rejuvenated Ed Grindley, before the route was climbed in August 1981. Meantime Mick Fowler had visited Neist and climbed Waterstein Arete. Pete Whillance, Dave Armstrong and party spent the following New Year at Neist. In cold conditions they put up a number of fine routes including Lightning Corner, Wind and Wuthering, and Cold Turkey (all at HVS), California Dreaming, Cold Comfort Corner, and Frigid Air (all at E1), as well as the slightly harder Breakfast in America (E2/3 6a).

Things really started to hot up in 1983, when over forty new routes were created. Some homework with a geological map helped identify the dolerite sills at Staffin. Grindley led Road to Ruin (E2) - the first line at Kilt Rock - at the end of April, and the following day Dick Swinden led Internationale (E3). Williams unearthed the tamer, but enjoyable Clandestine(VS), which had its second ascent by Pete Hunter and Willie Jeffrey the same day. Grindley returned to climb Wide Eyed and Footloose, and Richard McHardy led him up Fancy Free. Meanwhile Murray Hamilton and Rab Anderson, in company with Bob Duncan and Kenny Spence, were finding some fine lines at Neist including Groove-less Bodily Harm (E4 6a), Starfish Enterprise (E4 6b), and Cool Breeze (E4 6a). Bruce Kerr also succumbed to Temptation (E1) on the upper crag.

In July, Grindley signed off at Kilt Rock with the classic Grey Panther (E1). Hunter, Jeffrey and Williams stayed on and climbed another dozen routes, including Skyeman (E2), Edge of Beyond (E2), Ruination (E3), and some surprisingly good routes on the descent gully walls, including Electric Bagpipe (HVS), and Secret Service (HVS). Later that summer Bill Birkett made his first appearance at Staffin to climb Killer Whale (E4 6a). Finally, in November, Hamilton, Dougie Dinwoodie and Colin MacLean developed Lighthouse Wall at Neist.

The next three years were somewhat quieter. In 1984, Birkett, Bob Wightman and T. Walkington added several lines at Staffin including The Tempest (E3 6a) and Drop The Pilot (E4 6a), and N. Smith, G. Bisset and S. Reid had a Joint Experience (Severe) at Neist. In 1985 Birkett climbed Over The Rainbow on the sensational Chimney Stack to give the first E5 outwith the Cuillin. John Hargreaves and Bill Birkett climbed a stack at Rubha Hunish in 1986 - the first route recorded at the most northerly tip of the island.

There was more activity in 1987. Dinwoodie forced some good lines at Staffin including Iron Crow (E3 6a), and The Great Deep (E3 5c). He also opened up the Fallen Pillars area and climbed the first route on the Staffin Slip buttresses - Dawn of Time (VS). Grant Farquhar and Graeme Ettle girdled Kilt Rock with Brightside Crossing (E2), and Garry Latter added another hard line to the Chimney Stack with Sheer Sear (E5 6a). John Hargreaves, Bill Birkett and Fred Snallam climbed two more stacks and Opening Gambit (E1) at Rubha Hunish. C. Waddy and G. Percival had a productive three days in June adding Black Crow King (E3 6a), Fe Fi Fo Fum (E3 5c) and Ill Wind (E5 6b) at Staffin. Possibly the most notable event that year was Graeme Livingston's lead of Death Pirate at Neist - the first route on the island to attract an E6/7 6b grade. This was two years before the ascent of The Highlander (E6 6b) on the Cioch, which is the only route of comparable difficulty on the island to date.

Later in the summer Williams and Jeffrey pioneered the first routes on Suidhe Biorach near Elgol, with Fertility Right and Fertility Left. Birkett and Grindley teamed up to do Staffin Classic (HVS) - the first route on Staffin Slip North. The following spring saw the rapid development of Staffin Slip South by Ed Grindley, Ian Sykes and a strong team from Yorkshire and the Lakes - Ian Blakeley, Colin Downer, John Hargreaves, Gunars Libeks, Al Pounder, Ron Kenyon, Steve Suthorn, Luke Steer, and Bill Birkett. Among the many outstanding routes climbed were Green Vote (E3 5c), Gorbachev (E2), Experimental Learning (E3 5c) and Woman of the Eighties (E3 5c). The only other area to see activity that year was Neist, where Stoor and Birkett added Neist an' Easy (E1) and Golden Mile (E3 5c).

In early May of 1989 Willie Jeffrey jammed his way doggedly up Whispering Crack (E3 5c) at Rubha Hunish to snatch one of the plum lines on the island, (on the same day as the SMC's centenary dinner). The following day Jeffrey and Williams found a new crag for the lower grade climber at Flodigarry and opened their account with the immaculate Rock Island Line (Severe). The last weekend of May saw simultaneous activity in several different corners of the island. George Szuca and party climbed Karen (VS) among a number of routes on the upper crag at Neist. Four new routes were added at Staffin Slip. These included Birdman of Bewaldeth (E3 5c) with Colin Downer leading. Meanwhile at Rubha Hunish Keith Milne lead The Red Barron Flies, so named because Ian Barron took a spectacular fall the same day attempting Fly Man. Jeffrey and Williams also visited Rubha Hunish and were astonished to encounter other climbers. They retreated to Flodigarry the next day, where they climbed Buoy Racer (VS).

In June, Dave Leaver took Jeffrey and Williams up to inspect Carn Liath. They could not believe that such an impressive crag of good rock was still untouched. In cold conditions they climbed a scrappy route on the right-hand side of the main crag, although their attention was drawn to the compelling line up the highest section of the face. They returned to this later in the year, and carried out two mammoth cleaning sessions. Jeffrey lead the direct start pitch (of what was to become Prospect of Rona) before rain stopped play. A delay in following up this effort proved costly and Mark Hudson, his father and friends were soon to make the crag their own.

In July, Mark Worsley forged his way up The Cruiser (E1) at Neist, and the following month McLeod and Moody found The Danglers (E1) at Kilt. In September Williams and Jeffrey added another line at Flodigarry. Grindley stumbled upon their belay stakes a few weeks later. He was so incensed about this unreported activity, that he raced up the top pitch of Tresspassers Will be Prosecuted, before climbing the bottom one. He then planted decoy stakes on the cliff top above unclimbed lines. Having found out that Jeffrey and Williams were the competition, he returned a few weeks later with Gunars Libeks to add two more routes.

The following spring Williams and Grindley joined forces and between them added more than a dozen routes to the Flodigarry buttresses. Grindley put up Councillor Dubh (E2 5b/c), and Williams lead Jeffrey up Lucy in the Sky (HVS), and the amazing Spantastic (HVS). Grindley, Libeks and Williams went out on a limb to make the first ascent of Stac Buidhe. Grindley's Sasha (E3 5c) was the best of four new routes done at Staffin Slip. Grindley took in The View (HVS) on Ellishadder Wall, and later Colin Moody grabbed Bandasky (E1).

George Armstrong and George Szuca were active at Neist in September, and among their finds was a superb pitch on the upper crag - Wish You Were Here (E1 5b). Grindley and Williams shared leads to pioneer Goofus Band (HVS), the first route on Sgeir nan Eathar Bàna at Kilmaluag.

Not as many new routes were done in 1991. Colin Moody led Entrevennes (E1) on Ellishadder Wall and Horny Corner at Neist. However, the best crop appeared on Carn Liath where Mark Hudson scooped a number of routes including Prospect of Rona (E1) on the main cliff, and The Blade (HVS). Bill Birkett switched on the spectacular

Northern Lights (E2) at Rubha Hunish in September. Developments continued at Carn Liath in 1992, with Mark Hudson completing the original finish to Hearts Highway, and opening up Thief Buttress. Mark Garthwaite climbed a wall of superb rock on the upper crag at Neist to give Route with a View (E3 6a). He then forced the sensational crack line on The Fin to produce Heavenley's Pleasure (E5 6a). N. Carson and D. Carson climbed a very impressive finger crack on Ellishadder Wall to create Y Bilidowcar (E4 6a). Rob Macdonald stirred up interest in Suidhe Biorach, by climbing Jamie Jampot (VS) and Crack of Zawn (E1). Colin Moody started his campaign on the north side of Bay 3 at Neist by producing Tinderbox with N. Horn.

Activity showed no signs of abating in 1993. Neil Smith snatched the superb India (E3) at Suidhe Biorach. On Carn Liath, Dave Brown climbed The Judge (HVS) and The Big Easy (HVS), and Andrew Holden lead Arbocranker (E2). Luke Steer was still under the influence when he lead Frisky After Whisky (E3 5c) at Kilt. Bill Birkett experienced Northern Exposure (E2) to find the longest route at Rubha Hunish, and Simon Richarson completed a set of new lines on the sea-stacks there.

In 1994 Dominic Partridge powered up the outrageous prow at Suidhe Biorach to give Mother's Pride (E4 5c). Jeffrey found Reach for the Sky (E1) at Flodigarry. At Carn Liath, Dave Brown led Silence of the Lambs (E1), and Mark Hudson climbed the superb and photogenic Bengal Lancer (E2). At Neist, Colin Moody filled in a number of lines on the lower crag including Warmer Cleaner Better (E3 6a), and Williams found the enjoyable Baywatch on the upper crag. On the Staffin Buttresses Birkett deployed monster camming devices to climb the meaty Heracles (E2). At Rubha Hunish Jeffrey and Williams completed a long standing project by climbing Minch and Tatties (E1).

By 1995 developments at Staffin, Carn Liath and Suidhe Biorach were tailing off, but a burst of renewed activity at Neist yielded some surprisingly good routes. Supercharger gained a good companion when D. Holmes, A. Cave and C. Waddy climbed Perfectly (E5 6a) on An t-Aigeach. On the upper crag Williams and Abbott cleaned and climbed Wall Street (E2), Venture Capital (E1), Insider Dealing (HVS) and two pleasant VS routes, Sonamara, and Shocks and Stares. Colin Moody climbed A Haggis Called Wanda (E2) on Ellishadder Wall, a line which lots of climbers must have walked past before.

In 1996 Jeffrey climbed Blockbuster (HVS) at Neist, a route with an interesting leap back onto the cliff top to finish. Just as the guide was nearing completion, Stevie Abbott led Powerbroker (E1) and Terminal Bonus (HVS) at Neist, and Colin Moody slipped in a couple more routes on Lighthouse Wall. At the very, very last moment, Willie Jeffrey snatched three remarkably different E1s at Neist - A Fist Full Of Dollarite, Security Risk and Bridging Interest, and Bill Burkett found Friends of the North (E2), another big route at Rubha Hunish.

And the future? Well, the main phase of exploration seems to have passed, but there are undoubtedly still plenty of lines left to do. Some stiff challenges await the E5 climber on Carn Liath for example, and those prepared to spend time cleaning can still uncover good routes of all grades.

Notes on the Use of the Guide

CLASSIFICATION OF ROUTES

Summer

For summer rock climbs the following grades have been used: Easy, Moderate, Difficult, Very Difficult, Severe, Hard Severe, Mild Very Severe (Mild VS), Very Severe (VS), Hard Very Severe (HVS), Extremely Severe. The Extremely Severe grade has been subdivided into E1, E2, E3, E4, E5 and E6, in keeping with the rest of Britain.

Technical grades are given for routes of VS and above where known. Much effort has been made to elicit information from active climbers about routes, some of which will have all the relevant pitches graded while others will have only the crux pitch so described. The normal range for technical grades expected on routes of the given overall grade are as follows; VS – 4b, 4c, 5a; HVS – 4c, 5a, 5b; E1 – 5a, 5b, 5c; E2 – 5b, 5c, 6a; E3 – 5c, 6a; E4 – 5c, 6a, 6b; E5 – 6a, 6b. Routes with technical grade at the lower end of the range will be sustained or poorly protected, while those with grades at the upper end of the expected range will most likely have a shorter and generally well protected crux.

Although the British system is thought second to none by those familiar with it, it is known to confuse visitors from abroad. For their benefit, it can be assumed that 5a, 5b, 5c and 6a correspond to the American grades of 5.9, 5.10a/b, 5.10c/d and 5.11a/b respectively. Eurocraggers should note that there is little or no fixed protection on these routes and if they are used to cruising bolted French 6c, they may suffer some distress while attempting the corresponding 6a pitches here, with their sometimes spaced and fiddly protection. Grading information is in some cases scanty or even lacking, particularly in some of the older or more obscure routes; climbers should therefore be even more circumspect in their approach to such routes. Further information about any routes is always welcome.

Winter

Where possible, the harder winter climbs have been graded using the two-tier system in which the Roman numeral indicates the overall difficulty of the climb and the accompanying Arabic numeral represents the technical difficulty of the hardest sections of climbing. This is built on the old Grades of I to V, which was previously used. The grades of climbs from Grade IV downwards remain unaffected, and the new technical grades have been applied only to a minority of the harder routes where the information is available. Both parts of the grading system are open-ended.

Grade I — Uncomplicated, average-angled snow climbs normally having no pitches. They may, however, have cornice difficulties or dangerous run-outs.

Grade II — Gullies which contain either individual or minor pitches, or high-angled snow with difficult cornice exits. The easiest buttresses under winter conditions.

Grade III — Gullies which contain ice in quantity. There will normally be at least one substantial pitch and possibly several lesser ones. Sustained buttress climbs, but only technical in short sections.

Grade IV — Steeper and more technical with vertical sections found on ice climbs. Buttress routes will require a good repertoire of techniques.

Grade V — Climbs which are difficult, sustained and serious. If on ice, long sustained ice pitches are to be expected; buttress routes will require a degree of rock climbing ability and the use of axe torquing and hooking and similar winter techniques.

Grade VI — Thin and tenuous ice routes or those with long vertical sections. Buttress routes will include all that has gone before but more of it.

Grade VII — Usually rock routes which are very sustained or technically extreme. Also sustained routes on thin or vertical ice.

Grade VIII — The very hardest buttress routes.

The technical grades which are shown by the Arabic numbers, are based on the technical difficulty of classic winter routes of Grade V only. This is used as a basis for assessing the technical difficulty of the route, while the Roman numeral gives an indication of the overall seriousness of the climb, in a very similar way to which the E grades and the numerical grades are used in summer. In this way a V,4 is normally a serious ice route, V,5 would be a classic ice route with adequate protection, V,6 would be a classic buttress route and V,7 would indicate a technically difficult but well protected buttress route. Each route is of the same overall difficulty (V) but with differing degrees of seriousness and technical difficulty.

Equipment and Style
It is assumed that a good range of modern nuts and camming devices will be carried for the harder climbs, both in summer and winter. The summer climbs described in this guide are graded assuming the presence and stability of any of the *in situ* pegs that are mentioned. If

pegs are essential on new routes, it is hoped that they will be kept to a minimum and left in place; please keep to the Scottish tradition of bold climbs with leader-placed protection. Please make every attempt to find a safe alternative to pegs before resorting to them. Unfortunately, pegs are still necessary on some winter routes to make them acceptably safe. This tends to be more often the case on the harder gully climbs than on the better rock of the buttress routes.

Left and Right
The terms left and right refer to a climber facing the direction being described, i.e. facing the cliff for route descriptions, facing downhill in descent.

Pitch Lengths
Pitch lengths are in metres, rounded to the nearest 5m. The lengths are usually estimates, rather than measurements. Although 50m ropes are popular, 45m ropes should be sufficient for most climbs. Where pitch lengths greater than 50m are given, this does not indicate moving together, merely belay where required or desired.

Recommended Routes
No list of recommended routes has been given, instead a star grading system for quality has been used. Stars have been given as a selection guide for occasional visitors and consequently have been allocated throughout the grades. Many of the routes without stars are still very good. Starred routes on different cliffs may vary slightly according to the quality of the cliff. Winter stars are a problem because quality will vary with conditions, so stars, like the grade, have been applied for average conditions which may not exist at the time.
*** An outstanding route of the highest quality, combining superb climbing with line, character, situation and other features which make a route great. Could compare with any route in the country.
** As above, but lacking one of the features while having similar quality of climbing.
* Good climbing, but the route may lack line, situation or balance.

First Ascensionists
The year of the first ascent is given in the text. The full date and first ascensionists are listed area by area in chronological order at the back of the guide. Details of variations are given under the parent route. Winter ascents are listed under their corresponding summer route.

Litter and Vandalism

Litter is a continuing problem at popular camping sites, despite a slow improvement in recent years. All litter, including spare and unwanted food, should be taken out of the mountains. The justification for leaving food that is bio-degradable is spurious in these areas, as the breakdown of material in such a cold environment takes years. Likewise, leaving food for birds and animals is misguided as this only attracts scavengers into the area where they prey on the residents. If you take it in, take it out again; this includes finger tape and chalk wrappers, litter that climbers cannot blame anyone else for. Another problem is rings of stones used round tents; if you must use them, return the boulders where they came from. In the end, justified complaints by landowners can lead to access problems. Please co-operate by not leaving any traces behind you.

Mountain Rescue

In case of an accident requiring rescue or medical attention, telephone 999 (police). Give concise information about the location and injuries of the victim and any assistance available at the accident site. Try to leave someone with the casualty. In a party of two with no one nearby, there will be a difficult decision to make. If you decide to go for help, make the casualty warm and comfortable and leave him in a sheltered, well marked place. However, it is often better to stay with the victim.

Avalanches

Although avalanches are relatively rare in the Cuillin, because the frequent thaws reduce the probability of building an unstable snow pack, it is wise to be aware that they can occur. Climbers venturing onto the hills in winter should aquaint themselves with the principles of snow structure and avalanche prediction. There are a number of suitable books on the subject. A knowledge of what to do if involved in an avalanche, either as a victim or an observer, may help to save lives. A knowledge of first aid and artificial resuscitation is an obvious necessity.

Avalanches most often occur following heavy snow fall or during periods of strong thawing conditions, when slopes between 22 and 60 degrees are suspect, with the main danger area being between 30 and 45 degrees. Any danger will last longer in colder conditions when the snow pack takes longer to stabilise. The main danger is windslab avalanche, which occurs when snow is re-deposited by the wind. This snow bonds poorly with underlying layers and in these conditions lee slopes are the main danger areas, but pockets of windslab can be found in any sheltered location. Knowledge of the preceding weather, especially wind direction, is of great importance in predicting which slopes and climbs are avalanche-prone and this must always be borne in mind.

Climbers and walkers, however, should be able to make their own predictions by studying the pattern of snow deposition from the past and present weather conditions. Being able to dig a snow pit, study the snow profile and assess the relative strengths of the various snow layers and draw sensible conclusions from a profile is an important skill for those venturing on the hills in winter. A simple indication of severe avalanche risk is when the snow splits easily into slabs with defined boundaries when walked on; these small slabs indicate that much bigger ones may be waiting to peel off. Along with the means to make a realistic risk assessment, it is also necessary to understand the principles of movement in avalanche terrain to minimise any risk.

If avalanched, try either to jump free or anchor yourself for as long are possible. If swept down, protect your access to oxygen by 'swimming' to stay on the surface, by keeping your mouth closed and by preserving an air space in front of your face if buried. Wet snow avalanches harden rapidly on settling, so try and break free if possible at this point. If trapped, try to stay calm to reduce oxygen demand.

If a witness to an avalanche, it is VITAL to start a search immediately, given that it is safe to do so. Victims will often be alive at first but their chances lessen quickly if buried. Unless severely injured, some 80% may live if found immediately but this drops rapidly to about 30% after 1 hour and 10% after 3 hours. Mark the burial site if known, the site when last seen and the position of anything else found and search until help arrives. Again, a working knowledge of First Aid may save a life as many victims may have stopped breathing.

Remember IMMEDIATE SEARCHING CAN SAVE LIVES.

Maps and other sources of information

The Ordnance Survey 1:50,000 Sheet 32 covers the entire Cuillin range while the rest of the island is covered by Sheet 23. The Ordnance Survey 1:25,000 Outdoor Leisure Map *The Cuillin and Torridon Hills* is very useful. The double-sided map *The Black Cuillin, Island of Skye* by James Renny and Adam Kassyk with a scale of 1:15000 and published by the Scottish Mountaineering Trust is by far the best map for navigation on the ridge.

The Scottish Mountaineering Club District Guide *The Islands of Scotland including Skye* has a wealth of detailed information. *Scrambles in Skye* by J. Wilson Parker (Cicerone Press, 1983) and *Black*

Cuillin Ridge Scrambler's Guide by S.P.Bull (Scottish Mountaineering Trust, 1986) are also useful.

Safety

Climbing in the Cuillin is a markedly different experience from anything else in Britain. Not only are basic rock climbing skills and techniques necessary, but of equal importance are competent route-finding and mountaineering judgement. The 'easy way off', usual elsewhere in Britain, is often absent here and it is vital to plan descents in advance so that the pleasant day out does not become an epic. Far too many people have been hurt or killed while descending areas which are intrinsically loose and which require care and skill to negotiate safely. The Cuillin are not the place to learn how to abseil or climb safely. On the more remote routes, it is worth the second carrying a light sac with boots, waterproofs, food and First Aid to save complicated descents and to cope with sudden changes in weather, which are common. Sound rope retrieval methods, i.e. a Shunt or prussik loops, should be carried in case of jammed abseil ropes, and you should know how to use them! The rock in the Cuillin varies from excellent to execrable, from gabbro to basalt, often on the same route and can be treacherously soapy in wet or damp weather. Descents usually are on the poorer crumbly rocks, such as basalts and scree, a particularly unpleasant combination in the wet. About 90% of accidents in the Cuillin are caused by rockfall, usually by the victim pulling it onto themselves. Test holds and all blocks and double check abseil anchors. Remember that it is probably better to sacrifice a karabiner on a vital abseil than to risk a complicated and lengthy release of a jammed rope. Above all, treat the Cuillin as a mountain range with all the potential dangers, both objective and subjective, that you would expect if you were climbing abroad.

Leave a note of where you are going and when you expect to return, allowing a generous amount of time for the terrain. More time must be allowed here than elsewhere due this fact.

Much of the Cuillin are composed of magnetic rock which render a compass useless; in any case, navigation on the ridge is often complicated by the requirements of detailed route-finding to avoid tricky obstacles. Study the maps in clear weather, make careful appraisal of the terrain and any obstacles while approaching them, and read the relevant section of the guide which may provide helpful hints on how to find the best line.

Accommodation

For hotels and boarding houses, the main tourist information office is in Portree (tel. 01478 612137). Other information centres are open in the holiday season at Broadford (tel. 01471 622361) and Kyle of Lochalsh (tel. 01599 534276).

The two most useful camp sites are situated at Sligachan, opposite the hotel and at Glen Brittle beside the beach. Both are well appointed with modern facilities. Opportunities for wild camping at the roadside are rather limited, but camping at Loch Coruisk and in the Cuillin corries is possible.

There are two huts which are covenient for climbers. The Glen Brittle Memorial Hut is at the roadside about 300 metres north of Glenbrittle House. It has accommodation for 16 and a resident warden from April to September. It is owned by the BMC and MCofS, from whom booking details can be obtained. The Coruisk Memorial Hut is owned by the JMCS, Glasgow Section, and is delightfully situated on the shore of Loch na Cuilce, 100 metres north-west of the outflow from the Scavaig River. Access is by boat from Elgol or Mallaig, or on foot from Sligachan or Strathaird. It has accommodation for nine.

There are various possibilities for self-catering accommodation, of which perhaps the most convenient is that close to the Sligachan Hotel (tel. 01478 650303).

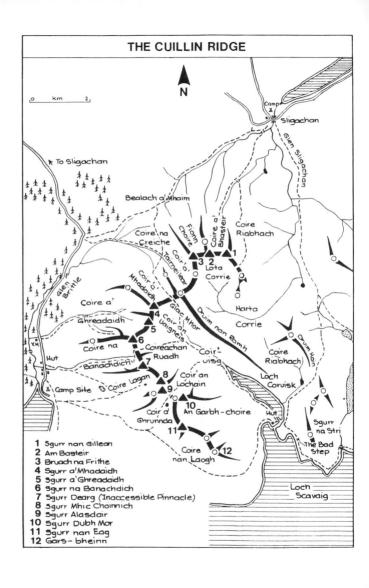

THE CUILLIN RIDGE

N

0   km   2

To Sligachan

Camp ✕
Sligachan

Glen Sligachan

Bealach a'Mhaim

Coire na Creiche

Fionn Choire

Coire a' Bhasteir

Coire Riabhach

Glen Brittle

Coir' a' Tairneilear

3   2
Lota Corrie

1

Coire a' Mhadaidh

Coir' an Uaigneis

4   Glac Mhor
5

Druim nan Ramh

Harta Corrie

Coire a' Ghreadaidh

Coire na Banachdich

6

Coireachan Ruadh

Coir' uisg

Drium Hain

Coire Riabhach

Hut

7

Camp Site

Coire Lagan

8

Coir' an Lochain

Loch Coruisk

Hut

9

10
An Garbh-choire

Coir' a' Ghrunnda

11

Sgurr na Stri

The Bad Step

12
Coire nan Laogh

Loch Scavaig

1 Sgurr nan Gillean
2 Am Basteir
3 Bruach na Frithe
4 Sgurr a'Mhadaidh
5 Sgurr a'Ghreadaidh
6 Sgurr na Banachdich
7 Sgurr Dearg (Inaccessible Pinnacle)
8 Sgurr Mhic Choinnich
9 Sgurr Alasdair
10 Sgurr Dubh Mor
11 Sgurr nan Eag
12 Gars-bheinn

The Traverse of The Cuillin

It is perhaps appropriate to begin this guide by describing the nearly Alpine expeditions to be enjoyed in the heart of the Cuillin. These outings require not only rock climbing and route-finding skills and fitness, but also careful planning of logistics and tactics. Years of patient anticipation may preceed a successful outcome, particularly of the winter traverse, and as such these are trips to be treasured. In truth, they are 'the stuff of which dreams are made'.

THE TRAVERSE OF THE MAIN RIDGE

This, the most famous expedition in Britain, involves over 3000m of ascent spread over a horizontal distance of 10km. It makes a fantastic outing provided certain criteria are met. The technical standard of the climbing is never more than Very Difficult by the easiest line, but since most of the ridge is sustained and exposed scrambling with extensive sections of Moderate and Difficult climbing, it is wise to be able to lead Severe in order that most parts can be soloed. Competence in abseiling is also necessary. Equally important are adequate fitness and competence in route-finding; there are many tricky sections of the ridge in clear weather, let alone in mist. Prior knowledge is not essential but could be useful, but if in doubt it is often wiser to keep on the actual crest rather than make obscure detours. Crampon scratches certainly point to the best ways on the narrower sections.

Little climbing gear is needed: one 45m rope per party, three or four nuts, one of them small, a couple of slings and a figure of eight descender for the abseils, which can double up as a belay brake. All the abseil slings are normally in place, but since *in situ* slings are often weak due to sunlight and abrasion, several spare slings should be carried. Also useful, particularly if the route has to be abandoned, is *The Black Cuillin of Skye* map, published by the Scottish Mountaineering Trust. The scale is 1:15000 and it shows every bealach that can be descended.

Sometimes overlooked is the need to carry adequate water and food supplies. Three litres per person in warm weather is usual, plus moist food such as oranges as well as suger-rich supplies for energy. The ridge is arid, the only reliable water in dry weather being in Fionn Choire, 60m below the ridge at an obvious small pool set amidst moss.

The ridge may be tackled from either end, but most parties prefer to complete the traverse from south to north. The route starts up Gars-bheinn and includes every peak on the main ridge, plus Sgurr Alasdair, and finishes at Sgurr nan Gillean. The total time taken will be approximately three hours to reach Gars-bheinn from Glen Brittle, ten to fourteen hours on the ridge itself, and a further two hours from the summit of Sgurr nan Gillean to Sligachan.

The main sections of difficulty along the route are decribed in the relevant chapters, but it is appropriate to describe them here within an overall description of the traverse. The start involves either a long plug up Gars-bheinn, soul destroying but easy, or a more interesting approach *via* Coir' a' Ghrunnda. Follow the camp site track towards Coire Lagan, but branch off right on a well defined path which contours around the broad base of Sron na Ciche before eventually entering Coir' a' Ghrunnda. Keep well left in the corrie itself, under South Crag, until Loch Coir a' Ghrunnda is reached. Climb east by a steep zigzag scree path to the narrow col which lies east of the loch. In mist it might be easier to continue up the path to Bealach Coir' an Lochain. Leave the sacs at Bealach a' Garbh-choire, then straightforward ridge scrambling leads to Gars-bheinn (about an hour or less from the bealach).

Now turn back north to start the adventure. The first part of the ridge is mainly straightforward. The square castle of Caisteal a' Garbh-choire can either be bypassed or traversed at Difficult standard, over exceptionally rough rock. The first technical section is the infamous Thearlaich-Dubh Gap.

The Thearlaich-Dubh Gap   Very Difficult
The ridge dramatically steepens into a tower as the gap nears. Steep Moderate rocks lead to the gap itself, a chasm with near vertical walls, that have to be abseiled *via* the 10m south-east wall (Severe) to a belay below the 25m north-west wall. The highly polished chimney-crack has a tight central section (small nut for protection) and leads strenuously to the easier upper groove. It is diabolical in the wet and there have been numerous incidents involving, for the most part, inexperienced climbers. It is the most technical section of the ridge. It is possible to escape from the gap down the Coir' a' Ghrunnda side.

The next section leads to Sgurr Thearlaich, but a diversion off the ridge to make an ascent of the final rocks of Sgurr Alasdair is quite easy and definitely worthwhile. Descending from the summit of Sgurr Thearlaich provides the next major difficulty.

The descent of Sgurr Thearlaich   Difficult
The difficulties are concentrated in the highly polished slabs just above the Bealach Mhic Choinnich. In descent, a steepening line leads down left to the bealach. It is also possible to traverse down right to the same point. The final few metres are interesting and even more so when wet.

The ascent of Sgurr Mhic Choinnich   Difficult or Easy
King's Chimney   Difficult
This is the spectacular but fortunately straightforward right-angled corner so prominently cutting the summit rocks on the south face. It starts about 20m above the bealach and is reached from Collie's Ledge, the obvious shelf cutting across the west face. Climb the corner on big holds, avoiding the overhang above by a right traverse on jugs. An excellent pitch.
Collie's Ledge   Easy
The ledge starts 6m above the bealach and traverses the west face in a spectacular manner to meet the main ridge north of the summit. The summit can also be gained by a Difficult wall from near the north end of the ledge.

From Sgurr Mhic Choinnich, there is no particular difficulty to the foot of An Stac. Here there is an option. Either follow the exposed crest of An Stac, a loose Moderate which is usually avoided, or the scree slopes and basalt shelves on its south-west side. It is important to keep close to An Stac during this approach, passing through a cairned notch, then going up to the foot of the Inaccessible Pinnacle *via* horrible basalt slabs and scree; easy but tiring. When descending this section, do not be led astray by the scree gully below which seems to offer an easier way; it ends in a nasty cliff.

The Inaccessible Pinnacle
The south to north traverse usually climbs the 'In Pin' *via* the east ridge and descends the west ridge by abseil.
The East Ridge   Moderate
A splendid way to the top. This is the archetypal arete, much beloved by the pioneers: "A razor-like edge with an overhanging and infinite drop on one side, and a drop longer and steeper on the other". It has huge holds.
The West Ridge   Difficult
This is extremely polished and not recommended in the wet. From the col, reach a sloping ledge (crux), then follow a crack to the summit.

There is a wire sling and fixed karabiner for the abseil down the edge facing Sgurr Dearg.

From the summit of Sgurr Dearg, keep left in the descent to Bealach Coire na Banachdich, not obvious in mist initially, then straightforward scrambling leads over Sron Bhuidhe to Sgurr na Banachdich. The ridge now turns from north-west to north-east near the bealach below Sgurr Thormaid. Sgurr Thormaid itself has a deceptive track which runs below the summit rocks on the west side. A cairn indicates the way up steep rocks to the summit. If this is ignored and the 'path' followed, a most interesting excursion is needed to regain the ridge. Continue left around the diminishing ledge until it fades into a sheer wall, the drop below being impressive. At this point, a slabby groove leads steeply up left, climbed on small holds to the summit. This is probably no more than Difficult, but it gives the most exposed climbing on the ridge. This could be considered Collie's Alternative Ledge!

The exposed and delightful crest of Sgurr a' Ghreadaidh now follows. The ridge is extremely narrow, but the next major difficulty is the traverse of Sgurr a' Mhadaidh, which has four tops on a ridge running south-west to north-east. Rather confusingly, the highest top at the south-west end of the ridge is called the fourth top, the first top being at the north-east end of the ridge.

The Traverse of Sgurr a' Mhadaidh   Moderate
There are two steep sections on the west faces of the third and second tops, the second top being best taken direct. Otherwise a tricky traverse right across polished slabs down to a shallow gully has to be taken to regain the ridge.

The Bealach na Glaic Moire lies below, an easy pass, before the most complex section of the ridge, the traverse of the three tops of Bidein Druim nan Ramh.

The tops of Bidein Druim nan Ramh   Difficult
These peaks form an impressive triangular cluster and can give serious route-finding problems, especially in mist. The main ridge here lies south-west to north-east. Climb easily from the Bealach na Glaic

Opposite: The East Ridge of the Inaccessible Pinnacle

Next page: Looking north from Sgurr Thearlaich to Sgurr Dearg and Sgurr na Banachdich (Climber, Guy Muhlemann)

Moire to the south-west peak, and at its steepening traverse left and return to the crest by a basalt staircase. Continue towards the summit of this top and go right to descend steeply with one overhanging move to a huge boulder at the col. Cross the col and climb steeply and fairly directly up the centre peak, finishing up a steep chimney, then turn right along a short ridge to reach the top. Return down the ridge on a bearing north to reach the top of a smooth slab on the east side of the ridge. Climb (or abseil) down to broad ledges, scramble down to the next steepening (which may also be abseiled) and descend to the col. From there, climb up leftwards onto the north-east peak and climb directly up to the summit by its north rib. Descend easily to the next col, the Bealach Harta.

The ascent to An Caisteal up its south ridge is easy. Just before reaching the summit, take a path to the left along a ledge and descend steeply. Do not take the ledge which descends to the right of the summit (the infamous 'Belly Ledge'). Moderate scrambling leads down to a final steep rock pitch just above the col. Climb down on good holds, leftwards at first, then go back right to the col.

Before the long haul up to Bruach na Frithe, in the vicinity of Sgurr na Bhairnich, there are a couple of vertical chasms formed by the weathering of dykes which are a good example of cols in the making. The first is unavoidable and a stride is needed to cross it, the second can either be jumped or more tamely turned to the right.

Sgurr a' Fionn Choire is turned on the left and some steep easy rocks ascended beyond to gain the system of ledges below the ridge's most impressive single sight, the Bhasteir Tooth. There are two ways of reaching the Tooth.

Naismith's Route   Very Difficult

A rather sensational climb with great atmosphere. From the ridge, traverse right in an increasingly exposed position on a system of ledges that overlook Lota Corrie. The route takes the right end of the face *via* a cracked wall. From the main ledge, continue up to a higher ledge, small nut belay (10m). From the right end of the ledge, either climb the wall to the cracked chimney or, if wet, traverse awkwardly out right to the diagonal crack and go steeply up this to the same point.

Previous page: On the ridge of Sgurr a' Ghreadaidh, looking towards Sgurr Alasdair (Climber, J.Sutherland)

Opposite: Naismith's Route on the Bhasteir Tooth

Continue up the easier crack-chimney to below a steep top crack. Traverse right to another crack (excellent protection) and make the crux move over the top (15m). From the belay, an easy step leads to the final straightforward slabs of the Lota Corrie Route to the summit of the Bhasteir Tooth.

Lota Corrie Route   200m   Moderate
This is an interesting and easier way of reaching the Tooth. It is as enclosed as Naismith's Route is exposed. Descend below the vertical south-west wall of the Tooth down into the Lota Corrie to where a shallow chimney-gully cleaves the south-west face. Either follow the pleasant slabs to the left of the gully to the neck under Am Basteir's west wall, or follow a groove, some scree and a short steep chimney to the same place. This route is feasible in the wet.

Am Basteir
From the summit of the Tooth, descend a short distance leftwards to reach a gully directly under the vertical west wall. Traverse right on shelves to a gully and ascend this *via* a dyke to arrive on a good ledge directly under a short overhanging wall with a polished crack to its left. This undercut wall, though only 4m high, is harder technically than anything on the ridge, but it has both incut holds and no exposure. The crack to its left is harder and is best overcome by a short abseil when traversing from north to south. From the ledge above the wall, continue up the crest of Am Basteir to the summit.
An inferior route avoiding this wall is to keep traversing out right on broken rocks on the Lota Corrie face of Am Basteir until it is possible to ascend to the summit. It is also possible to avoid both the Tooth and Am Basteir by simply walking under the vertical north face to Bealach a' Bhasteir. The combination of these two peaks form a fitting climax to the traverse of the ridge, especially for a tired party.

The West Ridge of Sgurr nan Gillean   Moderate
From Bealach a' Bhasteir, continue under the north wall of the west ridge for a short distance to the first obvious chimney. Climb this steep, well polished problem (the second chimney is harder and much looser) and traverse the short exposed crest over little pinnacles. Since the fall of the celebrated Gendarme, this section has lost much of its bite. Above, easy scrambling leads to the summit; it is traditional to thread the 'window' just below the top of the mountain.

In descent, follow the Tourist Route (the south-east ridge). Initially a narrow crest, it soon steepens into a fine polished ridge which can be turned on the right if required. This ridge ends in scree and a line of cairns leads down from the continuation of the ridge (Sgurr na h-Uamha being the true termination) towards Glen Sligachan, eventually forming a well marked track, passing west of the little Loch a' Choire Riabhaich, before joining the Allt Dearg Beag to Sligachan for a well earned pint (or, for some people, breakfast!).

THE GREATER TRAVERSE

This extension of the main ridge includes the traverse of Clach Glas and Bla Bheinn. It involves some 4000 metres of ascent and descent and will take a strong party in good conditions about 18-20 hours, first to last top. The traverse of the Bla Bheinn group is described in detail in a later chapter.

THE WINTER TRAVERSE

This is probably the greatest single outing to be had in Britain, at least five stars on a three star scale! Good conditions are comparatively rare and opportunities for a sucessful traverse must be grasped quickly before a thaw sets in. An easterly wind and high pressure bode well. It is usual to travel from north to south because the major difficulties can be avoided in this direction by abseil. The hardest technical sections of the ridge will be no more than Grade IV, but there are a very large number of Grade II and III pitches. Although many will prefer to solo large sections of the ridge, it is worth considering adopting the alpine techniques of moving together roped. Done properly, this is almost as fast as climbing unroped, and it will avoid the consequences of a simple slip which would otherwise be fatal at innumerable points along the way. Some of the major problems are as follows:

The West Ridge of Sgurr nan Gillean
It is usual to abseil from just above where the Gendarme used to be down Tooth Chimney, then to traverse back to the ridge at Bealach a' Bhasteir.

The Bhasteir Tooth
Descend Lota Corrie Route for 60m before abseiling, or abseil down to the boulder ledge of Naismith's Route and follow a hard traverse.

The Traverse of Bidein Druim Nan Ramh
It may be necessary to abseil from the north top to the gap and again from the central top to the next gap.

The Traverse of Sgurr a' Mhadaidh
When going from north to south, abseil the steep sections on the third and second tops.

The Inaccessible Pinnacle
Either avoid it by a traverse below it and An Stac on the south-west side, or climb the east ridge, which can sometimes be hard.

Sgurr Mhic Choinnich
It can be hard to find the abseil point above the top of King's Chimney; go down a little left at the end of the summit. From the bealach, the ascent of Sgurr Thearlaich can be awkward. To take in Sgurr Alasdair, it will probably be necessary to make a short abseil down the short steep wall below the ridge.

The Thearlaich-Dubh Gap
This will be at least Grade IV on the short side and may need devious tactics to overcome it. Otherwise, descend into Coir a' Ghrunnda to avoid all the difficulties.

Allow two or three days for the ridge. Most parties will leave food dumps on the ridge beforehand in anticipation of a speedy crossing. It would be wise to alert the Mountain Rescue Team as otherwise your lights might be misconstrued. A final hazard is that the Police have been known to remove the climber's car, thinking the owner to be irretrievably lost; leave a note on the dashboard.

The Northern Cuillin

The northern limit of the main Cuillin ridge is Sgurr nan Gillean (*peak of the young men*), which despite its name, holds some of the oldest climbs in Britain. Combined with more recent additions, this region now offers climbs varied in both grade and style.

LOTA AND HARTA CORRIES
(*Map Ref 470 240*)

These two fine and remote corries are hidden away on the south side of the northern Cuillin peaks. Lota Corrie is effectively an upper level of Harta Corrie and is separated from it by a broad slabby rock band. The River Sligachan originates in Lota Corrie, initially flowing south, then east before eventually draining northwards down Glen Sligachan. The western side of Harta Corrie is dominated by the complex peak of Bidein Druim nan Ramh, which lies at the junction between the main ridge and an important lateral ridge running south-eastwards called Druim nan Ramh. This ridge and its indefinite north-eastern extension to Meall Dearg form the southern side of Harta Corrie.

Three major peaks, Bruach na Frithe, Am Basteir and Sgurr nan Gillean are situated on the main ridge overlooking the head of Lota Corrie. A further section of ridge which curves southwards from Sgurr nan Gillean to Sgurr na h-Uamha forms the eastern side of Lota Corrie.

The corries are infrequently approached from below as it is a long slog from Sligachan. Follow the path along the east bank of the River Sligachan, leaving it at Lochan Dubha, then follow the south-east bank of the river to Harta Corrie. A short distance up the corrie stands a huge boulder, the Bloody Stone, which offers both good shelter and bouldering, the name of the boulder being unconnected with the quality of bouldering.

The approach to Harta Corrie from Coruisk *via* Corrie Riabach is both shorter and more interesting, involving a crossing of the broad bealach at 270m between Druim nan Ramh and Druim Hain.

No less than four easy passes can be used to cross or gain the main ridge from these two corries. The first pass, known as the Bealach Harta, is on the western side of Harta Corrie and about 200 metres east-north-east of the northern top of Bidein Druim nan Ramh. It links with Coir' a' Tairneilear and is the only easy pass between Harta Corrie and Glen Brittle. At 760m it is the second lowest point on the main ridge, Bealach na Glaic Moire on the opposite side of Bidein Druim nan Ramh being marginally lower. To reach Bealach Harta, walk up Harta Corrie for 3km, making for the wide stony break which splits the corrie's very slabby western wall. Ascend this, trend right on scree below the summit buttresses of Bidein and ascend a scree shoot to gain the ridge.

The other three passes are approached from Lota Corrie. To reach them, find a way up the great sweep of rock forming the lip of Lota Corrie. The easiest way goes up to the right (east) of a small stream that tumbles down the right-hand side of the rock band. Once established in Lota Corrie, Bealach nan Lice, which connects with Coire a' Bhasteir, can be reached by following the main stream to the left of a rocky knoll. Ascend to the back of the corrie, and just before the angle noticeably steepens, reach the junction of two streams. Follow the left branch north-westerly to its source and continue in the same line on scree past the base of the Bhasteir Tooth. A large knobble of rock stands at the top of the pass. For Bealach a' Bhasteir, take a more northerly course between the two streams up the back wall of the corrie to the lowest point on the skyline. This side of the pass is not well used and has less scree.

The fourth pass, Bealach a' Ghlas-choire, is the low point on a southward extension of the main ridge from Sgurr nan Gillean to Sgurr na h-Uamha. It links with An Glas-choire and Glen Sligachan. Ascend the lip of Lota Corrie as for the previous bealachs, then immediately after passing a waterfall, turn right and ascend the steep eastern wall of the corrie, mainly on scree. This can be used as a descent route by those returning to Coruisk after traversing the ridge.

The rock climbing in the corrie is of a decidedly exploratory nature, largely neglected for the flesh-pots of Coire Lagan. If seeking solitude and acres of slabby, featureless, sound rock then this is the place for you. The main climbing interest is on the slabs of An Caisteal and Sgurr na h-Uamha.

KEY TO MAP OPPOSITE

1   An Caisteal, Harta Face
2   Sgurr na h-Uamha, South-West Face
3   Glen Sligachan Buttress
4   Nead na h-Iolaire
5   Sgurr nan Gillean, Pinnacle Ridge
6   Am Basteir and the Bhasteir Tooth

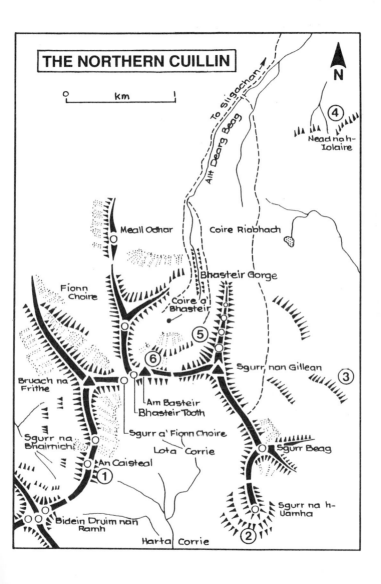

THE NORTHERN CUILLIN

N

0 km

To Sligachan

Allt Dearg Beag

Meall Odhar

Coire Riabhach

Bhasteir Gorge

Fionn Choire

Coire a' Bhasteir

⑤

⑥

Sgurr nan Gillean

③

Bruach na Frithe

Am Basteir
Bhasteir Tooth

Sgurr a' Fionn Choire

Lota Corrie

Sgurr na Bhairnich

An Caisteal

①

Sgurr Beag

Sgurr na h-Uamha

②

Bidein Druim nan Ramh

Harta Corrie

Nead na h-Iolaire

④

AN CAISTEAL, HARTA FACE
(Map Ref 462 243)

The Harta face of An Caisteal is a great slabby mass of rock, cleft by two long gullies (South and North) into three buttresses. A number of long lower grade climbs have been done, but since the rock is extremely user-friendly, countless variations are possible. Winter scope is manifestly better. The climbs start at an altitude of about 500m, and can be reached from Harta Corrie as described above. The easiest descent is from the Bealach Harta.

South Buttress   300m   Difficult   (1911)
Start by the lowest part of the South Gully. Make a downward traverse by way of a square platform, climb the face by steep slabs, then an easier 60m section. Above this the buttress narrows to an edge with a cliff on the left and the gully to the right. It is possible to vary the lower section to avoid the detour of the original route.
Variation   Direct Start: Very Difficult   (1946)
Climb direct from the bottom of the gully to the platform, then ascend a short vertical wall on the left of the gully where a large rock splinter projects.

Raeburn's Route   360m   Difficult   (1905)
This lies to the right of South Gully. Easy climbing leads to a steeper section where the rocks are slabby. Turn an overhang on the left to a point overlooking the gully. A fine chimney leads out above the overhang by easier rocks. The final wall, two-thirds of the way up, is cleft by several chimneys.

White Wizard   350m   III/IV **   (1983)
This fine winter route takes a line between Raeburn's Route and Archer Thomson's Route. Follow an obvious right-trending 90m gully formed by a basalt dyke. Break out left up snowfields for 90m, then follow a narrow gully line to the top. The top section of this route is particularly good.

Archer Thomson's Route   360m   Difficult   (1911)
This rather indefinite line is best described as being straightforward, very interesting but with no particular features. It lies to the left of North Gully and the climber is left to pick the most appealing line.

North Buttress   300m   Difficult   (1953)
Start right of North Gully, go up the left-hand edge of a steep wall, then
return to the centre of the buttress. Continue up a long stretch of slabs,
gradually getting steeper, to a terrace. Climb the front of the tower
ahead, moving from left to right and then back left again. The continuation to the final tower is easier. This can be climbed either by a central
chimney or a gully to the left, to its top. The summit of An Caisteal is
easily reached a little further on.

SGURR NA H-UAMHA
736m   (Map Ref 476 240)

This beautiful peak, 1½ km south of Sgurr nan Gillean, forms the true
northern termination of the main ridge. It boasts many rock faces, the
principal one being the south-west face, just below the summit and
facing towards Bidein. There is also climbing of a similar quality on the
east face overlooking An Glas-choire. The climbing is of good quality,
in the lower grades, and open to variation. The summit of the mountain
involves climbing above Bealach a' Ghlas-choire. A small top halfway
along the north ridge gives pleasant scrambling but the crux of the
ascent is the steep rise immediately after this top. The easiest line is
not obvious and at least Moderate. In ascent it is usual to spiral
upwards on the west side of the ridge, although a more direct line can
be taken in descent when the route is easier to see.

SOUTH-WEST FACE

Approach as for Harta Corrie until south of the peak, then head up a
small side corrie called Coire nan Clach. The only feasible descent is
down Bealach a' Ghlas-choire, north of the summit ridge. This gives
descents to both Lota Corrie and An Glas-choire.
   This extensive face is tiered and bounded on the left by West Gully.

West Gully   150m   Moderate
Climb the gully for 75m, then follow the left branch, going first by a
chimney then by several jammed blocks, followed by rather loose rocks
to finish just north of the summit. A possible route for wet days.

Braehead Climb   120m   Very Difficult   (1965)
This route ascends the face just right of West Gully as directly as
possible. Climb slabs and grooves to some overhangs, which are

passed on the right by parallel cracks. Move left and climb a pinnacle to a ledge with a perched block. Climb a small chimney to a large ledge under some overhangs. Continue up right past the overhangs, then go back left along an easy ledge. Go right to a groove which leads by easier scrambling to the North Ridge.

Murray's Climb   240m   Difficult   (1937)
The face springs up steeply from the upper part of Harta Corrie. This route starts at the base of the rocks where one can see into Lota Corrie on the left and lower Harta Corrie on the right. The climbing is steep and exposed, with much variation possible. In general the standard is harder to the right.

Smith's Climb   300m   Severe *   (1949)
This line, chosen to obtain the most continuous climbing, lies to the right of Murray's Climb and is roughly in the direction of the summit from the lowest point of the Druim nan Ramh ridge. The crag is in three tiers, the lowest one being broken, the middle one being the main face and the uppermost comprising the summit rocks. Climb a groove onto steep slabs for about 60m to a line of vertical rocks. From below this, follow a diagonal traverse left to the first steep, smooth groove. Gain the main face ahead and climb up until a left traverse is possible along a line of basalt. Climb up into a deep square-cut groove, visible on the skyline from the base of this section. Follow this for 60m to the summit ridge which eases to scrambling near the top.

EAST FACE

This face overlooks An Glas-choire, and is reached by fording the River Sligachan. When the river is in spate, it is necessary to walk well up Harta Corrie, then contour back right into the corrie. The best descent is *via* Bealach a' Ghlas-choire.

The face is characterised by a huge hanging tongue-shaped ridge. The rock is good and the climbing pleasant.

Aslan's Tongue   300m   Severe *   (1968)
This route takes the line of the tongue-shaped ridge. Start at the first break right of the cairn at the foot, trending right before breaking back on clean slabs to the crest, after which the climb is nowhere really difficult. After about 100m the route dwindles to a ledge with an undercut wall to the left; then follow two 50m steps leading to a further 90m of open slabs which end right at the summit.

On the first ascent of the peak in 1887, the pioneers found a way up from An Glas-choire by a steep break in the rocks on the north-east flank, describing their route as a "capital scramble".

GLEN SLIGACHAN BUTTRESS
(Map Ref 484 251)

This fine buttress is about 5km up Glen Sligachan, not far above the floor of the glen at an altitude of 150m and opposite Marsco's Central Buttress. It forms the lowest part of a rocky spur which descends to the east from the col between Sgurr nan Gillean and Sgurr Beag.

The cliff is in two main sections. There is a large steep slabby buttress on the left with a prominent nose and a broad expanse of slime beneath it (The Snot), and the buttress is girdled high up by a broad ledge. The other section, the steep right wing, is at a slightly higher level and comprises a high-angled slab separated from the left buttress by a recess which contains two deep chimneys. The sun leaves the crag early and due to the massive rock, blade pegs may occasionally be required for belays.

Descent is possible *via* either flank of the buttress.

LEFT-HAND BUTTRESS

Sidetrack   135m   Very Difficult   (1969)
Start near the left edge of the buttress.
1. 25m   Climb a left-slanting crack followed by slabs to a recess.
2. 35m   Climb directly above by a shallow slab corner and slabs, then veer right to belay below a steepening.
3. 20m   Go up right to climb a short steep groove, then move left to a ledge.
4. 30m   Climb up left to the final bulging barrier and make a long horizontal traverse right to a cracked block belay in a corner.
5. 25m   Ascend the groove directly above the belay, then trend diagonally left to the top.

Cheek of the Devil   155m   HVS 5a *   (1980)
A good, exposed route. Start at cairn on slabs just left of The Snot.
1. 25m   Climb the slabs to a niche just left of the nose.
2. 25m 5a   Pull over the niche and go up steeply leftwards into a blank groove with a bulging headwall. From the very narrow ledge beneath the headwall, go right up a faint groove to a wide ledge and peg belays.

3. 35m   Traverse right, then climb a small V-groove high on the right-hand side of the big wall. Climb the groove to a peg belay.
4. 35m 5a   Bold moves up the steep wall on good holds lead rightwards to the arete. Climb around the arete and go up to a superb eyrie (peg runner). Go delicately around the arete to a thin crack, climb this and walls above to the girdling ledge.
4. 35m   Finish up short walls and corners.

Blasphemy Chimneys   105m   Severe   (1969)
In the centre of the crag lie the chimneys that separate the two main buttresses. This route lies in the recess and is right of a steep grassy chimney-gully. Climb the prominent corner-chimney strenuously to a large grassy bay. Walk into the corner and climb the left-hand of two chimneys into a niche. Move up left and climb a crack to a grass ledge, then move back right to belay in a corner of the original line at a ledge. Finish up the corner.

RIGHT-HAND BUTTRESS

Rat Trap   95m   VS   (1980)
This route takes the middle of the wall right of the central chimneys. Scramble to a cairn at the foot of the wall.
1. 35m   Climb up and right to a peg belay in a niche at the foot of a slanting groove system.
2. 25m   Follow the slanting grooves to a short chimney, then climb this to a good peg belay beneath a prominent left-slanting crack.
3. 35m 5a   Climb the very awkward crack, then follow easier ground to the top.

Opal Creamer   80m   E1 *   (1980)
This route takes a fairly sustained line left of a white streak. Scramble up past Rat Trap to a cairn.
1. 45m 5a   Climb direct up a faint line for 12m, crux. Go slightly left and follow a narrow zigzag line to a crack at 30m. Go right, then left and up to a good chock belay under the first overlap.
2. 35m   Move over the overlap on the right and continue up to the overhang. Pull over this on good holds and finish up slabs on Rat Trap.

NEAD NA H-IOLAIRE
(Map Ref 484 275)

This crag lies low on the flanks of Sgurr nan Gillean at an altitude of 230m and faces north, being on the north-west side of a low ridge. The crag is rather heathery but has some quite reasonable climbing and can save a half-day. Up to 90m in height, it has a few easier climbs, including the prominent chimney, as well as several shorter chimney and face climbs. It is often wet and takes some time to dry out.

Approach the crag *via* the Tourist Route up Sgurr nan Gillean. Cross the Allt Dearg Mor by the footbridge 200 metres from the road at Sligachan, then follow the track, crossing the Allt Dearg Beag, to contour around to the crag at an altitude of 230m, approximately 3km in all.

The climbs are described from left to right. The descent route is to the right of the crag, down the wide scree gully

Left Rib   60m   Very Difficult   (1918)
This climb takes the rib bounding the left side of the central chimney. Climb slabs and heather to a large ledge. Continue *via* a steep 20m slab to a heather shelf, whence a higher ledge leads to the top.

Central Chimney   60m   Difficult
The prominent chimney is often wet.

Raptor   30m   Severe   (1994)
Start at the centre of a gabbro slab, 3 metres left of the second pitch of Eagle's Eyrie. Climb the crack in the centre of the slab to a heather terrace, no protection. Climb the broken left edge of a gabbro wall to a sloping heather terrace, then go up the short wall above. Belay up to the right

Eagle's Eyrie   85m   Very Difficult   (1993)
Start at a grassy ledge directly below the summit and left of a steep wall bounding the wide descent gully.
1. 35m   Climb the slab to a grassy ledge at 20m, move left and climb the slab to a wide ledge and block belay.
2. 25m   Climb the slab on its right-hand edge, continue boldly on good basalt and where the face steepens, traverse 6 metres right above a rowan to continue up a crack to a ledge and block belay.

3. 25m   Climb the gabbro face and move right to a small ledge on a steep slab. Climb the slab on good holds to easier ground and pleasant scrambling to finish.

Elizabeth   50m   Very Difficult *   (1994)
Probably the best of the routes here, with a bold first pitch. From the right-hand corner of the buttress adjoining the scree gully, go 15 metres along a path rising up left. Start at the middle of an undercut concave slab.
1. 25m   Climb the slab to a heather ledge and continue up a gabbro and basalt staircase to a block at the foot of a steep corner; belay on the right.
2. 25m   From the block, climb the corner to a sloping heather terrace and cross over left to a short steep gabbro wall. Climb this diagonally right on 'mouth-watering holds' to easy ground.

August Rib   90m   Severe   (1967)
The route lies up the right side of the face and starts a little way up a scree gully at a short slanting crack in the west wall (arrow). Go up the crack for 5m, then step awkwardly left round onto a rib which is followed to a stance and belay. Follow the rib on the right in two short sections to another good stance and belay. Climb the clean and exposed rib on the right to a ledge from which easy rocks lead to the top.

To the right of August Rib is the scree gully. Its left-bounding wall offers one route.

One Flew Over The Cuillin Ridge   50m   E3
Start near the entrance of the scree gully.
1. 30m 4c   Follow a right-curving line up the wall, a good pitch.
2. 20m 5b   This promising start does not continue. "The continuation of the line unfortunately goes through a basalt sill for 15m, no gear, falling to bits, to a final 4m of good gabbro". Futher advice to second ascensionists included 'frontal lobotomy needed'. Well, you can't win 'em all.

SGURR NAN GILLEAN
964m   (Map Ref 472 253)

The round of Coire a' Bhasteir provides a splendid expedition with climbing up to Difficult in standard. It can be done in either direction, but is described from the Sgurr nan Gillean end first. The details of the climbing sections are given in subsequent sections. The first objective is Pinnacle Ridge, which leads to the summit of Sgurr nan Gillean. Then take the west ridge to descend to Bealach a' Bhasteir, and continue *via* the east ridge to the summit of Am Basteir. A direct traverse of the narrow crest beyond is recommended; this suddenly ends at a big drop. A small block (sling usually in place) allows a short abseil to a ledge. Follow this ledge around leftwards, then scramble down a shelf to the right until it is feasible to descend onto the final slab section of the Bhasteir Tooth. Ascend this pleasantly, then either abseil down Naismith's Route or, equally interesting, descend Lota Corrie Route as follows: From the summit, descend pleasant slabs, then head off down the series of short but steep chimneys which lie immediately left of and below the summit slabs. These are easier to descend than is apparent from above. There is much loose scree between chimneys and they eventually give out to a long moderately-angled groove, slippery in the wet, which in turn marks the end of the difficulties. Scramble on down short steps to the foot of the gully in Lota Corrie.

Climb up close to the vertical wall on the right, where there is a path, and bear round to the left near the top to reach the Bealach nan Lice. Follow the path directly under the vertical north wall of Am Basteir to reach the Bealach a' Bhasteir and the descent down the left bank of the Bhasteir Gorge. A series of cairns leads through the slabs and keeps quite high before reaching the boggy low ground and the path back to Sligachan.

In reverse, (the west to east traverse) this expedition is equally fun and dry condition are more important than on the way just described. From the Bealach nan Lice the best way up the Bhasteir Tooth is *via* Naismith's Route.

COIRE A' BHASTEIR
(Map Ref 470 255)

This most impressive corrie has superb rock scenery. The surrounding mountain features include the north or Pinnacle Ridge and west ridge of Sgurr nan Gillean, Am Basteir and the Basteir Tooth. Entry to the corrie is guarded by glaciated slabs cut by a deep gorge. The corrie floor consists almost entirely of rock slabs and scree with only a small amount of vegetation near to the small lochan.

From the Sligachan Hotel go west, and cross the Allt Dearg Mor at a footbridge and follow the track to the Allt Dearg Beag. Continue along the north-west (right) bank almost to the Bhasteir Gorge, a deep ravine that divides the lower reaches of Coire a' Bhasteir. Cross over to the south-east bank some 200 metres before the gorge, then go up easy ground to the foot of the First Pinnacle of Pinnacle Ridge. Traverse right over broken ground into the corrie. Alternatively, a cairned path zigzags up the west bank of the gorge over slabs and ledges, keeping well away from its edge.

There are no particular difficulties in the corrie apart from rough going over scree and slabs. The main ridge can be easily reached at Bealach a' Bhasteir. It is also possible to reach the ridge close to the west side of the Bhasteir Tooth; this provides a rougher but more interesting route to Bealach nan Lice than the one up Fionn Choire.

To descend, Pinnacle Ridge is easily scrambled down from anywhere up to the summit of the Third Pinnacle. The gully between the First and Second Pinnacles is easy scree. From the col between Knight's Peak (the Fourth Pinnacle) and the summit, a scree gully gives a descent into Coire a' Bhasteir. The west ridge is also an obvious descent.

COIRE RIABHACH

This is the small corrie to the north-east of Coire a' Bhasteir.

The Tourist Route   Easy   (1836)
This follows the south-east ridge of Sgurr nan Gillean and is by far the simplest route of ascent or descent. If used in ascent, leave the Coire a' Bhasteir path 300 metres after reaching the Allt Dearg Beag at a footbridge and traverse the moor *via* a cairned path over the low ridge of Coire Riabhach. Pass a lochan on the left of the path, making for the col between Sgurr Beag and Sgurr nan Gillean. From Coire Riabhach, grass slopes and a stone shoot lead to the upper corrie. Scree then leads onto the south-east ridge itself, on the Sgurr nan Gillean side of the col. The ridge is straightforward, with a little mild scrambling on the last 60m or so. The route is well cairned and a substantial cairn exists on the ridge where the lower path joins it; a useful landmark on the descent.

SLIGACHAN FACE OF THE FIRST PINNACLE

A few rather indifferent climbs have been recorded on this face above Coire Riabhach. It is divided into two tiers by a broad shelf.

Lament   120m   III/IV   (1986)
This starts on the left of the two-tiered face which curves up below the south-east ridge and stretches across to Pinnacle Ridge. Start on the left and take an icy ramp which slants right to reach an icefall. About 10m before the icefall, break out left through overhangs to gain and climb a hidden chimney to easy ground.

Thor   40m   Mild Severe   (1963)
Start at a conspicuous chimney leading from a steep scree-covered ledge some 50 metres left of the start of Pinnacle Ridge. Climb the chimney to the level of large ledge on the left at 15m. Climb a thin crack from the left end of the ledge, crux, to a stance and belay. Continue up to join Pinnacle Ridge.

Naismith's Route   75m   Difficult   (1896)
Start on the lower tier, 70 metres left of a prominent gully (Black Chimney). Climb straight up steep rocks to the shelf. Climb the upper tier by an open shallow gully that leads left towards a chimney. Climb the chimney and the wall above to finish.

Black Chimney   75m   Severe   (1898)
This is the conspicuous gash-like gully on the lower tier. It contains a steep 15m pitch which includes a chockstone (passed on the left), an overhanging cave and finally a 10m vertical crack which is the crux.

Sligachan Buttress   90m   Difficult   (1911)
This lies on the top tier, left of Sligachan Gully, and follows steep rocks to the top of the buttress.

Sligachan Gully   100m   Difficult   (1907)
This lies beyond Black Chimney, but on the top tier. It is straightforward scrambling save for various boulder pitches. An alternative on the left, the Parallel Chimneys Variation, follows two parallel chimneys which branch from the gully. A feature of this climb is a fine cave carpeted with moss, juniper and blaeberries.

PINNACLE RIDGE AND FACE

Pinnacle Ridge throws down four pinnacles into Coire a' Bhasteir. The First Pinnacle is too broken to offer routes worthy of detailed documentation and the gully between the First and Second Pinnacle is Easy. The next two Pinnacles become increasingly impressive and the Fourth Pinnacle, or Knight's Peak, overlooks a col which has a scree gully running down to the corrie. The final tower of Sgurr nan Gillean is a well proportioned pyramid with a rather depressing series of chimneys that ooze loose rock and dampness into the corrie.

Pinnacle Ridge   Difficult **   (1880)
Climb the First Pinnacle via its north-west face, which gives approximately 150m of Moderate climbing and scrambling, decidedly tricky in the wet. The First Pinnacle can be easily descended via the scree gully between the First and Second Pinnacles into Coire a' Bhasteir.

Pleasant scrambling follows over the Second Pinnacle and onto the summit of the Third Pinnacle. The crux follows. Either descend the left ridge for a few metres, then go steeply down a crack with good holds (the popular way), or descend right to a little shoulder and go down a short slippery crack (the traditional way). Both routes end above a narrow gully. In wet weather it is advisable to abseil to the same point (numerous slings in place). Descend the narrow gully (tight but easy) to the col below Knight's Peak. Climb this by slabby ramps to a neck on the right. Descend by first traversing left below the summit to a col, then go easily down by following shelves right then back left to the gap below the final summit slopes of Sgurr nan Gillean. These can be climbed either directly above the gap, or by a traverse right. Follow numerous ways up on good rock, either on the left via a chimney, or right via ramps, or straight up the middle to the summit.
Winter: III ***   (1947)
This gives a superb climb, one of the best in Skye when in condition. Difficulties can vary greatly and can be time-consumimg, especially under powder snow. Follow the summer line.

Second Pinnacle   100m   Difficult   (1911)
There is much, usually easy, variation in the lower part and the easiest line penetrates the steeper rocks above the last terrace by an open chimney on the left. Climb the chimney for 10m, then traverse right across a slab for a few metres and traverse back left above it. An awkward move above (crux) is followed by climbing up and right for 20m to below an overhang. Finish up a steep edge to the summit.

Second-Third Gully   Difficult   (1896)
This is easy, apart from a large cave which requires much wriggling of
the back and foot variety.

The following climbs are on the Third Pinnacle.

Fria   90m   Very Difficult *   (1963)
This good climb lies on the Second-Third Gully face of the Third
Pinnacle. Traverse out of Second-Third Gully to the foot of steep rocks
some 60m from the base of the Third Pinnacle. Climb the conspicuous
fault on small holds, then take steep rock overlooking Second-Third
Gully for 60m to reach a large square cup, which has sloping floors
falling into the gully. Gain the top right-hand corner of the cup by a long
crack and leave by a short chimney to climb a further 15m to the
summit of the pinnacle.

1   Slingsby's Route   120m   Severe   (1890)
There is no difficulty from the foot of the pinnacle to a ledge level with
the top of the first pitch in Second-Third Gully. The next 30m concen-
trates the difficulties, starting some 12m left of a chimney. Steep rocks
lead to a sharply inclined slab, which is awkward to start. Difficulties
ease once a deep crack on the right is gained, whence it is easy to a
broad ledge below a cave. The crux is the exit from the cave (as always)
and is easier on the left. Easy rocks then lead to the top.

2   Luscher's No.1   120m   Very Difficult   (1920)
This is the chimney to the right of Slingsby's Route. The chimney
crosses a ledge running beneath a steep slab. Climb the chimney
direct to the ledge. Above, short pitches lead to another ledge. Continue up the rocks on the right to the ridge which falls steeply into
Third-Fourth Gully.

3   Luscher's No.2   90m   Difficult   (1920)
This starts from the Third-Fourth Gully at a deep black crack. Climb
the crack for 5m, cross the slab on the left, then climb straight up the
ridge mentioned in the previous route.

Third-Fourth Gully   100m   Very Difficult   (1905)
The climbing is confined to about 30m. The initial 20m consists of two
slimy chimneys followed by a large cave. The crux above is a loose
wall, and if you are still with us, the climb finishes up a short chimney.

KNIGHT'S PEAK

North Face   150m   Difficult   (1898/1920)
Two variations have been climbed on this face. The earlier route starts
below the difficult pitch in Third-Fourth Gully and follows a narrow ledge
before going straight up. The later route climbs a chimney in the right
side of Third-Fourth Gully to a cave. The line continues up a chimney
for a short distance before breaking out left up fine slabs to the summit.

4   West Face Direct   60m   Severe *   (1927)
An altogether more interesting way up the pinnacle. Near the middle
of the base of the pinnacle is a cave, well known as a shelter. Start a
few metres to the right.
1. 30m   Climb to the top of a slanting groove, then traverse up right
to a ledge on the skyline. Continue to a crack and follow it to an
awkward exit and a small stance. Traverse 5 metres right, then go up
a nose to a platform and belays. It is possible to traverse off right at
this point.
2. 30m   Climb a steep slab of magnificent rock a few metres above
and to the right of the last pitch. Continue by the West Face to the top.

5   West Face   150m   Moderate
To the right of Knight's Peak is Subsidiary Gully. Climb the face above
by a variety of routes on rather unsound rock.
Winter: IV **   (1962)
A good sustained climb, which takes the line of least resistance starting
as for West Face.

THE BHASTEIR FACE

6   Fourth-Fifth Gully and Face   150m   II
Climb up Fourth-Fifth Gully, then take the easiest line to the summit.

North-West Face Route   150m   II/III   (1986)
Start at the bottom of Fourth-Fifth Gully.
1. 50m   Ascend rightwards up a ramp (above MacLaren's Chimney)
until it steepens into a chimney.
2. 50m   Climb the chimney and move leftwards through a rock band
to the buttress crest.
3. 50m   Follow the crest to the summit rocks.

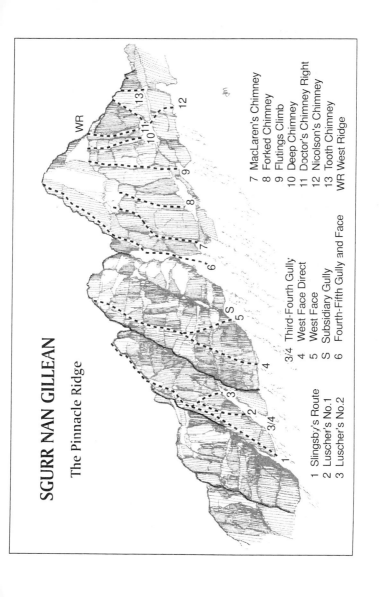

SGURR NAN GILLEAN

The Pinnacle Ridge

1 Slingsby's Route
2 Luscher's No.1
3 Luscher's No.2

3/4 Third-Fourth Gully
4 West Face Direct
5 West Face
S Subsidiary Gully
6 Fourth-Fifth Gully and Face

7 MacLaren's Chimney
8 Forked Chimney
9 Flutings Climb
10 Deep Chimney
11 Doctor's Chimney Right
12 Nicolson's Chimney
13 Tooth Chimney
WR West Ridge

Just a Boy's Game   170m   III *   (1993)
Although escapes are possible to the left, this is a good route. Start at
the ramp of North-West Face Route and gain an icefall. This gives the
first of four ice pitches with snow terraces in between, the third being
an ice bay. The route takes a fairly direct line finishing at a pinnacle on
the West Ridge less than 50 metres from the summit.

7   MacLaren's Chimney   50m   Very Difficult   (1911)
A rather loose chimney, climbed direct, which lies left of Forked
Chimney and near Fourth-Fifth Gully.

8   Forked Chimney   75m   Very Difficult   (1898)
Start 15 metres right of Fourth-Fifth Gully. The chimney is very steep
and deeply cut, and divides into two about 30m above the scree. Climb
the left branch, back and footing past an overhang. The right branch
of the chimney has also been climbed.

9   Flutings Climb   90m   Difficult   (1919)
To the right of Forked Chimney are three shallow gullies; this climb
takes the rightmost one and is reached by a 30m pitch.

10   Deep Chimney   70m   Difficult
The chimney starts at the upper left-hand corner of a scree shelf on
the right of the buttress. Loose scree is a feature in the lower part whilst
the upper is partially redeemed by a large jammed block near the top.

Doctor's Gully Left   60m   Moderate
There are two parallel gullies starting a few metres right of Deep
Chimney. Climb the left-hand one.

11   Doctor's Chimney Right   60m   Moderate
Climb the right-hand chimney.
Winter: 70m   II *   (1994)
Start at the snow bay left of Tooth Chimney and climb the gully going
straight up to the ridge over three or four enjoyable bulges.

12   Nicolson's Chimney   50m   Difficult   (1873)
This is one of the first recorded climbs in Skye, unfortunately hardly a
classic. More of a rake than a chimney, it runs up obliquely right from
near the Doctor's Gullies and strikes the western ridge of Sgurr nan
Gillean just above the initial step where the celebrated Gendarme used
to stand. It is not an escape off the West Ridge.

13   Tooth Chimney   30m   Difficult   (1956)
This is just round the corner from Nicolson's Chimney. Follow the left side of the chimney and back up around a chockstone to finish on a little col.

West Ridge   Moderate *
This gives a pleasant scramble from Bealach a' Bhasteir to the summit of Sgurr nan Gillean. From the bealach, contour around on the Coire a' Bhasteir side of Sgurr nan Gillean to a steep but straightforward chimney. This leads to a fine narrow arete formed of blocks which create steps in this section of the ridge. The celebrated pinnacle called the Gendarme, which fell in the winter of 1986, stood just beyond where the approach gully exits onto the ridge. The ridge has now consolidated at this section, but care should be taken as the blocks are in a constant state of attrition. Although this section is hardly more than scrambling, the drops are considerable on either side. The ridge becomes more broken higher up and it is customary to thread the 'window' formed by blocks near the summit.
Winter: II *
The ridge gives a fairly straightforward ascent under good consolidated snow, but under powder the approach gully and lower arete can be tricky. The difficulties are not sustained. In descent it is normal to abseil down the approach gully, or failing that the preceding chimney, Tooth Chimney. This was the traditional way when the Gendarme was still controlling the crowds.

AM BASTEIR
935m   (Map Ref 465 253)

The fine thin blade of Am Basteir has an impressive north face and harbours the distinctive Tooth on its western edge. The north face of Am Basteir is an impressive place, and if it was composed of solid rock it would undoubtedly attract climbers. Unfortunately, the basaltic dykes that form a large proportion of the face act as a deterrent. Exploration may reveal something better however.

The approach is as described above for Coire a' Bhasteir. The descent from Am Basteir is *via* the east ridge to Bealach a' Bhasteir. For the traverse of Am Basteir and the Tooth, see the descriptions of the traverse of the main ridge and the round of Coire a' Bhasteir.

Am Basteir Chimney   70m   Very Difficult   (1909)
This chimney lies to the immediate left of North Face. It is in three
sections, the first is straightforward, the next 20m is the crux with
classical chimney climbing, whilst the upper 25m is fine climbing on
excellent holds.

1   North Face   120m   Difficult
Climb the initial chimney section of Am Basteir Chimney. Traverse out
right on a series of ledges across the very steep face to below the
summit. A final short steep pitch leads to the crest of Am Basteir close
to the summit. Despite loose rock on the ledges, this is an extremely
atmospheric climb with impressive rock scenery.

2   King's Cave Chimney   30m   Very Difficult   (1898)
This is the north-facing chimney between Am Basteir and the Tooth. It
is completely enclosed and can seem hard for the grade when wet,
which is often. Despite a rock fall in 1924, the climb is still possible.
Climb 12m over chockstones to a large chamber, crux. At the back
there is a blockage, pierced by a small hole, which may require
excavation. Persevere to wriggle up the final 2m tunnel which will lead
to daylight and the col above. An unusual excursion which would
benefit from greater popularity.

3   West Wall   45m   Severe   (1960)
This is a direct route from the Tooth to Am Basteir. An easy shelf slants
leftwards up the face overlooking the Tooth. Follow this to a cairn, then
climb 4m to a cramped ledge. About 6m to the left, an awkward pull-up
leads to the foot of a prominent 10m diedre, which is not hard. There
is some loose rock on this climb.

Ordinary Route   45m   Very Difficult
This is the standard route to the summit of Am Basteir from the col
between it and the Tooth. Go right up easy broken rocks, then back left
up a gully to the well polished wall which lies right of a small undercut
groove. The short overhanging wall to the right of the groove is the
normal way; it has big holds but is decidedly strenuous. In reverse,
abseil down this wall to the ledge, then traverse off to the left to find
the descent gully. To reach the col, either reverse the Lota Corrie Route,
or abseil Naismith's Route.

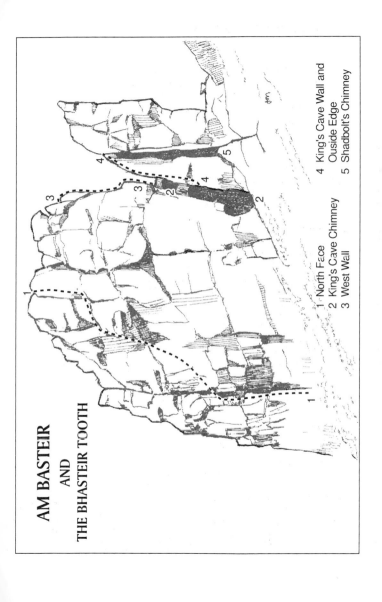

AM BASTEIR
AND
THE BHASTEIR TOOTH

1 North Face
2 King's Cave Chimney
3 West Wall

4 King's Cave Wall and
  Ouside Edge
5 Shadbolt's Chimney

BHASTEIR TOOTH
916m   (Map Ref 464 252)

This startling and fearsome fang juts out west of Am Basteir. Fortunately it is composed of sounder gabbro than Am Basteir and its ascent by the classic Naismith's Route on the south-west face is the highlight of many a tired party's ridge traverse.

   In the wet the surest way of reaching its summit is to climb Lota Corrie Route. The easiest descent is to abseil down Naismith's Route or to descend Lota Corrie Route.

THE NORTH FACE

4   King's Cave Wall and Outside Edge Continuation   55m   Severe*
(1960)
Start up the right wall of King's Cave Chimney, below the first chockstone, by a flakey crack; possible belay at 10m. Awkward climbing leads to a large semi-detached block. From just above this block make an airy though easy horizontal 20m right traverse to the edge of the undercut spur between King's Cave and Shadbolt's Chimney; belay. Climb the spur directly, adhering tenaciously to the extreme right edge, a very fine pitch.

5   Shadbolt's Chimney   50m   Very Difficult   (1906)
The chimney is in the middle of the face and is climbed by a tortuous through route. Approach either from the base of King's Cave Wall or by a traverse from the col. The initial 5m are the crux. Back and foot up the chimney above until barred by a roof. Traverse 5m horizontally outwards over jammed blocks until it is possible to see daylight behind and above. Climb towards this, to emerge on the roof by a small hole.
Variation: 50m   Very Difficult   (1932)
Instead of going into the back of the cave, back up outside to the roof, then go horizontally outwards under it and round to the end. The walls get rather too far apart for comfort, but a large slab which blocks the chimney affords relief by a crack between itself and the east wall. Constricted climbing leads to the jumbled blocks at the top; easier climbing to finish.

THE SOUTH-WEST FACE

Naismith's Route   35m   Very Difficult **   (1898)
A rather sensational climb with great atmosphere, and the scene of
many an anxious moment for tired leaders finishing the ridge. From
the ridge, traverse right in an increasingly exposed position on a
system of ledges that overlook Lota Corrie. The route takes the right
end of the face up a cracked wall. From the main ledge, continue up
to a higher ledge, small nut belay, 10m. From the right end of the ledge
either climb the wall to the cracked chimney, or if wet, traverse
awkwardly out right to the diagonal crack and steeply up this to the
same point. Continue up the easier crack-chimney to below a steep
crack. Traverse right to another crack (excellent protection) and make
the crux move over the top, 15m.

Naismith's Route Direct   35m   Difficult   (1934)
This provides a more direct start to the main route, beginning beside
a small cave some way below the col. The initial pitch takes a 15m
chimney. There are three more pitches that work up to the left, the final
one comprising some delicate traversing out left to rejoin the parent
route at the higher ledge.

Rainbow Warrior   40m   E3 **   (1989)
Start on the south face to the left of Naismith's Route.
1. 25m 6a   Take a left-trending line to reach a crack above a groove.
From the top of this, traverse left to a ledge on the arete; nut belay.
2. 15m 5c   Traverse left until it is possible to surmount the roof above.
Climb to a second, smaller roof and pass it by a crack on the left or right.

Lota Corrie Route   200m   Moderate
This is an interesting and easier way of reaching the Tooth, as enclosed
as Naismith's is exposed. Descend under the vertical south-west wall
below the Tooth into Lota Corrie where a shallow chimney-gully will be
seen cleaving the south-west ridge. Either follow the pleasant slabs to
the left of this gully to the neck under Am Basteir's west wall, or follow
a groove and short steep chimneys, separated by scree, to the same
place. This route is feasible in the wet.

SGURR A' FIONN CHOIRE
930m   (Map Ref 463 252)

This is the prominent boss of rock between the Bhasteir Tooth and
Bruach na Frithe, cleft by a gash at the top. The gash continues in the
form of a chimney some distance down the Lota Corrie face. The
easiest approach is from Bealach nan Lice.

Route One   Difficult
This lies on the Lota Corrie side. Start at a prominent nose and climb
it on the east side. Turn an overhang and climb the steep west wall *via*
a corner; the rest is easy.

Route Two   Moderate
This lies on the wall facing Am Basteir. Climb a steep chimney and
traverse a gentle slab to a steep corner on the right which leads to a
gash near the summit.

   Perhaps of more use than the climbs is one of the few springs to be
found high up near the main ridge. This lies 60m below the bealach on
the Fionn Choire side.

BRUACH NA FRITHE
958m   (Map Ref 461 252)

Approach either by the Fionn Choire from Sligachan or traverse the
main ridge from either direction to reach Bealach nan Lice. This gives
easy access to the north face.

North Chimney   Difficult   (1908)
This lies up the biggest chimney on the north face. The part of greatest
interest lies near the top where there is a chockstone "not easy to
pass", to quote the first ascensionists.

The Central Cuillin

This chapter describes the climbing in the three fine corries which lie on the west side of the central portion of the main Cuillin ridge: Coire na Creiche, Coire a' Ghreadaidh and Coire na Banachdich.

COIRE NA CREICHE

This is one of the great Cuillin corries, well seen from the Glen Brittle road. It is drained by the Allt Coir' a' Mhadaidh and the corrie itself is split into two portions by the spur of Sgurr an Fheadain. The northern part is known as Coir' a' Tairneilear and the southern part as Coir' a' Mhadaidh. The corrie is backed by Bruach na Frithe to the north, Bidein Druim nan Ramh centrally and Sgurr a' Mhadaidh to the south. It is a wild and impressive place and is not often visited by climbers. The whole atmosphere is in marked contrast to Coire Lagan and some of the climbs deserve to be more popular. Unfortunately, not all the rock is perfect, largely due to the numerous basalt dykes that cut through many of the climbs. All routes in this corrie need circumspection, but this should enhance and not detract from their quality.

The northern portion, Coir' a' Tairneilear, has rather limited climbing possibilities but the spur of Sgurr an Fheadain and the southern portion, Coir' a' Mhadaidh, have many long routes. This southern section has a great back-wall of slabs split by three prominent gullies, with the Bealach na Glaic Moire above them. Right of the slabs is the huge rock face of Sgurr a' Mhadaidh which forms a precipice nearly 300m high.

The easiest approach from Glen Brittle is *via* a path that leaves the road on the east side of the glen just below two forestry plantations at Map Ref 424 258. There is limited parking near a forest entrance. Take the path downhill from there to the river in the floor of the glen. Follow the path on the north bank past some lovely pools and waterfalls for 2km towards Sgurr an Fheadain. Just before the mouth of the corrie, cross over to the other bank of the Allt Coir' a' Tairneilear. A path which originates from Bealach a' Mhaim also crosses the stream at this point and continues round into Coir' a' Mhadaidh.

The approach to Coir' a' Mhadaidh is the same as for Coir' a' Tairneilear, but branch off after 1½km, cross the Allt Coir' a' Tairneilear at a stream junction and follow the right-hand stream into Coir' a' Mhadaidh. It is possible to walk over the Bealach na Glaic Moire to Coir'-uisg *via* this path.

The descent from the main ridge down to Coir' a' Tairneilear is by scree slopes from the col between Sgurr na Bhairnich and An Caisteal, or from the col between An Caisteal and the north top of Bidein Druim nan Ramh. This is the only easy pass over to Harta Corrie, and it is known as Bealach Harta. It is at the very back of the corrie just to the north-east of Bidein Druim nan Ramh. The descent from the main ridge into Coir' a' Mhadaidh follows a scree slope to the north of the three prominent gullies on the back wall of the corrie below the Bealach na Glaic Moire. This can also be reached by scree from between Bidein Druim nan Ramh and Sgurr an Fheadain. The descent from Bealach na Glaic Moire is the only safe way in mist off the main ridge into Coir' a' Mhadaidh. An easy descent into Coir'-uisg is also possible down the path from the Bealach na Glaic Moire.

Descents from the summit of Sgurr a' Mhadaidh are best taken *via* the col of An Dorus down to Glen Brittle, which is a very easy scree descent into Coire a' Ghreadaidh. The descent into the Coruisk basin is more complicated, with scrambling and involved route-finding. It finishes by joining the lower part of the Bealach na Glaic Moire route. Just south of An Dorus lies the Eag Dubh, a notch which is fairly easy on the west side but involves a pitch of Difficult standard on the Coruisk side. Another more interesting descent is down the Thuilm Ridge from the summit of Sgurr a' Mhadaidh. This has a section of Moderate down-climbing above the col which lies below the ridge of Sgurr Thuilm.

KEY TO MAP OPPOSITE

1   Sgurr An Fheadain, North-West Face
2   Coir' a' Mhadaidh, The Slabs
3   Sgurr a' Mhadaidh, North-West Face
4   Sgurr Thuilm, South-West Buttress
5   Sgurr a' Ghreadaidh, North-West Face
6   Sgurr Eadar da Choire, South Wall
7   Coire a' Ghreadaidh, South Branch
8   An Diallaid
9   Coire na Banachdich, Window Buttress
    and North-West Buttress

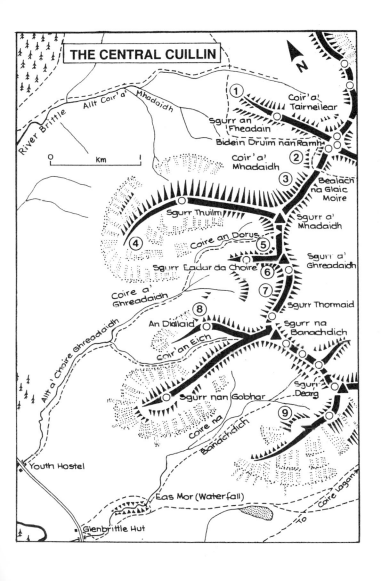

COIR' A' TAIRNEILEAR
(Map Ref 452 248)

The floor of this corrie lies at about 400m.

Sinistra Crack   150m   Severe   (1980)
This route is located on the crag on the right of the corrie, which has
two crack systems. Climb the left-hand crack, which slants slightly left,
in three long pitches to the crest of the ridge leading from Sgurr an
Fheadain to the main ridge.

SGURR AN FHEADAIN
687m   (Map Ref 453 245)

This is well seen from the road as a fine symmetrical peak, split by the
central gash of Waterpipe Gully. Its fine and open north-west face, set
at an altitude of 300m, sports a number of fine climbs in both summer
and winter. It lies just left of Waterpipe Gully. The rock tends to be better
here than elsewhere in the corrie.

1   Drainpipe Gully   120m   Difficult   (1980)
Climb the gully left of the main face *via* some pleasant pitches.

2   Edgeway   120m   Difficult *   (1980)
This climb initially follows the pleasant right-hand edge of Drainpipe
Gully, then continues straight up an obvious line.

3   The Rent   120m   VS 4c   (1980)
This climb starts left of the open gully on the main face and initially
rises to meet an open corner. Climb up the break in two pitches and
take the third and crux pitch up a tricky chimney. More straightforward
climbing leads to the top.

4   Revelation   150m   VS 4c   (1980)
To the right of the open gully is a wall. Climb this to gain a curving line
parallel to the face. A bit scrappy lower down, the climb gains in quality
with height.

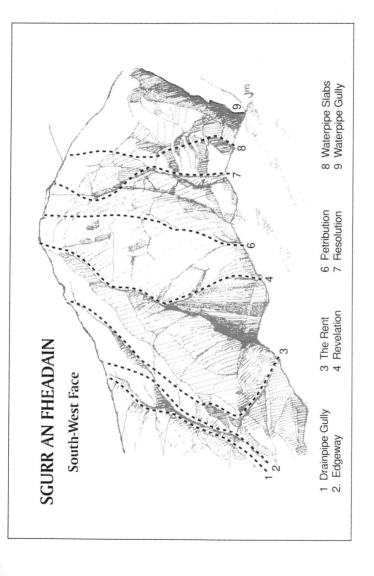

SGURR AN FHEADAIN

South-West Face

1 Drainpipe Gully	3 The Rent	6 Fetribution	8 Waterpipe Slabs
2. Edgeway	4 Revelation	7 Resolution	9 Waterpipe Gully

5   Hearthammer   105m   E3 ***   (1990)
This route takes the prominent slanting dyke high in the centre of the
face. Low in the grade. Start 3 metres left of the flake crack of
Retribution.
1. 35m 4c   Climb a slabby wall directly to a grass ledge at 25m, gain
the wall above by a large block on the right, then move back left and
go up to belay in a short corner at the base of the dyke.
2. 40m 5c   Follow the dyke diagonally rightwards to a ledge, move
right and climb the right-hand side of an overhang to rejoin the dyke
which is followed to its conclusion at a good ledge. A tremendous pitch.
3. 30m 4b   Continue more easily to the top.

6   Retribution   145m   HVS 5a   (1980)
Start at a prominent flake crack and follow this line up the central wall,
left of the two chimney systems.

7   Resolution   150m   VS 4b   (1974)
Left of the start of Waterpipe Gully is a steep wall with two chimney
systems. The route takes the right-hand chimney initially, then transfers
to the left. Start at an easy slab; cairn.
1. 40m   Climb the slab to a sapling, go up a corner for a few metres,
then move up a wall on the right to a chimney. Follow this to a spike
belay.
2. 20m   Follow the grass rake to its top, then move across the wall
on the left to a good stance and ash belay.
3. 40m   Traverse left to join the other crack system and climb this
diagonally right to a steep grassy recess. Climb a short corner on the
left, or the slab on the right, to a good ledge and poor peg belay.
4. 10m   Move a few metres right and go up to a good stance at the
foot of a short corner.
5. 40m   Climb the corner and an easy diagonal line left to the top.

8   Waterpipe Slabs   150m   Hard Severe 4b *   (1981)
This route starts centrally between Waterpipe Gully and Resolution. It
follows a parallel course to Resolution, always taking the line of least
resistance to the top.

9   Waterpipe Gully   400m   Mild VS 4b *   (1895)
The first ascent of the prominent central gully, which cleaves the peak
in two, was a remarkable feat for the time and it has produced one of
the major gully climbs in Scotland. Although many of the pitches can

be turned on the right wall, thus reducing the climb to Severe standard, the following description probably takes in the best climbing. It is more of an expedition than a pure rock climb and when reasonably dry can be climbed in rock boots. Although the rock is loose in places, it is not unreasonable, and escapes are rarely hard to find.

There are several pitches of note. The first obstacle is a streaming pitch, best turned by the steep right wall. If taken direct it is VS and can be split halfway. To turn it, climb up then right to trend back left past a tired tree to poor belays. Above this section a loose scramble leads back into the gully. A chockstone pitch leads to the third pitch, a fine but wet back and foot chimney. Higher up, the direct route on the left is a wet and nasty green chimney. Taken direct this is VS 4c, with precarious back and foot work. However the broad chimney on the right is much more amenable.

Further up, an impasse presents itself in the form of a wet pitch. Go up the short wall on the left to gain a chimney on the right. Climb this, then step left to cross a rib (crux, 4b) to reach a shallow chimney and a small spike belay on the left. Climb the chimney to a heather rake, then go back right to regain the gully above the overhung chimney pitch. Easy scrambling now leads into a deep and impressive cleft. Climb a usually wet and poorly protected pitch on the left to a stance below huge chockstones. A grand finale leads past impressive but not very difficult chockstones.

Winter: 400m   IV *

Expecting the chance of a lifetime, the first ascensionists were a little disappointed that the pitches were mostly short and separated by walkable snow. The hardest and longest pitch was the first, of 30m. Leaner but icy conditions could well produce an entirely different sort of climb.

The Hose   360m   III   (1978)

About 50 metres right of Waterpipe Gully is another shallow gully. Two 45m ice pitches and several smaller ones were encountered *en route*. Escapes are possible to the right.

Moon Raker   60m   VS   (1963)

The line is well seen from the Foxes' Rake on Sgurr a' Mhadaidh. It follows a prominent boomerang-shaped corner well right of Waterpipe Gully. There are three pitches, one of 30m and two of 15m. The second pitch is the crux.

The Spur and Summit Gullies   Moderate   (1907)
These are on the north buttress, starting some distance up from the screes. The gully has a prominent rounded boulder capping the first pitch, well seen from below. Above the boulder, the gully continues as a deep-cut cleft which gives quite a good climb. There is another gully further to the left in the same buttress, containing three good pitches.

COIR' A' MHADAIDH

Right of Sgurr an Fheadain at the head of the corrie lie sweeps of slabs split by three prominent gullies, very visible on the approach walk.

Stag Gully   120m   II/III   (1994)
Left of North Gully is a thin chimney slot. Climb this in three pitches to a terrace where a further pitch leads to the top. This gully is only 2 metres wide in places.

Stag Buttress   200m   III   (1994)
This is the buttress to the right of Stag Gully. Take a more or less central line to the crux section halfway up at some slabby rocks. Below and above this section the climbing is much easier.

North Gully   120m   Moderate   (1914)
This can be used as an alternative to the ascent to the Bealach na Glaic Moire. The first obstacle is an overhanging slab extending across the gully, which is avoided by a crack on the left wall. The final cave pitch gives a through route.
Winter: III *   (1983)
The gully gave a fine ice pitch at mid-height and a through route up to the Bealach na Glaic Moire.

Central Buttress   220m   II/III   (1995)
This climb is on the broad area of rock between North Gully and Central Gully, taking a chimney line to the right of the large area of slabs. Easy climbing for 100m leads to a steeper central section where the chimney gives three long pitches to the top. The middle pitch has a rock barrier which can prove tricky in thin conditions.

Central Gully   100m   Difficult   (1952)
The initial bridging pitch is the best. Above, the angle lessens and the walls become shallow and after a while the gully ends on the slabs at mid-height.

1   South Gully   210m   Severe ***   (1937)
Probably the perfect gully and definitely not to be missed, quite a different proposition from the other two. An excellent climb for a hot day when the pool is at its most tempting. Climb over a succession of excellent pitches, seven or eight depending on conditions, all of about Difficult to Very Difficult in standard. Then a 20m pitch follows, which usually has a greenish-blue pool at its foot. Climb this pitch direct, or in wet weather by the right wall. The next pitch has not been climbed direct, so climb out on the slabs on the right to regain the gully. After several more interesting pitches the final chasm is climbed by back and foot between smooth walls past two chockstones.
Winter: III/IV *   (1986)
On the first ascent the gully was largely banked out, but it provided two good pitches. An earlier attempt failed due to thin conditions, so it has to be concluded that an ideal ascent will require much ice and moderate snow. When thin, it will be harder, at least Grade IV.

The following route is located on the left of the corrie as you walk along the burn towards South Gully, about 350 metres before it.

Stepped Buttress   II   (1995)
The bottom of the route is a steep wall with a line of small left-slanting ledges. Start about 30 metres from the burn. Climb the initial steep wall by a line of left-slanting ledges with one awkward section. Continue to the top of the first step in another pitch, then walk to the second step. Climb this in two pitches to a scree slope. It is possible to descend rightwards back into the corrie or to climb another route on the headwall.

SGURR A' MHADAIDH
918m   (Map Ref 446 235)

This fine mountain offers some superb climbing, especially on the north-west face. Approach along the Allt Coir' a' Mhadaidh path, as for Sgurr an Fheadain, then branch off right into Coir' a' Mhadaidh.
The north-west face is a complex series of cliffs and ledges at an altitude of about 600m. The main features include a large amphitheatre left of centre, from which two prominent rakes lead diagonally right. The lower one is Foxes' Rake, which provides a Moderate climb, crossing some loose ground. It finishes by a short chimney at a broad notch high up on the north-west ridge. The upper rake is of comparable standard,

but better quality. It is reached by a right-slanting gully from the back of the amphitheatre and finishes between the third top and the main summit of Sgurr a' Mhadaidh. Neither route is obvious in poor visibility.

Several large buttresses lie left of the amphitheatre; to its right, and below Foxes' Rake there is a massive wall of rock, the true north-west face, split by the groove of Shining Cleft. Right of this, the angle becomes more amenable and slabs stretch right towards the long diagonal gully of Slanting Gully. Right again, the buttress rears up, forming a rib that abuts Deep Gash Gully. The right wall of this forms a splendid buttress of excellent rock, which effectively marks the right-hand end of the crag.

Many of the climbs are on sound rock, but several have either sections of general unsoundness or have basalt dykes crossing them. Allow several dry days before attempting the major lines as they retain water well.

The climbs are best described from left to right; all the routes lie right of South Gully.

2   North-West Buttress   360m   Very Difficult   (1896)
This is the broken buttress right of South Gully, starting left of a shallow gully. It has three sections of equal height, the lowest and uppermost sections being easy. The middle section has one steep pitch which is usually turned on the right by the shallow gully. Climb up the gully for 20m, then traverse back left to the middle line of the buttress by a narrow groove, 20m. There is much variation on this climb and greater difficulties can be sought if desired.

Clap Trap   240m   Severe   (1966)
This is a disappointing climb up the west spur of North-West Buttress. From the corrie it looks like a steep unbroken rib, but in fact it consists of a series of steep walls between broad scree ledges sloping down into the amphitheatre. Take a direct line from just above the main waterslide at the mouth of the amphitheatre. The climb deteriorates after three pitches.

3   Goliath Buttress   345m   HVS *   (1964)
This climb takes the easiest line up the prominent buttress between the slabby rocks of North-West Buttress and the amphitheatre. After about 20 metres of scrambling, start beneath a crack at the left end of the block overhangs which guard the base of the crag, about 25 metres left of Sanguinary Cracks.

1. 40m 4a   Climb slabs to the foot of the crack and follow this to a stance in a niche under a large overhang; peg belay.
2. 25m 4a   Step left onto a rib and continue straight up to a block belay.
3. 35m 4a   Continue up the fault by a double crack to a large overhang, then traverse 5m to a stance on the right edge of the buttress; peg belay.
4. 25m   Climb to a large terrace.
5. 20m 4a   The line of overhangs above is broken by a dyke in the centre. Climb to a ledge beneath this; peg belay.
6. 20m 5a   Surmount the overhanging dyke, exit using one peg for aid and continue to a good ledge.
7. 30m 4c   Move up to a large block perched on a slab, cross the block to a very steep wall on the left and climb this strenuously, but on large holds, to a terrace.
8. etc. 150m   Easier climbing now leads to a junction with North-West Buttress, 60m, which is followed to the summit, 90m.

4   Gargantua   360m   HVS 5a *   (1969)
This climb follows the right-hand edge of Goliath Buttress. At the bottom right-hand corner of the buttress a line of cracks slopes up to the right. Start just below this at a shallow groove (arrow).
1. 30m   Climb the groove, then follow the edge of the buttress to flake belays below a slightly overhanging wall.
2. 25m   Traverse 6m left, then go up slabs and grooves to a large ledge below the right end of block overhangs girdling the front of the buttress; peg belay.
3. 20m 5a   Follow the dyke right for 4m, go up then left below one overhang and out onto a lip of the overhang above the previous stance, crux. Climb the wall and slab above to a ledge; peg belay.
4. 35m   Climb to a large terrace.
5. etc. 250m   Now follow the crest of the buttress for several pitches to join North-West Buttress.

Sanguinary Cracks   210m   Severe   (1958)
This climb follows the prominent line of cracks on the right flank of Goliath Buttress. Start left of the amphitheatre, just above the level of the foot of Foxes' Rake, at a chockstone belay at the base of the cracks.
1. 30m   Climb a crack and the slabs on its right to a shelf.
2. 30m   Continue up the shallow chimney above to a horizontal shelf.
   Easier climbing leads for 75m to another shelf. Above, a short steep pitch leads to a ledge where the line of cracks finishes. Scrambling is

possible either left or right, but it is better to continue directly to the summit. The last pitch is somewhat loose.

5   Foxes' Rake   Moderate
This is the lower of the two right-slanting rakes. Starting from the screes below the amphitheatre, follow the broad easy-angled rake of overlapping slabs, crossing the face diagonally to finish on the north-west or Thuilm Ridge *via* a short chimney at a broad notch. Care should be taken as the climb crosses some loose ground. This route should be used as a descent only in clear weather.

Upper Rake   Moderate *
This route, a better climb than Foxes' Rake, is reached by a right-slanting gully from the back of the amphitheatre. It finishes between the third top and the main summit of Sgurr a' Mhadaidh.

Gauger's Gully   100m   Difficult   (1939)
From Upper Rake, a deep-cut gully splits the middle of the second peak of Sgurr a' Mhadaidh. The gully has three principal pitches. Climb easily up the bed of the gully to a stance and belay below a chockstone. Climb the left wall and continue past the chockstone to a chimney above. Climb the back and foot chimney past a large chockstone to the top.

Icicle Factory   205m   VI,6 ***   (1986)
A superb route taking the prominent ice-choked corner in the back right-hand side of the amphitheatre, up to the left of The Smear.
1. 30m   Climb into an ice groove and continue to a ledge on the left.
2. 30m   Climb an ice curtain on the left to gain a right-slanting ramp which is followed to a belay below the main difficulties.
3. 30m   Ascend the narrowing ice ramp and surmount the capping icicle to belay on the right.
4. 25m   Continue up an icicle and the steep ice above to belay beneath the very impressive final pitch.
5. 45m   Climb the ice column to the overhang and transfer to an icicle on the right which leads to an easy gully. A superb pitch.
6. 45m   Continue to the ridge.

The Smear   90m   V/5 **   (1979)
This is the prominent icefall that flows down between Foxes' Rake and the Upper Rake. It gives a very good climb when in condition.

SGURR A' MHADAIDH
North-West Face

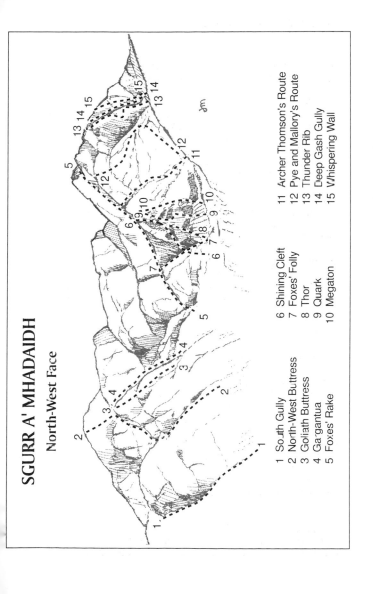

1 South Gully
2 North-West Buttress
3 Goliath Buttress
4 Ga'gantua
5 Foxes' Rake

6 Shining Cleft
7 Foxes' Folly
8 Thor
9 Quark
10 Megaton

11 Archer Thomson's Route
12 Pye and Mallory's Route
13 Thunder Rib
14 Deep Gash Gully
15 Whispering Wall

6   Shining Cleft   270m   Hard Severe 4b *   (1952)
A long rather rambling climb that has considerable atmosphere. It starts left of the long diagonal gully, Slanting Gully, crosses it, then continues up the great V-cleft at the top. It should be noted that the cleft is a natural drainage line and due to the amount of basalt present the grade will escalate alarmingly if greasy.

Start at the lowest point of the slabby rocks left of Slanting Gully and cross them to a cairn. Climb up right to a ledge, then go up a 4m slab to a slanting chimney in a long low overhang. Trend right across slabs to a recess above the big cave in Slanting Gully and cross the gully at that point. Follow a narrow gangway, then a broad slabby ledge under big overhangs, to a slabby amphitheatre topped by a basalt sill. This amphitheatre runs up to form the great V-shaped cleft of smooth basalt which is overhung at its top. Follow the cleft, easily at first, to the sill and belays. Now traverse delicately right on basalt to reach a right-slanting ledge, 4b. Climb a short chimney to a platform on the crest of the rib, which forms the right wall of the V-cleft. Follow the rib, at first by a chimney on the left, then by easier rocks on the crest, to finish in Foxes' Rake.

7   Foxes' Folly   105m   Severe *   (1950)
A very pleasant climb. Start at the base of the dyke 6 metres left of Slanting Gully.
1. 40m   Climb the dyke to steeper rocks and a block belay near the gully.
2. 10m   Traverse left until the steep rocks can be climbed back to the right to a small broken overhang with spike belays.
3. 10m 4a   Climb the fault through the overhang above to reach a steep slab which leads to Slanting Gully above a wedged block.
4. 30m   Easy climbing on the edge of the gully leads to the final pitch below Foxes' Rake.
4. 15m   Climb a crack on the left of the gully to the rake. Finish up Foxes' Rake.

Slanting Gully   210m   Severe   (1907)
Despite rockfall, this climb is still possible but has areas of unsound rock. The grade will depend on the current state of the climb. The gully is divided into two parts where Foxes' Rake intersects it rather more than halfway up. An easy initial pitch leads to a stance in the gully. Either bridge up the narrows or climb the left wall by a narrow ledge, 25m. Minor pitches follow to where Foxes' Rake bisects the gully. Above

lies the 'Cracks Pitch'. Climb up to and out of a small cave with an overhanging roof; this can be avoided on the left. Just below the Upper Rake is a good 25m pitch.

Two Pitch Gully   75m   Very Difficult   (1911)
This is the deep, vertical, chockstoned rift in the rock wall of the third peak of Sgurr a' Mhadaidh. It starts from the Upper Rake and lies 90 metres right of the top section of Slanting Gully. The start of the climb is the crux, where a short entry gains the chimney above.

Fox Trap   60m   Very Difficult   (1951)
This short climb lies on the south-west face of the third peak of Sgurr a' Mhadaidh, right of Two Pitch Gully. It can be seen from the south-west peak of Sgurr a' Mhadaidh as a narrow right-slanting dyke-chimney. If required, it can be reached from the ridge by descending Upper Rake from the col between the third and fourth peaks of Sgurr a' Mhadaidh; it is the first fault encountered. The route follows the chimney throughout, passing a few chockstones higher up, and finishes on the ridge.

The cliff now dramatically steepens and presents a huge diamond-shaped wedge of rock, 200m high, where three high quality lines find their way. It should be pointed out that there are considerable areas of loose or brittle rock on this crag.

8   Thor   240m   E2 **   (1967)
A fine hard route, taking the steep rocks right of Slanting Gully, which represented a considerable breakthrough at the time of its first ascent. Start 12 metres right of Slanting Gully where a short gangway leads left into a corner above its undercut base.
Follow the gangway into the corner and go directly up this on a narrow dyke to a stance on the left (25m 5a). Continue directly up the dyke to a stance on an easy traverse line about 10m below the lower overhangs. Go up to the right for 12m to a stance on a wide sloping ledge, 4b. The next section is the crux. Move up left onto the wall, then traverse a horizontal gangway with difficulty to an old peg. Make a tricky move across an overhanging dyke to a sloping ledge on the left, 5c. Continue up the steep but easier corner directly above, stepping across left at the top to a stance and peg belay, 4c. Continue directly towards the large corner which splits the upper buttress (The Shining Cleft), 4b. Climb it until forced off, and finish by its right-hand arete, 4b.

9   Quark   210m   E3 **   (1976)

The second great route of the trilogy, which takes a direct and fierce line in an excellent position between Thor and Megaton. Start 25 metres right of Thor.

1. 45m 5b   Climb a slab to below a steep wall, possible belay at 15m, and climb grooves on the left past large poised blocks to a vertical basalt dyke. Move left and follow a shallow fault to the upper slab, then go up left to a good ledge.

2. 45m 5c   Go diagonally right to a steep groove (often wet), climb 7m to a standing place, then traverse right with difficulty, crux, to a small stance and possible belay. It is probably better to continue. Climb a hanging black groove to move right to a belay.

3. 45m 4c   Continue up the groove, then move left to easier ledges. Follow the ramp back right to a belay. This pitch is unpleasantly loose with small stones on the ledges.

4. and 5. 75m   Continue more easily to the top, taking the line of choice.

10   Megaton   250m   E1 ***   (1972)

This was an excellent route, but it has had no recorded ascent since the crux ramp collapsed leaving unstable and blank areas of rock. Subsequent to the rockfall, there have been two known attempts, one of which freed the combined tactics move at 6a. Both parties retreated on reaching the remains of the ramp. As one of the best climbs of its grade in Skye, the route is recorded both for posterity and as an obvious challenge. Start centrally, below the widest part of the over-hangs, 75m above and right of Thor.

1. 35m   Climb the lower slab to belay below overhangs.

2. 40m 5a   Traverse right to a basalt breach in the overhanging wall, then climb to a large ledge; escape possible.

3. 25m 5a   Gain the upper slab, then traverse horizontally to its lip, small stance and peg belay.

4. 25m 5b   Using combined tactics, gain and climb the left-slanting ramp, peg runner, to a small stance and peg belay.

5. 35m 5a   Climb up for 12m, then traverse left to easier slabs.

6. and 7. 90m 4b   Continue more easily, finishing close to Shining Cleft on the rounded rib.

The cliff now becomes slabby once more and the rock improves. The following lines are open to many adventurous variations.

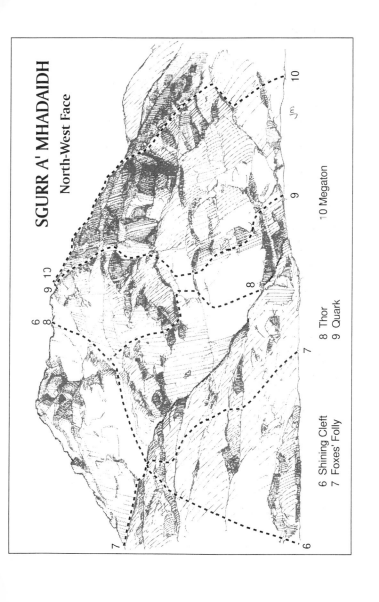

SGURR A' MHADAIDH
North-West Face

6 Shining Cleft
7 Foxes' Folly

8 Thor
9 Quark

10 Megaton

Vixen Groove   135m   Severe   (1968)
Start as for Archer Thomson's Route and follow this for 45m to a slabby bay. Then climb the groove above to the top in four pitches, with an awkward and loose chimney-cave at 90m.

11   Archer Thomson's Route   225m   Severe *   (1911)
A real mountaineering route with a nominal grading; be prepared for harder climbing! A fault lies midway between Slanting Gully and Deep Gash Gully; easy rocks lie to the right of this. Using route-finding skills, try to find the easiest way up the cliff.

Mantrap   200m   Hard Severe   (1958)
This climb lies up a fault line about 15 metres right of Archer Thomson's route. Climb easy rocks to the right of the fault, which is at first wide and broken; belay on a broad ledge. Continue up right of the fault to a stance. Above, the fault steepens and becomes harder. Climb up left over slabby undercut rocks to a bottleneck in the fault. Traverse awkwardly right, then climb steepening rock and pass a final bulge at the narrowest section of the fault, crux, usually wet. Easier climbing leads to a very wet, steep and loose overhanging exit; turn this on the left. Easier pitches lead to Foxes' Rake.

12   Pye and Mallory's Route   225m   Very Difficult **   (1918)
A fine and historic route with yet more intriguing route-finding. The start is artificial but traditional, the alternative being more direct. Start as for Archer Thomson's Route, then after 10m make an easy 45m right traverse, parallel to the scree, until close to the dyke gully. Keep left of the dyke for 60m, trending away from it. Move left to a shallow chimney and climb it, finishing by the left wall. After 45m the climbing becomes easier. An interesting finish is to traverse right and climb a shallow chimney which leads to Foxes' Rake.

To the right of the dyke gully the crag rears up into a fine-looking rib.

13   Thunder Rib   240m   E1 5a   (1960)
A fine name for a loose climb, which takes the rib left of Deep Gash Gully. Start at the centre of the rib and climb it to a stance. A few metres above, gain a traverse line left and follow it, descending slightly, to the lip of some overhangs. Continue traversing hard left, crux, around the

corner until it is possible to resume upwards progress. Go up, then right, passing right of three old pegs, then continue diagonally up through bulges to the edge of Deep Gash Gully. Finish up the crest of the gully. There are several variations, all harder. Unfortunately the state of some of the rock leaves doubt as to its overall stability.

14   Deep Gash Gully   120m   HVS 5a **   (1949)
This is the prominent, usually wet gully on the right of the north-west face. An historic climb, scene of epic sorties and a fine outing. It was first investigated by W.W.Naismith and G.B.Gibbs in August 1898 (who reached the second pitch), then by several others, including Shadbolt, who soloed the lower pitch. The Cuillin's equivalent of Glen Coe's Raven's Gully.
1. 20m 4c   Back up to the topmost of a series of chockstones which form the roof of a large cave. The exit is contorted and leads to a belay.
2. 20m 5a   Continue up the narrow gully across another interesting roof. Easier rocks lead to the top of the chimney.
   Two easier pitches now follow, the second of which involves a left traverse and a 12m overhanging chimney which leads to a cave. Climb out of the cave by descending for 2m, then go up awkward loose rocks on the right wall until a strenuous chimney (arm pulls and knee jams) leads to a belay (4c). Three easier pitches lead thankfully to the top.
Winter: VI,7 ***   (1991)
A formidable and atmospheric winter climb.
1. 30m   Climb a short step, then easy snow to a large roofed cave.
2. 15m   Back and foot to huge chockstones in the roof, then go out and under the lip of the overhangs to an awkward exit. Belay in the recess immediately above.
3. 40m   Climb a short step and easy snow to a hollow on the right wall.
4. 40m   Go up left into the extremely steep upper gully. Bridge up past an ice pillar, then climb iced grooves to a hidden cave recess below the final overhangs.
5. 30m   Climb 3m on the right wall, then make very committing moves to bridge the gully and enter a narrow chimney. Surmount the final capstone direct and climb steep snow to belay at the next chockstone recess.
6. and 7. 90m   Bridge past the chockstone, then climb the snow gully to a short exit pitch.

Dyke and Buttress Route   180m   Severe **   (1956)
The first half of this climb follows the slanting dyke gully left of Deep
Gash Gully, while the top half takes the buttress to its right. The
situation is superb.
1. 30m   From the bottom of Deep Gash Gully, traverse horizontally
15 metres left on a grass ledge to the dyke. Climb the gully, mainly by
the left wall, to below the overhanging cave pitch.
2. 10m   Climb the crux overhang *via* a tricky move.
3. 50m   Climb more easily up the gully to where jammed blocks form
a shallow cave. Above this, the gully peters out in an area of broken
ground.
4. 15m   From the top of the jammed blocks, traverse up and right
across the right wall of the gully to a massive flake belay beneath a
vertical wall.
5. and 6. 75m   Turn the vertical rocks on the left by an awkward
sloping shelf, then make straight up the buttress on interesting rocks
to finish.
   Further scrambling, first left to avoid a prominent tower, then right
above it, leads across the top of Deep Gash Gully to the final rocks of
the Thuilm Ridge.

15   Whispering Wall   180m   Very Difficult ***   (1960)
This excellent sustained climb is one of the best routes in the Cuillin.
The large crag on the right side of Deep Gash Gully faces across to
Thunder Rib. A choice of routes leads to a slanting terrace at 45m.
Above the terrace, follow a vertical dyke which provides the nearest
feasible line to Deep Gash Gully and lies just outside the gully wall.
After 60m, leave the dyke, which swings away to the left, and continue
on the original line up a steep 20m pitch. Now climb easier rock, then
finish by a series of cracks and chimneys, turning the uppermost on
the left.

   Right of Whispering Wall lies the Thuilm Ridge of Sgurr a'Mhadaidh.
This can either be approached by traversing over Sgurr Thuilm or by
ascending fairly directly to the Thuilm - Mhadaidh col from Coire an
Dorus.

Thuilm Ridge of Sgurr a' Mhadaidh   Moderate
This is the north-west ridge of the mountain. Two rock ribs rise quite
impressively from the col. Weave a way up the slabby left-hand one,
awkward and exposed in places. The ridge then levels off and a dip on
the crest marks the top of Foxes' Rake. The rest of the ascent is easy

and soon leads to a minor top (900m) on the main ridge. Turn right and follow ledges on the right (west) of the narrow crest, reaching the main summit after some 120 metres. The ridge also provides a good descent after climbing in the corrie.

COIRE A' GHREADAIDH

Coire a' Ghreadaidh is a huge open corrie lying west of Sgurr a' Ghreadaidh. It is bounded on the north by the ridge linking Sgurr Thuilm with Sgurr a' Mhadaidh and to the south by the western ridge of Sgurr na Banachdich. The surrounding mountains are, from north to south, the ridge of Sgurr Thuilm leading to Sgurr a' Mhadaidh, the col of An Dorus, Sgurr a' Ghreadaidh with a short spur leading north-west to Sgurr Eadar da Choire, Sgurr Thormaid, the col of Bealach Thormaid, then a south-westerly pronged ridge leading to An Diallaid on the north prong and Sgurr nan Gobhar on the south one.

The corrie has two subsidiary recesses in its upper reaches. The left-hand (northern) one, high up under the summit of Sgurr a' Mhadaidh, is known as Coire an Dorus. It is situated under the important gap on the ridge known as An Dorus. Coire an Dorus is separated from the main corrie by a small spur which leads out to Sgurr Eadar da Choire. The main corrie, the south branch of Coire a' Ghreadaidh, is much larger, very rocky and has no simple route to or from the main ridge. To the south-west lies a subsidiary corrie known as Coir' an Eich. It is a minor scree bowl between Sgurr nan Gobhar and An Diallaid, two small tops on the ridges leading west and north-west respectively from Sgurr na Banachdich.

Coire a' Ghreadaidh is approached from the bridge at the Youth Hostel by a path on the south bank of the Allt a' Choire Ghreadaidh. In its lower reaches this lovely stream presents a series of pools and waterfalls.

The easiest descent from Coire an Dorus is down the easy scree of the An Dorus col. The Glen Brittle side is easy, but it is a more complicated scramble down to the Coruisk basin, with tricky route-finding, joining the lower section of the Bealach na Glaic Moire route down to Coruisk. A notch just south of An Dorus, Eag Dubh, is fairly easy on the Glen Brittle side but has one pitch of Difficult standard in a gully on the Coruisk side. To the right of An Dorus is the north-west face of Sgurr a' Ghreadaidh, which has a broad rake running up right from below. From the top of this rake, easy scrambling leads to the summit of Sgurr a' Ghreadaidh. This is not recommended as a descent route in mist due to the difficulty of identifying the top of the rake.

The descent from the main or south corrie is more complicated. There are two unattractive descents, both Moderate, from cols either side of Sgurr Thormaid. The north-easterly col has a gully which slants down to the left. To reach the south-westerly col, Bealach Thormaid, if on the Ghreadaidh side, skirt the three teeth of the north-east ridge of Sgurr Thormaid by a ledge on the west, which leads down to the col. From there, descend a gully and a rake which passes under a massive overhang on the north-west face to the corrie. An easy descent from Coir' an Eich is down the scree, or from An Diallaid down a scree slope into Coir' an Eich.

The climbing in the corrie is mainly centred around the interesting north-west face of Sgurr a' Ghreadaidh and on the lower south-west flank of Sgurr Thuilm.

SOUTH-WEST BUTTRESS OF SGURR THUILM   (Map Ref 430 237)

This buttress can be approached in about an hour from Glen Brittle by the path, as described above. It is the first crag in the corrie, and being low (about 400m) it often escapes the worst of the Cuillin weather, being frequently below the mist level. It is fairly quick drying and has one very good route and others of interest. The crag is split by a prominent central corner, taken by Gail, which has a slab on the right. The rock is never above suspicion and much of the crag is for steady climbers only. It would vastly improve with a little more traffic.

The descent follows scree down the left flank of the crag. The climbs are described from left to right.

Black Slab   60m   Moderate *   (1992)
The left end of the crag is composed of firm gabbro slabs. Near the left end is an undercut cave. Start just left of the cave and take a delightful line straight up the slabs.

Soft Options   60m   Hard Severe   (1992)
1. 30m 4c   Climb the prow on the right of the cave, then go straight up the slabs above.
2. 25m 4b   Continue up the slabs to a bulging headwall, and pull over the first bulge to a stance and belay.
3. 5m 4b   Climb the short headwall.

Fosdyke   60m   Hard Severe   (1971)
Start about 5 metres left of Gail.
1. 25m   Climb the prominent vertical dyke to a small stance below
roofs.
2. 5m 4b   Traverse the slab on the left below the large roof, using
undercuts, to a small stance.
3. 30m   Climb the slabby corner above until it becomes grassy, then
move right and follow a steep groove to a scree terrace.

Gail   95m   E1 **   (1965)
This very fine route takes the slabby corner in the centre of the crag.
Most of the loose rock has been removed, and the climbing is well
protected on the second and third pitches.
1. 25m 4a   Climb the rib right of the mossy groove, then trend left to
a big spike.
2. 20m 5b   Climb the corner direct to a small ledge above the crux
steepening.
3. 15m 5a   Climb to the band of overhangs, then traverse right on
underclings to a ledge.
4. 35m 4b   Rather than climb the easy groove above, step boldly left
onto a ramp and go around the edge onto a slab. Climb this to easy
ground.

Pincer   65m   HVS   (1965)
This is the vertical dyke just right of the Gail slab. It gives a sustained,
interesting and worrying pitch which is much more solid than it looks,
requiring a patient approach. Protection is adequate.
1. 25m 4c/5a   Climb the right-curving dyke past a broken ledge and
continue to a heathery nook.
2. 15m   Climb easily up the dyke to the stance on Gail.
5. 25m   Finish up the groove.

NORTH-WEST FACE OF SGURR A' GHREADAIDH
(Map Ref 445 233)

This is the large mass of rock at an altitude of about 750m, stretching
from An Dorus to Sgurr Eadar da Choire. It is an excellent cliff, split
into two distinct buttresses by the notch of Eag Dubh. The buttress to
the left of Eag Dubh, An Dorus Buttress, is larger, firmer and friendlier
than the long crag to the right, Summit Buttress. The latter has several

distinct corner and groove lines plus some areas of friable rock. The prominent split below the highest point is taken by Hamish's Chimney.

The approach follows the path to Coire an Dorus as described above. Descents are best made to the left of An Dorus Buttress, which is easy, also to the right of Summit Buttress as mentioned in the preamble to Coire a' Ghreadaidh. It is also possible to descend the Eag Dubh, which is fairly easy on the west side but involves a pitch of Difficult on the Coruisk side down a chimney, which can be abseiled.

AN DORUS BUTTRESS
The climbs are described from left to right.

1   Trapist   85m   VS   (1976)
This pleasant route follows the pronounced dyke on the left side of the buttress.
1. 45m 4a   Climb the dyke on the left side of the buttress.
2. 40m 4c   Climb easily to a steepening, then climb the wall left of the dyke to reach a diagonal ramp leading back right to the top.

2   Simplicity   170m   Severe *   (1976)
A very good route indeed, with the most enjoyable climbing on the crag. Start below the smooth-looking slabs towards the left of the face.
1. 40m   Follow a dyke up the slabs, then move right to belay under a large overhang; an excellent pitch.
2. 35m   Climb the overhang on the right, then continue easily to a grass ledge.
3. 40m   Climb the wall above.
4. 30m   Scramble to the base of the final wall.
5. 25m   Climb the rough juggy wall to the top; a good pitch.

3   An Dorus Buttress   130m   Very Difficult   (1955)
The more broken rocks right of Simplicity give the original route on the crag. Start at the lowest rocks and follow a central route throughout, with much moderate scrambling on excellent rock. There is considerable scope for variation and some of the difficulties are avoidable.

4   Gauche   150m   VS *   (1976)
Another good line, following the crack in the right side of the buttress. The second and fourth pitches are both good.
1. 40m 4a   Climb the crack direct to a stance.
2. 35m 4b   Climb to the overhang and turn this on the left wall.
3. 40m   Scramble to below the final wall.
4. 35m 4b   The exposed arete between the chimney and grooves leads to the top.

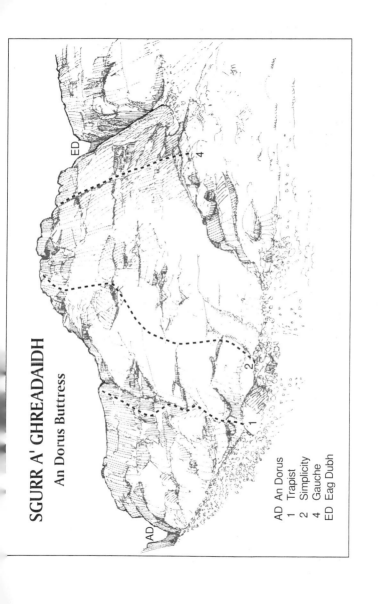

SGURR A' GHREADAIDH
An Dorus Buttress

AD An Dorus
1 Trapist
2 Simplicity
4 Gauche
ED Eag Dubh

SUMMIT BUTTRESS

To the right of the preceding routes is a gully which leads to the notch of the Eag Dubh. Beyond the Eag Dubh lies the imposing Summit Buttress of Sgurr a' Ghreadaidh. Due to basalt dykes, there are areas of unsound rock interspersed with excellent gabbro.

1   Scimitar   80m   VS *   (1968)
Left of Hamish's Chimney are a pair of steep left-curving corners. This route takes the left-hand one, starting near the centre of the crag, 60 metres left of Hamish's Chimney. The climb is high in the grade.
1. 35m 4c   Climb shallow grooves to the large overhang. Traverse left, crux, and go up and left to the start of the crack.
2. 45m 4a   Follow the crack to the top.

2   Hamish's Chimney   90m   Difficult   (1965)
This is the obvious chimney on the right-hand side of the crag. It provides interesting climbing and leads directly to the summit cairn.

3   Virgin Arete   75m   VS   (1965)
This route lies up the buttress immediately right of Hamish's Chimney. The first pitch is good, but the climb is easier and looser above.
1. 20m 4c   Climb a groove and a strenuous overhang on the edge overlooking the chimney.
2. 45m 4a   Continue in the same line to the terrace.
3. 10m   Scramble up easy rocks to the ridge.

SGURR EADAR DA CHOIRE
(Map Ref 443 234)

South of the north-west face lies a prominent ridge which divides Coire a' Ghreadaidh into its north and south branches. It contains a double-topped peak, Sgurr Eadar da Choire. The ridge gives a fine line of ascent, particularly under winter conditions, as well as some other routes.

North-West Ridge of Sgurr a' Ghreadaidh   Moderate   (1898)
This ridge provides 320m of pleasant scrambling. Rotten rock at its foot can be avoided by traversing a rake from the screes below Hidden Gully in the south branch of the corrie, or by an easy rake from Coire an Dorus. The direct ascent of the ridge gives climbing that can be harder than Moderate if a suitable line is chosen.

SGURR A' GHREADAIDH
North-West Face, Summit Buttress

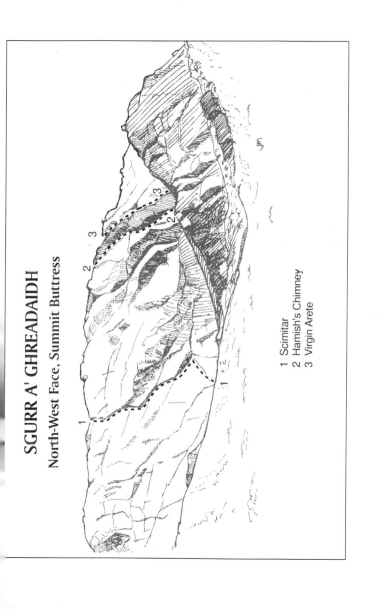

1 Scimitar
2 Hamish's Chimney
3 Virgin Arete

Winter: II **   (1976)
Follow the left flank of Eagle's Gully to its termination. Traverse up and
left to a small ridge below a short steep slab. Climb the slab to the crest
of the ridge, then follow the ridge to its junction with the west face of
Sgurr a' Ghreadaidh. Climb the face by a steep shallow 60m gully, then
climb more easily to the summit crest.

Eagle's Gully   Moderate   (1910)
This is the long and narrow gully in the centre of the north face of Sgurr
Eadar da Choire. It gives a good alternative to the summer route up
the north-west ridge.

SOUTH WALL OF SGURR EADAR DA CHOIRE
(Map Ref 443 234)

Approach as for Coire an Dorus, but head straight for the spur of Sgurr
Eadar da Choire and follow screes under the south wall of the ridge.
The crag is at an altitude of about 600m. To descend, either go back
north along the ridge and descend the Eag Dubh, or take one of the
descents from the south branch of the corrie (as described below).
    There are two recorded lines on this wall. In the centre of the face
lies a prominent corner at three-quarters height.

Ceo   110m   Very Difficult   (1965)
This climb lies up the highest part of the buttress, following a left-slanting groove.
1. 25m   Climb the groove to a ledge.
2. 30m   Continue up the groove, which becomes indefinite, then go
up a short wall to a ledge.
3. 45m   Enter the undercut groove above from the right and continue
to a ledge.
4. 10m   Move right along the ledge and go up a final wall.

Gael Force   135m   HVS *   (1977)
This climb takes the corner in the centre of the face, starting directly
from below at a groove.
1. 45m   Climb the groove and the steep wall above to the terrace.
2. 45m 4b   Continue steeply to a detached flake, then trend right to
the foot of the main corner and a peg belay.
3. 25m 5a   Traverse under the corner, then climb directly up the crux
crack to finish over a steep wall to a terrace.
4. 20m 4b   Finish by a steep wall on good but loose holds.

SOUTH BRANCH OF COIRE A' GHREADAIDH

This is the large main corrie with extensive west-facing masses of rock at an altitude of about 700m. There is no simple route to or from the ridge, and despite the extensive exposure of rock, the climbing has proved broken and limited.

The descent from the main or south corrie is complicated and involves a couple of unattractive options, both Moderate, from cols on either side of Sgurr Thormaid. The north-easterly col has a gully which slants down to the left. To reach the south-westerly col, Bealach Thormaid, if on the Sgurr a' Ghreadaidh side, skirt the three teeth of the north-east ridge of Sgurr Thormaid by a ledge on the west, which leads down to the col. Now descend a gully and a rake, which passes under a massive overhang on the north-west face, to reach the corrie. An easy descent from Coir' an Eich is down the scree. From An Diallaid descend a scree slope into Coir' an Eich.

White Wedding   100m   IV *   (1986)
This route takes the straight shallow gully on the back wall of the corrie. It is very prominent from the approach and starts about 250 metres right of Gael Force.
1. 25m   Two ice steps lead to a ledge on the right at the start of the steep section.
2. 45m   Excellent ice climbing leads to a ledge on the left.
3. 30m   The ice ahead is steeper but shorter and leads to easier ground. The ridge is now about 150m above.

The following routes lie on the west-facing wall of the corrie.

Hidden Gully   120m   Difficult   (1908)
This gully cuts obliquely into the crags and faces Sgurr Eadar da Choire. It is difficult to locate, being hidden until at its foot. The chief features are a large cave, a black chimney followed by a second cave, then scrambling to finish.

Overhanging Gully   135m   Very Difficult   (1947)
Climb the first two pitches of Hidden Gully as far as the chockstone below the black chimney. Traverse 5 metres left, then climb a basalt dyke for a further 25m to a belay. Continue 30m up the dyke, using the left-hand gabbro wall. Climb the gully to an overhanging wall and cave,

then take the right-hand side of the cave to a scoop. Climb the scoop to a large ledge, then finish up a gabbro ridge *via* a gendarme.

Hidden Gully Buttress   140m   Very Difficult **   (1952)
An excellent route, making a visit here well worthwhile, which takes the buttress right of Hidden Gully. Start in the gully. Steep but Moderate climbing leads to a small rock amphitheatre on the right-hand side of the buttress. Traverse horizontally left along a fault to a niche near the crest. Continue up the right retaining wall of the buttress above the niche, climbing a steep and exposed groove running diagonally right across a seemingly impregnable wall. Now climb a light-coloured wall on excellent holds to the finish of Hidden Gully.

Vanishing Gully   120m   Difficult   (1910)
The gully right of Hidden Gully contains several interesting pitches, then fades out into the face above at two-thirds height.

Diagonal Gully   275m   Easy
This is the long slanting gully immediately below the col between Sgurr a' Ghreadaidh and Sgurr Thormaid. It leads diagonally up to the ridge and contains one pitch near the bottom which can be turned on the north side.
Winter: II
Apart from a minor pitch near the bottom, snow leads to the top.

North-North-West Spur   250m   I/II   (1993)
This is the rib that lies to the north-east of the Bealach Thormaid and is well defined higher up.

AN DIALLAID   (Map Ref 435 229)

This is the short spur separated from Sgurr nan Gobhar by the scree bowl of Coir' an Eich. It has a few rather unattractive climbs (there are better places to climb in the Cuillin than here), although it is very accessible. The rock on the lower slabs is firm gabbro but the steeper buttress near North-East Gully has much basalt.

To approach, follow the path leading into Coire a' Ghreadaidh from the Youth Hostel; the crags are on the north-facing wall above the path, at about 700m. The easiest descents are down the screes of Coir' an Each or by keeping high from the top of the climbs and descending into the main corrie beyond Footrot.

Footrot   120m   Difficult   (1970)
The easy-angled slabs above the path are composed of immaculate
gabbro, devoid of cracks or any sort of protection. Although easier lines
can be taken straight up, this route climbs the slab from left to right,
taking the line of least resistance.

The next climbs lie further up, near North-East Gully, which splits
the slabby buttress.

Diamond Buttress   240m   Very Difficult   (1965)
This is the long rambling buttress left of North-East Gully. Start 30
metres left of the gully and follow the edge of a slab. After 30m, keep
to a definite ridge and make for a large slab higher up. In the middle
section there is a steep undercut wall. Turn this on the left and scramble
up to the slab. Start the slab at an obvious corner, move into a groove
on the left and follow a series of corners to the top. Apart from the top
corners, the rock is excellent

Nearer My God to Thee   155m   VS   (1980)
Start immediately left of and below the start of North-East Gully's first
pitch, where a flake leans against a big slab which forms the gully's
left wall. There is very little protection, but the first and last pitches are
interesting.
1. 35m 4b   Climb the flake and crack to the top, go up the wall above
and step right to a narrow ledge. Now climb the wall left of a mossy
crack to a narrow ledge. Continue straight up the wall above on better
holds to a spike belay.
2. and 3. 80m   Follow the edge of the slabs to a ledge below a steep
undercut wall.
4. 40m 4a   To the right is a large poised flake with a crack on the right.
Climb the crack to the top of the flake, then continue up an easier
corner to the top.

North-East Gully   150m   Severe   (1929)
This is the deep narrow gully, which appears as a deep chimney when
viewed from below. There are about seven pitches, of which the first is
the crux.
Winter: III *   (1978)
A fine line which usually presents two good pitches in full conditions.
It will certainly be harder when lean.

Verucca   120m   Very Difficult   (1970)
This route starts right of North-East Gully. Climb the rib by the line of least resistance; belays are hard to find.
Direct Start: 60m   Severe   (1970)
Start almost at the entrance to North-East Gully at the edge of a steep wall.
1. 40m   Climb the unprotected wall to a peg belay.
2. 20m   Continue directly to the ridge.

Branching Gully   120m   Difficult   (1908)
This is the prominent gully that lies up right of North-East Gully and faces north-west across Glen Brittle. It is easily seen from the path into the main corrie. There are several interesting pitches.

COIRE NA BANACHDICH
(Map Ref 435 220)

This is the third great corrie on the Glen Brittle side of the main ridge. It lies due east of the Glen Brittle Memorial Hut and is the most accessible of all the Cuillin corries. There are three main peaks surrounding the corrie; Sgurr nan Gobhar (630m), Sgurr na Banachdich (965m) and Sgurr Dearg (978m). The approach follows the south bank of the Allt Coire na Banachdich. A path leaves the road 50 metres south of the Glen Brittle Memorial Hut, crosses to the south bank after 300 metres, then joins a path starting from Glenbrittle House. Continue along the rim of a deep hollow where the stream pours over a fine waterfall, the Eas Mor. Be sure not to take the paths forking off to the right for Coire Lagan, but instead continue by the Allt Coire na Banachdich.

The headwall of the corrie is composed of slabs and cliffs split by terraces. Between the southernmost top of Sgurr na Banachdich and Sgurr Dearg lies an important pass over to Coruisk - Bealach Coire na Banachdich. This is the easiest pass between Glen Brittle and Coruisk, providing the correct route is followed. The west side of the bealach is guarded by a deep black gully, Banachdich Gully, so the normal line of approach goes well right, close to the flank of Sgurr Dearg. A scree terrace then slants left below a buttress to the bealach. The Coruisk side is a straightforward scree descent.

The round of the corrie is a popular outing, affording dramatic views eastwards of Coir'-uisg. It involves relatively uncomplicated scrambling. Sgurr nan Gobhar is easily ascended or descended by its south-western shoulder. The only difficulties are on the south ridge of Sgurr na Banachdich. This involves some pleasantly exposed scrambling over the three lower tops. The first unnamed top is a short distance north of the bealach and directly above the shoulder of Sron Bhuidhe, which divides Coireachan Ruadha to the east. The second, or south top, lies 300 metres further north. All this is little more than walking. The difficulties lie in the traverse of the third or centre top, which has an awkward descent to the gap before the main summit. This ridge can be avoided by following exposed scree-covered ledges on the west side, but this is not attractive or recommended. A descent should not be attempted before the main summit is reached. The mountain is precipitous on the Coireachan Ruadha side and falls into the Coire na Banachdich in a series of loose screes, slabs and crags. Sgurr Dearg is easily ascended or descended by its north-west ridge from Bealach Coire na Banachdich. Its west ridge, which forms the south side of Coire na Banachdich, provides some pleasant scrambling after the minor top of Sgurr Dearg Beag (929m) It has stupendous views across to Coire Lagan. The true summit of Sgurr Dearg is the Inaccessible Pinnacle and the round of the corrie would not be complete without an ascent.

SGURR NAN GOBHAR   (Map Ref 427 224)

The prominent black gash of a gully splitting the south flank of the hill (631m) provides a poor route. The descent follows the west ridge.

Goat's Gully   210m   Difficult   (1950)
This rather esoteric climb follows the black gash over all sorts of obstacles. The first ascent party preferred the option of soloing as this was more in keeping with the character of the route.
Winter: 180m   II/III   (1993)
Climb the gully in four pitches. Turn the first small icefall on the right.

The large gully that splits the slabs in the backwall of the corrie provides the following route:

Banachdich Gully   120m   Very Difficult   (1898)
This gully lies centrally within the band of slabs below the bealach. It contains four pitches, the last being the best. Some pitches are best turned on either wall if the gully is too wet.
Winter: III
The gully is far better under winter conditions, with several ice pitches.

North Rib   120m   Difficult
The north or left bounding rib of Banachdich Gully gives much drier climbing than the gully.

South Slabs   120m   Moderate
The slabs to the right of the gully give amusing scrambling that can be varied at will, providing a more interesting way to the bealach than the normal scree approach. This is not advisable as a descent route.

WINDOW BUTTRESS and NORTH-WEST BUTTRESS

By far the best climbing in Coire na Banachdich is found on the two separate buttresses on the north side of the west ridge of Sgurr Dearg. The lower buttress is known as Window Buttress (altitude 600m) because of the remarkable hole which pierces its summit tower. In the right light, this feature can be seen from the Glen Brittle Hut. Immediately above Window Buttress is Upper Window Buttress. North-West Buttress lies some 350 metres further up the corrie and its base is level with the top of Upper Window Buttress (altitude 750m). It is distinguished by two prominent black chimneys. Between the two buttresses is a minor one. The rock on North-West Buttress is some of the best and roughest in the Cuillin, so some routes can be climbed when wet. Window Buttress also has good rock, but not quite up to North-West Buttress standard. On the other hand, Upper Window Buttress has areas of loose rock.

Window Buttress is easily reached by following the Coire na Banachdich path, which runs below it. North-West Buttress can either be reached from the corrie by walking up past Window Buttress, or from Sron Dearg by descending the scree slope between it and Window Buttress. The descent from Window Buttress is *via* screes down to the west, or by a scramble down a large rake above the finish of the buttress. The easiest descent off North-West Buttress is down broken ground to the west.

Window Buttress   90m   Difficult *   (1906)
There are three possible starts to this popular climb. A large cairn defines the start of the normal route. About 10 metres to the left, a fine Mild Severe crack gives by far the best start, but awkward in the wet.

The third alternative climbs the arete bounding the gully on the right. All these options lead to easy middle ground. Above, a fine corner leads either through the 'Window' or, better, straight up the crack. Traverse over the pinnacles to finish on a neck of rock. From the neck it is possible either to descend easily down the gully or to scramble directly above to a large rake.

There are three alternatives to the neck route:

Bishop's Climb   35m   Difficult   (1914)
A few metres below the neck of Window Buttress is a sloping shelf. A steep and often wet chimney starts a few metres left along this shelf. Climb straight up the chimney to a large rake. A much cleaner alternative at the same grade is to climb the fine open rocks a few metres left of the chimney.

Durham Slabs   35m   Severe   (1962)
This constitutes a rather pointless variation to the large rake. Descend the gully behind Window Buttress for a few metres on easy rock to gain a slanting shelf *via* some steep but straightforward rocks, all highly polished. Gain a slabby corner-ramp to the left, then follow the slabs to a wall. Climb this, stepping right to easy ground and the rake.

Widow's Eye   40m   Severe   (1970)
Traversing left beyond the foot of the rake below Durham Slabs is a steep open corner overlooking upper Coire na Banachdich. Climb the corner over three prominent shelves on the left to a belay. Climb the corner direct, avoiding an overhang by delicate climbing on the right wall, then continue to the top.

Upper Window Buttress   130m   Severe   (1957)
Follow the wide rake above the finish of Window Buttress leftwards for 60 metres to the end of the ledge.
1. 30m   Trend left up a steep wall (some loose rock) to a crack.
2. 10m   Traverse easily right.
3. 30m   Climb the prominent crack.
4. 30m   Continue up the crack, turning a chimney delicately on the left, then climb a steep wall using an undercut crack on the left.
5. 30m   Finish up a steep broken wall on the right.

Between Window Buttress and North-West Buttress is a minor crag, Inbetween Buttress.

Val   90m   Very Difficult   (1980)
This good route follows the right-hand arete of the crag directly. It provides a reasonable alternative when Window Buttress is crowded.

The last climbs in this section lie on North-West Buttress.

Toolie Grooves   90m   Hard Severe 4b **   (1953)
Start below the left-hand of the two black chimneys, where the chimney has opened out to form a groove. Climb the groove, which has a hard start, for 25m. Exit *via* an obvious gangway on the left to a platform, then continue up a corner to a similar platform. From the highest point of this platform, climb to below the final overhang, then move right to where the crux mantelshelf leads to the base of a steep little slab. Climb the slab, then a notch in the ensuing overhang, to finish by a little crack on the right. A very good route.

Black Chimney   90m   Very Difficult   (1909)
This is the right-hand of the two black chimneys, a basalt intrusion. About 10 metres right of Toolie Grooves is a steep sloping gangway. Climb this to a large ledge, which can also be reached by a scramble up from the right. Climb the basalt staircase and chimney, escaping on the left wall at the top to a second scree ledge. Finish by a short vertical chimney. Alternatively, follow a sloping ledge to the right, then go round a corner, up a narrow chimney and onto the roof.

Valkyrie   90m   HVS **   (1959)
Left of the direct start to Aesculapius is a cracked corner. Climb it strenuously to the terrace. Cross the terrace and continue up the corner, which now slants to the right. More delicate climbing on excellent rock leads to a small triangular ledge. Climb the overhanging crack to an outward-sloping mantelshelf. Continue up steep cracks and a chimney to finish up the last pitch of Aesculapius. The original line took the final overhang on Aesculapius directly using aid, but this is avoidable.

Aesculapius   70m   Hard Severe 4b ***   (1958)
An excellent climb on perfect rock which can be climbed in the wet.
Start on the same sloping gangway as Black Chimney and follow it to
a scree ledge.
1. 15m   Go up right to a basalt dyke, climb up a few metres, then
traverse left and go up to a ledge.
2. 20m   Follow the right side of the chimney, then enter it and climb
to a small triangular ledge.
3. 20m   Climb a steep wall on the left to a shelf under an overhang,
then move back across the top of the wall to a ledge. Climb to a narrow
chimney above and so to a ledge.
4. 15m   Traverse right up a rising ledge, then continue right to easy
ground.

The Hygeia Variations   VS 4c and A2   (1958)
This forms a direct start to the left of the normal route, climbing directly
to the sloping gangway. The direct finish takes the final overhang on
aid.

The Southern Cuillin

When thinking of rock climbing on Skye, the routes on Sron na Ciche jump immediately to mind. These are the most popular destinations in the whole of the Cuillin, easily accessible from the Glen Brittle camp site. Steeped in history both ancient and modern, there is something for everyone here.

COIRE LAGAN

The round of Coire Lagan gives an excellent 11km expedition. Climbing up to Very Difficult is encountered on the south-west ridge of Sgurr Alasdair and there are several ascents and descents of Difficult standard. If all the difficulties are bypassed, the standard remains around Difficult.

Follow the path to Coire Lagan from the camp site or youth hostel. Either gain the southern end of the plateau of Sron na Ciche by scree, or take the following more difficult and exciting route:

Collie's Route   Moderate
Walk up the Sgumain Stone Shoot to beyond the toe of Eastern Buttress, then scramble up the terrace to Eastern Gully. Cross this to the left edge of the Cioch Slab. Climb the deep cracks on the left edge of the great slab to re-enter Eastern Gully. Continue scrambling up the top section of Eastern Gully *via* a chockstone squeeze and scree, or visit the Cioch by descending right along a shelf leading down across the top of the slab to the neck of the Cioch. From the neck, either climb straight to the top, or follow a chimney a short distance to the left. Return from the Cioch to Eastern Gully *via* the shelf.

KEY TO MAP OPPOSITE

1 Sgurr Dearg, South Buttress	7 Sron na Ciche, Cioch Buttress
2 Sgurr Mhic Choinnich, West Face	8 Sron na Ciche, Western Buttress
3 Sgurr Alasdair, Coire Lagan Face	9 Coir' a' Ghrunnda, South Crag
4 Sgurr Sgumain, West Buttress	10 Coir' a' Ghrunnda, North Crag
5 Sgurr Sgumain, Eastern Buttress	11 Alasdair – Thearlaich Crags
6 Sron na Ciche, Eastern Buttress	

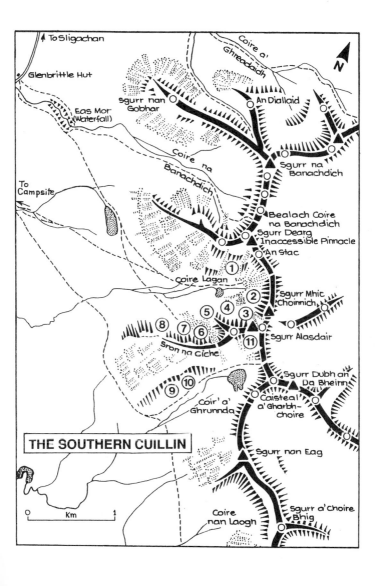

THE SOUTHERN CUILLIN

The traverse continues easily over Sgurr Sgumain to the Bad Step below the south-west ridge of Sgurr Alasdair. This can be taken direct for the most interest, the crux being just above the Bad Step (Very Difficult). For easier options, traverse right just below the col for about 30 metres to an open corner. Now climb up and left to the crest. A recent rockfall here has created areas of instability.

From the summit of Sgurr Alasdair, scramble down to the top of the Great Stone Shoot (a fast descent to upper Coire Lagan), then scramble to the summit of Sgurr Thearlaich. The descent of Sgurr Thearlaich is one of the tricky sections (Difficult), but it can be abseiled if necessary. The difficulty is on the last section above Bealach Mhic Choinnich, where highly polished slabs give a steepening descent down left to the bealach. It is also possible to traverse down right to the same point; the final few metres are entertaining.

Now ascend Sgurr Mhic Choinnich by either of the following routes:

King's Chimney   30m   Difficult   (1898)
This is the fine open corner that looks so fearsome from below. Start from a shelf about 20m above the bealach, reached from Collie's Ledge. Climb the corner and turn the overhang on the right; huge holds all the way.

Collie's Ledge   Easy   (1890)
Gain a ledge about 5m above the bealach, then follow it across the west face of Sgurr Mhic Choinnich (easy but exposed) to the north ridge. Follow the ridge to the top. A variation (Difficult) leads more directly from Collie's Ledge to the summit.

The traverse continues along the north ridge of Sgurr Mhic Choinnich to the foot of An Stac. Either skirt An Stac on the left (west), passing through a cairned nick to slithery slabs below the Inaccessible Pinnacle, or climb the impressive-looking crest of An Stac (Moderate) to its summit. Take care with the rock. The next and most famous obstacle is the Inaccessible Pinnacle, which can be climbed with surprising ease along the exposed east ridge (Moderate). Much beloved of the early pioneers, it fulfils the definition of an arete to near perfection, but its description can hardly be bettered by the following: "A razor-like edge with an overhanging and infinite drop on one side and a drop longer and steeper on the other". From the blocks on the summit, abseil from the fixed chain to the col below the west ridge. This provides an alternative line of ascent, giving a polished route (Very

Difficult), which starts up a wall to gain a ledge, then follows a platform and easy rocks to the top.

Walking now remains to the top of Sgurr Dearg, from which the easiest descent follows the long but easy west ridge back to Glen Brittle.

SGURR DEARG
978m   (Map Ref 444 216)

There are two areas of climbing on this otherwise tame side of Coire Lagan. The first is essentially a practice area, situated well down the corrie, and the second the fine crag of South Buttress.

PRACTICE CRAG   (Map Ref 440 207)

This slabby crag of sound gabbro is some 50m long and about 25m high, and is set at an altitude of about 440m. It has been exhaustively climbed on and can otherwise save a wet or indifferent day. Most of the climbs are in the middle grades and there is scope for short nasties of a harder nature. Low and high-level traverses are popular, but only one line is of particular note.

Approach as for Coire Lagan, but continue to the Matterhorn Block (see description of the approach to Sron na Ciche on p125). The crag lies left and above this, a minute or two from the path.

Central Crack Direct   25m   VS 4c
Climb the thin central crack.

To the immediate right of Practice Crag crag lies a much more impressive rib, bounded on the left by a narrow gully.

Sally's Climb   100m   Severe *   (1956)
This takes the rib right of the narrow sloping gully which is blocked by a big chockstone. Climb the rib more or less directly in three pitches; a very pleasant climb.

SOUTH BUTTRESS   (Map Ref 444 212)

This fine south-east facing buttress of sound gabbro lies low in upper Coire Lagan at an altitude of 620m. It is roughly triangular in structure, with a steep upper left wall on the left and a rib on the right. A grassy terrace below the main frontage of cliff is easily reached by scrambling. The neighbouring ridge of East Corner is separated from the parent crag by a gully. Unlike its bigger neighbour, Sron na Ciche, it gets the morning sun and the routes provide the most interesting approach to Sgurr Dearg and the Inaccessible Pinnacle.

The approach follows the path from Glen Brittle as described. Continue past the Matterhorn Block on the path to the lochan in upper Coire Lagan; the crag lies 120m above on the left. The descent takes broken ground and screes keeping well left of Western Drainpipe.

1   Western Drainpipe   150m   Difficult
This is the gully bordering the left edge of the buttress. The start avoids the Great Cave by taking slabs on the left.
Direct Start: 15m   Severe   (1952)
Climb past the Great Cave by parallel cracks on the right, which later merge into a smooth groove. "Socks may be required " to quote the first ascensionists.

2   Baly's Route   150m   Difficult   (1909)
Ascend Western Drainpipe for 45m, then climb the buttress on the right.

3   Western Drainpipe Ridge   145m   Hard Severe 4b (1952)
Start at the foot of the right-facing ridge which lies right of Western Drainpipe. Climb the rib direct to a bulge at 30m. Make an awkward move up and left, then climb the rib with only minor deviations over a succession of slabs and walls.

The following routes start from a central grassy bay, The Terrace, which can be reached by a variety of scrambling lines.

4   Barber's Route   110m   Severe   (1937)
This route lies between Baly's Route and Central Route. Start at a cairn below a sentry box.
1. 20m   Climb to the sentry box, then go up the chimney to a sloping ledge on the right. Awkwardly gain a groove and continue to a small stance.
2. 20m   Ascend the left wall to a flake and cross this to the right wall of the groove. Climb up to a large platform on the right.
3. 20m   Follow the groove to belays.
4. 50m   Follow a line of choice to the top of the buttress.

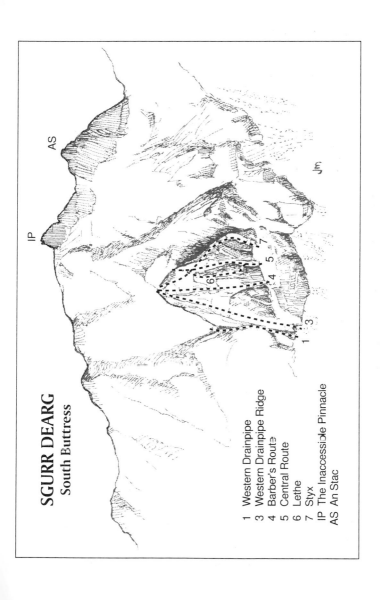

SGURR DEARG
South Buttress

1 Western Drainpipe
3 Western Drainpipe Ridge
4 Barber's Route
5 Central Route
6 Lethe
7 Styx
IP The Inaccessible Pinnacle
AS An Stac

5   Central Route   120m   HVS *   (1950)
The initial section of this good climb follows a steep impressive fault, whilst the upper part takes the line of a prominent chimney. Start at a corner in the centre of the buttress near the left end of the upper grass terrace. Climb the corner (possible escape left at 5m), then go up a steep slab on the right to where it forms a corner (15m 5a). Zigzag up slabs and climb a chimney and a groove to a broken recess, which is followed by a corner and an overhanging chimney (4b). Climb the prominent chimney above, which rises to the right. Easier rocks lead to the arete connecting the buttress to the main mass of the mountain.

6   Lethe   105m   VS   (1965)
1. 35m 4c   Follow Central Route for 10m, then step left into the prominent right branch of the Y-shaped crack on the left wall. Climb to an overhang with a peg belay.
2. 35m   Move right to a crack, then climb it to the top of a corner.
3. 35m   Finish up the chimney of Central Route.

7   Styx   120m   HVS 5b *   (1979)
Start 15 metres right of Central Route at a moss patch where a hidden stream runs behind the rock. The first and last pitches are good.
1. 15m 5b   Climb the strenuous V-crack to a small ledge.
2. 20m   Climb the crack to a platform on the left, then continue up the corner-groove to the foot of a chimney.
3. 30m   The original line takes the chimney. However, it is better to go up right and climb a corner followed by slabs to a steepening and belays below a chimney.
4. 25m   Climb the chimney to a grass ledge.
5. 30m 4c   Climb directly to an overhung alcove, traverse right to the edge, then go up and back left to a ledge. Above, 60m of scrambling leads to the rather shattered arete, which rises to the summit.

Lagan Route   90m   Severe   (1947)
A red wall in a raised alcove lies 20 metres right of Styx. On its left wall is a dyke and a crack. Follow the crack, then step across the dyke to a flake which leads to a belay (20m). Continue up an easy crack on the left. Move left, then climb slabs above (left of an inverted flake) to a grassy recess. Climb the groove above to a ledge, then bear right to climb slabs. From the top of the easy crack it is possible to climb straight up the slabs (VS 4c).

East Corner   150m   Difficult
Starting from its east corner, climb to the top of the buttress.

WEST FACE

The west face of South Buttress has two obvious chimney lines high up in the upper left-hand corner. The following climb takes the right-hand one.

Mistaken Crack   50m   Hard Severe   (1955)
1. 20m   Ascend the chimney to an overhanging block and pass this on the left wall.
2. 20m   Climb the wall close to and left of the crack, pass a chockstone and belay on a stance above.
3. 10m   Pass another chockstone to reach a small cave, then climb its left wall.

A partly aided variation to the third pitch of Mistaken Crack takes the overhang on the right **(Oedipus**, Severe/A2, 1958).

THE INACCESSIBLE PINNACLE
986m   (Map Ref 444 216)

This remarkable plinth of rock projects on the south-east side of the summit of Sgurr Dearg, overtopping the latter by some 7m. It has been a popular outing for over 100 years and the two most travelled routes reflect this visibly, and are adversely affected by rain.

Being a Munro, the 'In Pin' sees traffic jams more than most routes, so it is wise to remember that a good summer's day will see a queue for the two older routes; there is always the option of the south face climbs instead.

There are several climbing options to reach the In Pin, either by one of the routes from Coire Banachdich *via* the Window and North West Buttresses, or from Coire Lagan *via* a route on the South Buttress of Sgurr Dearg, or by the Bealach Coire Lagan *via* the Moderate rocks of An Stac.

The descent involves an abseil off the summit down the west ridge. Descend Sgurr Dearg either by the easy slopes of Sron Dearg or by the An Stac screes. To reach the latter, skirt the base of the south face of the In Pin, then traverse below An Stac over slabs and scree. Pass through a cairned nick and continue to descend close to An Stac until a near horizontal traverse leads to the top of the An Stac screes. Do not be tempted to follow the obvious scree gully seen from the descent slabs on the right. This ends in a nasty cliff.

The classical routes of the west and east ridges have been described above as part of the Coire Lagan round. In winter, the east ridge is about Grade III.

North-West Corner   20m   Difficult
This starts from the screes 3 metres left of the West Ridge. Climb the prominent crack along the edge of the north face.

SOUTH FACE

The Cutter   25m   VS 4c   (1994)
Start at the extreme left end of the face. Climb a left-slanting groove capped by two roofs, pull right under the second, then climb a groove directly to the summit block.

Varicose   30m   VS 4b *   (1964)
This good and exposed climb lies up the left side of the face. Start by white marks on the rocks at the right end of the overhangs. Climb to an overhang, surmount this on good holds, then continue to a ledge with a perched block. Climb the wall above directly to the summit.

Route I   30m   Mild VS 4b   (1921)
This route takes the left-hand of two lines of weakness which run up the face a few metres left of the prominent South Crack. Climb the wall direct to join Route II at a ledge below the summit ridge.

Route II   30m   Mild VS 4b   (1921)
The right-hand line of weakness. Climb straight up the wall to a small ledge, continue to a second ledge, then step right into a corner and finish up the face.

Hadrian's Wall   30m   VS   (1962)
Start 5 metres left of South Crack at a ledge 2m off the ground.
1. 20m 4c   Traverse left to a diagonal crack, then climb straight up the face on small holds to a platform.
2. 10m   Step off the right end of the platform, then climb the face, finishing over a slight overhang.

South Crack   30m   Hard Very Difficult *   (1906)
A good classic climb, recommended when there are queues at either end of the In Pin. It takes the fairly strenuous prominent crack running up the centre of the face, with a short detour at 10m.

AN STAC
954m   (Map Ref 445 215)

This is the bold-looking buttress under the Inaccessible Pinnacle, which projects from Sgurr Dearg in the direction of Sgurr Mhic Choinnich. Moderate in ascent, it is not quite as rotten as most would believe and was descended in 1891 by Gibson, Morse and Wicks.

Approach as for the Inaccessible Pinnacle; it lies immediately south-east of it on the main ridge. The descent is towards the Inaccessible Pinnacle.

An Stac Chimney   70m   Moderate   (1908)
This is the line of the dyke which ends under the summit of An Stac.

SGURR MHIC CHOINNICH
948m   (Map Ref 450 210)

This fine mountain lies at the back of Coire Lagan. The Lagan face is very large but unfortunately broken by a great number of ledges which preclude satisfactory summer climbing. The traverse of the mountain is interesting and enjoyable and can be achieved in a variety of ways. The south side drops precipitously to Bealach Mhic Choinnich, and the best route to the summit from that side is by King's Chimney. An easier alternative is the atmospheric Collie's Ledge. Both these climbs were described above, in the section on the Coire Lagan traverse.

The approach follows the track into upper Coire Lagan to where the Lagan Face stretches below the summit. Bealach Mhic Choinnich can be reached directly by following the Sgurr Alasdair Stone Shoot until a left branch leads up to the bealach where an easy rock scramble takes one to the crest; King's Chimney is immediately to the left. The north-west end of the mountain is easily reached by taking the An Stac screes to Bealach Coire Lagan.

The descent requires care. Accidents have happened to parties attempting to descend directly from the summit to Bealach Mhic Choinnich. Either abseil down King's Chimney, or descend to the north-west and the An Stac screes, or reverse Collie's Ledge to Bealach Mhic Choinnich.

1   Jeffrey's Dyke   300m   Very Difficult   (1948)
This is the conspicuous dyke to the left of the long West Buttress. Start at a slabby bulge, then follow straightforward rock for 60m to the base

of the dyke. Follow this with occasional deviations onto the walls either side. Cross a grass terrace low down and climb a steep rib on the left. Above, a steeper wall leads to another steep wall and a further grass terrace. A few metres to the right along this, climb straight up steep rocks, soon traversing obliquely back left, then move up on good holds over the rim of a wall to reach a little mossy terrace. A deep narrow cleft lies just to the right; follow this (a continuation of the dyke) to Collie's Ledge. Cross this and climb a wall to the summit ridge.
Winter: III
When in good winter conditions, the summer line gives a run of snow-ice with the final wall often verglassed. In thin conditions the route will be much harder.

2   The Twister   300m   III   (1978)
This follows the wide shallow gully immediately left of and parallel to West Buttress. Turn a vertical step at mid-height on the left.

3   West Buttress   300m   Difficult   (1906)
This long buttress runs up from the floor of the upper corrie to the summit. Much variation is possible in the lower and middle sections. In the upper section, follow a central chimney on excellent rock. After completing this climb, A.P.Abraham commented that "a few holly trees planted on top of Sgurr Mhic Choinnich would generally improve the appearance of such a desolate summit".

WEST FACE

This is the short clean wall at the back of Coire Lagan just below the ridge. The routes start from a narrow ledge. The best approach is from Jeffrey's Dyke. At the right side of the face are three right-slanting corners, the right-hand one being the descent. The routes are described from right to left.

Vanishing Beads   50m   VS 4b *   (1994)
Right of the descent route is a rib, and on its right side is a short, bulging, wide crack. Climb it and the slab above to reach twin cracks. Follow these to a large ledge, then climb the cracked buttress above.

Raven's Rib   30m   E1 5b *   (1994)
Start at the left side of the rib. Move up right and climb it to the large ledge.

Mud Wrestler   30m   Very Difficult *   (1994)
Climb the corner left of the descent route, above the chockstone.

Huffy Messiah   30m   Severe *   (1994)
The next corner to the left. Avoid the large overhang by stepping left
and climbing the corner-crack.

Up the Down Stoneshoot   30m   Severe *   (1994)
Start below the jutting overhang and climb the corner-crack leftwards
past hollow flakes, then trend left and climb flake cracks to the top.

Starless Bay   40m   VS 4c   (1994)
Climb the bay by a series of corners.

Flap Cracker   60m   HVS 5a **   (1994)
Approach from the base of the previous route by Very Difficult climbing.
Start up a dyke, then climb the obvious left-slanting corner-crack. Step
left and finish up a corner. It should be possible to extend the route by
adding a pitch below the start.

SGURR THEARLAICH
984m   (Map Ref 451 208)

The climbing on Sgurr Thearlaich in Coire Lagan is on the rather
uninviting west face, which sees little traffic. So far only a buttress and
the five gullies which run down into the Stone Shoot have been
climbed. They are imaginatively named A to E, going from north to
south. The rock cannot be described as perfect.

To approach, take the path into upper Coire Lagan. The easiest
ascent of the peak is *via* the Stone Shoot. From Bealach Mhic
Choinnich, the only difficulty on the traverse of the peak is immediately
above the bealach where polished rocks are best taken slightly left,
then right to gain the crest (Difficult). Winter alternatives depend on
the state of the snow; normally the lower slabs are turned on the right,
but a snow shelf to the left leads to the ridge about 75 metres from the
summit.

In descent, the only difficulty is just above Bealach Mhic Choinnich
where the Difficult slabs can either be abseiled or down-climbed. The
difficulties are concentrated in the highly polished slabs just above the
bealach.

4   Lower Rib   90m   Hard Severe 4b   (1960)
This is the leftmost and best defined of the ribs and buttresses on the Stone Shoot face. After a promising start up the conspicuous crack running up the right side of the buttress, the climb degenerates into an undignified scramble.

5   Gully A   90m   Difficult   (1908)
This route lies 10 metres left of the Great Stone Shoot. Ascend a narrow cave pitch on the left wall, through a tunnel into an enclosed chimney. Climb the chimney, then a chockstone pitch and finish up a narrow chimney.
Winter: III *   (1970)
The gully contains three short ice pitches and gives an interesting climb.

6   Gully B   90m   Difficult   (1908)
There are three easy pitches followed by a good one up a chimney.

7   Gully C   90m   Difficult   (1908)
The highlight of this route is a deep fissure with jammed blocks at the top, followed by a cave with a through route.

8   Gully D   90m   Very Difficult   (1908)
A gradually improving climb with the *pièce de resistance* being a 30m pitch near the top.

9   Gully E   90m   Difficult   (1880)
Of historic interest as the probable route used by Charles Pilkington on the first ascent of Sgurr Thearlaich. The gully is more open than the others and the route follows slabby rocks on the right near the top.

SGURR ALASDAIR
993m   (Map Ref 450 208)

This graceful peak is the highest in the Cuillin. It is named in honour of Alexander Nicolson's first ascent.

   The easiest route of ascent takes the path from Glen Brittle into upper Coire Lagan and the foot of the Stone Shoot. Follow this to the top, where a simple scramble leads to the summit of the peak. However, the south-west ridge is better, as described below. The quickest descent is down the Stone Shoot.

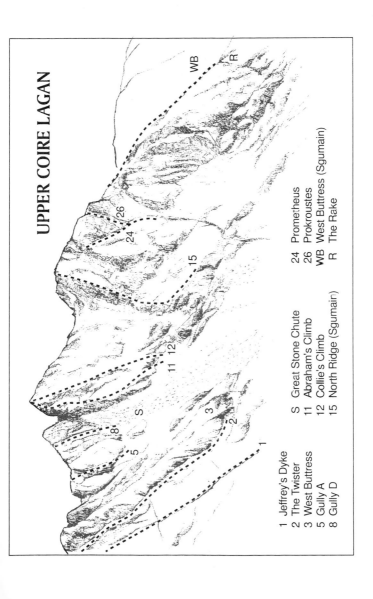

UPPER COIRE LAGAN

1 Jeffrey's Dyke
2 The Twister
3 West Buttress
5 Gully A
8 Gully D

S Great Stone Chute
11 Abraham's Climb
12 Collie's Climb
15 North Ridge (Sgumain)

24 Prometheus
26 Prokroustes
WB West Buttress (Sgumain)
R The Rake

THE STONE SHOOT FACE

This face forms the right wall of the Stone Shoot. It is dark and forbidding with much loose rock, and receives little traffic. An adventurous expedition onto this face in the 1930s was so grippingly described that the original description is printed below in order that someone may be tempted to find out what it is really like.

10   Stone Shoot Face   120m   VS   (1937)
The length excludes parts of other climbs. "Climb the first few pitches of Abraham's Route, and where it overlooks the Stone Shoot take to this face and bear left and upwards. The rocks are not much more than Difficult until a small amphitheatre is reached with overhangingly forbidding rocks all around. Climb up to the foot of the wall, and from there follow a sloping ledge leading to a corner on the right; the holds on the wall are satisfactory, 30 feet. Getting round the corner is very awkward as at first glance there does not seem to be any handhold to get round but there is an undercut one for the right hand that supplies the key. The position now is an imposing one as the next move is up a greasy chimney with splayed out walls (basalt) overhanging the Stone Shoot. The chimney has to be forced by faith, friction and some jamming and has to be one continuous movement as it is devoid of positive holds (boots). No belay for the traverse or the chimney could be found. The climb finishes up the North Arete."

COIRE LAGAN FACE

This face is thankfully sunnier and less intimidating then the Stone Shoot Face, although it also has much loose and broken ground. It throws out a broad buttress that forms a prominent rib overlooking the Stone Shoot. The routes stretch right from above the scree of the Stone Shoot, before the narrows.

11   Abraham's Climb   300m   Difficult *   (1907)
This rather loose classic is best treated with care. The Stone Shoot passes through a narrow neck about 90m above the floor of the corrie. Above this, a short wall faces the corrie and the climb starts at a chimney slanting left from the right end of this wall. Follow the chimney and its left retaining wall, then continue on this line over broken rocks

First ascent of Uhuru, Eastern Buttress (Climber, Kevin Howett)

to the crest of the wall overlooking the Stone Shoot. Climb up the steep
ridge with minor deviations to finish on the summit.
Winter: III/IV **   (1952)
Follow the summer line throughout; a sustained climb of quality.

12   Collie's Climb   270m   Difficult   (1896)
This climb is easier than Abraham's, but even looser. It follows the ridge
to the right. Climb to the base of the ridge. In poor visibility it is better
to approach the ridge by climbing a further 120m up scree towards the
Sgurr Alasdair - Sgurr Sgumain col to reach a short wall facing the
corrie. Start at the left-hand end of the wall and climb left to join the
ridge. Pleasant climbing leads up the ridge, but the upper section is
more broken and rather loose.

13   North-West Face   270m   IV
This winter route is to the right of Collie's Climb and ends on the summit.

14   South-West Ridge   Very Difficult
The ascent of this popular ridge from Sgurr Sgumain is generally Easy
with one short Very Difficult step near the bottom, the 'Bad Step'. This
can be avoided on the right but recent rockfall has created loose
sections in the vicinity which can be avoided. Traverse below the col to
the right for 30 metres, dropping only slightly, to an open corner facing
the col. Climb this, then go left to the crest of the ridge. It is best to keep
to the crest for maximum enjoyment.

SGURR SGUMAIN
947m   (Map Ref 448 206)

To the south-west of Sgurr Alasdair lies Sgurr Sgumain. The mountain
throws out a long north ridge and has an impressive north face. The
easiest approach is from Sron na Ciche, but the North Ridge is more
interesting. The easiest descent is towards Sron na Ciche, then down
the Sgumain Stone Shoot. Alternatively, carry on up the south-west
ridge of Sgurr Alasdair and descend its Stone Shoot.
    To reach the base of North Buttress, follow the second terrace right
beyond the Final Tower and descend Difficult rocks to a point where a
left traverse leads to the rake at the base.

Conjuror, Eastern Buttress (Climber, Bruce Kerr)

15   North Ridge   350m   Moderate *   (1887)
This is the well defined ridge which runs straight to the summit of Sgurr Sgumain from near the lochan in upper Coire Lagan. It gives enjoyable scrambling, but care should be taken with the rock in places.

Left of North Ridge an easy scree slope leads to the col. To the right lies the very impressive North Buttress, with the well defined Frankland's Gully bounding its left edge.

NORTH BUTTRESS

This is the steep face high on the mountain looking west into upper Coire Lagan. It is separated from the West Buttress by an easy gully. This cliff has several excellent climbs in impressive situations, although the rock is very loose in places. The crag ends in a jutting tower, which forms a fitting finale to routes on the lower West Buttress. Two terraces traverse across the buttress, rising to the right. The lower terrace is taken by Wood-Johnson's Route and the upper one is a useful finish for several climbs, avoiding the top of the buttress which is decidedly loose. Two gullies slant up left; the lower left-hand one is Frankland's Gully and the other is taken by Prometheus.

16   Frankland's Gully   120m   Hard Severe *   (1925)
A nice route through impressive scenery. Start at Wood-Johnson's Route and move up left until a step can be made at 7m around the edge into a triangular niche. Overcome a short sharp wall by a tricky mantelshelf, then traverse easily into the gully. About 45m of scrambling leads to the next pitch, cave belay. Traverse up on the left wall to a recess at 7m (possible belay), then traverse back to the bed of the gully on a rising ledge which gradually diminishes to a final awkward move. Finish by a steep but not difficult crack that leads to the north side of Sgurr Sgumain.
Winter: V, 6 **   (1981)
An excellent and technical expedition. Climb the gully direct to the end of a left traverse. Climb the rib above to finish at the top of the summer route. Continue up the easier gully, crossing the upper part of Prometheus, and climb the narrow gully by a through route to the ridge.

17   Grannie Clark's Wynd   140m   E1 5b **   (1971)
The impressive buttress above Frankland's Gully is bounded on the right by Direct Route, which finishes on the side of the buttress, as for

Frostbite. This line steers a course between a large blank wall and slab on the left and some very steep loose rocks on the right. The excellent climbing is rather spoilt by a loose finish. Start right of the lowest point of the buttress.

1. 45m 5a   Climb Frankland's Gully *via* a direct overhanging start.
2. 10m 4b   Make a rising traverse below a roof, then climb over it and go past a large block to a platform.
3. 35m 5b   Go up left into a shallow corner, passing a loose flake on the right. Trend up left to a small ledge and good belay.
4. 50m 5b   Climb up and left to a bulge and go through it at the easiest point, crux, then continue up loose rock to the top.

18   Wood-Johnson's Route   180m   Mild VS *   (1932)
This route wanders across the face following the lower terrace. Right of the start of Grannie Clark's Wynd is a prominent corner-crack.
1. 30m   Climb the corner to a large ledge.
2. 15m 4b   Step round a corner on the left and climb an open chimney, trending back right, then left through an overhang.
3. 10m 4b   Traverse right for a few metres, then climb to the left-hand end of the lower terrace.
4. 50m   Continue along the terrace to a belay below a steep crack at its end.
5. 30m   Climb the steep crack on good holds and move right, continuing to the second terrace.
6. 45m   It is safer to follow the second terrace rightwards to finish, as the summit rocks are loose. Otherwise ascend directly to the top of the buttress.

19   Direct Route   180m   VS 4c *   (1957)
This route provides some good climbing. Climb the first three pitches of Wood-Johnson's Route, then branch up a wide open groove to a rake sloping steeply to the right. Climb the rake for 25m, then climb a prominent slab on the left to below the final pitch. Climb an overhanging wall on good holds, crux, and move left to a steep slab which ends on top of the buttress.

In the centre of the face is an overhanging wall bounded on the right by a line of corners and chimneys, and on the left by two prominent corners 30m up.

20   Raynaud's   110m   HVS **   (1994)
1. 45m 4c   Start close to Frostbite and climb up to the left-hand of the
two corners. Follow the corner, moving left at the top to belay on the
slanting fault.
2. 40m 5a   Gain the corner left of the bay of Direct Route, directly
above the belay, *via* a bulge. Climb the corner and, after mounting a
shelf at the top of the corner, move out left and continue to a belay.
3. 25m   Climb easily up right, and traverse off right to finish.

21   Frostbite   140m   VS 4c **   (1968)
This good sustained climb takes the right-hand of the two corners. It
is well protected after the initial 20m. Start about 20 metres right of
Wood-Johnson's Route, at a stone terrace under the initial overhang.
1. 25m 4b   Climb up to a ledge below the right-hand corner; poor
belay. It may be wise to continue.
2. 35m 4c   Go up the corner on good holds to a ledge and climb a
short wall to a grass ledge.
3. 40m 4c   An easy diagonal break leads up right (part of Wood-
Johnson's Route) to a big corner. Belay below the corner to avoid rope
drag. Climb the corner, which is capped by a large overhang. Avoid this
on the left to reach the arete; a good pitch.
4. 20m 4a   Continue to a big rocky terrace and move up to the
prominent final groove.
5. 20m 4c   Climb a layback crack to a good ledge, surmount an
overhang on dubious holds, then continue to the top.

22   Purple Haze   95m   E1 ***   (1968)
Good climbing up a fine natural line; low in the grade. Start from the
stony terrace 5 metres right of Frostbite.
1. 40m 4b   A small orange slab forms the first break in the overhangs
as one descends the terrace. Climb up right along the prominent fault,
move up, then continue diagonally to the foot of a corner.
2. 35m 5b   Climb the corner above to a large sloping ledge. Go
straight up three short steep corners to the foot of a groove.
3. 20m 5a   Go up the groove towards an overhang. Move left on a
ledge to the arete, then climb this boldly to the second terrace below
the final wall.

23   Reluctance   100m   Hard Severe **   (1970)
This pleasant route gives some exposed climbing through a break in
the wall 12 metres left of Prometheus. Climb a fault leading up left to
a ledge. Move right and continue to the second terrace, as for Wood-
Johnson's Route. Follow the terrace right to finish.

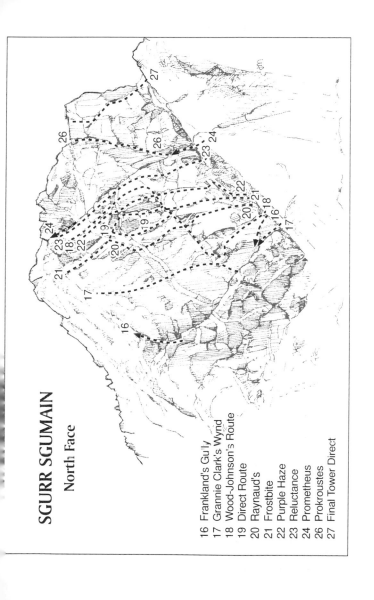

SGURR SGUMAIN
North Face

16 Frankland's Gully
17 Grannie Clark's Wynd
18 Wood-Johnson's Route
19 Direct Route
20 Raynaud's
21 Frostbite
22 Purple Haze
23 Reluctance
24 Prometheus
26 Prokroustes
27 Final Tower Direct

24   Prometheus   110m   HVS 4c   (1957)
This climb takes the prominent gully on the right-hand side of the face.
1. 20m 4c   The initial pitch is an unpleasant overhang. Climb left through the overhang to a block belay before the chimney of Prokroustes bears right.
2. and 3. 90m   Continue up the main gully, passing a large chockstone on the left.

25   Theseus   120m   HVS *   (1958)
This climb is about Hard Severe after the initial pitch.
1. 30m 4c   Climb the first pitch of Prometheus, then go 6m beyond the junction with Prokroustes to climb an open corner on the right. Follow an obvious line parallel to Prokroustes to a large block belay. (It is possible to continue right along the fault to join Prokroustes below the last two pitches).
2. 30m   Climb a steep wall to an exposed 20 metre traverse left.
3. 30m   Easier climbing leads to a terrace. Go right to the foot of some open corners.
4. 30m   Climb the corners and continue to the summit ridge above a line of red basalt.

26   Prokroustes   120m   HVS 4c ***   (1957)
A classic traditional route without a traditional history.
1. 20m 4c   Climb Prometheus, pitch 1.
2. 20m 4c   Climb the chimney on the right on greasy rock, past a bolt and a peg, to a good belay above a pointed chockstone.
3. etc. 80m 4b   Scramble up for 20m, then climb a narrow chimney to a steeper top section. Climb an overhang on large blocks, then crawl under a chockstone to ascend a thin crack to another chockstone.
   Two pitches lead to the top of the Final Tower. Alternatively, climb easier cracks on the right to the second terrace.

27   Final Tower Direct   60m   Hard Severe 4a *   (1920)
This climb is high up on the west end of North Buttress, forming a convenient finish to the West Buttress climbs. Start at the north-west corner of the Final Tower and follow a crack up the north face, trending back right on easier rocks near the top.

28   Willit   45m   VS   (1959)
The terrace below the Final Tower is broken centrally by a watercourse emerging from a gully with an enormous block in it. This climb follows the sharp arete on the left.

1. 25m 4c   Climb the overhanging arete, then follow the ridge crest to a belay.
2. 20m   Traverse 12 metres left, then climb the cracked wall on the left.

WEST FACE OF THE FINAL TOWER

This is a much friendlier but far less impressive place than North Buttress. It overlooks the Sgumain Stone Shoot. A prominent terrace halfway up the face divides it into two tiers. Approach as for Eastern Buttress, but continue up the Sgumain Stone Shoot where the crag lies up left. The climbs are described from left to right.

29   Introduction   60m   Very Difficult *   (1958)
This route takes the middle of three prominent grooves on the lower tier.
1. 30m   Climb the groove to a sloping shelf and chockstone belay.
2. 30m   Continue up a delicate slab above and finish on the terrace near the start of Final Tower Direct, which makes a good continuation.

30   Laceration   65m   Severe *   (1965)
This climb makes a fine prelude to Penitentiary Grooves. Start 15 metres right of Introduction.
1. 25m   Follow the left-slanting groove line to a stance and belay.
2. 40m   Move right into another groove with a large flake. Climb this, then traverse left into a broken groove which leads to the top.

31   Penitentiary Grooves   45m   E1 5b **   (1971)
A very fine route in the middle of the upper face, forming a big diedre capped by a triangular roof. It is the continuation of the right-hand groove line. A curiosity is the jammed bolt at the top of the crack.
1. 15m   Climb the diedre to a stance.
2. 20m   Surmount an overhang and continue up the diedro over two small overhangs to below the top roof. Cross this by the right wall to gain a ledge.
3. 10m   Finish up a groove.

32   Hermaphra and Ditus   95m   Mild Severe   (1958)
Takes the line directly beneath Penitentiary Grooves.
1. 20m   Climb a chimney to a sentry box and chockstone belay.
2. 35m   Follow the chimney to a ledge.
3. 10m   Continue easily to the terrace.
4. 30m   Above and right lies a chimney. Climb up, then go right to the chimney which is often wet. Climb it on the right to the top.

33   Priam   60m   Mild Severe   (1958)
A variation start to Hermaphra. Start 10 metres to its right at a
companion chimney. Climb this direct to a left traverse to reach the
sentry box stance at the top of the first pitch of Hermaphra.

WEST BUTTRESS

This important and slabby crag stands between upper Coire Lagan
and the Sgumain Stone Shoot. An entertaining rake crosses the lower
part of the buttress, passing under a prominent blaze of white rock.
The rake starts near the lochan and provides a reasonably quick way,
with some scrambling, from the lochan to Eastern Buttress of Sron na
Ciche. The rock on West Buttress is far sounder than on most of the
nearby crags.
   To descend, gain the Sgumain Stone Shoot on the right.

34   Superstition   80m   Very Difficult   (1951)
The side of the buttress overlooking Coire Lagan has a prominent
steep 45m wall about 60m up. This route starts directly under the left
edge of the wall, at the foot of a left-slanting gully.
1. 25m   Traverse diagonally left up the right wall of the gully to a large
sloping ledge.
2. 20m   Easy slabs on the right lead to a grassy terrace. Climb a wall
and go over slabs to the foot of a chimney in the left corner of a
prominent wall.
3. 10m   Climb slabs to the immediate left of the chimney.
4. 10m   Traverse into the chimney and climb to a large ledge and
belay.
5. 15m   Move right along a sloping ledge and go up a steep corner.
Traverse left across a steep slab and finish up another corner.

35   The Slant   120m   Difficult *   (1958)
This good and pleasant climb on sound rock follows a natural line
which crosses the face diagonally. Start at the rake at some slabby
rocks left of the white blaze. Climb slabby rocks diagonally left under
a large vertical wall to a chimney. Climb the open chimney and finish
up a wall of very rough rock.

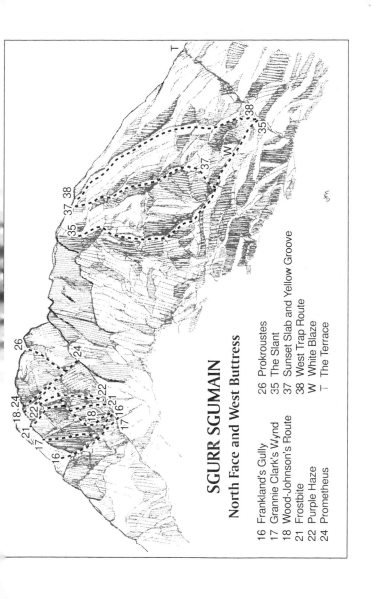

SGURR SGUMAIN
North Face and West Buttress

16 Frankland's Gully
17 Grannie Clark's Wynd
18 Wood-Johnson's Route
21 Frostbite
22 Purple Haze
24 Prometheus
26 Prokroustes
35 The Slant
37 Sunset Slab and Yellow Groove
38 West Trap Route
W White Blaze
T The Terrace

36   The Klondyker   135m   HVS ***   (1988)
A recommended route with some fine climbing. Start about 8m below the white blaze, directly below a chimney on The Slant.
1. 30m 4b   Climb diagonally left up a slab to a corner left of the chimney on The Slant. Layback up the corner until it is possible to move right to a cracked slab which leads to a belay at the foot of a steep impressive wall.
2. 30m 5a   Climb a small corner and cracks to gain the left side of a large sloping ledge about halfway up the steep wall. Gain the weak crack line above from a perched block on the left, then follow this and the wider crack above through an overhang to a large ledge and an old peg at a junction with Sunset Slab. An improbable pitch for the grade.
3. 20m 4a   Climb the groove above the peg until an easy left traverse leads to a ledge at the foot of an obvious groove with a yellow left wall.
4. 30m 4c   Move left around an edge into an exposed position and climb up left past an overhang to a basalt recess. Climb to a small well positioned ledge, then go up a short wall to a belay.
5. 25m   Move right and finish up the painfully rough arete.

37   Sunset Slab and Yellow Groove   200m   VS 4c ** (1951/64)
A very fine logical combination of routes giving the most popular climb on the crag. Scramble to a belay below the white blaze.
1. 50m   Follow a left-slanting slab, above and parallel to the larger line of The Slant, to the base of a steep crack on the right wall.
2. 25m   Climb the crack for 15m, then traverse easily right to a belay. (The original route now traverses easily right for 35m, then follows a steep strenuous crack before finishing up West Trap Route).
3. 20m   Climb to a corner below an overhanging crack.
4. 30m 4c   Climb the wall left of the crack to a ledge, then continue by the crux upper crack to a grassy ledge. (An escape right by a line of cracks and grooves to West Trap Route is now possible).
5. 15m 4b   Climb an easy slab, move round a corner and climb a steep groove. Traverse under an overhang to a broad ledge with a vertical yellow wall on the left.
6. 10m 4a   Move right to a stance and belay on the arete.
7. 30m 4a   Climb the arete, avoiding the steep upper section on the right.
8. 20m   Climb a steep corner to easier rocks and the top.

38   West Trap Route   240m   Very Difficult   (1924)
The upper part of this climb follows the conspicuous dyke (as seen from the lower corrie) right of the white blaze. Start from the rake about 15 metres right of the white blaze. Climb broken rocks to join a fault line rising to the right. Make for a small broken chimney at 25m, then climb it. Continue in the same line, with one deviation on open slabs on the left, to a dark chimney. Climb the strenuous chimney, crux, to a ledge. Climb a crack behind a flake on the left, continue up the slabs, then traverse left to join the dyke 30m above the ledge. Follow the dyke to finish.

39   Lost Hope   240m   VS   (1959)
The length includes sections of West Trap Route. Follow West Trap Route to the crack behind a large flake above the crux chimney. Move over to the large grassy ledge on the right. Climb slabs and grooves to a right-angled corner with a crack in the back, 45m. Climb the thin crack in the right wall, then traverse right into a steep and difficult groove which leads to a belay, 20m. Continue up the buttress, parallel with West Trap Route, by short pitches and grassy ledges.

40   West Buttress Route   480m   Difficult
Start immediately right of a long fault which splits the lower section of the buttress right of West Trap Route. Pleasant slabby climbing leads to a central chimney at half-height. Now follow several possibilities left of centre to gain the arete *via* a chimney. Continue along the narrow, rather shattered arete to the terrace below the Final Tower.

SRON NA CICHE
859m   (Map Ref 444 213)

This is deservedly the most famous cliff in Skye. It offers an unrivalled collection of routes of all grades and lengths with the additional attraction of a relatively short approach from Glen Brittle. The crag is well over a kilometre long and exceeds 300 metres in height in places. Like many of the Cuillin cliffs, it has a massive appearance that leads to confusion in mist. There is no substitute for a reconnaisance on a clear day, both from the path leading to upper Coire Lagan and by identifying the start of climbs from the base of the crag.

The cliff is composed of great sheets of gabbro that have formed slabs and walls, intersected by basaltic intrusions which have weathered preferentially to give gullies and chimneys. Sron na Ciche is divided into three main sections: Eastern Buttress on the left; Cioch Buttress and Cioch Upper Buttress in the middle; and Western Buttress on the right. The crag is bounded on the left by the Sgumain Stone Shoot. Eastern Buttress is to the right and ends at Eastern Gully, a deep slit that runs up to the summit plateau. From above the lower rocks of Eastern Buttress, a well defined but discontinuous terrace runs rightwards across the face. This terrace crosses Eastern Gully, runs below the Cioch, then is cut by Cioch Gully before re-appearing below Upper Buttress. It then continues up right, above Amphitheatre Wall, to emerge on the plateau beyond.

The next buttress right of Eastern Gully and below the terrace is the superlative Cioch Buttress, a massive area of steep slabs and grooves up to 180m high, bounded on the right by the deep Cioch Gully. The big bald slab above, bordering Eastern Gully, is Cioch Slab. This contains the famous Cioch pinnacle which appears to overhang the surrounding rock. Cioch Gully itself terminates immediately behind the Cioch, although from a distance the fault line is seen to continue as a shelf running diagonally left across the top of Cioch Slab to terminate in Eastern Gully. The much steeper slabs and grooves behind Cioch Slab and the Cioch, which continue to the right above the terrace, are known as Cioch Upper Buttress. This buttress has a lower continuation below the terrace, right of Cioch Gully, which terminates at the next major fault, Central Gully. This lower area of crag contains a curiously-shaped rock, Hexagon Block, which is roughly in the centre.

Central Gully runs up to the plateau. It begins as an easy-angled shallow chimney which cuts first through massive slabs and then a bowl of slabs, The Amphitheatre, at half-height. Above, it steepens, crosses the terrace, and finishes on the plateau. The very steep wall that lies above The Amphitheatre is known as Amphitheatre Wall.

Western Buttress is the huge mass of rather featureless rock to the right of Central Gully and Amphitheatre Wall. It can be conveniently described as anything right of the prominent blunt Amphitheatre Arete.

The approach to Sron na Ciche starts either from the camp site and follows a path which has recently been greatly improved, or from the Memorial Hut by a grassy path up the south side of the Allt Coire na Banachdich to the Eas Mor and then south-east to Loch an Fhir-bhallaich. This path is usually rather boggy and goes along the north side of the loch. A short distance beyond the loch, it joins the path which goes directly up the hillside from the camp site. The Sron na Ciche path branches rightwards off the main path (cairns), and after crossing the Allt Coire Lagan takes a rising diagonal line that eventually mounts the scree below Western Buttress near Mallory's Slab and Groove. If, in mist, you miss this turn off and are inadvertently heading up to the upper corrie, then the large pointed boulder of the Matterhorn Block is a little further on to the right of the path. You can either backtrack to the cairns or cut straight across to Sron na Ciche.

EASTERN BUTTRESS (Map Ref 446 204)

The buttress contains a wide variety of climbs, mostly on excellent rock. Being quite high (600m or higher), it can be rather colder here than one might expect, particularly up on Vulcan Wall. The climbs are on the east face overlooking the Sgumain Stone Shoot and on the west face overlooking Cioch Slab. The buttress is bounded on the left by the Sgumain Stone Shoot and on the right by Eastern Gully. About 60m above the base of the rocks lies the terrace, which starts at the Stone Shoot and slants up rightwards over Eastern Buttress. A further 60 metres up the Stone Shoot is an impressive slabby wall, Vulcan Wall, with a huge flake to its right. Some of the most recent and best hard climbs lie on this wall, and most of the older routes are also of high quality. The best collection of hard routes in the Cuillin lie on this buttress.

To approach, follow the track to Western Buttress (see above), then follow the path below Cioch Buttress, past Eastern Gully to arrive at the buttress. The path continues to the Sgumain Stone Shoot a little further on. The quickest and safest descent is down the Sgumain Stone Shoot, which is straightforward over large scree and boulders, painful in rock boots. A short smooth rock step bars access to the Stone Shoot: skirt right, then descend easy polished rock to the top of the scree. The slabby ramp behind the finish of the routes can also be descended into the Sgumain Stone Shoot.

If necessary, a more laborious descent of Eastern Gully can be undertaken. Minor pitches lead down from the top and the first obstacle lies down a subterranean route behind a chockstone. (Large climbers should read the description of Eastern Gully!). The next difficulty is a cave ("Abseil" is scratched on the rock above on the right); there is usually an assortment of slings. Lower down, follow the terrace rightwards across Eastern Buttress to the Sgumain Stone Shoot.

Why   60m   VS 4c   (1990)
This climb takes the slabby buttress left of Kinloss Gully. Start by scrambling over a chockstone and climb a steep corner until it is possible to move right onto a slab under a basalt bulge. Follow a line of big flakes rightwards, then move back left to under the headwall, belay. Traverse down left along a crack, then finish up a corner.

Kinloss Gully   55m   VS 4c   (1957)
Start in the bay left of Vulcan Wall and climb the large corner-crack to the top; often wet.

Confession   60m   E4 *   (1982)
A serious route with some dubious rock which takes an impressive line up the right wall of Kinloss Gully.
1. 15m 5a   Climb a small groove, often wet, then continue up a corner to a cramped stance at the start of an obvious traverse.
2. 45m 5c   Traverse right, then climb the crack to the top.

1   Spock   70m   E3 ***   (1980)
A very fine route with excellent bold climbing at the bottom of its grade. Start 5 metres left of Vulcan Wall.
1. 40m 5c   Climb overhanging cracks on the arete, then continue up the arete on small holds through a shallow groove to belays above an obvious roof.
2. 30m 5a   Go diagonally right to finish up the steep crack left of Vulcan Wall.

2   Vulcan Wall   70m   HVS ***   (1957)
A magnificent route with enjoyable climbing. Start at 'VW' scratched on the rock.

1. 20m 5a   Climb to a ledge and block belay.
2. 40m 5a   Move up to a ledge to the left of the block, then continue by a line of cracks to a small ledge on the right (possible belay - The Chambre Finish rises above this ledge). Make a rising traverse left to bigger holds; a sustained pitch.
3. 10m   Traverse left to the edge of the wall and climb to a glacis. Belay well back.

Variation: **The Chambre Finish**   25m   E2 5c *   (1982)
A purist's finish giving a logical conclusion. Where the normal route goes left onto easier ground, ascend the thinner and left-hand of two parallel cracks above; the right-hand crack is taken by Uhuru.

3   Uhuru   70m   E3 ***   (1990)
Excellent climbing up the fine crack line in the silver-streaked wall between Vulcan Wall and Dilemma. Start at cracks just left of the vertical crack of Dilemma.
1. 25m 5c   Climb to a small overlap and follow the crack above to a hard move right to the Vulcan Wall ledge. Traverse left to a flake block belay.
2. 45m 5c   Step right off the block, climb cracks and go right over a curving overlap. Move up and right to pull into the main crack, then follow it with difficulty to better holds. Continue up the excellent crack to finish right of the large precarious block.

4   Dilemma   80m   E3 ***   (1977)
This route climbs the delicate slab and strenuous overhang between Vulcan Wall and Creag Dhu Grooves. It is quite straightforward for the grade. Start at a thin vertical crack in the slab between these two routes.
1. 45m 5c   Climb the crack until level with the stance of Vulcan Wall. Continue up the crack to its finish, then climb up right to the overlap. Move under the overlap into a faint groove, then climb over the overlap to gain a descending traverse line which leads to a small niche just left of the large stance on Creag Dhu Grooves.
2. 35m 5c   Follow the crack diagonally left up the slab, then struggle up its continuation through the impressive overlaps.

5   Pocks   85m   E2 ***   (1988/92)
A very fine and varied route.
1. 35m 5b   Start up Creag Dhu Grooves, then climb the crack on the left to where Dilemma crosses the overlap. Move right under the

overlap to a ledge, step right, then climb the overlap and move up right to the belay on Creag Dhu Grooves. A superb pitch.
2. 50m 5c   Climb a steep crack, just right of Creag Dubh Grooves, to a slab and follow this rightwards to an arete. Continue up right to finish up the crack on Enigma.

6   Creag Dhu Grooves   95m   E3 ***   (1957)
Another superb climb, which follows the chimney between Vulcan Wall and the huge flake on the right. Start on the ledge below Vulcan Wall at the corner of the wall and great flake.
1. 40m 4b   Climb the chimney behind the flake to a chockstone, then continue to a large ledge above the flake.
2. 10m 5c   Climb the superb technical corner.
3. 20m 5c   Continue up the equally good corner to a good ledge.
4. 25m   Continue to the top.

7   Zephyr   85m   E5 **   (1982)
This fine climb follows the right arete of Creag Dhu Grooves. Start just right of that route at a slab leading to a small roof.
1. 40m 5b   Turn the roof on the left, then follow flakes and grooves to a large ledge.
2. 20m 6a   Gain a small ledge on the arete, ascend to a horizontal break, then move left around the arete into a slim bottomless groove. Climb this and the slab above to a small ledge.
3. 25m 4c   Move left and continue up the wall to the top.

8   The Plunge   90m   Scottish VS   (1962)
A traditional Cuillin route for all of those satiated with technical grades and the galaxies of stars on this crag. It has been deliberately left unchecked! Start just right of Creag Dhu Grooves at the bottom of the prominent flake. Traverse 4 metres diagonally up right, then go over a bulge to a belay (25m). Climb a corner to a sloping ledge, go left under an overhang, then surmount it to reach a block belay on top of the flake. Traverse right and go around an overhanging wall, then climb to a stance and belay near the arete. Climb to a small ledge and traverse 12 metres right (crux) to a large platform. Climb a thin flake to easier ground.

9   Enigma   135m   E3 **   (1979)
The main pitch of this fine climb follows the crack in the steep upper wall, well left of The Snake. Start about 12 metres right of Creag Dhu

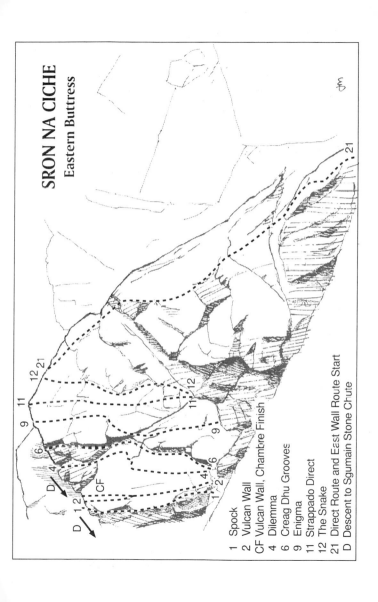

SRON NA CICHE
Eastern Buttress

1 Spock
2 Vulcan Wall
CF Vulcan Wall, Chambre Finish
4 Dilemma
6 Creag Dhu Grooves
9 Enigma
11 Strappado Direct
12 The Snake
21 Direct Route and East Wall Route Start
D Descent to Sgumain Stone Chute

Grooves at the right-hand end of a large flat ledge with a deep crevasse at the back.
1. 35m 5a   Climb the wall above, first by a left-slanting groove then slightly rightwards by cracks; belay over on the left.
2. 25m 5b   Climb easily right and up, crossing the right side of the prominent flake, to reach a thin right-slanting corner crack. Climb this until below a large overlap, then traverse right to nut belays on a well situated ledge.
3. 35m 5c   Above and left is a thin crack splitting the wall. Gain and climb the crack to a belay beyond the final overhang.
4. 40m   Continue up the crack.

10   Strappado   105m   HVS *   (1957)
This climb follows the right side of the prominent flake to the right of Creag Dhu Grooves. Start below the broken rocks which lead to the top of the flake.
1. 45m 4a   Climb the right side of the flake to a belay 5m from its top.
2. 10m 5a   Traverse horizontally right to an exposed ledge on a steep wall, then follow a small dyke.
3. 20m 5a   Where the dyke joins a small fissure on a slight overhang, make a hard right traverse to a ledge, followed by another difficult descending traverse to belay on a further ledge.
4. 30m 4c   Cross The Snake and climb a wall on the right on small holds to easier ground.

11   Strappado Direct   90m   E2 **   (1980/88)
This worthwhile climb takes a direct line to the right of the normal route, giving some fine climbing.
1. 25m 5a   Start up Strappado or The Snake to reach a crack in a slab just left of The Snake. Climb the poorly protected crack to a ledge.
2. 30m 5b/c   Climb Strappado for 10m, and where the original route makes a descending traverse right, continue straight up the crack above to a niche.
3. 35m 5a   Go up the arete on the left to easy ground.

12   The Snake   110m   VS ***   (1965)
This is the classic medium grade route of the crag, but protection is not plentiful. The route follows a very obvious fault line, starting 3 metres right of Strappado.
1. 35m 4c   Follow the fault to a belay.
2. 35m 4c   Continue up the fault to a belay in a groove.
3. 40m 4a   Finish up the dyke to the crest of the buttress.

13   The Team Machine   165m   E4/5 6a **   (1982)
A fine girdle of East Buttress. Start at Kinloss Gully.
1. 30m 4c   Climb Kinloss Gully to a belay.
2. 25m 6a   Follow a horizontal crack to belay on a slab under a roof, just beyond Confession; a well protected pitch.
3. 40m 5b   Climb to the right end of the roof and follow a thin descending crack which leads into the corner of Creag Dhu Grooves; belay on the large ledge above.
4. 30m 5a   Gain a small ledge on the arete and ascend to a thin horizontal break. Follow this to a junction with The Snake, which leads to a ledge and belay.
5. 40m 4a   Finish up The Snake.

14   Zigzag Route   Moderate   (1907)
This route takes the easy rake that starts below Vulcan Wall and trends right to the crest before crossing over to the top part of Eastern Gully.

15   Schadenfreude   85m   Mild Severe   (1957)
Start on the terrace, 15 metres right of Zigzag Route.
1. 30m   Climb optional cracks leading to the upper ledge at 10m. Go easily right for about 8m, then climb a crack to a big ledge.
2. 20m   About 10m of easy climbing is followed by a fault on the right wall.
3. 20m   Continue bearing left on sloping ledges to gain a dyke, then go up to a ledge and spike belay.
4. 15m   Climb the sharp arete to finish.

16   Magic Casement   100m   VS   (1953)
Above the point where the terrace meets the Stone Shoot lie some prominent boulders abutting a bulge on the buttress. Above these is a slabby bay, immediately above which a small squat buttress is split by a crack. Climb the crack to scree (10m). Climb the right-hand of two open grooves and gain an edge before stepping left under flakes to belay on the scree ledges of Zigzag Route. Walk 10m up the rake until below the uppermost crack leading to the upper rake of Zigzag Route. Climb the crack, then walk 3m up the rake to an imposing vertical crack. Climb the crack past a spike and chockstone, then climb a difficult groove and cracked overhang to a ledge (20m). Climb a left-slanting groove, return right to a ledge, then continue to another ledge (10m). Climb a steep crack right of a basalt dyke and cross it to finish on a glacis (20m). Scramble to the top.

17   Caravan Route   85m   Hard Severe   (1949)
Leave the Stone Shoot at the bay above the terrace. Start at a bulging
corner 10m along a flat ledge, at the top of the first pitch of the Girdle
Traverse of Sron na Ciche.
1. 30m   Climb the corner, then trend right up a wall and slab until it is
possible to cross right across a wall, *via* a break, to belays. The climb
briefly joins Direct Route here.
2. 30m   The blocks above and left of the stance lead to a corner. Climb
slightly left above the corner to a wall split by slanting cracks. Climb
the cracks to a belay.
3. 25m   Easier slabs on the right lead to Direct Route below its
penultimate pitch.

18   Magic   45m   E4 6a ***   (1982)
Some distance up from the foot of the buttress is an area of recessed
rock. This climb takes the prominent left-hand crack, giving a superb
and well protected pitch. Climb the flake and slab leading to a small
overhang in a corner, move right and go up the crack to a corner which
leads to the top.

19   The Conjuror   45m   E3 5c **   (1983)
This climbs the right-hand companion crack, 6 metres right of Magic.
Follow the thin crack up the wall to gain a corner. Climb the corner to
a roof and follow the crack to the top.

20   Presdigitateur   45m   HVS 5a   (1987)
This route takes a crack starting just right of The Conjuror. Climb the
right-leaning crack to a ledge beneath a roof, pull over this and climb
the groove to the top.

21   Direct Route   180m   Mild Severe **   (1912)
A very popular classic, highly polished in places, which gives an
exhilarating climb up the front of the buttress, starting from the terrace.
Since it is well scratched, little trouble should be had following the edge
overlooking Eastern Gully as closely as possible. The crux, a steep
wall near the top, should be avoided in the wet. An alternative is to
climb loose flakes to the right, traversing back left above the crux.

22   East Wall Route   270m   Severe *   (1947)
Start at the very foot of the buttress, just left of Eastern Gully. Climb
diagonally up left, traverse left to a scooped slab and cross this
leftwards. Trend left across an open corner, then go across slabs to a

good ledge. Continue easily up a gully, then go left to the terrace. Cross this, then climb diagonally up left across a slab to an overhung ledge. From here, an awkward left traverse leads to a small stance. Continue the left traverse below the overhang, then go up the edge of a groove left of a basalt dyke. Climb the dyke and go up a slab, then move left up a prominent fault which exits from an amphitheatre. Climb steeply up a crack to a perch. Struggle over perched blocks to the base of a wall (Orient Wall). From below a thin flake, traverse up right to a steep crack, take the slab on the right, then go up the right-hand crack to a ledge. Step left to split blocks and traverse up right to a good ledge. Step up right to a shelf to finish above. This last pitch is just right of Direct Route, and the lower pitches can be used as a direct start to Direct Route.

23   Hangover Route   60m   VS   (1947)
This route starts at a corner 10 metres left of Eastern Gully. Climb to a stance and belay at 15m. Climb the corner and the slab on the right to gain a recess on the left. Continue up the corner to a 'cat-walk' crack slanting up left; from its top move up towards Eastern Gully to finish.

The following two routes lies on the most southerly section of the west wall, on a slabby crag identified by MMS scratched on the rock.

24   Protect and Survive   E2 5b   (1990)
Start 6 metres right of the large triangular block. Go up right following a thin diagonal crack to an awkward move to gain a good ledge at a big flake. Keep moving up and right past a small spike to belay at a block in the groove.

25   Hindsight   E1 5c   (1990)
There are two left-slanting cracks 8 metres apart. Climb the slab just right of the left-hand crack.

The west wall of Eastern Buttress has some very attractive climbs on sound rock, overlooking Eastern Gully. Approach the face *via* the terrace; the routes lie right of Direct Route.

26   Chimney Route   180m   Difficult *   (1912)
Start 10 metres right of Direct Route and follow a series of enjoyable chimneys and corners. There are eight pitches, of which the fourth is a fine 20m chimney.

Two striking open corners rise above the terrace, well left of the upper pitches of Chimney Route. Climb broken rocks to reach the base of the corners.

27   Trojan Groove   25m   HVS 5a *   (1965)
Climb the left-hand of the two corners.

28   Helen   E3 6a ***   (1994)
This excellent route, so called because it lies between the Trojans and the Spartans, climbs the formidable-looking arete between Trojan and Spartan Grooves. Climb the initial bulge of Spartan Groove, then move up left to a slanting crack which starts from a horizontal crack. Climb the slanting crack, crux, then the wall just right of the arete to a finish up the arete.

29   Spartan Groove   40m   E1 5b **   (1965)
Climb the right-hand of the two corners, following it to a left-trending overhang. Traverse right with difficulty under this and continue to join Direct Route.
Variation: E1 5b   (1980)
A direct alternative is to pull through the overhang by an undercut to a small ledge on its left; gain the slab above and finish more easily.

30   The Joker   35m   Very Difficult *
This follows the dyke left of Jack O'Diamonds, with a bulge low down.

31   Jack O'Diamonds   100m   Hard Severe **   (1953)
A very good climb, well seen from the Cioch, named after the diamond-shaped block left of the 20m chimney of Chimney Route.
1. 35m   Start in Eastern Gully, 12m above the terrace, and climb open rocks direct to the foot of the 20m chimney of Chimney Route.
2. 20m   Climb a steep wall left of the chimney and, after a mantelshelf at 5m, follow a steepening groove to the conspicuous diamond-shaped block. Go right across the top of the block, and finish up a short crack.
3. 35m   Follow a line of blocks and grooves directly above to the foot of the final V-chimney.
4. 10m   Climb the chimney to join Direct Route below its crux pitch.

32   Searcher   100m   Very Difficult   (1964)
Start from Eastern Gully, 30m above the terrace.
1. 40m   Follow the left-hand of two lines of grooves to a ledge and large spike. Avoid the vertical groove above (this is VS 4c) on the left

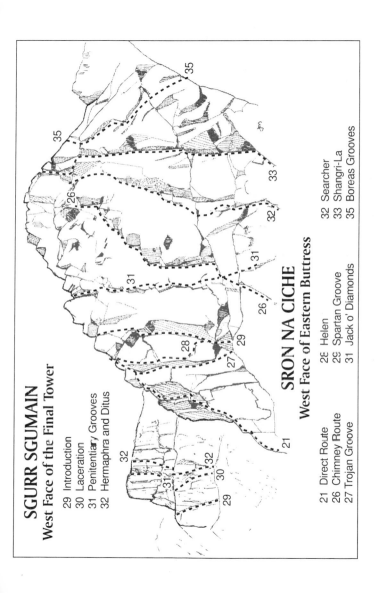

SGURR SGUMAIN
West Face of the Final Tower

29 Introduction
30 Laceration
31 Penitentiary Grooves
32 Hermaphra and Ditus

SRON NA CICHE
West Face of Eastern Buttress

21 Direct Route
26 Chimney Route
27 Trojan Groove

28 Helen
29 Spartan Groove
31 Jack o' Diamonds

32 Searcher
33 Shangri-La
35 Boreas Grooves

wall and return right by a ledge to a large block below the continuation of the groove.

2. 40m   Follow the groove rightwards to a ledge near the corner of the fourth pitch of Shangri-La.

3. 20m   The last pitch is the crux. Climb the fierce-looking groove above, at first in the corner, then by a good crack on the left, to exit near the top of Chimney Route.

33   Shangri-La   130m   VS ***   (1964)

A superb classic climb, the best on this face, which takes the fine series of corners right of Searcher. Start at the foot of Searcher, where a series of corners slants up right. Easy grooves lead to a stance below a steep wide crack. Ascend this, or the wall on the left, to gain the grooves above *via* awkward cracks (4b); flake belays. Climb the excellent corner above and take the final overhang direct in a fine position (35m 4b). Climb the deceptive groove to a wide platform (20m 4b). Above are two corners; climb the strenuous left one (20m 4c). Finish up easy rocks. A Skye curio is (or was) the lashed boulder below the final pitch. This 'Damoclean' object will, sometime in the future, obliterate anyone unfortunate enough to be below in Eastern Gully.

34   Mistral Buttress   105m   VS **   (1992)

This route gives good climbing up the buttress right of Shangri-La.

1. 40m 4c   Start 15 metres right of Shangri-La and climb a cracked ramp up right. Step right and follow a corner to an overhang, moving right to a block belay. (The corner can be reached by moving left from the abseil point on Eastern Gully).

2. 50m 4b   From the block, step left onto a slab, move left to a dyke which leads to the crest of the buttress and climb this to a ledge.

3. 15m 4c   The left-hand corner above is taken by Shangri-La. Left of the right-hand corner are twin cracks. Climb the right-hand crack to an overhang, step left and follow both cracks to the top.

35   Boreas Grooves   90m   VS   (1958)

This lies well right of the last route. Start 10m below the point where the shelf from the top of Cioch Slab enters Eastern Gully, and 12m above the top of the Gully's second pitch.

1. 20m   Climb to the foot of an obvious corner and ascend this to a ledge.

2. 35m   Climb a large groove to a terrace below an overhung corner.

3. 20m 4c   Climb the left-hand corner, as for Shangri-La.

4. 15m   Scramble over easy rocks to finish.

Eastern Gully   Hard Severe   (1938)
Not an attractive route of ascent. The difficulties lie in the first two
pitches, particularly the second. This can be avoided by starting about
15m below the cave, where a 3m wall on the left can be climbed by a
steep crack to a pinnacle. The rest of the gully is easy, either branch
of the forks being straightforward.

In descent, minor pitches lead down from the top and the first
obstacle lies down a subterranean route behind a chockstone. Here
those of great girth or bust invariably get stuck. They will empathise
with a lone Englishman who complained: "Difficult pitch in upper part
of Eastern Gully ... there is an unjustly neglected through route which,
I found, called for unusual exposure, having to remove my trousers to
get through. The critical chest or hip measurements appear to be about
36 inches. There is no technical difficulty - except for mixed parties. "
Dare you risk it? If you do, the next difficulty is a cave, the crux of the
gully; ('Abseil' is scratched on the rock above on the right.) There is
usually an assortment of slings. Leave the gully at the terrace, and
follow the latter rightwards across Eastern Buttress and down to the
Sgumain Stone Shoot.

CIOCH BUTTRESS   *(Map Ref 445 204)*

From below, the massive perfect gabbro slabs appear to be easy-angled, however this illusion is rapidly rectified once you have stepped
off the scree. The climbs follow lines of weakness and have a steep
lower section with easier slab climbing higher up. The open chimney-
gully of Cioch Direct, which is two-thirds of the way west along the crag,
is easily recognised in mist by the waterfall and polish. The routes on
the right-hand side are longer and sport a steep headwall that forms
the crux of most of those climbs. There are extensive easy slabs below
the terrace, and many of the climbs are much longer than the early
guide books made out. In fact the climbs (and grades) have grown with
successive guides!

The approach is described in the introductory notes to this section.
Cioch Buttress is the area of rock between Eastern Gully and Cioch
Gully at an altitude of about 450m, and its upper limit is defined by the
terrace that runs below the Cioch.

The descent from the terrace that runs below the Cioch follows it
into Eastern Gully *via* a little slab. This gains the scree a short way
above the lower continuation of the terrace, which is followed to the
Sgumain Stone Shoot. A brief walk downwards and back west leads
to the foot of the buttress.

1   Tennatte   40m   E2   (1990)
Start 10m up the left wall of Petronella and follow a steep layback crack
to an obvious down-sloping spike. Use this to gain holds on the right,
then climb straight up to the *in situ* thread on Petronella.

2   Petronella   55m   Mild VS 4b **   (1952)
This fine little climb is on the small buttress between Eastern Gully and
Little Gully. From the screes, climb an awkward prominent crack which
curves leftwards up the centre of the buttress. The overhangs above
are turned by a shelf followed by an airy pull-up.

3   Stormy Petrel   50m   HVS 5b *   (1985)
Climb the crack right of Petronella, move left as the crack fades and
climb to a stance. Traverse right to avoid a big overhang, then finish
straight up.

4   Little Gully   70m   Difficult *
This is the small but worthwhile gully to the west of Eastern Gully. Care
should be taken with occasional loose rock. Easily follow either of the
two branches until they converge below a cave. Climb this by backing
up and out through a window above the entrance. The next pitch can
be climbed direct or turned on the left. Above, the climb deteriorates
into a groove, so traverse left onto the face where scrambling leads to
the terrace.
Winter: III/IV   (1970)
A good low-level route requiring cold conditions. Steep ice bosses lead
to the easy entrance of a cave chockstone. Exit from this *via* a funnel,
sometimes awkward. Above this, snow with short ice walls lead to the
terrace.

5   Acapulco Wall   110m   E3   (1980)
This serious route takes a direct line up the buttress 6 metres left of
Bastinado. Start just right of Little Gully.
1. 25m 5b   Climb a ramp and a short wall to a ledge. Gain and climb
a short steep crack to the large block belay of Bastinado.
2. 35m 5c   Climb awkwardly left until it is possible to pull right into a
very thin crack. Climb this and a bulge to a small ledge 5 metres left
of the crux of Bastinado. Continue up the wall above to a niche with an
overhang, then climb this to a tiny spike runner. Trend up right and go
up a wide crack to block belays.
3. 50m 4b   Climb slabs and cracks to ledges and the terrace.

6   Bastinado   90m   E1 **   (1956)

A good and well protected climb needing a positive approach. Start 20 metres left of Cioch Grooves.

1. 35m 4c   Ascend to an obvious crack, which slopes slightly left, then climb it to a broad grassy ledge.

2. 10m 5b   Climb the corner direct, then trend left to a sloping ledge.

3. 10m 5b   Step left to below a groove which overhangs at its lower end. Climb this strenuously until good holds allow a move right to a triangular corner and belay.

4. 35m 4b   Climb a crack immediately behind the corner to a small rock ledge. Continue up a crack to the terrace.

Variation: 10m   E1 5b *   (1983)

Climb a groove and jam crack right of the normal crux.

7   The Nipple   125m   E2 *   (1977)

This route takes a direct line between Cioch Grooves and Bastinado. Start at a thin crack 6 metres left of Cioch Grooves.

1. 45m 5b   Follow the crack, avoiding a steepening on the left, to reach easier-angled slabby rock.

2. 35m 5b   Move up diagonally left past an ancient peg towards a prominent groove with a smooth left wall. Step across the top of the groove to enter a deeper groove which leads to a stance on the left.

3. 45m   Finish up the slab between Cioch Grooves and Bastinado.

8   Cioch Grooves   150m   HVS **   (1957)

A superb and exciting climb, the only drawback being the possible escapes into Cioch Direct. Start left of Cioch Direct where a shelf lies above the scree. A prominent crack lies parallel to Cioch Direct.

1. 30m 4c   Climb the crack to where it steepens, then step left to a parallel crack which is followed to easier slabs. Traverse right to belay near the crux chimney of Cioch Direct.

2. 25m 5a   Traverse back left below a steep wall and go up this on the left to a block. A thin traverse right, crux, enables a delicate step onto the slab above. Belay below a fine crack just left of Cioch Direct.

3. 25m 4b   Climb the crack to easier slabs and belays.

4. and 5. 70m   Continue up the left-hand crack, then follow easier slabs to the terrace.

Variation: E1 5a

An alternative to the crux pitch is to continue straight up from the step onto the slab and climb this *via* a 'mental mantel' which leads to the top of the fine crack.

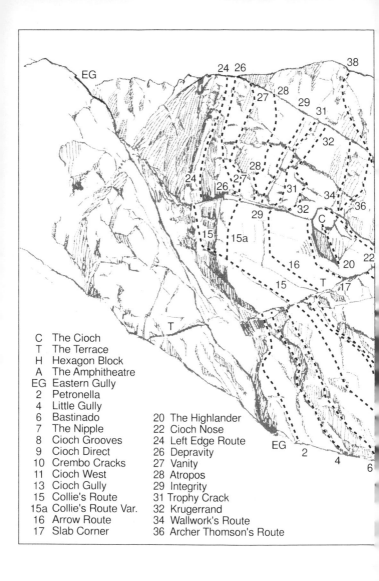

C   The Cioch
T   The Terrace
H   Hexagon Block
A   The Amphitheatre
EG   Eastern Gully
2   Petronella
4   Little Gully
6   Bastinado
7   The Nipple
8   Cioch Grooves
9   Cioch Direct
10   Crembo Cracks
11   Cioch West
13   Cioch Gully
15   Collie's Route
15a Collie's Route Var.
16   Arrow Route
17   Slab Corner

20   The Highlander
22   Cioch Nose
24   Left Edge Route
26   Depravity
27   Vanity
28   Atropos
29   Integrity
31   Trophy Crack
32   Krugerrand
34   Wallwork's Route
36   Archer Thomson's Route

SRON NA CICHE

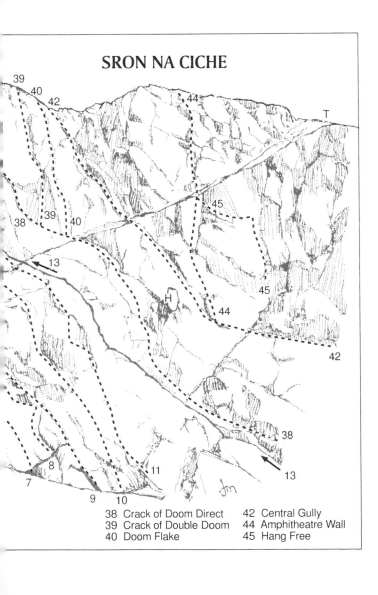

38 Crack of Doom Direct 42 Central Gully
39 Crack of Double Doom 44 Amphitheatre Wall
40 Doom Flake 45 Hang Free

9   Cioch Direct   150m   Severe 4a *   (1907)
Probably one of the most trodden climbs in Skye, after Window
Buttress and the Inaccessible Pinnacle. Such heavy traffic has caused
the inevitable polishing and this can be detrimental in the wet. The
climb starts 10m up the screes from the lowest rocks of the buttress
and takes an open gully. There are two main methods of attack for the
lower section: Poise and Elegance, or Elephantine Struggles. Either
way, climb the open chimney-gully, following a polished corner and a
long easy groove, before climbing a series of entertaining chimneys.
The topmost chimney is the tight crux, the scene of an historic rockfall
on the first ascent. Above, a sloping shelf leads up and left to a jumble
of boulders which include a yardarm. Traverse left across a broken slab,
then climb parallel cracks on impeccable rock to easier slabs and the
terrace.

10   Crembo Cracks   155m   HVS **   (1958)
A superb but serious climb which lies left of the toe of Cioch Buttress,
easily identified by a pair of cracks.
1. 40m   Either climb the right-hand crack (which has an inverted-V
10m from the base) and follow the dyke up left to a ledge (4b) or, far
better, climb the left-hand jamming crack to step up left on a nose and
follow a slabby corner past flakes to the same ledge (4c).
2. 35m   Continue up a very pleasant chimney and cracks to the base
of a steeper slab. Traverse right to a ledge and climb the steep corner
crack to the grassy ledge of Cioch West.
3. 40m 5a   The route now attacks the unlikely wall above, sometimes
easily identified by signs of retreat! Climb the steepening corner above
to a square corner at the base of the wall, old peg runner. Traverse 5
metres delicately right across the slab to a hidden corner. Climb the
steep creaky flakes above and go up a series of awkward poorly
protected steps, passing an old peg, crux. Now climb the impressively-
situated bulge above by the undercut wobbly flakes, taking care with
the cuddly jug above. Step up right to a fine ledge. A serious but
excellent pitch which requires steady climbing.
4. 40m   Continue much more easily over slabs to the foot of the steep
little wall of Cioch West.

11   Cioch West   215m   Severe **   (1919)
A fine climb, polished in places, giving constantly interesting climbing
with a splendidly exposed crux. Start a few metres left of Cioch Gully
below a notch-like chimney.

1. 35m   Climb polished grooves into the strenuous chimney. Above, easier grooves lead to a stance and belays.

2. and 3. 60m   Easy grooves lead up the slabs on immaculate rock to a belay on an overhung ledge below an off-width crack.

4. 20m   Climb up right across a steep slab on polished incut holds to reach a fine ledge. Easy rocks lead to the ledge that encircles the upper bastion of the climb; belay below a well scratched wall.

5. 25m   Climb the right-trending break with interest to ledges.

6. 15m   The chimney on the left leads to the crux, a 'hand-traverse' that leads left onto a narrow ledge; a fine pitch.

7. 30m   From the left end of the ledge, climb easier rock to a large ledge.

8. 30m   Easy slabs lead to a short vertical nose overlooking Cioch Gully. This leads strenuously to a belay. Now scramble left across the slabs below the Cioch to a jumble of boulders and the ledge system running below the Cioch itself.

Variation: 35m   Hard Severe 4b   (1951)
About 100m above the start, where the original route traverses right across the polished slab, it is possible to climb the wall above (the off-width!) to meet the left end of the 'hand-traverse' pitch.

12   West Ridge of the Cioch   140m   Severe   (1932)
This route takes the rib that bounds the left edge of Cioch Gully.

1. 40m   Start below a corner just left of Cioch Gully. Climb the left wall near the edge over several steepenings.

2. 20m   Continue up the edge to a platform below an overhanging wall.

3. 30m   Climb the wall by a strenuous crack, then follow the easy ridge to the next short wall. Climb this to belays.

4. 50m   Climb along the ridge to the top of the Cioch.

13   Cioch Gully   200m   Very Difficult   (1906)
Start either in the gully or by the dykes either side, or by the rocks leading in from the foot of Cioch Buttress. Long sections of easy climbing lead to two pitches. The first of these involves strenuous backing-up through a tunnel formed by a large fallen block, whilst the second is a short sharp layback that finishes on the shelf behind the Cioch.

Winter: III
Quite a good climb, but the last pitch needs a reasonable build-up.

14   Banana   40m   Hard Severe 4b   (1992)
This route provides a harder alternative to Cioch Gully. Scramble
halfway up the gully until a small subsidiary gully appears on the left.
Scramble up this smaller gully to the foot of a short steep corner above
a chockstone. The corner contains two cracks; climb the one on the
left awkwardly to the top of the corner. Trend right around a bulge, then
follow a rising traverse across a slab to a corner. Continue rightwards
around this corner to a second slab which leads to the terrace.

THE CIOCH AND CIOCH SLAB

This massive slab, which steepens at the top, is pockmarked with
weathered augite crystals, and is composed of the finest gabbro
available. At its west end lies a noble tower, one of the Cuillin's most
famous landmarks, the Cioch. It rests, somewhat implausibly, on the
slab, cracked around the base but presumably very stable. It is a
superb viewpoint and should be visited by every climber in the area.
The Cioch has become a playground for technical test-pieces, short
but hard, as well as some well polished favourites in the lower grades.
   Approach as for Cioch Buttress as far as the Sgumain Stone Shoot.
Now follow the terrace across Eastern Buttress to Eastern Gully, as
described for Collie's Route. To descend from the shelf that runs along
the crest of Cioch Slab, traverse left easily in an exposed position to
Eastern Gully and descend this as described above.

15   Collie's Route   Moderate **   (1906)
This varied route, the original, is recommended for novice parties.
Starting from the Sgumain Stone Shoot, follow the terrace across
Eastern Buttress into Eastern Gully. Here a curving polished shelf
leads right to the base of the slab, rising above a grassy ledge. Climb
the deep cracks on very polished rock, following the left edge of the
slab for 50m to the edge. Easy blocks now lead back into Eastern Gully
which is followed to the narrow shelf which runs across the top of the
slab. Traverse right easily and downwards along the exposed 'Collie's
Ledge' and gain the Cioch itself by a highly polished arete (The Neck).
Climb to the top either by the slabs or by the more secure chimney a
few metres west of its eastern edge. Return by the same way.
   A recommended Very Difficult variation is to climb the steep slab up
right of the cracks to Collie's Ledge, instead of entering Eastern Gully.

Cioch Upper Buttress. Climbers on Integrity (left) and Wallwork's Route (right)

16   Arrow Route   60m   Very Difficult ***   (1944)
To the left of the Cioch is the unique Cioch Slab, a 50 degree plane of
dimpled rock, gabbro at its very best. The easiest line is as follows.
From the base of Slab Corner, follow the diagonal crack up the slab
easily for 15m to belay at a triangular flake. Now climb up and left
towards a hidden shallow ramp utilising the magnificent dimples. Either
finish up the ramp or, slightly harder, climb another break to the right,
45m. No longer the unprotected pitch it used to be, it is now possible
to place well spaced protection. There are obviously more direct and
harder lines nearer Slab Corner which can capture the bold flavour of
this magnificent slab.

17   Slab Corner   50m   Difficult
This is the big polished corner between the right edge of the Cioch
Slab and the Cioch, much used by beginners.

There are several climbs on the Cioch itself, which are reached from
the terrace.

18   Slanting Crack   60m   Severe *
Follow Slab Corner to about 6m below the Neck, belay. Gain the
slanting crack *via* jammed flakes and traverse diagonally up right to a
platform, followed by an easy crack to the top; often wet.

19   Overhanging Crack   35m   E2 5c **   (1978)
Follow Slab corner for 30m to where an obvious overhanging crack
runs straight up the eastern face of the Cioch. Traverse right into the
crack, climb it with difficulty, then finish by open slabs.

20   The Highlander   45m   E6 6b ***   (1992)
A stunning pitch up the frontal arete of the Cioch. Climb easily up slabs
to the arete. Climb boldly up the right side of the arete to an obvious
hole (runners in the flake to the right). Continue *via* a thin diagonal
crack to a resting ledge (crucial Friend runners). Move up to a large
flat hold on the arete (poor micro nuts) and attempt to stand on it. A
tricky mantelshelf gains the upper slabs and easy ground; belay on top
of the Cioch.

The Cioch Slab and the Cioch

21   Erotica   25m   E3 6b **   (1983)
This route climbs the small frontal face of the Cioch, *via* the obvious thin crack line. Start up easy slabs, then climb the crack (well protected in the top part) with a rest out left on a ledge. Finish by easy slabs.

22   Cioch Nose   45m   Very Difficult **
An airy and rather smooth climb up the western edge of the Cioch. Start from the terrace and climb a groove to a belay in a corner. Traverse left to a delicate slab and go up this to mantelshelf the edge above, using a hidden hold. Gain and climb the knife edge to the top. A superb little climb, but nasty in the wet.

CIOCH UPPER BUTTRESS

Cioch Upper Buttress stretches from Eastern Gully in the form of a steep slabby wall cut by impressive overlaps. Several prominent and famous crack lines pierce this wall, giving challenging and direct lines of great quality. Some of Skye's finest routes are to be found here. The buttress extends as far as Central Gully on the right, and its base is the shelf as far as the Cioch, then the terrace as far as Central Gully. It includes the steep rock above Cioch Slab as well as the rocks above the terrace further right.

Access to the routes above Cioch Slab is easiest *via* Collie's Route. For the climbs above the terrace to the right of the Cioch, it is easiest to follow a section of the Girdle Traverse (Very Difficult), by a rather exposed and awkward traverse, as follows: From the neck behind the Cioch, follow a ledge under the buttress, traverse around a little pinnacle and across some slabs, then descend an exposed oblique chimney to the terrace. From the plateau it is possible to descend Eastern Gully to the start of the shelf.

To descend from the shelf below Cioch Upper Buttress, reverse Collie's Route to Eastern Gully. The descent from the large glacis above the buttress goes left onto the plateau, following huge blocks of gabbro. The quickest and safest descent is down the Sgumain Stone Shoot. A short smooth step bars access to the Stone Shoot; skirt right, then descend easy polished rock to the top of the Shoot. If necessary, the more laborious descent of Eastern Gully can be undertaken.

23   Slabby Wall Crack   80m   VS   (1994)
This quite good but slow-drying route lies on the true left wall of Eastern Gully, just above the exit of the shelf from the Cioch. The wall is bounded on the left by a corner.

1. 5m 4c   Pull through the initial bulge and belay at the foot of the corner.
2. 50m 5a   Move up the corner until it is possible to step right into the obvious crack which splits the wall, then climb the crack to its top; less deceptive than it appears.
3. 25m   Climb a short crack to easier ground.

24   Left Edge Route   75m   Severe   (1937)
This route starts in the innermost corner of the deep recess on the left extension of the shelf, left of the face of the buttress. The recess is well seen from below. Ascend the recess to a belay (20m). Traverse up and right to the buttress edge to belays. From there, climb directly up the edge to the glacis.

25   Piety   90m   VS **   (1985)
Climb the corner between Left Edge and Depravity to its top, then move left to Depravity's belay, 4c. Go back right to a hanging arete and climb this and slabs to the glacis, 4b.

26   Depravity   90m   VS 4c *   (1958)
A pleasant route, quite hard for the grade. Start about 10 metres right of Left Edge and just left of an overhanging sentry box. An awkward start leads left to an overhang with a tiny stance just above, 4c. Climb a rib on the right for a short distance, then cross a groove on the left and climb to a platform and belay, 4b. Continue to the top, keeping slightly to the right of Left Edge Route.

27   Vanity   90m   E2   (1980)
Start at the overhanging sentry-box just left of Depravity.
1. 20m 4c   Climb rightwards round the sentry box and go up into a corner. Belay on a small stance.
2. 35m 5b   Climb the corner, and halfway up it move left onto the upper slab. Climb this to below overhangs, then climb the double overlap above, move right and go straight up to belays.
3. 35m 4a   Finish directly above.

28   Atropos   100m   E1 **   (1978)
Start well left of Integrity and climb a steep wall onto a slab. Go up this, trending slightly left before making a diagonal traverse up right across a slab to belay below an overhang, 5b. Climb the overhang on the left, then go up to a belay below roofs, 4b. Traverse left and up through the overhangs (loose blocks), then move up right to a belay, 5a. Finish straight up.

29 Integrity   75m   Mild VS ***   (1949)
A magnificent classic that breaks through intimidating slabs by an
arrow-straight line; the best climb of its grade in Skye. Start about 6m
up the shelf left of the grass patch behind the Cioch.
1. 40m 4b   Surmount a strenuous overhang on good rough holds to
arrive on the slab above. Continue up the thin crack in a superb
position, excellently protected. A little block overhang inset by a corner
is awkward, belay on the flat ledge above.
2. 35m 4b   Continue up the crack more easily. Purists will take the
top, steeper, crack direct. The easiest line bypasses this with a step to
the right.

30 Ajax   30m   Hard Severe 4b
An additional pitch directly above Integrity, starting from the glacis.
Beware of a sharp 2 metre flake in the upper section that is
alarmingly loose; it needs vigorous use and may expire sooner
rather than later.

31 Trophy Crack   80m   E1 **   (1956)
Probably the easiest Extreme in the Cuillin, with an excellent initial
pitch, this well protected climb takes the crack to the right of Integrity,
above the grass patch. Start by a pinnacle at the base of the crack.
1. 40m 5b   Go over the initial steepness, then follow a groove and a
short overhang. A layback above is followed by the crux and a step left
to a good ledge and belays.
2. 40m 4b   Climb the much easier crack above. Either climb the big
overlap direct (5a), or step left through a narrow sentry box and climb
the slab above. Step back right to the main crack, which widens before
finishing on the glacis.

32 Krugerrand   80m   E3 *   (1980)
This climb sports a difficult but well protected crux. Start 5 metres right
of Trophy Crack.
1. 25m 6a   Climb the slab to a large roof and surmount this using
finger jams. Climb the crack above, crux, to a hanging stance.
2. 25m 5a   Go up slightly left and over the next roof, then traverse
back right to a crack and follow it to the Trophy Crack belay.
3. 30m   Climb the slab parallel to Trophy Crack and cross the roof by
a small ledge. Finish straight up the slab above.

33   Ghost Riders   85m   E2 *   (1981)
This line is directly behind the Cioch, between Krugerrand and Wallwork's Route. Follow an arching dyke until an obvious hold can be used to surmount the overlap. Gain a ledge by a long reach and follow the wall up left for 10m to ledges which lead back right to a jammed block recess beneath an overhang (5b). Gain the pinnacle up on the right and surmount the overhang slightly right of this. Continue to a sloping ledge, then move right around a corner. Follow the arete directly to the glacis (5b).

34   Wallwork's Route   75m   Very Difficult ***   (1915)
A splendid route of character which used to be graded Difficult when real men (and women) still wore nailed boots. Start at the grass patch behind the Cioch. Traverse right along a broken rake, then swing left along a tottering pile of blocks; belay under a roof. Pull over on excellent holds to a platform and belay. Above is a fearsome crack. Avoid this by stepping right into a right-angled corner capped by a small roof. The corner is surprisingly tricky but well protected and leads over the roof to a stance and belay. Follow a wide crack through a slab and outflank a roof by a traverse right past perched blocks to the upper glacis.

35   Fidelity   70m   Severe   (1970)
This climb takes the obvious line starting 6 metres right of Wallwork's Route. Climb the large crack behind a big loose block, surmount a small bulge at 15m direct and belay at a small block on the right-sloping ramp of Archer Thomson's Route. Climb up and left to a loose block, turning the overhang on the left, and follow the crack to finish at the bottom of the glacis.

36   Archer Thomson's Route   75m   Very Difficult **   (1911)
Another character-crunching route which used to be graded Difficult. Start on the grass patch behind the Cioch. Follow Wallwork's Route for 25m, and 12m up the groove, break out on the steep shelf on the right which finishes at the base of the upper glacis.

The following routes lie above the terrace, and can only be reached from the grass patch behind the Cioch by following the Very Difficult traverse mentioned in the approach to the crag. Otherwise, either climb Cioch Gully to near the top, then take the slabs on the right (Severe) to the terrace, or climb Crack of Doom to the same point.

37   Rib of Doom   75m   VS 4c **   (1949)

This is the fine rib to the left of Crack of Doom. There are two alternative starts, either from the foot of the oblique chimney at the start of the traverse up left to the grass patch behind the Cioch, or by following Crack of Doom to a point below the crack. Traverse towards the rib, gaining it *via* a subsidiary groove. Follow the rib in a tremendous position to the top.

38   Crack of Doom   165m   Mild VS **   (1918)

This famous and historic climb is vastly improved by the Direct Start and Direct Finish. The actual crack is an insecure thrutch, memorable for its polish and dampness, but the rest makes up for it. The actual crack can be seen from the corrie as a prominent curving crack, which can be gained from the grass patch behind the Cioch. From the terrace, 40m of Moderate slabs lead to the foot of the crack.

Climb the crack to a chockstone (12m). Above, the crack steepens and narrows, forming the crux, 4b. This is strenuous and can be hard if grease is present on an already polished surface. It is possible to avoid the crux by Severe climbing on the left wall. The original climb finishes at the foot of the sloping glacis.

Direct Approach:

There is a choice of two routes to the foot of the Direct Approach. Either climb Cioch Gully to a point 10m above the grass terrace which leads rightwards from below a large chockstone in the gully, or climb Cioch West to reach a chimney which rises from Cioch Gully, then descend to the start of the climb.

Climb a square corner to a short slab and hence to a line of holds leading diagonally right to an open 'V'. Climb this by its left side to a small stance and belay by a detached block (20m). Descend again to the foot of the 'V', climb right around another slab, then go up a steep corner to a narrow ledge (20m). Traverse briefly right from the ledge, then ascend a steep shallow groove which joins the lower section of Crack of Doom about 15m below the terrace.

Direct Finish: Hard Severe

This is immediately above the Crack of Doom and right of the sloping glacis, and leads straight up very steep rocks to the plateau.

39   Crack of Double Doom   90m   Mild VS 4b ***   (1947)

This is an excellent classic climb despite some dubious rock. A clean-cut fault lies right of Crack of Doom. Start immediately right of Crack of Doom and follow the fault to the apex of the slab. The climbing gets progressively harder with the crux in the last 10m below the apex.

Above the slab, a crack runs up a steep right-angled corner. Climb the corner to the top. There are several harder variations to reach the belays above the apex of the slab, but none are as good.

40   Doom Flake   90m   Severe *   (1947)
A good and quite strenuous climb. Start 25m up the terrace from Crack of Doom, where a large fallen flake forms a right-angled corner with the main face. Climb a thin crack in the wall from the left-hand side of the flake, then climb a basalt jigsaw with an awkward mantel into a corner above on the right. Climb the crack above, then a wall above a large flake. Go right over perched blocks and climb a corner to finish.

41   Pearly Gates   170m   VS   (1964)
This is the girdle traverse of Cioch Upper Buttress, and it has some good climbing in fine positions. Start 10 metres along the ledge from Eastern Gully and 5 metres left of Left Edge Route.
1. 30m   Traverse right and cross a diedre to a ledge and peg belay.
2. 20m 4c   Continue 10m right, with some difficulty, then pull over the overlap before descending to a ledge.
3. 40m 4c   Traverse right to a large slab and make an ascending traverse across the slab to belay on Integrity.
4. 30m 4b   Move right across Trophy Crack to belay on Wallwork's Route.
5. 30m   Move across and up Archer Thomson's Route to belay in the niche.
6. 20m 4c   Finish by going right and continuing up the Rib of Doom.

WESTERN BUTTRESS   *(Map Ref 442 202)*

Western Buttress covers all the rocks to the west of the Cioch and Cioch Upper Buttress. It includes The Amphitheatre and Western Buttress proper. The Amphitheatre is the large depression immediately right of the upper section of Central Gully and is composed of great sheets of slabs extending from the gully to an arete on the right (Ampitheatre Arete), with a vertical back wall, Amphitheatre Wall.

Western Buttress has a few very prominent features from which it is possible to locate the routes. It is best seen from the other side of the corrie as at close quarters the features merge into the cliff, which is 300 metres in height. Slanting up left from the base of the crag are several gullies or rakes, the most prominent being Central Gully, which starts in the middle of the buttress, crosses the floor of The Amphitheatre and finishes on the summit plateau west of Cioch Upper Buttress.

West Central Gully starts near the west end of the buttress, slants up the face parallel to Central Gully, then peters out under a large overhang about halfway up the cliff. In the lower section of the cliff between these two gullies is a vast diamond-shaped area of slabs.

To the west of Amphitheatre Arete and across an open gully is another arete, West Central Arete. This commences at half-height just above the overhang at the termination of West Central Gully. About 90 metres from West Central Arete, and again high on the face, are three prominent overhanging corners.

The whole buttress is on a vast scale with several types of features recurring. Route-finding is the most problematical single difficulty on many of the climbs and in consequence a great number of usually accidental variations, some better than the original climb, have been done. The essence of this cliff is exploration and it is a fine place to get lost; guidebooks may hint to the way, but an eye for a likely line will be of more use. It should therefore be pointed out that due to the above factors and the presence of basalt, climbers should be capable of leading a full grade above the standard of their chosen route; this is especially true on some of the easier lines.

The approach is described in the introduction to Sron na Ciche. By far the easiest descent is down the open gully well to the west of the crags; scree and a little scrambling.

42 Central Gully 400m Very Difficult (1907)
A fairly straightforward climb, at times interesting. Follow the gully to The Amphitheatre. Some steeper pitches ensue, including one best turned on the left. Above, the gully forks and the left branch gives the better finish.

43 East Wall and Central Gully Arete Very Difficult (1909)
This is a variation to Central Gully. From above The Amphitheatre, follow the east wall of the gully to the terrace and climb the interesting arete to the summit plateau.

44 Amphitheatre Wall 180m VS 4b * (1932)
There are several routes and variations criss-crossing this wall and sharing pitches; this is the original route. Start in The Amphitheatre to the west of and slightly lower than the Hexagon Block. The climb is in two sections, split by the terrace. Although some of the pitches are short, many can be linked to give longer runouts if desired. This is a very fine climb which deserves more attention. However, there has recently been substantial rock fall in the vicinity and care should be taken with all blocks.

The climb initially goes 15m up steep slabs to belays. Now traverse 7m right, and climb straight up to a terrace. Follow two 'embryonic' chimneys for 10m, then a slanting crack and an exposed crack with three jammed blocks to a belay above. A bridging pitch then leads to a stance (7m). Continue up the easier-angled crack to a spike belay (25m). The terrace is just above.

The upper wall starts at a cairn 5 metres right of the flake. Go first left, then turn right to a large corner and a huge poised block (10m). Traverse 5 metres right to a spike belay. Above and to the right is an overhang followed by a 5m groove which leads to a stance. From there go straight up for 3m, then move obliquely up right across a steep rake and so to a stance. Climb the pinnacle on the right, then step up to a hand-traverse left which leads to a belay. Continue up left over jammed blocks to the plateau.

45 Hang Free   90m   E2 *   (1980)
This good route lies up and right of Amphitheatre Wall. In the right half of the wall is a line of cracks.
1. 20m 5b   Climb the thin crack past an old peg until it is possible to rest on the right.
2. 30m 5b   Move up the overhanging crack and a slab to make a hard move left to a nest belay.
3. 20m 5b   Reverse the slab, moving right to regain the crack and groove. Jam and bridge up the groove to pull into a niche.
4. 20m 5a   Follow the groove to the headwall, climb this using twin cracks and follow easier ground to the terrace.

46 Amphitheatre Arete   270m   Moderate *   (1907)
A sporting mountaineering ramble. Start from Cioch Gully and ascend slabs towards The Amphitheatre. Cross Central Gully where it reaches The Amphitheatre, then go right across waterworn slabs to the nose of the arete. Follow this to the top.

47 Mallory's Slab and Groove   300m   Very Difficult * (1918)
The grading assumes rock boots and the easiest line. It is an enjoyable line, popular and best finished by West Central Arete. Start from the screes midway between Central and Cioch Gullies, at a prominent crack immediately right of a large overhang. Climb the crack and the exposed slab above to reach Central Gully. Follow the gully for roughly 45m (depending on where one joins the gully) to a prominent crack going up to the right. Climb this and continue on a line towards the overhang on West Central Arete. Pass the overhang on the left to reach

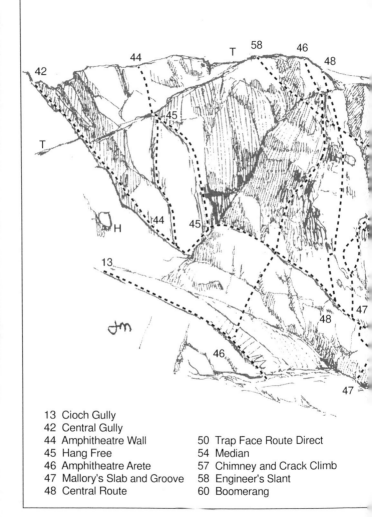

13 Cioch Gully
42 Central Gully
44 Amphitheatre Wall
45 Hang Free
46 Amphitheatre Arete
47 Mallory's Slab and Groove
48 Central Route

50 Trap Face Route Direct
54 Median
57 Chimney and Crack Climb
58 Engineer's Slant
60 Boomerang

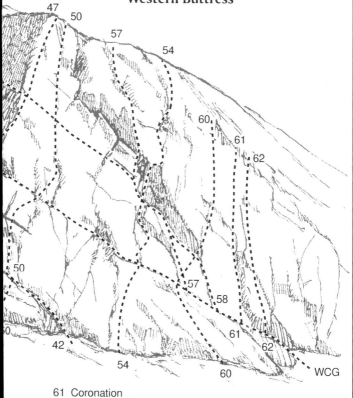

SRON NA CICHE
Western Buttress

61 Coronation
62 Parallel Cracks Route
H Hexagon Block

T The Terrace
WCG West Central Gully

the gully on the left of the arete. Either finish up the loose gully, or much better up the arete on the right. It is also possible to finish up Engineer's Slant.

48 Central Route   255m   Hard Severe **   (1957)
A splendid expedition. Start on a steep wall just left of where Mallory's Slab and Groove leaves Central Gully.
1. 25m   Follow Central Gully to a point just left of its prominent crack. Climb steep juggy rock to a sloping platform with a block belay.
2. 10m   Climb over a bulge above the block, then go right across a short slab to a break in a small overhang above. Climb this to a sloping gangway and move left to a crack and flake belay.
3. 20m   Climb the crack, step right to another crack and step left at the top. Climb the wall for 5m, bearing right to the edge of a shallow gully.
4. 15m   Climb steep rock directly above to a small stance and flake belay.
5. 25m 4b   Step up left of the belay, then go up and right until near a block by the gully. Move onto a gangway, traverse left to a bulge and surmount this, continuing for 4m and bearing right to a sloping ledge; spike belay on the left.
6. 30m   Surmount the bulge above the belay to an easing, then go up an easy-angled slab. Scramble easily up the slab to the foot of steeper rocks above.
7. 25m   Climb the wall *via* a small dyke that has a 'sinuous offshoot' in its upper section. After 10m, follow a slab easily to another steep section.
8. 25m   Climb the groove above and a short steep slab. From the top of the groove, follow an easy arete to a thread belay under a block 10m higher (the top part of Amphitheatre Arete).
9. 25m   Go easily along the arete, then descend into a small gully on its right to a triangular grass patch below the final tower.
10. 25m   Steep rock leads to a belay on the edge of the gully at the right-hand side of the tower.
11. 30m 4b   An exposed crux follows. Traverse up and left on small holds to a break in the overhang above. Climb the break avoiding a block, then climb the left wall of a steep groove to the top.

49 Trap Face Route   300m   VS 4b *   (1914)
This route seems particularly prone to the mists of uncertainty, which is perhaps not surprising since the variations seem directly related to the number of ascents. Some of the upper reaches, particularly in the

chimneys, are very loose and care is needed. Be warned, this is not a route for wet weather: 'The cracks are inclined to be greasy and not too pleasant in wet conditions' (to quote the original description). To clarify, or confuse, here are some of the possible ways to get lost:-

Climb Central Gully or, better, the first two pitches of Mallory's Slab and Groove to Central Gully. Follow the gully to where Mallory's Slab and Groove continues, then traverse right round a corner (stance) into a prominent chimney, which lies below the line of West Central Arete. Climb the chimney for 20m, then trend right and go up to below a small rock nose in a corner. Above, steep and awkward cracks lead to a depression. Follow this right of overhangs, then pass a bridged boulder to a rake. Follow the dyke to a small amphitheatre. From here there are several possible lines to the summit. Either climb an easy groove leading right, then a left-trending crack before moving more easily right to a ridge below and right of the summit ridge of the buttress. Or, climb directly up a short way, then follow a diagonal fault up and left to a huge detached flake with a fine crack separating it from the buttress. Climb the crest of the West Central Arete, or just right of it.

Variation: 45m   VS 4c *   (1950)
From the stance after rounding the corner from Mallory's Slab and Groove, climb a short layback crack in the corner. Ascend the right wall of the corner, then move diagonally right to an undercut ledge which is right of a shallow chimney. Climb this and move right to a difficult shallow groove. At its top, move back left into the corner and climb to a stance and belay.

50   Trap Face Route Direct   300m   VS 4c **   (1976)
This direct and recommended variation borrows parts of older climbs, starting up Diamond Slab, the large diamond-shaped area of slabs lying between Central and West Central Gullies. Start 15 metres right of Mallory's Slab and Groove at a small overhang. Climb the overhang, then follow easier slabs to Central Gully. Go 5m up the gully, then climb straight up to cracks in the middle of the slab, belaying 10m below them. Climb the cracks through an overlap and belay in the basalt dyke 3m above and right. Climb the slab above to a large overhang, then pull onto a glacis under the overhang *via* the left-hand corner of a brown wall; belay. Turn the overhang by the right-hand of two grooves and 5m up layback the finger-crack right of the groove to exit from the overhang; belay. The next two pitches take the large overhang above, followed by a chimney, then go up left and belay on top. Continue straight up and follow the dyke to join West Central Gully Arete. Finish up this, or keep to its right.

51   Diamond Slab   180m   VS   (1946)
Start at a small overhang 15m right of Mallory's Slab and Groove.
1. 30m   Climb the overhang, traverse right, then go up a crack to a
slab below an overhang; belay in the crack.
2. 25m   Traverse left and climb a crack to a grass platform and a
boulder belay in Central Gully.
3. 35m   Cross the gully onto a steep slab. Climb this direct on large
sloping holds, then trend left to a 'knob belay' in a shallow corner.
4. 20m   Traverse up right, then climb straight up to a grass ledge with
small flake belays.
5. 30m   Traverse up right on a good ledge broken by sloping slabs to
a small flake belay.
6. 40m   Continue the traverse to a vertical dyke, then follow this to
West Central Gully and thence to the top.
Direct Finish: 70m   VS 4c *   (1964)
A more logical but harder finish.
4. 35m   From the belay at the top of pitch 3, continue directly up the
slab instead of traversing right. At 25m, traverse under an overhang
and across a wall on its right, crux, to a grass ledge.
5. 35m 4c   Continue 5m along the ledge to a dyke, then follow this to
a junction with West Central Gully.

52   Angel's Pavement   100m   Severe   (1955)
This climb starts from Central Gully at a point 60m above the screes
(arrow).
1. 50m   Climb steep rocks, trending left towards the top, to a poor
stance.
2. 25m   Move up and slightly right over steep rock to a belay.
3. 25m   Ascend up and right to a prominent V, well seen from Central
Gully.

53   Central Slabs   90m   Severe   (1932)
Start at a grsssy patch in Central Gully, just above where the gully
becomes almost horizontal.
1. 45m   Climb steep slabs to a sloping grass stance and belay.
2. 15m   Climb a loose overhang by a crack and belay just up and left
of the overhang.
3. 30m   Follow easier-angled slabs to finish in West Central Gully just
under the crack in the upper overhangs. A variety of routes can now
be followed to the top.

54   Median   300m   Hard Difficult **   (1909)
One of the best routes of its grade in Skye, this excellent climb is serious for the grade and needs basic route-finding ability.

Start 40 metres west of Central Gully; the route name is scratched on the rock at the foot of a long crack line. Climb the crack and continue to West Central Gully (90m). Go up the gully to the foot of a deep chimney cutting rightwards through slabs. Climb the chimney to its end (40m). Above is a big overhanging wall. Follow the chimney line leftwards beneath it for 45m, and belay on the more open crag above. Climb a wall some 5m to the right, then traverse right and go up to a belay at the foot of an easy-angled slab. This leads left to the base of the big fan-shaped corners which form such a noticeable feature from the corrie floor. Belay at the foot of the corners and go rightwards up a depression, often greasy and poorly protected, until the line turns left again up a chimney (45m). A further two pitches follow either the chimney, or the buttress on its left, to the terminal arete.

Many variations are possible, particularly from the base of the fan-shaped corners. An escape is possible from the foot of the easy-angled slabs beneath them: go right and emerge onto Moderate slabs which lead in some 90m to the terminal arete.

55   West Central Gully and Arete   400m   Hard Very Difficult (1908)
West Central Gully forms a long rake parallel with and higher than Central Gully. Climb the rake to where it terminates in a corner with an overhang. The crux section turns this overhang on the left, then crosses to the right of the arete past a large block. Keep to the general line of the arete, bearing slightly left of the crest where necessary.

56   Zigzag   300m   Difficult   (1911)
Climb West Central Gully for about 90m to gain a dyke and follow it for 30m. Climb two chimneys above to a grass platform. Follow two ledge systems, the first to the left, the second to the right. A grassy chimney leads to the arete of West Central Gully and Arete, and the top.

57   Chimney and Crack Climb   300m   Severe   (1911)
Follow West Central Gully for about 75m to where slabs can be climbed on the right to a vertical cave. Climb the cave by its left wall and continue direct to a deep-cut chimney. Gain a steep sloping ledge and follow it for a few metres, then traverse back right past a steep corner to a platform. Finish up the long crack above over a bulge (crux).

58   Engineer's Slant   390m   Very Difficult *   (1912)
A more interesting and continuous climb than West Central Gully and Arete, this route goes from the foot of West Central Gully across the face of Western Buttress to finish by Amphitheatre Arete. It crosses scenic ground and is a fine mountaineering route. It should be noted that there are several harder variations that link West Central Gully to Engineer's Slant. The first part of the climb is the better.

Start from the foot of West Central Gully and climb this until the gully becomes a crack. Branch to the right, following a line that crosses Median just below the prominent overhanging corners. An easy-angled traverse left now leads beneath these corners, which has occasional steep pitches and reaches West Central Gully Arete by a grassy chimney. Continue in the same line, crossing the arete and the wide open gully beyond, which separates West Central Gully Arete from Amphitheatre Arete. Cross Amphitheatre Arete and finish up a shallow chimney which leads to the plateau.

59   A.B. Route   400m   Severe *   (1936)
This climb starts halfway between the foot of Central Gully and West Central Gully, well to the right of Median. Climb 100m of easy slabs, then traverse 20 metres left on a grassy ledge. Above, climb steeper slabs for 60m to a point level with a dyke. Traverse for 30m in an exposed position, crossing the dyke to a grass ledge. Now climb 75m of very steep and exposed slabs on good holds to where West Central Gully meets Trap Face Route. Finish either up Trap Face Route or West Central Gully Arete.

60   Boomerang   210m   Mild Severe   (1952)
Start 30 metres east of West Central Gully and climb up and left over slabs and a waterworn slab corner into West Central Gully, just below where Median crosses it. Take an easy line up rightwards, crossing Engineer's Slant, into a conspicuous fault below a light-coloured wall. The fault, twice awkward, runs up and right to a grassy finish.

61   Coronation   150m   Severe   (1953)
The entrance of West Central Gully has a short pitch set in the grassy entrance tongue, approximately 20 metres left of Parallel Cracks. Start below this short pitch at an overhung recess in the upper wall. Climb the recess by the right, then trend left to a layback crack. A long groove now leads more easily up to a patch of grass. Climb an undercut bulge, then a short 'leftward trend'. Turn the formidable wall above by a fine

crack on the left; easier than it looks. Climb the next overhang by the wall on the left, crux; this leads to an easier crack to finish.

62 Parallel Cracks Route   150m   Very Difficult **   (1920)
An interesting climb. Start at the foot of the tongue of West Central Gully where a steep rib bounds a large slabby depression on the right. Two parallel cracks go up the rib; climb the rib right of the right-hand crack, then step left to join it. Follow the line of cracks, which give interesting short pitches, to a more difficult crack that leads to a chimney containing an arched block. Easier ground leads to the edge of Western Gully, which provides a scrambling descent route with minor Moderate pitches.
Direct Start: Severe   (1963)
The cracks can be gained directly from below.

63 Cooper's Gangway   240m   VS
Start at a steep slab 15 metres right of the foot of West Central Gully and just right of two small overhangs. Climb the slab until forced to the left edge; stance and belay a little higher (25m). More easy climbing up and right leads to a large grass platform, which is above and between two grass patches (45m). A brief traverse up left leads to a ledge at the foot of a steep wall. Climb up left towards a wide dyke at 15m, cross this and traverse left across the slab above, climbing over a short wall to a belay. The exposed wall above is not as rotten as it appears, and is easily climbed by a short steep crack. Easy rocks now lead to a steep wall of light-coloured rock. The crux follows, a steep sloping gangway which leads to a stance on the left edge of the wall. Climb the easy rocks above to the top.

64 Apex Route   240m   Severe   (1946)
This climb takes a line on the buttress between West Central Route and Western Gully. When seen from the corrie, it lies directly up the centre of the narrow pointed buttress, crossing Parallel Cracks and appearing to keep right of Cooper's Gangway.
   Start at a crack at the lowest point of the slabs forming the base of the buttress. At 60m, cross a rake and climb above this, always trending left across a number of slabs and over several steep ribs. Above, there are a number of more difficult pitches, including a vertical chimney, a crack in an overhanging wall, a strenuous slanting chimney and two steep narrow slabs flanked on the right by vertical walls. Finish at the apex of the buttress.

66   Western Gully   Moderate   (1906)

The gully starts 60m above the screes and contains numerous minor pitches.

The Girdle Traverse of Sron na Ciche   700m   Very Difficult *
(1912)

A real expedition to end the holiday with. Leave the Sgumain Stone Shoot above the easy terrace leading to Eastern Gully and traverse round Eastern Buttress to the foot of the 20m chimney on Chimney Route. After ascending a slanting ledge on the gully wall for about 30m, and descending a narrow 12m chimney containing serpentine rock, some narrow ledges and a delicate hand-traverse lead to the chockstone of the second pitch of Eastern Gully. Cross Cioch Slab to the neck behind the Cioch, then follow a ledge under Cioch Upper Buttress. Traverse a little pinnacle and some slabs and descend an oblique chimney to the terrace. Follow this westwards for 6m and descend a shallow gully for 30m. Move left to the sloping mossy roof of the Hexagon Block.

   Cross Central Gully to The Amphitheatre (the lowest point reached) and traverse water-worn slabs to above the nose of Amphitheatre Arete (cairn on skyline). Cross West Central Gully Arete, taking an ascending line, passing above the overhanging fan-shaped corners to the left of Median. Eventually, arrive at a point beyond Western Gully, at the same approximate level as the starting point.

COIR' A' GHRUNNDA
(Map Ref 450 200)

This is the next large corrie south of Coire Lagan. From the campsite, follow the path as for Coire Lagan, but branch off right on a well defined path around the broad base of Sron na Ciche before eventually reaching Coir' a' Ghrunnda itself. Keep well left to reach the first major crag, South Crag. Continuing on the path takes one to Loch Coir' a' Ghrunnda in the upper corrie, then the path continues up to the main ridge at Bealach Coir' an Lochain. Above and left of the loch is the Coir' a' Ghrunnda face of Sgurr Alasdair. To the east of the loch a fainter path goes to the little pass of Bealach a' Garbh Choire on the main ridge, just south of Caisteal a' Garbh-choire. It is a wildly impressive place with huge areas of glaciated slabs and an excellent example of a terminal moraine.

On descent, reach the cairned path to the true right of the burn which flows out of the loch and keep to the right, under South Crag. Although there is easy access to the main ridge at the head of the corrie, the ascent of the col between Sgurr Alasdair and Sgurr Thearlaich is Severe.

The main cliffs are South Crag and North Crag on the Ghrunnda face of Sron na Ciche and the Alasdair-Thearlaich crags further up the corrie. These cliffs are very different in character, the first two being suitable for long easy to medium grade climbs whilst the latter gives shorter and harder routes taking well defined lines.

Cuckoo Groove   60m   VS 4c   (1980)
This route is on the small buttress to the left of the path before the final scree ascent up to South Crag. The buttress is marked by a slabby ramp on the left and a deep chimney on the right. It has a lower tier of slabs and a steeper upper tier with a conspicuous two-stepped groove near the middle. Start at a grass-topped pedestal near the middle.
1. 35m   Climb up for 6m, then work right towards a break at the top of the slabs. Step right to an overhung stance and belay.
2. 25m   Work left under the overhang until it is possible to pull over it into the groove. Take the first step of this direct, then turn the second by a rib on the right which leads to the top.

GHRUNNDA FACE OF SRON NA CICHE

Several cliffs lie on the south-east side of Sron na Ciche, facing Sgurr nan Eag. The approach is described above.

SOUTH CRAG   (Map Ref 445 196)

This cliff is at an altitude of about 500m and is reached first on the approach. It is fairly steep and slabby and rather confusing in mist, whilst the more broken North Crag is separated from South Crag by a watercourse. South Crag has a few prominent features, one of which is a white slab high up. Other features in clear visibility include; Stony Rake, a shelf which starts from the centre of the lowest rocks and runs diagonally left across the face; a horizontal ledge about 35m up from the base of the crag; and Pinnacle Rake, which contains several large pinnacles and slants up from the right-hand end of the crag. In mist, the only certain identification is the inscription 'White Slab' at the foot of the route, and South Crag Gully just beyond. It is possible to scramble up to the horizontal ledge *via* a slanting rake left of White Slab. Like many slabby crags, it is climbable more or less anywhere and the routes, especially at the left hand end, can be picked at will.

By far the easiest way off South Crag to Coire Lagan is the loose but easy descent gully that lies at the extreme western end of the West Buttress of Sron na Ciche; unfortunately this is not exactly handy for gear collection. For those who wish to return to the base of the crag, moderate rocks beyond the south-west end of the crag provide a route for dry weather, leading down to Stony Rake. It is also possible to descend Pinnacle Rake, following the broken ground at the extreme north-east end of the crag. It is longer, but more straightforward, to descend into upper Coir' a' Ghrunnda by making a traverse north-eastwards above North Crag until it is possible to go down to the lochan and follow the path down the corrie below the crag.

1   Far South Buttress   150m   Moderate   (1920)
This is the left-bounding buttress of Green Recess Chimneys. Ascend slabby rocks for about 75m to the foot of a tower. Climb this by its left edge to Pinnacle Rake. Above, another pitch leads to a second tower which is climbed on the left.

2   Green Recess Chimneys   180m   Very Difficult *   (1920)
This is quite a good sheltered climb, suitable for wet or windy weather.

The chimneys form the first continuous break at the south-west end of the crag. Start from Stony Rake and take entertaining chimneys which lead to a small grassy recess below Pinnacle Rake. Take care with some loose blocks just below the rake. The top section of the crag is confusing, and various ways are possible, both left and right of one of the large pinnacles. In wet weather it is possible to take the corner right of the pinnacle (as for White Slab), and then quit this for an easy leftward line to rejoin the top of Green Recess Chimneys.

Direct Start: Very Difficult
This starts halfway up the slanting rake which leads to the horizontal ledge *via* a corner of a pinnacle.

3   Central Buttress   210m   Difficult **   (1920)
An excellent route. From Stony Rake, a horizontal ledge runs across the central part of the face. Climb the smooth rocks below the horizontal ledge by a narrow curving dyke. Now attack the buttress on the left side of a projecting rib. After this, climb the centre of the buttress as closely as possible, with a traverse to the left edge below Pinnacle Rake. The tower above the rake provides fine climbing to finish.

4   Trap Dyke Route   180m   Difficult   (1920)
The long dyke right of Central Buttress gives an interesting but not particularly difficult climb. The route crosses Pinnacle Rake at a lofty pinnacle, one of the two after which the rake is named.

5   White Slab   180m   Very Difficult **   (1920)
A very good and popular climb. The start is identified by 'White Slab' emblazoned on the rock. Start from Stony Terrace, left of a big rock depression below the white slab. Climb up for 12m, then trend left by a dyke line to the horizontal ledge. Variation is possible as far as a ledge below the white slab. The original route traverses right from the ledge, over the root of the rock depression, then follows the right-hand of two chimneys. Move onto the rib on the right and follow this to a ledge below and right of the white slab. Climb steep rock to a small ledge, followed by a short left traverse, then ascend to a recess. Easier rocks now lead to Pinnacle Rake. Climb the corner to the right of the pinnacle to a 12m chimney, which in turn leads to an open buttress and the top.

Direct Finish: 40m   Severe   (1970)
An optional finish above Pinnacle Rake. Start 12m left of the final chimney of the normal route. Climb a prominent crack for 5m, then traverse right onto a steep loose wall, which is climbed direct.

6   White Slab Direct   180m   Severe ***   (1950)
This is another excellent climb. Start in the rock depression left of South Crag Gully, to the right of the ordinary route. Climb slabby rocks to a stance and belay. Follow a crack in the V-shaped groove above for 5m, then climb a slab on the left past three thin ledges. Traverse left, then continue straight up to the top of the depression to cross the ordinary route at the horizontal ledge; chockstone belay. Climb a prominent crack and continue up to the base of the white slab. From the middle of the lower edge of the slab, an upward traverse leads to the outer edge and thence to Pinnacle Rake. Finish as for the ordinary route.

Oxford Variation   35m   VS 4b *   (1950)
This variation climbs the small buttress between the large rock depression and South Crag Gully on the right. Climb for 12m to a stance and belay at the foot of a small scoop. Climb the scoop, then trend first left then right to gain the foot of a slab, the lower edge of which overhangs. The slab is cut by two cracks; climb the overhanging right-hand crack (often wet) to a small platform at 20m. Now move over to the outer and lower part of the horizontal ledge.

7   Mega Route   125m   VS   (1968)
This climb follows the left edge of South Crag Gully.
1. 35m 4c   Climb the crack on the left of the gully, past an overhang, to a spike belay.
2. 15m   Continue up the crack to the horizontal ledge.
3. 25m   Climb a depression and the corner above, then exit left to easier ground.
4. 50m   Scramble up to Pinnacle Rake and finish by the corner above.

8   South Crag Gully   150m   Very Difficult   (1920)
This is the gully which forms near the right end of South Crag. Climb the shallow trenches on the right for 60m, followed by a short mossy pitch, then a chockstone pitch and a chimney. Above, climb a cave pitch and a flake of rock, then several smaller pitches lead to Pinnacle Rake. Beyond, the gully diminishes to a crack and the climb continues up the rocks to the right.

9   Girdle Traverse of South Crag   180m   Severe   (1947)
Start at the left end of the crag on a large mossy ledge. Traverse into Green Recess Chimneys at about the foot of the first chimney proper, then keep as near as possible to a level of about 12m below the foot of the white slab. A delicate crack traverses past the white slab to a groove, 12m, followed by 10m of ascent to a large ledge. From the

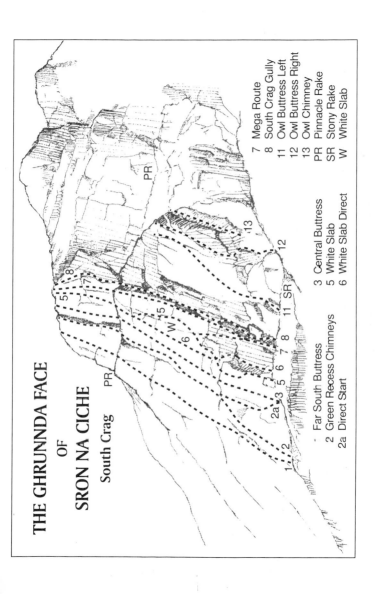

THE GHRUNNDA FACE
OF
SRON NA CICHE

South Crag

7   Mega Route
8   South Crag Gully
11 Owl Buttress Left
12 Owl Buttress Right
13 Owl Chimney
PR Pinnacle Rake
SR Stony Rake
W   White Slab

-    Far South Buttress
2   Green Recess Chimneys
2a   Direct Start

3   Central Buttress
5   White Slab
6   White Slab Direct

right-hand edge of the ledge, climb a steep broken corner for 6m, followed by a delicate traverse across the gully to finish.

10   Intermediate Traverse   95m   Severe   (1957)
Start 100 metres left of the foot of Stony Rake and just left of a large overhang 30m up.
1. 25m   Climb an easy foot-wide dyke to a diagonal fault.
2. 40m   Climb the fault for 6m, then traverse right and around the base of an overhang.
3. 30m   Climb the rib on the right to a ledge, then continue easily to Stony Rake.

11   Owl Buttress Left   55m   Very Difficult   (1924)
Start right of South Crag Gully and trend gradually right up a series of slabs. From a horizontal shelf, a V-shaped chimney leads to Pinnacle Rake, just left of Owl Pinnacle, the second major pinnacle on the rake. The rocks above are easy but pleasant.

12   Owl Buttress Right   55m   Mild VS 4b   (1932)
Start right of Owl Chimney and left of some very steep rocks. Move diagonally right to a belay above the steep section. Climb the slab above slightly to the right, avoiding easier rocks to the left. The final pitch is a steep little wall ending on rotten rock at the top of Owl Pinnacle.

13   Owl Chimney   45m   Difficult   (1920)
At the extreme right end of the crag is a chimney. The lower part is constricted, the middle part V-shaped and the upper part overhangs, but is easily climbed on the right.

NORTH CRAG   (Map Ref 447 197)

At an altitude of about 700m, North Crag is higher and more broken than South Crag. It is divided into two buttresses - Stack Buttress and Slab Buttress. The easiest descent from the top of the crag is to traverse north-east until it is possible to descend into the upper part of Coir' a' Ghrunnda.

Stack Buttress Direct   150m   Difficult *   (1920)
This worthwhile climb on excellent rock lies to the left of North Crag Gully. Climb the right-hand side of the buttress, overlooking the gully and on rough clean rock, to a rake below the Stack. Ascend a steep

slab, then climb the face of the Stack by a narrow vertical crack. The rocks above are easy.

Red Wall Variant   Difficult   (1920)
Start a little left of the parent route. Climb a reddish basalt wall, a broken gabbro rib and a long chimney to the rake beneath the Stack.

The Stack, seen from the slabs of lower Coir' a' Ghrunnda, has two prominent right-facing corners and a steep corner-groove system to the left. The rightmost corner curves rightwards and is formed where the Stack abuts the slab, leaving a 30cm wide crack in the corner. The first of the routes described below takes the large corner to the left of this, whilst the second takes the steep groove.

Gonzo Jamming   50m   E1 5b   (1988)
Scrambling and easy climbing lead to a left-rising terrace at the base of the Stack. Belay 20m up the slab in the rightmost corner. Step left and continue up to the base of the second corner. Climb the lower corner to a large stance and belay. Climb the upper corner direct *via* a slippery jam.

Stormwatch   50m   E3 *   (1988)
A good climb at the lower limit of its grade. Take a belay 5m up the slab from the terrace, below a niche.
1. 25m 5a   Step left to a short crack, climb this and step left to another corner. Climb to a large terrace and belay on the left at the foot of the groove proper.
2. 25m 6a   Climb the groove and the steep slab by strenuous fingerlocks in the right-slanting crack, crux. Pull into a pod, swing back out left to a crack, then break into the steep corner to emerge on the notched arete.

North Crag Gully and Black Knight's Wall   165m   Difficult
                                                        (1920)
The lower part of the gully is avoided by the rocks of Slab Buttress. The upper part widens out with an overhanging cave pitch on the right. The centre of the wall is climbed past a large block, The Black Knight.

Slab Buttress   240m   Moderate *   (1920)
A good ramble. The buttress is in three sections divided by rakes. Start at the lowest point and follow the buttress at will and as directly as possible; the rock is rough, clean and reliable throughout.

VAGABOND BUTTRESS   (Map Ref 447 200)

This is the prominent buttress at an altitude of about 750m between North Crag and the Alasdair-Thearlaich crags. Where the Glen Brittle path meets the glacis barrier, climb up left and scramble to an obvious slab which is easier than it appears from below. To descend from the top of the buttress to Coir' a' Ghrunnda, traverse north-east and descend towards the lochan. To return to Coire Lagan, go up to Bealach Coir' a' Ghrunnda and descend the Sgumain Stone Shoot.

On the left side of the slab is a crack which bounds the right edge of the buttress. Left again is an overlap and a wide flared groove with a crack in the corner, a large horizontal flake at its foot and two large flakes at the top. The following climb takes this crack.

Vagabond Crack   130m   HVS *   (1984)
1. 30m   Easy slab climbing leads to the horizontal fault.
2. 10m   Step left to a ledge and make an awkward move up onto the ledge with the large flake.
3. 40m 5b   The crack lies above. After initial difficulty, ascend and finish steeply over doubtful flakes to belay on a slab; an excellent pitch.
4. 50m   Step left to the arete and climb easily to the top.

THE ALASDAIR-THEARLAICH CRAGS (Map Ref 450 207)

The steep crags just below the summits of Sgurr Alasdair and Sgurr Thearlaich, overlooking Coir' a' Ghrunnda at an altitude of about 850m, provide an excellent series of shortish but concentrated climbs on sound rock. The crags present a very steep frontage of well defined grooves and walls, compact and up to 120m in height. They are split by the Thearlaich Dubh Gap, the crags on the left being the Alasdair-Thearlaich cliffs and that to the right is Thearlaich-Dubh Buttress. The rock is usually firm and is often quite fine grained, but compensates in very positive holds.

The shortest way to the foot of the crags from Glen Brittle is by Coire Lagan and the Sgumain Stone Shoot to Bealach Coir' a' Ghrunnda, followed by a traverse northwards across scree and boulders below the east face of Sgurr Sgumain. Most of the climbs finish near the top of the Stone Shoot, which provides the quickest descent. To return to the foot of the climbs, traverse Sgurr Alasdair and descend its south-west ridge to the Alasdair-Sgumain col, avoiding the Bad Step by the chimney on its left (looking down). The easiest descent from the climbs on the Thearlaich-Dubh Buttress is along the main ridge south-east to Bealach Coir' an Lochain and so down to Coir' a' Ghrunnda.

1   West Gully   105m   Very Difficult   (1912)
This is the first definite gully at the west end of the cliffs. It is narrow and steep, and consists of a quick succession of short pitches on clean, sound and water-worn rock for the first 60m. Above, climb the open face to the summit.

2   W.C. Route   105m   Very Difficult   (1965)
Between West Gully and Central Route is a big obvious corner. Climb the corner to a belay shortly before the overhang. Move diagonally right over slabs, then go horizontally left across a wall to climb the corner crack to a stance and belay. Climb the steep cracks above to the top.

3   Central Route   105m   Severe   (1921)
This climb starts 25 metres right of West Gully and about 90 metres left of Thearlaich-Dubh Gap Gully, on a buttress immediately left of a prominent cave a few metres up. From the lowest point of the buttress, follow the left edge to a smooth wall. Trend right towards a chimney and climb this to an overhang, where it is possible to climb the left wall. The climbing above is easier.

4   Commando Crack   105m   Severe ***   (1950)
A very good and quite exciting climb which takes the prominent chimney-crack to the right of the cave mentioned in the previous description. It is 25 metres left of a second and more prominent cave. Start below a crack between two overhangs.
1. 10m   Climb the rib right of the crack for 3m, traverse left into a chimney, then climb to a pinnacle belay high on the left.
2. 20m   Ascend the right wall for a few metres, then traverse into the chimney. Ascend the awkward overhang to a belay on the left.
3. 10m   Continue up the crack on the right to a belay in a sentry box below an overhanging chockstone.
4. 10m   Thread the chockstone, climb the nose on the left and climb to a stance and belay.
5. 25m   Layback the right-hand crack, then cross to the left-hand crack, which is followed by a short scramble.
6. 30   Easier climbing leads rightwards to the top of the Stone Shoot.

5   The Asp   75m   E2 5b/c ***   (1965)
An excellent well protected climb which takes the steep crack 7 metres
right of Commando Crack. Climb the crack, largely by chimneying, to
an overhang, then pull out onto an inclined ledge beneath the overhang. Move up to the overhang where a difficult move left (crux) gains
the upper crack (large Friend protection); belay on the ledge above.
Climb the crack above, then scrambling leads to the top.

6   Oneshotbang   130m   VS   (1977)
Climb the obvious gully-cleft immediately left of Con's Cleft.

7   Con's Cleft   60m   HVS **   (1965)
A very good climb with good protection. Some 30 metres left of the
Thearlaich-Dubh gap is a prominent diedre, starting 7m up from the
base of the buttress.
1. 15m 5a   Climb with increasing difficulty to an overhang, then gain
the crack above (crux, beware of a loose block) and belay on a ledge.
2. 10m 4c   Climb the crack to another ledge.
3. 35m 4c   Continue up the crack directly. At one point make a couple
of moves on the right wall to avoid loose rock, then regain the crack
immediately.

8   Atlantis   90m   VS   (1980)
This route climbs the wall and groove just right of Con's Cleft. Climb
the lower wall by a series of left-trending cracks to gain the upper
groove. Climb this to the top of the buttress.

9   Bower's Climb   90m   Very Difficult   (1919)
Climb the first pitch of Thearlaich-Dubh Gap Gully, then break out onto
the left wall and climb the face to finish near the head of the Stone
Shoot.

10   Thearlaich-Dubh Gap Gully   Moderate
This is the deep gully that leads up to the Thearlaich-Dubh Gap. It is
mostly loose scrambling and forms the best descent from the main
ridge back to the foot of the crag.

11   Thearlaich-Dubh Gap   Very Difficult or Severe   (1891)
Ascend Thearlaich-Dubh Gap Gully to the floor of the gap. If wishing
to proceed south-east, climb the right (south-east) wall which is 10m
high and Severe with good holds. If proceeding north-west towards the
main summits, climb the left (north-west) wall (25m), which is very

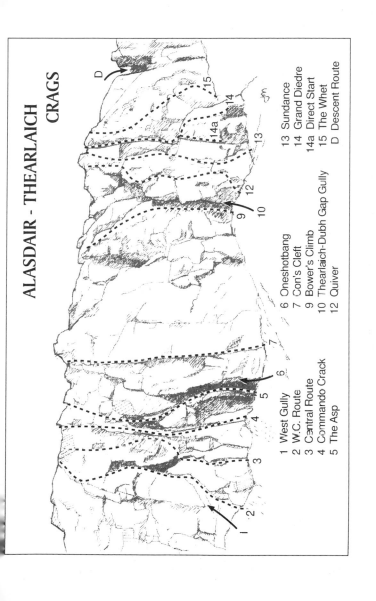

ALASDAIR - THEARLAICH CRAGS

1 West Gully
2 W.C. Route
3 Central Route
4 Commando Crack
5 The Asp
6 Oneshotbang
7 Con's Cleft
9 Bower's Climb
10 Thearlaich-Dubh Gap Gully
12 Quiver
13 Sundance
14 Grand Diedre
14a Direct Start
15 The Whet
D Descent Route

polished and a tricky Very Difficult. Climb the basalt chimney to a step left and an easing. Do not underestimate it in greasy conditions. During the main ridge traverse, it is common to abseil down one side and climb out the other. In winter, traversing towards Sgurr Dubh, the short side may be too time-consuming, in which case descend Thearlaich-Dubh Gap Gully into Coir' a' Ghrunnda to rejoin the main ridge beyond.

THEARLAICH-DUBH BUTTRESS
(Map Ref 452 207)

This is the buttress immediately right of the Thearlaich-Dubh Gap.

12   Quiver   90m   Very Difficult **   (1951)
A climb with some fine positions. Start under a small overhang near the left edge of the buttress and make a short traverse right, then follow a shallow groove until a corner leads onto a terrace. At the left end of the terrace is a steep slab topped by two overhangs. Climb a crack in the slab and take the first overhang direct. From under the second overhang, step left onto the edge of the buttress, and follow it to a stance and belay. Continue up easier rocks until progress is barred by another series of overhangs. Traverse across the left wall of the buttress to a projecting nose, then finish by a steep shattered groove.

13   Sundance   95m   HVS   (1976)
1. 35m   Start up an overhanging recess immediately left of Grand Diedre and exit left. Trend up and right into a small corner which leads to easier ground.
2. 35m   Climb the steep slab above, which is split by a higher crack, and continue to a ledge.
3. 25m   Climb up steeply on a left-slanting slab, move out right to gain the arete, then continue to the top.

14   Grand Diedre   70m   VS **   (1958)
This excellent, popular and well protected climb takes the prominent diedre running up the buttress. Start below and right of the diedre.
1. 20m 4c   Climb a slab with a left traverse at the top to a good ledge.
2. 30m 4c   Continue up the diedre across an overhang (crux) to a small ledge.
3. 20m   Follow the diedre directly to the top.
Direct Start: 20m
It is better to climb directly up the corner.

15   The Whet   65m   HVS   (1970)
This route climbs the buttress to the right of Grand Diedre, slanting from right to left. Start 12 metres right of Grand Diedre at a broad crack slanting right towards a recess.
1. 30m   Climb the crack for 7m, then go straight up and left to below a prominent layback crack. Climb this, then move left to a peg belay.
2. 35m   Continue up the groove above, move left around an overhang and finish up steep walls near Grand Diedre.

16   Victoria Buttress   45m   Very Difficult *   (1992)
Right of a small gully to the right of The Whet lies a small buttress. Climb the corner on the left of the buttress.

17   Victoria Sponge   45m   HVS 5a   (1992)
Climb directly up the smooth wall to the right of Victoria Buttress.

CAISTEAL A' GARBH-CHOIRE
(Map Ref 454 202)

This fierce-looking castle stands athwart the main ridge between Sgurr Dubh an Da Bheinn and Sgurr nan Eag. It is composed of exceptionally rough gabbro and peridotite and the traverse, following the crest, is Difficult. A more direct climb up the north end is Very Difficult.
Approach as for upper Coir' a' Ghrunnda and from the loch. The castle stands just north of Bealach a' Garbh-choire. Descend by Bealach a' Garbh-choire to either Coir' a' Ghrunnda or to Coruisk.

Lumps   45m   Very Difficult   (1963)
This climb of curiosity value takes a direct line up the south-east face, via curious lumps of rock protruding from an otherwise smooth wall.

ANTLER BUTTRESS   (Map Ref 450 194)

This steep gabbro buttress is on the west flank of Sgurr nan Eag, overlooking Coir' a' Ghrunnda and opposite South Crag. The easiest way off is to descend a gully to the right of the crag.

The Stag   80m   VS 4c   (1979)
Start 15 metres right of a shattered gully by a crack.
1. 40m   Climb the crack and the slabs above to a stance.
2. 40m   Continue up the crack above.

COIRE NAN LAOGH
(Map Ref 460 192)

This is the southernmost and most open corrie in the Cuillin. It is a lonely and seldom visited spot which may repay a winter visit. The climbing is not extensive and consists of a back wall of slabs around 150m in height cut by gullies. The slabs are continuous only for the first 60m.

To approach from Glenbrittle camp site, take the path that leads to Coir' a' Ghrunnda, keeping to the main (Coruisk) track. Cross the Allt Coir' a' Ghrunnda and continue up into Coire nan Laogh, skirting the southern slopes of Sgurr nan Eag. The descent follows either the southern slopes of Sgurr nan Eag or Gars-bheinn.

West Gully   150m   Easy   (1912)
The leftmost gully is largely a scramble.

Central Gully   150m   Difficult   (1912)
A square chockstone is taken on the left followed by an undercut pitch, turned by a slab on the left, then a traverse back to the left. Above this, a long dyke chimney leads to a pitch of bridged boulders.

East Gully   150m   Difficult   (1912)
A less interesting gully than Central Gully.

The slabs themselves offer climbing up to Severe in standard.

Lambda   120m   Difficult   (1958)
Start 30 metres left of Central Gully and 15m above a grassy terrace, left of a recess. Climb a chimney formed by the recess and go up the slabs above; unfortunately the climb deteriorates soon after.

Mu   65m   Mild Severe   (1958)
This climb takes the buttress left of West Gully, and is worthwhile if you happen to be in the vicinity. Start in the gully below a chockstone and 3m below a square-cut overhang in the left wall.
1. 20m   Climb the wall and follow the edge of a slab to an overhang.
2. 25m   Traverse 10 metres left until the wall steepens, then climb it direct. Go right, then climb a left-sloping crack in the slabs above, to belay in a crack
3. 20m   Climb two short walls to the left of the crack to finish.

Coruisk

This chapter describes the corries that lie east and north-east of the central and southern Cuillin peaks. Water flowing from these corries eventually drains into Loch na Cuilce, the innermost part of Loch Scavaig. The following corries extend in a clockwise direction around the Coruisk basin, starting at Gars-bheinn and ending at Sgurr na Stri:- Coire a' Chruidh and Coire Beag; An Garbh-choire; Coir' a' Chaoruinn and Coir' an Lochain; Coireachan Ruadha; Coir' an Uaigneis and Glac Mhor; Coir'-uisg; Coire Riabhach.

If one had to choose one central, magical spot, which epitomised all of what the Cuillins are about, then that spot has to be on the shore of Loch Coruisk. It is the heart of the mountains and possibly fits the description of a wilderness area better than most mainland sites. The sheer amount of rock surrounding this basin, much of it unexplored, should be incentive to any rock climber, and if the area were blessed by better weather there would be little excuse for staying in the better known corries of the west.

Loch Coruisk is some 2½km long and nearly 500 metres wide. Paths, often boggy, run along either side. At the outflow from the south-eastern end of the loch, there are stepping stones across the River Scavaig which are often impassable in spate. This river only flows for a few hundred metres before spilling into the sea not far from the Coruisk Hut.

There are several ways of reaching Coruisk. The low-level walking routes are from Glen Brittle, Sligachan and Camasunary.

Glen Brittle to Coruisk - The Coastal Path.

This is the route around the southern end of the Cuillin from Glen Brittle, often called the Coastal Path. It continues around the coast to Camasunary. It is rather indefinite in the second half towards Coruisk and cannot be thought of as easy going; it is often described as 'a gruelling tramp'. Leave the east end of the campsite in Glen Brittle and follow a path leading uphill from the shore. After 500 metres, take the right fork, cross a stream and head for the base of Sron na Ciche. Cross the Allt Coire Lagan, then follow a lower path which eventually passes the mouth of Coir' a' Ghrunnda and Coir' nan Laogh. Continue to the foot of Gars-bheinn. When the path fades, contour for some distance at a height of about 230m, then follow a long gently rising traverse line to a point overlooking Loch Scavaig. Go round the shoulder at the south-eastern foot of Gars-bheinn and cross a small stream, the Allt an Fhraoich, at a height of about 280m. Continue northwards along a cairned shelf as far as the Allt Coir' a' Chruidh. Cross this above a waterfall and contour at about 300m until a large crag appears on the left. Then descend, at first by a short line of slabs, all the way to the shore, passing the Mad Burn Buttress *en route*.

Cross two streams, the second of which is the Allt a' Chaoich, or Mad Burn, aptly named when impassable in spate. Continue to some rock slabs which dip into the sea. These can only be avoided when the tide is out, but otherwise are similar in scrambling interest to the 'Bad Step'. Situated not far away, below a long rock face, is the Coruisk Memorial Hut. There is also ample opportunity for nearby camping. It is about 11km from Glen Brittle campsite to the Coruisk Hut.

Coruisk to Sligachan

The short River Scavaig spills down rock slabs into Loch na Cuilce some 100 metres south-east of the Coruisk Hut. A path leads from the hut across some rock slabs and down a small step to the side of the river. It then turns upstream and eventually leads to some stepping stones near the head of the river by Loch Coruisk. These are usually awash after bad weather and can be either hazardous or even impossible to cross. Two paths lead off from the other side of the river. The right-hand one leads round the coast to Camasunary, the one on the left goes to Sligachan. It skirts around the end of Loch Coruisk, then ascends north-eastwards to a low point on the long ridge of Druim Hain.

The path then descends northwards to the head of Srath na Creitheach. It crosses to the other side of the glen just before Lochan

---

KEY TO MAP OPPOSITE

1   Mad Burn Buttress
2   Sgurr nan Eag, North-East Face
3   Dubh Ridge
4   Sgurr Mhic Choinnich, East Face
5   Bealach Buttress
6   Sgurr na Banachdich, East Face
7   Sgurr a' Ghreadaidh, South-East Face
8   Sgurr a' Mhadaidh, South-East Face
9   Druim nan Ramh, Dubh View Buttress
10   Druim nan Ramh, Coruisk Slabs

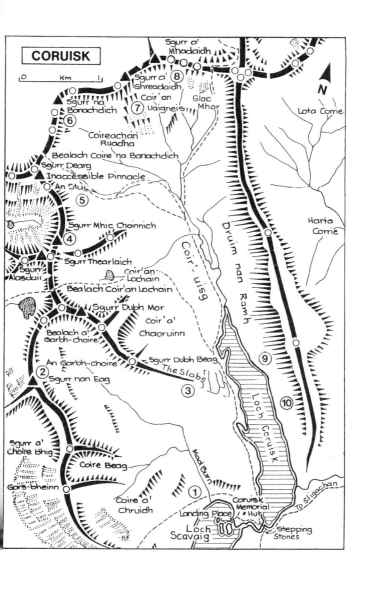

Dubha and joins a path which leads north from Camasunary. It continues north along the east side of Glen Sligachan, past the shapely peak of Marsco, all the way to Sligachan itself. The route is fairly obvious, but fairly tedious, being 12km from the Coruisk Hut to Sligachan.

Coruisk to Camasunary
From the Coruisk Hut, follow the path to the stepping stones across the head of the River Scavaig. Take the right-hand path on the far side of the river to a small bay at the head of Loch nan Leachd. Continue around the shore for some 400 metres to the famous Bad Step. This is a steep slab of rock that is traversed by a short crack-gangway, which slants down the slab. This gives a fairly straightforward scramble, which can be awkward when heavily laden. Continue along the coast over other rock slabs and cut across the small headland of Rubha Buidhe. Follow the obvious path without further difficulty until a large bay, Camus Fhionnairigh, and a bothy come into view. Head north until a suitable place can be found to ford the Abhainn Camus Fhionnairigh. This river is tidal and can be difficult to cross at high water or after continuous bad weather.

Elgol to Camasunary
The normal approach to Camasunary starts 1km south-west of Kirkibost on the road to Elgol; there is a small car park just south of this point. Follow the track for rather more than 2km to Am Mam. After crossing the pass, continue for a further 1km to a hairpin bend. Take the path which leads straight down to Camasunary. The bothy provides good shelter.

A longer, but more scenic coastal path starts 300m above the car park at Elgol, keeping fairly close to the shore and giving a simple but rough path to Camasunary.

LOCH SCAVAIG

The crags immediately north-west of the hut provide some climbing. The crag just outside the hut door has several routes from Very Difficult upwards and by linking pitches, as much as 100m of good climbing on excellent rock is possible. The lower wall has seen considerable activity and though there are three main starts ranging from Very Difficult to VS, there are also other much harder variations plus much bouldering. One harder climb has been recorded:

Beached Whale   20m   E3 5c *   (1994)
A good wee route which is protected by small Friends. Start 5 metres
right of the hut and climb directly to the big horizontal break. Follow the
break leftwards with difficulty to finish.

Meall na Cuilce, between the Mad Burn and Loch Coruisk, also
provides some fine exploratory climbing.

MAD BURN BUTTRESS   (Map Ref 479 195)

This is an excellent, quick-drying diamond-shaped crag of perfect
gabbro, giving attractive climbing in the middle grades. It is a good
choice when cloud is low over the tops since it lies at an altitude of only
150m. It lies 150m above sea-level and west of the Coruisk Hut, at the
base of the blunt north-eastern spur of Gars-bheinn. It is less than 30
minutes walk from the hut. Descents are to be found either side of the
crag.

Mayday   90m   Severe *   (1961)
On the left-hand side of the face is a conspicuous left-sloping diedre,
starting 25m up the face.
1. 25m   Start 15 metres left of the lowest rocks where a line of
weakness on a steep smooth wall leads to the diedre *via* a mantelshelf
and a left-trending crack.
2. 30m   Climb the diedre by delightful climbing on small holds to a
small stance.
3. 35m   Move left, then climb a crack, walls and ledges to easy
ground.

Warsle   90m   Hard Severe *   (1962)
The lowest point of the buttress is formed by a 6m pulpit, above which
a deep crack cleaves the rock. Either gain the pulpit from the right, or
better directly from below (HS is scratched on the wall to the right).
Climb the crack above the pulpit, then an easy-looking corner on the
left to reach a broad grass ledge. The face above is seamed by two
left-slanting ledge-crack systems. Gain the upper one by an exiguous
crack near the north end of the grass ledge and traverse along until it
is possible to move up and right to a good stance (30m). Climb a
delicate slab and a thinnish wall, crux, to reach the first terrace which
is immediately above.

Diagonal   135m   Severe *   (1962)
This is the longest possible climb on the crag. Start as for Warsle and
gain the broad grass ledge. Ascend 6m of the next pitch of Warsle to
reach the lower of the two diagonal crack systems, and climb it to a
stance (15m). Continue along the ledge-crack system until below the
south end of the first terrace and under an overhang. Regain the ledge
system 3m higher by climbing a steep nose to a stance (30m). About
50m of interesting climbing by the easiest line leads to the top.

COIRE BEAG

This is the relatively small corrie at about 600m, enclosed by the
north-east ridges of Gars-bheinn and Sgurr a' Choire Bhig. The
north-east ridge of Gars-bheinn is little more than a scramble but gives
by far the best route of ascent on the mountain and can be easily
combined with a route on Mad Burn Buttress. From the Coruisk Hut,
follow the coastal path until just after the Allt a' Chaoich, then ascend
the hillside beside the next small burn. From a knoll, turn left and head
south-west and follow the more westerly branch of a stream which
drains from Coire Beag. The ridge is easily gained by moving left before
the normal approach into Coire Beag enters the upper corrie.
    To enter the upper corrie, slant right along a shelf to reach the corrie
proper. To reach the summit of Gars-bheinn, follow the left-hand of the
two obvious scree gullies to reach a gap on the ridge a short distance
west of the summit.

SGURR A' CHOIRE BHIG
875m   (Map Ref 465 193)

The north-east face of this mountain presents a long rock face which
can be reached either by an approach from An Garbh-choire, or by
descending a rake rightwards from the col on the north-west ridge. Two
gullies were climbed at an early date but there is little else of note.

North-East Ridge of Sgurr a' Choire Bhig   600m   Moderate *
This is a shorter but in many ways similar excursion to the Dubh Ridge,
but far less popular. It gives a superb hard scramble. Follow the
approach to Coire Beag, then trend right towards the ridge. The initial
section of slabs is open to much variation and this freedom of choice
remains higher up where the ridge narrows. A prominent curving band

of overhanging rock is situated to the right of the crest, whilst near the top a steeper section of rock is usually turned on the right.

One particularly obscure route has been recorded here. However its exact wherabouts are uncertain and it either lies to the left of the north-east ridge or to the right on the north face of Sgurr a' Choire Bhig. Whatever the location, the crag's altitude is 600m.

Dwindle Wall   120m   Severe   (1968)
Left of the North-East Ridge is a buttress with a spring at its foot. Climb a chimney above to a glacis (30m). Continue leftwards up broken slabs to a broken ledge. Continue to a grassy rake and belays (25m). Climb much steeper rock up a tapering wall, overcome a small overhang, then traverse left at 25m on a gangway to belay on a small flake. Continue directly to a steep exit on a grass ledge.

AN GARBH-CHOIRE

This is the huge and chaotic corrie that lies on the east side of the main ridge, bordered by the east ridges of Sgurr a' Choire Bhig and 'The Dubhs'. It is drained by the Allt a' Chaoich. Above 500m, the entire floor of the corrie is a mass of jumbled boulders with sizeable gaps between. The exceptionally abrasive peridotite of these boulders and the rough terrain - the roughest in the Cuillin - make the name 'The Rough Corrie' particularly apt.

The corrie headwall has the prominent tower of the Caisteal a' Garbh-choire just north of the Bealach a' Garbh-choire which is a landmark from near the Coruisk Hut. There are two approaches from the hut. The more direct follows the Coastal Path over the Allt a' Chaoich, then ascends beside the next burn, as for Coire Beag. The alternative is to follow the River Scavaig to Loch Coruisk and to take the path on the south-west shore for 1km before turning up a wide depression on the left; both routes lead to the broad level expanse of the lower corrie floor, from where a westerly line leads to the upper corrie. Bealach a' Garbh-choire, which leads to Coir' a' Ghrunnda, is the only easy pass from the corrie. This entails clambering over the infamous huge boulders, but it is marginally easier towards the Sgurr Dubh side. At the top, it is possible to pass either side of Caisteal a' Garbh-choire, the left side being straightforward whilst the right side involves crawling under a giant block.

SGURR NAN EAG
924m   (Map Ref 458 195)

Lying north-east of the east ridge of the mountain is an important crag facing An Garbh-choire. The crag lies just west of the crag on Sgurr a' Choire Bhig and is characterised by a splendid cleft called The Chasm, an obvious landmark. Most of the other climbs lie to its left. This is a remote high altitude crag lying at around 700m. It takes several days to dry and as The Chasm is one of the more reliable winter climbs in the Cuillin, it often retains snow patches well into the summer.

Approach either from An Garbh-choire as described above, or from the main ridge *via* the col between Sgurr nan Eag and Sgurr a' Choire Bhig. The easiest way back to Loch Coruisk is down from this col.

Ladders   110m   VS 4c *   (1957)

This is a good, sustained and pleasant route giving varied and at times steep climbing. It starts in the second corner 25 metres left of The Chasm. Gain a line of holds on the left wall of the corner; a shoulder is traditional but not essential. Go up and swing left to a jutting platform. Climb the steep wall above to join the corner crack at a nose projecting from the right wall, then follow the crack to a broken terrace and block belays on the right (30m). From just left of the start of the second pitch of Left Edge, traverse 10m left then go up to the base of the shallower of two dykes. Follow this back up right to come out near a small ledge on the edge. Traverse 5 metres left to a narrow dyke-chimney and climb this to the top.

Leviathan   115m   E1 *   (1968)

A rather serious route with areas of loose rock, albeit in good positions. Start at a corner 15 metres left of The Chasm.

1. 35m 5a   Climb a crack to a sloping ledge at 10m, then continue up the wall by a basalt dyke to a large ledge with a jammed boulder thread belay.

2. 40m 5a   Step left from the belay and climb a short wall to gain a left-rising ramp. Follow the ramp to an area of rotton rock. Where the ramp ends under a small overhang (small wire runner beneath the overhang), move down a little and step left into a bottomless groove. Climb the groove until a traverse can be made left to a large basalt boulder jammed in the bottom of the crack system.

3. 40m 4b   Climb the crack directly, passing a small overhang without difficulty; belay on the summit ridge.

Left Edge   95m   E1 5a *   (1957)
This serious route takes the clean-cut edge above the left wall of The
Chasm. Fine, unprotected climbing.
1. 30m 4a   Climb the edge to broken rocks and belays on the left.
2. 30m 5a   Climb just left of the edge in a fine position to a small ledge,
then traverse 5 metres to an overhung nook and inadequate belays.
3. 35m 5a   Return to the edge and climb it to easier rocks.

The Chasm   120m   Very Difficult **   (1919)
A popular classic, sometimes thwarted by unexpected snow. There are
four good pitches of which the topmost is the hardest. Highly recommended.
Winter: III ***   (1987)
An excellent route, somewhat variable in grade but sometimes quite
straightforward. The first ascensionists described it as 'wonderfully
old-fashioned with superb rock scenery. The very recessed position
should ensure a build-up in all but the leanest conditions'.

Western Buttress   180m   Very Difficult   (1948)
The buttress is split into three indistinct ridges; this route is on the
left-hand and most prominent of these. Start at the foot of the steep
lower section and follow a line of short cracks and chimneys up the
centre of the ridge. The final steep section gives 30m of climbing to a
broad terrace. A short traverse to the right leads to a steep little groove
in the right-hand corner of the ridge. Above, a few minutes' walk leads
to the northern summit of Sgurr nan Eag.

THE DUBHS

The northern boundary of An Garbh-choire is the long ridge which
comprises the three summits of 'The Dubhs', namely Sgurr Dubh
Beag, Sgurr Dubh Mòr and Sgurr Dubh an Da Bheinn. The southern
flanks of these mountains are steep and craggy but have not yielded
any worthwhile routes to date. By far the most popular route to the
summit of Sgurr Dubh Beag and Sgurr Dubh Mòr is the justifiably
famous Dubh Ridge.

The Dubh Ridge   920m   Moderate ***
This is the best easy climb in Skye and a contender for the best easy
climb in Britain. Experienced scramblers with climbing aspirations
should not find the going too hard. The start is at Map Ref 475 206.

From the Coruisk Hut, follow the path on the south-western shore of Loch Coruisk to an obvious apron of slabs at the foot of the east ridge of Sgurr Dubh Beag. Depending on aptitude and skill, avoid the lower rocks by a grassy bay, then transfer to the slabs on the left. There is much variation and avoidable difficulties on this lower section. From a large ledge at 100m, head up right to join a continuation of the slabs. Continue for over 600m up perfect boiler-plated rough slabs, at a perfect 'padding' angle, with a few minor steps of steeper rock, all the way to the summit of Sgurr Dubh Beag. If desired, it is possible to escape at about 470m down a grassy runnel on the left into An Garbh-choire.

Just past the summit on the south-west ridge of Sgurr Dubh Beag is a drop of 15m where it is normal to abseil an overhanging section. It is possible to avoid this by returning down the crest for some distance and following grass and scree ledges on the south side, but the best line is not obvious. It is a short distance to the col at the foot of the east ridge of Sgurr Dubh Mor. If retreat is necessary, a tricky but feasible escape can be made northwards down steep scree and intervening slabs into Coir' a' Chaoruinn. The Garbh-choire side of the col is not recommended. From the col, a long section of easy walking leads up the east ridge until steep rocks are encountered below the summit ridge of Sgurr Dubh Mor. A way onto the ridge is normally found by ledges on the south flank, with the summit lying at the far western end. A scramble down the steep south-west spur leads onto Sgurr Dubh an Da Bheinn, although there is an easy descent into Coir' an Lochain on the right from the intervening col.

COIR' A' CHAORUINN and COIR' AN LOCHAIN

This pair of corries lie between the Dubh Ridge and the peak of Sgurr Coir' an Lochain to the north. They both overlook Coruisk but are wildly contrasting. Coir' a' Chaoruinn is the more easterly, and is the first corrie encountered on the left at the head of Loch Coruisk. It is overlooked by Sgurr Dubh Beag. There are slabs and waterslides at its entrance and much scree higher up. The col between Sgurr Dubh Beag and Sgurr Dubh Mor can be gained by scrambling leftwards at the head of the corrie. It also provides a convenient approach into neighbouring Coir' an Lochain, from where Bealach Coir' an Lochain connects with Coir' a' Ghrunnda and Bealach Mhic Choinnich leads to Coire Lagan.

About halfway up Coir' a' Chaoruinn (360m), a fairly obvious grass rake slants right onto the north-east ridge of Sgurr Dubh Mor. This can be identified by a large flake at the bottom, which forms a natural arch. Continue rightwards to a prominent stream, which leads up to the superbly-situated lochan nestling in upper Coir' an Lochain. A direct line from the lochan up the corrie headwall leads to Bealach Coir' an Lochain.

The right-hand side of the corrie is formed by a ridge which runs north-east from the northern end of Sgurr Thearlaich and ends in the spectacular top of Sgurr Coir' an Lochain. To reach Bealach Mhic Choinnich, continue past the lochan and ascend sharply rightwards to reach the low point on the ridge leading to Sgurr Coir' an Lochain. Turn left and follow the ridge south-west for a short distance until an obvious scree gully on the right can be ascended to Bealach Mhic Choinnich. It is also possible to reach the col between Sgurr Dubh Mor and Sgurr Dubh an Da Bheinn by heading left up scree from the back of the corrie.

The crags below the north sides of Sgurr Dubh Beag, Sgurr Dubh Mor and Sgurr Dubh an Da Bheinn have so far escaped exploration, though there are considerable exposures of rock. The first line of any consequence leads into the Thearlaich-Dubh Gap from upper Coir' an Lochain.

Aladdin's Route   Difficult   (1950)
This is the intriguing cleft that forms a chimney on the north-east side of the Thearlaich-Dubh Gap. There are several entertaining problems finishing by a through route. Unless using this route as a means to approach Coir' a' Ghrunnda, all return journeys will entail climbing at a higher standard than the route itself.

North-East Ridge of Sgurr Thearlaich   Moderate   (1913)
This is probably the quickest way of reaching the summit from Coir' an Lochain. The ridge is steep but fairly broken, and gives interesting scrambling all the way to the top. Start from the low point on the Sgurr Coir' an Lochain ridge and ascend this as for Bealach Mhic Choinnich, but instead of taking the the scree gully on the right, continue up the slabby crest. Where it abuts the main ridge, follow the north ridge to the summit.

SGURR COIR' AN LOCHAIN
729m   (Map Ref 454 214)

This superb peak with steep rock on three sides projects as a nose above Coir'-uisg. It was possibly the last British summit to have been ascended and the crags that fall to the north and north-east typify the route-finding confusion that Skye is famous for. A eye for the best line and the ability to climb with a grade or two in hand is advisable here.

The South Ridge   Difficult
This is the easiest route to the summit. Start from the col on the ridge leading south-west to Sgurr Thearlaich. Initially not well defined, it soon narrows and a level section leads to a minor top. Some distance after this, the only difficulty is descending into a prominent gap that cuts across the ridge. Gullies on either side of the gap give more direct but less attractive routes of a similar standard. A short scramble then leads to the small rocky summit, a great viewpoint.

THE NORTH-EAST FACE

This is the steep slabby face which is approached from Coir'-uisg. It consists of steep overlapping slabs and walls which steepen as they swing west. The rock is of a reasonable quality, but lines of weakness are few.

   The original route up the mountain lay somewhere on the north face. Pioneered in 1896 by Collie, Howell and Naismith with John Mackenzie, their tortuous route followed nearly 300m of confusing slab climbing. Such is the nature of the face that it is unlikely that their exact line has ever been repeated.

Raeburn's Route   300m   Very Difficult   (1913)
The very steep edge that faces Bidein Druim nan Ramh is the vague starting point for this route. The original description fully encapsulates the flavour of the crag: "Start below the overhang of the very steep edge facing Bidein. After 300 feet or so a traverse is forced on steep slabs round to the east. There does not appear to be any way through the overhang until right on the other corner of the tower facing the head of Coir'-uisk." Obviously there are possibilities of much harder variations to this climb. It can best be described as a secluded climb with route-finding problems, most suitable after a dry spell.

Shelf Route   150m   Mild Severe **   (1949)
An interesting and enjoyable mountaineering route on the north face.
It follows the 100m right-sloping shelf above the overhanging section
of the north face, some 75m above the lowest rocks. Start either by a
traverse from the right, or directly from below by a left-slanting line of
weakness which continues beyond the shelf which is 45m from the
start of the traverse or at 75m when approached from below. The shelf
is initially a metre-wide ledge, widening to a 12m sweep of slabs. There
are three 35m pitches along it, with the difficulties concentrated at the
slabs. From the top of the slabs, an easy traverse leads to broken rocks
at the right end of the shelf. Climb steep rocks for 12m to a ledge and
block belay. A short wall of slabs on the right leads to easier ground.

COIREACHAN RUADHA

This group of corries lie on the Coruisk side of the peaks of the central
and northern sections of the main ridge. The difficulty of approach
ensures a secluded atmosphere, but the quality of the climbs has
established the reputation of these remote corries.

SGURR MHIC CHOINNICH
948m   (Map Ref 450 210)

The eastern cliffs of Sgurr Mhic Choinnich are second only to Sron na
Ciche in terms of relative importance. They are steep and continuous
for over 210m, giving great routes both old and new. Were it not for the
long approach from Glen Brittle and the necessity of three days drying
time after wet weather, these crags would be much more popular. The
Upper Cliff conjours up the essence of the Cuillin, and its very
seclusion at the heart of the 'Forgotten Corrie' is an attraction for the
real mountaineer.

THE LOWER CLIFF

This lies below the terrace that supports the Upper Cliff. It is best
reached from Coire Lagan from either Bealach Mhic Choinnich, continuing on scree from where the terrace branches off, or from Bealach
Coire na Banachdich. Rotten Gully is not recommended as an approach. From Loch Coruisk the approach is straightforward. To
descend, follow the terrace back left to the foot of the crags, then back
right towards Rotten Gully.

The part of the Lower Cliff adjacent to the large gully is J Buttress. The gully itself, Great Gully, is still unclimbed and the St Andrew's U.M.C. party of 1958 found it 'unclimbable'. To the right of Great Gully lies The Amphitheatre, a pronounced bowl starting halfway up the crag. Right again, further steep crags separated by gullies and clefts stretch up towards Rotten Gully. The few recorded routes lie on either side of Great Gully and are described from left to right.

Magpie Cracks   65m   VS   (1968)
Left of Great Gully and 30m up lies a huge sloping terrace. Start on the terrace immediately left of a smooth overhanging wall.
1. 35m 4c   Make a rising traverse left across slabs to reach and climb a corner crack.
2. 30m 4b   Move left and climb to the top by cracks and walls.

St Andrew's Crack   105m   HVS   (1958)
Definitely a climb for lovers of wide cracks! The route follows the left-hand of two cracks which run up the lower cliffs just to the right of Great Gully. It is slow to dry as it acts as a drain. Start 10 metres right of Great Gully at the foot of the crack.
1. 30m 4c   Climb the right side of the crack, traverse left, then go up right over a small slab to a stance.
2. 25m 5a   Climb the left-hand crack which overhangs in two places.
3. 20m   Follow the crack over two jammed blocks, then easier rocks lead to a pinnacle with a stance at its crest.
4. 30m   Climb the harder crack, then continue under and over jammed blocks to the terrace.

Chemist's Constitutional   120m   Very Difficult   (1958)
Start 30 metres right of Great Gully at the lowest rocks, and just right of another gully. Climb a buttress for 60m to The Amphitheatre. Traverse left across its mouth, then go over the left wall to the first gully; climb this to the terrace.

Sue's Chimney   35m   Very Difficult   (1959)
Start right of Chemist's Constitutional at the foot of a gully on the left side of The Amphitheatre, halfway up J Buttress. Climb the gully, then its right wall to the terrace.

THE COIREACHAN RUADHA FACE OF SGURR MHIC CHOINNICH

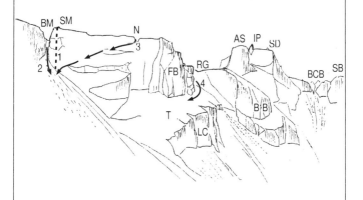

BM   Bealach Mhic Choinnich (Easy ascent or descent route)
SM   Sgurr Mhic Choinnich
 N   The Notch on North Ridge of Sgurr Mhic Choinnich
FB   Fluted Buttress
RG   The head of Rotten Gully
LC   The Lower Cliff
 T   The Terrace
BB   Bealach Buttress
AS   An Stac
IP   The Inaccessible Pinnacle
SD   Sgurr Dearg
BCB Bealach Coire na Banachdich
SB   Sron Buidhe
 1   Forgotten Groove
 2   Descent from Bealach Mhic Choinnich
 3   Descent from The Notch, exposed and difficult to find in mist.
 4   Descent by Rotten Gully, descend 90m and traverse onto
     The Terrace. Loose.

THE UPPER CLIFF

The Upper Cliff is best approached from the main ridge by the evil Rotten Gully, which lies on the left side of the cliff in descent. This gully is best reached from Glen Brittle by scrambling up easy rocks to the right of the An Stac screes on the Coire Lagan face of Sgurr Mhic Choinnich. The gully has become progressively looser and nastier and it is possible to leave sacs about 20m down on the left side by some blocks. This saves (assuming success!) the frightening return journey to retrieve them from the foot of the crags. Descend the gully for 90m and exit right (facing out) onto a terrace below the Upper Cliff.

Other methods to reach the crag require some route-finding skill. From the foot of the Stone Shoot, scramble up broken rocks to Bealach Mhic Choinnich and descend rough scree on the north side into Coireachan Ruadha. Join the terrace and follow it northwards under the main crags.

Alternatively, from near the top of Fluted Buttress there is a rake which starts approximately one-third of the way along towards the summit of Sgurr Mhic Choinnich. Descend the rake to the foot of Forgotten Groove and the terrace. This method is only advisable in clear weather and for those with some knowledge of the crag.

It is also possible to reach the Upper Cliffs from Loch Coruisk or from Bealach Coire na Banachdich, either *via* Chemist's Constitutional or the lower section of Bealach Mhic Choinnich.

The available descents include Rotten Gully, The Rake and Bealach Mhic Choinnich.

Going left along the terrace from Rotten Gully, the slightly smaller North-East Buttress is reached first, separated from Fluted Buttress by North-East Gully. Fluted Buttress, with its characteristic 'flutes', has the prominent cleft of Cocoa Cracks on its front face before swinging back south-east. The south-east wall contains the cleft of Mongoose Direct; to its right a prominent crack that forms a chimney after 45m forms the starts of both Crack of Dawn and Dawn Grooves. Left of the cleft of Mongoose Direct is a steep grooved buttress, taken by King Cobra. The south-east wall finally ends in a big bay, from the back of which springs an exiguous gully. Left of this are the slabs of Hanging Slab, and left again are unexplored crags, unfortunately marred by basaltic dykes.

The routes, which end on the main ridge north of Sgurr Mhic Choinnich, are described from left to right.

1   Forgotten Groove   75m   Very Difficult   (1951)
Approach from Bealach Mhic Choinnich and descend the scree on the
north side to below a huge groove that runs up to the summit. The
groove, formed by a slab on the left and a vertical bounding wall on
the right, is well seen from the west ridge of Sgurr Coir' an Lochain.
Scramble up to the foot by easy rocks from the start of an easy grassy
rake. Enter the groove directly or by a traverse from a slab on the left.
Very steep to start with, the angle eases and the groove finishes after
60m. From there, awkward climbing over friable rock leads to the
summit rocks.

2   Hanging Slab   205m   HVS   (1971)
This route takes the slab left of the exiguous gully which lies just left
of the start of King Cobra. Scramble up the gully to a belay at 45m.
1. 15m   Climb the left wall of the gully to a stance in the gully.
2. 45m   Traverse 35m across an undercut slab on the left to a line of
vertical cracks. Climb these, then make a short traverse left to a small
stance and high flake belay.
3. 15m   Move up and left again to climb a steep little rib to a large
ledge.
4. 30m   Climb cracks behind the ledge.
5. and 6. 100m   Follow cracks and chimneys more easily to the top.

3   Exiguous Gully   145m   VI,6   (1995)
This impressive line gives fine climbing up the obvious gully left of King
Cobra. Start at the foot of the gully.
1. 40m   Climb the left-hand corner of the gully until about 10m below
a marked steepening. Transfer to the right hand corner and belay 5m
below an obvious groove line forming the right-hand corner of the
steep section ahead.
2. 25m   Steep strenuous climbing in the groove-corner leads to a
good belay at a slight easing in the angle.
3. 45m   Continue up the groove line by more fine climbing, which
eventually eases at a broad snowy ramp.
4. 35m   Follow the ramp up left and break out right to join the ridge
at the first opportunity.

4   King Cobra   165m   E1 ***   (1960)
This, one of Skye's great routes, is low in the grade with good
protection and situations. Towards the north end of the face is an
impressive buttress. From the large bay on the left, an exiguous gully

goes to the top of the cliff. The climb follows the buttress on its immediate right, but left of the cleft of Mongoose Direct. Start 45 metres left of the Crack of Dawn. Scramble up the gully for 45m, as for Hanging Slab. Just below where it steepens, traverse easily right to a large flake at the foot of the 25m diedre.

1. 25m 4c   Climb the right wall of the diedre to a big ledge.

2. 25m 5b   Traverse right into another diedre and climb this, crux. It soon eases, then easier climbing leads to belays.

3. 15m 4b   Climb easily up a rib on the right to a comfortable shelf below a big overhang overlooking Dawn Grooves.

4. 35m 5a   Climb the wall 5 metres right of the continuation groove to a slab below the roof. Traverse right to avoid the overhang, then climb a ramp to a V-shaped groove which leads to large overhangs. Climb out on the left wall of the groove, swing across to jammed spikes on the left, then climb a short chimney on good holds.

5. 40m 4c   Traverse left across a slab into a chimney which leads to a good ledge on the right. Continue up the chimney to a large platform.

6. 25m   Climb a further chimney set in a narrow buttress to the top.

5   King Cobra Direct   145m   E3 *   (1992)

1. and 2. 50m 5b   Climb the first two pitches of King Cobra.

3. 45m 5c   Follow King Cobra to the shelf at the left end of the big overhang. Go through the left end of the overhang into a groove, crux, and follow this to a ledge with a chockstone in a wide corner crack.

4. 50m 4c   Climb the corner and a chimney to a large ledge, then climb a corner behind the ledge to belay on easy ground a short way from the top.

6   Mongoose Direct   195m   E1 5b ***   (1974/7)

This fine climb takes the great cleft in the buttress directly. It is a drainage line and is often wet. Start at a corner crack 5 metres left of Crack of Dawn.

1. 25m 5a   Climb the crack to a sloping ledge.

2. 20m 5a   Continue up a similar crack, then move up a slab to a belay beneath the deep groove of the main cleft.

3. 35m 5b   Climb a crack in the right wall, then the groove itself. Where it splits in two at a junction with Dawn Grooves, climb into the prominent clean-cut V-groove of the left-hand branch, crux, to a stance in a niche on the left.

4. 35m 5a   Continue up the chimney-groove to a spacious ledge.

5. and 6. 80m   Step up left across the overhang in the chimney line, then continue up the fault to easy ground.

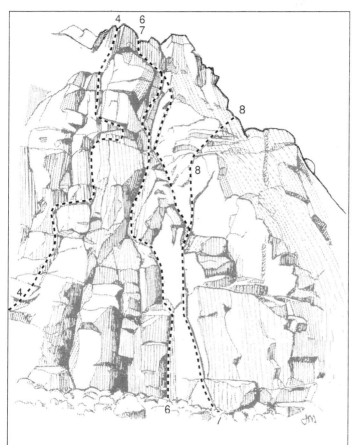

SGURR MHIC CHOINNICH
Coireachan Ruadha Face

4 King Cobra
6 Mongoose Direct

7 Dawn Grooves
8 Crack of Dawn

7   Dawn Grooves   175m   VS ***   (1958)

An excellent line, highly recommended, which takes a line of grooves right of the central cleft of Mongoose Direct and forms the left-hand boundary of Fluted Buttress where the south-east and front walls meet. Start at a crack line in the wall which forms a chimney after 45m.

1. 25m 4b   Climb the crack to a niche and belay.

2. 20m 4c   Climb out of the niche, go up the overhanging crack for a few metres, then traverse onto the exposed wall on the right to reach the platform which crosses the face.

3. 45m   The platform steepens on the left to form grooves. Climb the groove to below a point where the main groove becomes a clean-cut V (Mongoose Direct) and throws a lesser groove up to the right.

4. 35m   Traverse 5 metres right to a crack in the right wall of the lesser groove. Climb the crack up the slabby edge of the buttress to a good ledge. A steep 15m wall leads to a ledge girdling the upper part of Fluted Buttress. (This route can be joined here by either climbing up for 15m or by traversing right along the ledge).

5. 35m   Traverse 12 metres left to a chimney marking the line of the grooves. Climb the chimney to an overhang and exit left to a flake by a ledge. Climb the steep slabs above, trending right to regain the grooves; belay at the foot of a narrow chimney topped by a 5m V-corner.

6. 15m   Climb the chimney and the corner to the summit ridge.

8   Crack of Dawn   180m   VS *   (1951)

This is a very good climb if the Direct Finish is taken. The route follows a prominent slanting crack up the south-east wall of Fluted Buttress, then the continuation crack across the buttress. It originally finished by easier rocks (The Escape Route), but the Direct takes the true line. The Escape Route is useful for wet conditions. Start as for Dawn Grooves.

1. and 2. 45m 4c   Climb the first two pitches of Dawn Grooves.

3. etc., 135m   Climb the easier but steep chimney directly above to the top of the south-east wall, then follow the easier-angled crack which slants across the face to where it becomes indefinite; cairn. Climb the short steep crack immediately left of a little rib of clean rough rock, moving across the rib at the top and passing a big flake. Climb to the left end of the terrace; cairn. The Escape Route continues up Difficult slabs on the right-hand edge, finishing near the summit ridge. The Direct Finish climbs the little rib to the left of the cairn by a crack on its crest to where it steepens and ends at a ledge below a 'stupendous overhanging nose' split by a crack. Climb its right wall by a hard crack in a groove, step left to a ledge, then go back right to an

easy groove. From the recess at the top of the groove, traverse right to a ledge, go along it, moving up and right over two little corners, and finish at a cairn on the ridge.

9   Cocoa Cracks   165m   E2 **   (1969)
A very fine route, unfortunately rarely dry, following the huge right-angled corner in the front of Fluted Buttress, midway between Crack of Dawn and Fluted Buttress. Scramble up a slab below the corner.
1. 25m   Climb the corner, often wet, to the ledge on the right.
2. 20m   Climb a chimney above to a peg belay below an overhang.
3. 15m 5c   Climb the overhang, often wet and the crux, then continue up a wide chimney to belay in a nook.
4. 15m   Climb the narrowing, often wet chimney above by its right arete to reach easy ground; belay at the next steepening.
5. etc., 90m   Easier rocks lead to the finish of Crack of Dawn.

10   Fluted Buttress   210m   VS 4b **   (1950)
This splendid route offers exciting climbing which is not high in the grade. The largest buttress on the face is bounded on the left by the deep cleft of Dawn Grooves and on the right by North-East Gully. About 60m up on the right-hand section are three flutes which give the climb its name. Start on the terrace to the right of the corner of Cocoa Cracks.
   Climb a little rib for 7m, then traverse up under overhangs for 15m to where the overhang can be climbed to a ledge above (30m). Follow the ledge to the right, then go up an easy-angled chimney. Climb this to where it steepens under the flutes, then traverse out right to a slab (The Gangway) below a huge overhang. Follow the slab rightwards, with the overhanging flute on the left and the wall of the buttress dropping into North-East Gully on the right, until the slab steepens. Traverse out to the wall on the right where delicate and exposed climbing, crux, leads right and up to an easement above the overhangs. Follow a broken groove, trending back left to the centre of the buttress, then climb a short groove to the small terrace of Crack of Dawn and the cairn at its left end. Either continue up The Escape Route or, better, take the Direct Finish of Crack of Dawn, described above.

11   Populace   180m   HVS   (1977)
On the left wall of North-East Gully is a very obvious corner system. This climb follows the corners for 105m to where the system splits into a very steep V-groove on the right and a steep chimney on the left. Climb the chimney to exit onto slabs (45m). Above, climb an obvious fault that splits the final buttress (30m).

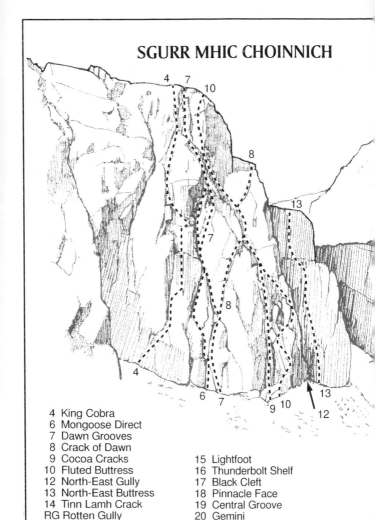

SGURR MHIC CHOINNICH

4 King Cobra
6 Mongoose Direct
7 Dawn Grooves
8 Crack of Dawn
9 Cocoa Cracks
10 Fluted Buttress
12 North-East Gully
13 North-East Buttress
14 Tinn Lamh Crack
RG Rotten Gully

15 Lightfoot
16 Thunderbolt Shelf
17 Black Cleft
18 Pinnacle Face
19 Central Groove
20 Gemini

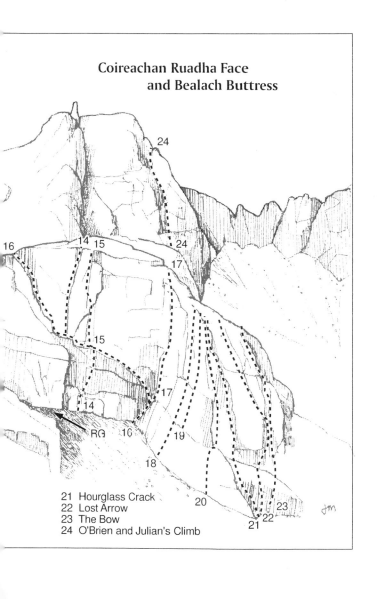

Coireachan Ruadha Face
and Bealach Buttress

21 Hourglass Crack
22 Lost Arrow
23 The Bow
24 O'Brien and Julian's Climb

12   North-East Gully   120m   Mild VS 4b *   (1912)
This climb was by far the hardest route in Skye when first ascended, and it has been unjustly neglected since. It represented a considerable step forward in the technique of its day. A good route to do when dry, it follows the conspicuous gully on the right of the face. After 60m of interesting climbing, climb a large flake on the right followed by an exposed right traverse across its top to a stance. From the ledge, climb a steep groove for a short distance, then move left across and up a steep broad rib, a delicate move which is the crux. Much easier climbing then leads up the right-slanting groove which ends at a broken platform 12m below the summit ridge.

13   North-East Buttress   120m   Very Difficult *   (1950)
This is the buttress between North-East Gully and Rotten Gully. Start near North-East Gully, and from a cairn climb a series of broken walls and corners. At about 60m there is a short steep pitch, followed by a shelf with an awkward wall at the back. Climb this and the steep wall above by a 15m crack on the left. The crack slants back to the right and from it an easy slab leads back to the neck of the buttress where North-East Gully and the small gully on the right join. Above, a steep final wall leads to the ridge. Start this wall on the left, then trend up right to the ridge.

BEALACH BUTTRESS
(Map Ref 448 214)

This is the buttress immediately north of the Sgurr Mhic Choinnich cliffs, lying between Rotten Gully and Bealach Coire Lagan. The approach from Coir'-uisg is simple, but from Glen Brittle it is more complicated. Each of the four options has disadvantages:
1. From Bealach Mhic Choinnich, traverse below the cliffs of Sgurr Mhic Choinnich, crossing scree to the cliffs.
2. Descend Rotten Gully to the terrace which leads under Upper Crag. The descent of the crags under this terrace starts down a little chimney on the true left of Rotten Gully, then more easily to the screes.
3. From Bealach Coire Lagan, scramble down loose grass and boulder slopes passing many outcropping basalt dykes, descending first right-wards (southwards), then back left and down a short wall to a scree fan. From here, traverse south across scree under broken rocky slopes, descending gradually until on the terrace which sweeps round the buttress. It is then possible to climb down under the Arrowhead.

4. From Bealach Coire na Banachdich.
   The return journey can be made by any of these routes.

   The south-east part of the buttress, overlooking Rotten Gully, is a large vertical wall of sound gabbro which has more broken rock to the left. To the right of the wall, the buttress is more amenable with several good medium grade routes. Towards the bealach the crags become broken again.

   The big vertical wall has a couple of striking lines, with room for more. A left-slanting shelf, Thunderbolt Shelf, runs up beneath it and is reached by three distinctive vertical walls. The vertical wall is bordered on the right by the chimney-crack of Black Cleft, before turning south to an area of numerous cracks and chimneys which are marked by three converging cracks that form a down-pointing arrow-head. This marks the starts of Hourglass Crack, Lost Arrow and The Bow. A pale rock scar left of Hourglass Crack decorates the central part of this area of crag. Two terraces run across the face, making the climbs somewhat disjointed.

14   Tinn Lamh Crack   105m   E1 **   (1969)
This is the striking vertical crack near the centre of the vertical wall. Despite a loose approach to Thunderbolt Shelf, the upper section is excellent with good positions. Start below the crack at the level of the foot of Rotten Gully.
1. 45m 4c   Traverse right along a prominent fault, surmount a shattered overlap and climb loose slabs to grass. Go right and through a break to reach Thunderbolt Shelf some 12 metres right of the crack.
2. 15m   Follow the shelf to belay left of the crack.
3. 45m 5b   Traverse right into the crack and climb it to a horizontal break. Continue up the crack to the final steep wall. Where it narrows, the crux move brings good holds within reach near the top of the wall.

15   Lightfoot   80m   E3 **   (1983)
This finds a way up the vertical wall to the right of Tinn Lamh Crack, cutting through a pronounced right-trending corner. It is a good steep route amidst impressive surroundings. Start from Thunderbolt Shelf. An abseil approach was made on the only recorded ascent.
1. 40m 6a   Climb the obvious leaning corner in the middle of the face over a small roof and continue until moves left can be made below a roof. Surmount this, then move up right above the roof, overlooking the corner, until hard moves enable a small ledge to be gained.
2. 40m 5c   Climb the splendid crack line above to the top.

16   Thunderbolt Shelf   150m   Severe *   (1953)

This is the shelf at the foot of the vertical wall. Despite rather scrappy climbing, the great position makes the route worthwhile. The lower part consists of three short vertical walls, each about 20m high. Turn the first by climbing the initial pitch of Black Cleft, the huge chimney that borders the right side of the vertical wall. From the chimney, traverse 10m left along a ledge and climb the wall to another ledge. Then move 25m left and climb the third tier to another ledge below the vertical wall. The route now slants up to the left, keeping close to the wall, one pitch going over a huge semi-detached flake on the wall itself. Higher up, take a direct line and finish by a prominent vertical chimney.

17   Black Cleft   120m   VS   (1954)

The deep chimney-crack right of the vertical wall gives a strenuous and good climb. The first 25m gives scrambling with a little chockstone pitch leading to a platform. Climb the steep narrow chimney above, passing a chockstone, to a ledge at 15m. Turn the chimney above on the immediate left, then steep and delicate climbing on loose rock for about 15m leads to an easier section. After 12m, the climbing steepens, going over an awkward slab in the chimney to the foot of a small chockstone overhang. Climb the overhang to a jammed block belay, then surmount another short strenuous overhang. Continue over a large and doubtful jammed block to a chockstone in the recesses of the cleft. A final 20m pitch goes up the chimney ahead until it is possible to climb out on the left wall and so up to the top.

18   Pinnacle Face   135m   Hard Severe *   (1954)

A very pleasant climb on sound clean rock. The route starts halfway between Black Cleft and the foot of the arrowhead, aiming for a prominent pinnacle on the face of the buttress. Climb an easy shallow crack for 30m to the lower terrace. Climb the clean crack in the face above, then traverse right across the foot of the pinnacle to a stance in its right corner. From the top of the pinnacle, step back left into the crack and go up to a ledge. Easier climbing up the face of the buttress leads across a grass patch and up a short steep wall behind, climbing to the right of a basalt fault. From the upper terrace, about 60m above the pinnacle, climb up and right over pleasant rock to the summit slopes.

19   Central Groove   75m   Very Difficult   (1960)
Start from the lower terrace a short distance right of Pinnacle Face.
Climb vertically for 5m into a groove, initially shallow but soon deep-
ening, avoiding loose blocks at the top. Easy climbing now leads to a
junction with Pinnacle Face and Gemini below the upper rocks. The
final slopes are enlivened by climbing a remarkable flying buttress,
more difficult and exposed than it appears from below.

20   Gemini   155m   VS *   (1954)
A good route on clean rough rock despite some loose sections. Start
immediately right of a shallow broken groove on the flat face, and left
of the arrowhead recess.
1. 45m   Pleasant climbing up the slabby face to the right of the groove
leads to the lower terrace. Cross this to a chockstone belay in a corner.
2. 30m   Climb 5m to the right of the crack, following an obvious
right-rising traverse, then trend back left to a small terrace.
3. 30m 4c   From a pair of shaky pinnacles, step onto the face and
climb to the foot of a steep groove. Traverse right to twin cracks on the
steep section of the face, then climb the right-hand crack, crux, to an
easing. Now follow the left-hand crack to a belay on the left.
4. 20m   A good pitch now follows; climb the pinnacle immediately
above the belay to its top, then climb the face beyond to the top of the
right-hand of twin pinnacles. Go up and over another pinnacle to the
upper terrace.
5. 30m   Easy climbing up the buttress above to the summit slopes.

21   Hourglass Crack   150m   Mild VS 4b *   (1950)
Start from the scree where the three downward pointing cracks form
the arrowhead. Climb the left crack to the lower terrace. Cross this and
a little to the left the continuation of the left-hand crack of the arrowhead
leads up a steep wall. Climb the tight crack, crux, to where it deepens
to an impressive clett. Follow this easily over a few small pitches to a
huge overhanging cave. Climb the right wall of the cave on smallish
holds, or back up between the walls to pass the cave; an enjoyable
and unusual pitch with fine views to Sgurr Coir' an Lochain. The wide
crack continues to the final cave; back up out of this and cross to the
left wall to reach the buttress left of the overhang. Scrambling above
leads to the ridge.

22   Lost Arrow   160m   VS   (1954)
A dry weather route only, with vegetated sections. The grade assumes
the usual damp conditions, if dry it is probably easier.
1. 45m   Ascend the centre chimney of the arrowhead past awkward
chockstones to finish up the left wall. Cross the lower terrace to belay
below the continuation of the same.
2. 25m   Climb the easy and broad grassy crack, then cross The Bow
and belay in a wet cave in the steeper chimney.
3. 20m   Climb the chimney, normally mossy and wet, to belay in a
cave below a large pointed chockstone.
4. 10m   Climb down, out and round the chockstone, then go over it
to the foot of another overhanging section.
5. 15m   Continue up the crack, surmounting the overhanging loose
chockstone on huge holds, then scramble up the gully to the upper
terrace.
6. 45m   The fault line finishes here. Either climb the easy top crack of
The Bow, or the face straight ahead which gives good climbing on
friable rock to end in a scramble to the summit slopes.

23   The Bow   165m   VS *   (1954)
A pleasant and enjoyable route with a short sharp crux. Start below
the right-hand crack of the arrowhead.
1. 45m   Climb the crack and the slab on the right. Walk across the
lower terrace to the right-hand of two faults which cross the cliff above.
2. 10m   Now climb a short greasy chimney and the fault which
crosses Lost Arrow to where it becomes an overhanging crack.
3. 15m 4c   Climb the overhanging crack, which splits higher up and
leads to an isolated slab.
4. 20m   Continue pleasantly up the slab by the crack in its right corner,
which steepens near its top.
5. 30m   Scramble to the upper terrace, with the deep-cut section of
Hourglass Crack on the left, and pass a weird rock bridge on the left.
6. 45m   Climb the broad and easy crack above the upper terrace.

SGURR DEARG

978m   (Map Ref 444 215)

The Coireachan Ruadha faces of An Stac, the Inaccessible Pinnacle
and Sgurr Dearg are steep, impressive and mostly loose. However
there is undoubtedly scope for exploration to supplement the one
recorded route on this large and slabby face of Sgurr Dearg.

The approach to the north-east face of Sgurr Dearg from Glen Brittle is *via* the Bealach Coire na Banachdich. This is the most popular crossing from Glen Brittle to Coruisk and descends from the main ridge as a loose gully hemmed by steep rock walls. Follow the path, then contour round to the base of the crags. From the Loch Coruisk path, head south-west, then go west up the line of a burn on tedious scree as for Bealach Coire na Banachdich, before contouring around to the base of the crag. The descent is *via* the Bealach Coire na Banachdich.

24   O'Brien and Julian's Climb   150m   Mild Severe * (1912)
A good but seldom visited climb, but fairly serious due to route-finding difficulties and often slippery rock. At the centre of the foot of the north-east face is a well formed cave, not easily visible from the south. Do not confuse this cave with a rib and damp recess 50 metres further left. Climb the lowest slabs, initially steep for 20m, which ease to a scree terrace. Climb the left wall of the cave, then a further 20m of steep rock to a long slanting shelf. The climbing gradually eases above the shelf and trends right to an upper shelf and a prominent rock tower on the north-north-east ridge. The summit is easily gained from there.
Winter: VI,5   (1996)
A fine climb up a big face. Climb to the cave (60m). A strenuous pull onto its left rib leads to sustained mixed climbing up the rib. Traverse left to a short cracked corner (40m) which leads to the slanting shelf. Climb another corner on the left to an obvious rising traverse (45m). Follow this up right for 70m to an icy gully leading to a subsidiary crest. Climb to the ridge.

SGURR NA BANACHDICH
965m   (Map Ref 440 225)

The north-east face of Sgurr na Banachdich presents extensive but broken areas of separate crags that lie below the various tops. Whilst only four routes have been recorded in this area, it should be pointed out that the rock varies from quite sound to deplorable, often on the same route. This does not preclude further exploration, but prior cleaning will be essential.
  The first two routes lie just north of Bealach Coire na Banachdich under a minor top; if approaching from Glen Brittle they can be reached by descending from the bealach and traversing across scree. From Loch Coruisk, they can easily be reached by following the path to the bealach from Loch Coruisk to the same traverse.

The Twins form a pair of prominent steep buttresses separated by a dark gully.

South Twin   75m   Difficult   (1953)
At the foot of the buttress is a huge slab topped by an overhang. On the left flank is a chimney which marks the start of the route. Climb the right edge of the steep and pleasant chimney to a level crest. From there, trend left across a wall and go up the crest to the summit. The rock is rather shattered in places.

North Twin   105m   Severe   (1953)
From a recessed platform 6m up, climb a steep crack to a ledge on the left flank. From the far end of the ledge, climb the steep slabby left wall of the buttress until it is possible to traverse right to the crest. A vertical knife-edge leads up on good holds to a level arete of solid rock ending at a neck. Finish up shattered rock.

The following climbs lie further to the north, near the summit of Sgurr na Banachdich. To approach them from the main ridge, continue past a minor top north of Bealach Coire na Banachdich, which houses The Twins, then descend to an incipient col. From the col, easy ground leads down to a level scree terrace below the summit cliffs. For the first route, traverse below steep black cliffs to a prominent narrow arete, the line of the route. For the second route, continue past the arete for 100 metres, passing a section of imposing vertical walls, to a big gully. The route lies to the right, directly under the summit of the mountain. From Coruisk, leave the Bealach Coire na Banachdich path, skirt the spur of Sron Bhuidhe to the right and gain the scree terrace.

Midget Ridge   120m   Moderate *   (1953)
A recommended little route. The narrow arete trends slightly right. Follow the edge exactly by pleasant climbing on good rock. Higher up the arete narrows to a knife edge, and finishes on the south top.

Clouded Buttress   180m   Severe   (1953)
This is the big buttress to the right of the gully which ascends directly to the summit. Despite many attractions, the climb is marred by some desperately loose rock and caution is advised. The climb follows the main line of weakness. From the foot, trend first right, then left. Cross some steep slabs to the left until it is possible to climb up and right towards a slabby shelf. Traverse left along the slabs to a short shallow chimney, then continue left and up to a recess in the left-hand corner

at a great white scar. Exit from this recess by the right-hand corner, crux, then go straight up for over 30m to a terrace. The final tower above may be avoided, but it gives a pleasant finish.

SGURR THORMAID
927m   (Map Ref 442 227)

The south buttress is well seen from the summit of Sgurr na Banachdich and can be approached from Glen Brittle via the Bealach Thormaid and from Coir'-uisg by following scree to Bealach Thormaid. The buttress lies to the right (east) and below the bealach. The descent is via Bealach Thormaid, a loose scree gully.

The buttress is fairly impressive, with the most obvious line of weakness taken by the only recorded route to date. The rock is much better than on some of the Sgurr na Banachdich routes, although there are still areas where care is needed.

Peridot   215m   HVS *   (1968)
The most obvious line of weakness forms a peridotite dyke overlooking the descent from Bealach Thormaid. Although the route is rather unbalanced technically, it takes a fine line to the summit. Start left of and above the lowest point of the buttress at some pale grey rock. Climb slabs and a corner to a large sloping grass ledge (35m 4b). The dyke is initially undercut and its entrance forms the crux; it can either be tackled direct or traversed into from the left (5a). The dyke then becomes much easier, but gives good climbing to the top where it forms a terrace. Instead of following the final section back towards the descent gully, continue up right towards the summit of Sgurr Thormaid by short walls (35m).

SGURR A' GHREADAIDH
973m   (Map Ref 445 232)

The south-east face of Sgurr a' Ghreadaidh is a huge mass of rock, broken into individual buttresses and gullies. It includes the longest climb in Britain, excluding the scramble of The Dubh Ridge, as well as several routes of more than 200m. Due south of the summit, at a height of 720m, is a large grass terrace. Above and to its right is the south-east ridge, the north-eastern limit of Coireachan Ruadha. Below the terrace, facing south, is a prominent rock mass cleft by two gullies; the deep right-hand one is Terrace Gully with East and West Buttresses flanking it. Well to the right there are a few other climbs, which continue up the rocks of the extreme left end of Coir' an Uaigneis. In general, most of the rock below the terrace is sound, whilst above it is very loose. The crags give some good traditional climbs which dry fairly quickly.

To approach from Coir'-uisg, follow scree slopes to the base of the crags; from Glen Brittle descend either Bealach Thormaid or Bealach na Glaic Moire and in both instances contour around on scree below the crags. From the summit of Sgurr a' Ghreadaidh, the quickest descent is down Bealach Thormaid.

The routes are described from left to right.

1   Terrace West Buttress   330m   Difficult *   (1924)
Start near the foot of Terrace Gully at some steep rocks. Climb these past a vertical section at 35m, which leads to a stretch of open slabs. Above the slabs, follow a left-sloping chimney-gully to a shelf at 120m. On the right, a fine 25m wall leads to a ledge of shattered rock. Climb a section of steep basalt, tricky in the wet, to an excellent wall of fine rough gabbro which leads to the terrace, 200m from the foot. Cross the terrace and gain a narrow ledge which runs up towards the Thormaid-Ghreadaidh gap. Follow this until it 'threatens to become non-existent'. Climb a dyke chimney, with a difficult exit, to open ground above. Reach the main ridge a short distance below the summit.

2   Terrace Gully   210m   Very Difficult **   (1920)
As this is a natural route of drainage, so it is infrequently dry. When dry, it gives a very good climb of its type. Start from a broad green ledge which runs along the foot of the cliff above a low vertical wall. The first pitch is a deeply-cut cave, then a ledge on the left leads to an enclosed chimney. Emerge from this by an aperture between the chockstones. Take the small obstacles above directly, and turn a wet chockstone pitch by the edge of the buttress to the left. A short distance higher, a fine unclimbed branch chimney rises to the right. A wet and slippery pitch in the main gully leads to the Great Cave Pitch. Ascend waterworn slabs, then at the start of a short scree slope climb the right wall of the cave to a small ledge. Traverse up left to enter a recess beside the capstone. The recess is difficult to enter but easy to leave. Above, the gully forms a long chimney, usually wet, containing an arched block high up. This has not been climbed, so instead climb the narrow crack on the right, then traverse back left into the gully. Scrambling remains to the terrace.

The first winter ascent of O'Brien and Julian's Climb (Climber, Brian Davison)

A suitable continuation above Terrace Gully is to follow the well defined rib in the centre of the face to the south top of Sgurr a' Ghreadaidh, giving 500m of climbing in all.

3   Terrace East Buttress   200m   Difficult   (1922)
This is the large rounded buttress to the east of Terrace Gully. Start at a large cairn near the east angle of the buttress at the right-hand end of the broad grass rake. A shelf and chimney lead to a large grass patch at 35m. From the top of the grass patch, follow a long left-slanting chimney-fault for 100m. Gain another grassy shelf and make an exposed left traverse across a vertical wall to a ledge above a long drop into Terrace Gully. Climb the steep wall above for 20m to a region of easy slabs and the terrace. The final rocks are best taken by the finish of the previous route, giving a total of 500m of climbing.

4   South-East Ridge   700m   Difficult *   (1896)
The true south-east ridge of the mountain starts from the scree of the terrace some 250m below the summit. Collie's original line is open to much variation lower down. Start left of where two gullies meet higher up like an inverted-U, well seen from Loch Coruisk. Either follow the left-hand gully or the rocks to its left, a mixture of climbing and scrambling, for over 400m, to where it is possible to traverse diagonally left by walking to the start of the south-east ridge proper.

5   South-East Ridge Direct   400m   Difficult   (1920)
This route starts well left of Collie's original route, and 20 metres left of a deeply-cut gully marked by a rowan tree. Work up and left by a series of steep pitches connecting dyke lines to reach the terrace. Finish up the south-east ridge proper.

6   Slab Route   350m   Severe   (1939)
This lies to the right of the prominent inverted-U formed by the two gullies. Start 7m right of the right-hand gully at some red slabs. Climb the slabs for 30m to the gully and go up to a cave. A short steep wall on the right leads to about 45m of easy rocks. Cross the gully, then climb slabs for over 150m, making for a large perched block. Pass this on easier ground either side. Walk up to the final crags, then climb a left-slanting slab that lies 15 metres right of a large black overhang. The slab is quite delicate at 13m; traverse across and at 45m climb a basalt wall to a large grass terrace. The final buttress is situated between two gullies and has an overhanging base. A steep start on

On the third pitch of The Great Prow, Bla Bheinn

the left leads to very loose rocks until the buttress steepens to a tower. Start by a mantelshelf on the left and either climb direct or by a traverse left to easy ground. The loose rock on the final tower requires great care.

SGURR A' MHADAIDH
918m   (Map Ref 446 215)

Coire an Uaigneis, the aptly named corrie of solitude, lies immediately south-east of Sgurr a' Ghreadaidh and below Sgurr a' Mhadaidh. It is guarded by crags and its boundaries are the south-east ridge of Sgurr a' Ghreadaidh on the west and the crags below the north-east top of Sgurr a' Mhadaidh on the east.

The access to the upper cliffs from Coir'-uisg is by the rocks to the right of the main stream draining the corrie. There is one easy route from the corrie to the ridge by a rake from the start of Second-Third Gully to the col between the third and fourth tops. The fourth top is the highest one, at the south-west end of the summit ridge.

COIR'-UISG BUTTRESS

This is the very attractive crag that lies below Coir' an Uaigneis proper, easily reached from Loch Coruisk. The initial 80m are steep and sound black gabbro with several overhangs. There is a prominent white scar in the centre of the buttress. It has some good routes and offers accessible climbing of a more continuous difficulty than the longer but more broken crags to the left on Sgurr a' Ghreadaidh.

To descend, a grassy terrace slopes down the steep frontal face to the foot of the east gully; this provides the easiest way down as the gullies either side of the crag contain rock pitches.

7   Rebound   180m   Severe   (1966)
This lies to the left of Original Route and follows the first feasible line round the corner to the left on the west gully wall. Start from the gully, just above the first waterfall.
1. 25m   Climb diagonally right to a break in the overhang close to the right skyline. Gain a small slab and follow this to a grassy ramp.
2. 35m   Follow the gangway rightwards, then go back left to an obvious chimney-groove with a small overhang at the top.
3. etc. 120m   Escape directly or on the right wall. Continue to the top by easier climbing.

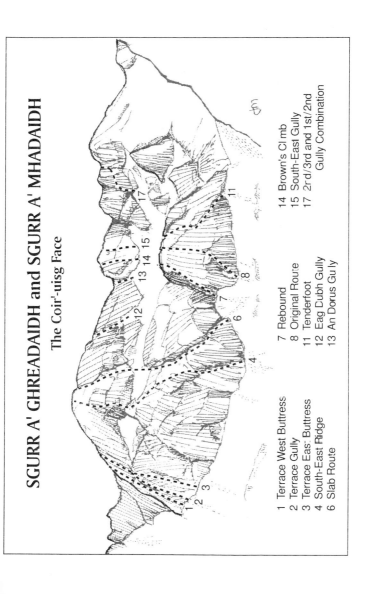

SGURR A' GHREADAIDH and SGURR A' MHADAIDH
The Coir'-uisg Face

1 Terrace West Buttress
2 Terrace Gully
3 Terrace East Buttress
4 South-East Ridge
6 Slab Route

7 Rebound
8 Original Route
11 Tenderfoot
12 Eag Dubh Gully
13 An Dorus Gully

14 Brown's Climb
15 South-East Gully
17 2nd/3rd and 1st/2nd
     Gully Combination

8   Original Route   240m   Severe *   (1949)
A conspicuous line of weakness runs diagonally up from the bottom left of the buttress, forming the greater part of the climb. Start at the lowest tongue of rock and move diagonally up left into the groove until checked by a small overhang beneath a big black one at 60m. Escape right, crux, to gain a series of continuous grooves. Follow the grooves to a point about two-thirds of the way up the cliff where they form a vertical corner. Climb this, continuing on the same line. Above, the angle eases to slabs and an easy crack leads straight up to finish.

9   Rawhide   95m   E1 5b *
Start 20 metres right of Original Route at a vertical crack line, just right of a white scarred overhang.
1. 30m   Climb up to the white scarred overhang and belay.
2. 35m   Climb the crack on the right to a belay on slabs.
3. 30m   From the right-hand end of the slabs climb a shallow groove, then move left to join Original Route. Finish as for Original Route.

10   Rongwrong   210m   VS   (1966)
Start as for Original Route. From the grass ledge below the main diagonal weakness, follow an obvious rising traverse line to below a prominent steep groove breaking through the left-hand end of the central overhangs. Continue on the traverse line to a gangway, then climb this rightwards to below a steep corner crack in the centre of the left-bounding wall of the main groove. Climb this crux crack to a platform level with a big black roof on the right. Easier climbing leads to the top.

11   Tenderfoot   195m   Severe   (1966)
At the right-hand side of the main face is a prominent sloping corner topped by an inclined roof at 40m. Climb the corner to the roof, then traverse right across a slab to chimney-cracks (45m). Climb these to a platform, then head back up the wall on the left past a flake to reach a sloping ledge with a perched boulder (15m). A groove on the right leads to the grassy terrace, then easier rocks lead to the top.

THE UPPER CLIFFS

These are more broken than Coir'-uisk Buttress, but contain some long easier routes where solitude is guaranteed. Some of the gully climbs are quite intriguing for dry days and there remains some scope for exploration.

An easy descent to Coir'-uisk is *via* the scrambling rake that descends slanting left from between the third and fourth summit tops of Sgurr a' Mhadaidh. This leads to the foot of the gully which lies between the second and third tops. An alternative is to descend the largely scree-filled An Dorus Gully to the west of the main summit, which is Easy in standard and requires some elementary route-finding in places. Both of these descents meet up with the lower section of the Glac Mhor. To reach Glen Brittle, both An Dorus and the harder Eag Dubh, which lies a little higher up Sgurr a' Ghreadaidh, give largely scree-filled descents. The Eag Dubh gully descends adjacent to the north-west face of Sgurr a' Ghreadaidh. If these options are not attractive, descend from the Bealach na Glaic Moire to either Glen Brittle or Coruisk.

The routes are described from left to right.

12   Eag Dubh Gully   Difficult   (1913)
This gully leads up to the prominent notch of the Eag Dubh from the Coruisk side. There are eight or nine pitches, the hardest being about midway.

13   An Dorus Gully   Easy   (c1600)
Much used as a pass in the bad old days of rape and pillage, this has some interesting scrambling and route finding from the Glac Mhor and finishes up the prominent gully that is largely scree.

14   Brown's Climb   240m   Difficult *   (1897)
This gives some fine straightforward climbing on reasonable rock. It lies on the main peak's south east buttress, to the left of South-East Gully. Start on the left-hand side by the lowest rocks. The first 150m are on steep sound rock. However, as the angle eases, the climbing gets harder.

15   South-East Gully   240m   Severe *   (1910)
This gully divides south-east buttress. There are ten pitches in all, the third being the hardest. Above this is a fine cave pitch, complete with a through route. Above pitch 7 an escape can be made into Third-Fourth Gully if necessary. Continue straight up, then take the right branch where the gully forks near the top.

The following gullies take their names from the corresponding tops of Sgurr a' Mhadaidh:-

16   Third-Fourth Gully   150m   Moderate
This is the largely scree-filled gully that lies east of the main or fourth peak. It has one 15m pitch and near the top it forks; the right branch leads to the col between the two tops whilst the left branch is a narrow chimney that leads to the gap between the main top and a prominent pinnacle north of it.

17   Second-Third Gully   150m   Very Difficult *   (1913)
This lies right of Third-Fourth Gully, starting near the foot of the easy descent rake. The steep lower section contains some fine pitches, including a large cave turned by a chimney a few metres to the left. Rejoin the main gully by traversing over an intervening rib. At half-height the gully turns to scree and it is usual to traverse over to the top half of First-Second Gully to get a more continuous climb.

18   First-Second Gully   150m   Difficult   (1913)
This lies to the right of Second-Third Gully. The lower half is scree and easy ground, but above half-height the gully narrows and deepens to give three fine pitches on continuous rock.

DRUIM NAN RAMH

The south-west flank of the Druim nan Ramh ridge that rises above the north-eastern shores of Loch Coruisk contains large amounts of slabby rock that have given several climbs. The Coruisk face of the ridge is very accessible and at a low level. There are two main areas of slab, about 500 metres apart, both rising from above the path.

DUBH VIEW BUTTRESS   (Map Ref 479 213)

This is the biggest buttress on the north-east shore of Loch Coruisk. It lies above a huge block by the lochside and the crag is split at half-height by a large grassy terrace.

Approach *via* the path along the north-eastern shores of Loch Coruisk to a point almost directly opposite the slabs of the east ridge of Sgurr Dubh Beag. The descent follows slopes down to the south-east.

JMCS Buttress   270m   Hard Severe   (1964)
The last 150m of this climb are of broken crag and heather but the lower section is quite good. Start at a fault below a white wall about 45m from the base of the buttress and on its right flank. This point can also be reached by scrambling on the lowest rocks. Follow the fault up

left below the white wall to more open rocks. Climb to below a large overhanging nose of white rock. Traverse left along a broad slabby terrace to the arete on its left, then follow the arete and the gully on its right; the crux is at the top corner. Easier rocks now lead to the half-height terrace, from where it is possible to escape to either side. Above the terrace, the climb degenerates, starting initially up the right edge from where a variety of lines lead to the ridge.

CORUISK SLABS   (Map Ref 484 210)

The slabs stretch over a fairly large area of hillside, with the maximum interest being towards the centre. The slabs merge with the general hillside to the right.

Approach as for Dubh View Buttress; the slabs are 500 metres to the right. The descent is to the south-east of the slabs.

Coruisk Slabs   210m   Severe   (1962)
Some pleasant climbing that becomes exciting in the wet. Start some 30 metres right of the first boulder at the foot of the slabs, when approaching from the River Scavaig.
1. 20m   Climb the left side of the cracked wall for 7m, then trend right to a belay below a damp basalt corner fault. Surmount this by the left wall, then climb the slab to a grass terrace.
2. 30m   Trend right and climb the slab on small holds, crux, then go up left to a cracked block belay.
3. 20m   Traverse left on the waterslide, then go up to the second grass terrace.
4. 45m   Walk right along the dyke to a belay below a steep slab.
5. 25m   Climb the slab to a grass field and continue to a corner with a block belay on the right.
6. 35m   Climb a rib direct to a fault and another block belay in the corner.
7. 35m   Continue up the ledge until the angle eases.

SGURR HAIN CRAG   (Map Ref 508 201)

This crag faces south-east and consists of two main buttresses separated by a wide gully. The rock varies from perfect gabbro to looser sections. Scope exists for more routes, but they would probably require cleaning.

To approach, take the path from Elgol to Camasunary. The crag lies 300 metres west of the southern end of Loch na Creitheach and 1½km north of Camasunary bothy. Being at low level, it may prove to be an attractive alternative in unsettled weather.

It is easiest to descend the east flank of the left-hand buttress.

LEFT-HAND BUTTRESS

Peterless Crack   120m   E1   (1990)
Start 4 metres left of a small bay, which is just left of the toe of the buttress.
1. 15m 5b   Climb over initial bulges, moving right then left, to gain a crack line in the slabs.
2. 20m 5b   Continue up the crack line through an overhang to block belays.
3. 20m 5a   Climb directly above the belay, following the crack line through overhangs. Go up to a grass ledge, then traverse left to the foot of a corner.
4. 35m   Climb the corner-groove until steep heather leads to trees.
5. 30m   Move round to the right and follow slabs to the top.

Bryantless Crack   125m   HVS   (1990)
Start at the small bay.
1. 15m 4c   Climb the overhanging corner to slabs.
2. 25m 4c   Continue up the corner to a block. Make an awkward entry into a gangway up to the left, then continue up left to a block belay on Peterless Crack.
3, 4 and 5. 85m   Climb Peterless Crack, pitches 3, 4 and 5.

The next three routes lie on the bounding walls, high up in the wide central gully. The first two climbs are on the left wall, the third on the right wall.

Assault Course Bimbo   20m   E4 6a **   (1990)
An excellent pitch on perfect rock, both very sustained and well protected. It takes the thin crack line up the centre of a vertical wall high up on the left bounding wall. Scramble 10m to a belay at some blocks. Climb to the top of the blocks just left of the crack. Make a short traverse along a quartz band to the crack, then climb it to the top.

Witchless Corner   20m   VS 4c *   (1990)
This is the prominent corner several metres right of and slightly higher than Assault Course Bimbo. Another well protected pleasant route on good rock.

RIGHT-HAND BUTTRESS

James's Crack   85m   HVS   (1990)
This is the prominent continuous vertical crack line in the right-bounding wall of the gully. It lies at the same level as Witchless Corner. The crack starts about 12m beneath a large jammed block in the gully and is not the wider crack 5m below the boulder.
1. 25m 5a   Climb the crack.
2. 25m 4c   Continue in the same line.
3. 35m 4b   Continue up the crack. This pitch is poorly protected and much loose rock was removed on the first ascent.

The Slabs   210m   Moderate
The broken slabs well right of the right-hand buttress provide a means of gaining the ridge of Sgurr Hain.

SGURR NA STRI
497m   (Map Ref 499 193)

This superb little pointed peak is the culmination of a broad ridge which extends south-west from Sgurr Hain. It rises directly above Loch Scavaig and thereby blocks easy access to Coruisk from the east. Although it has a rather indefinite summit, it is worth ascending for superb views of the whole Cuillin range. The north ridge gives the easiest line of ascent and is a walk. A prominent ramp on the north-east flank gives a good scramble. The infamous Bad Step lies below the west face near sea-level. The east face is rugged but has no notable climbing.

The west face gives all the recorded climbs. Rather dismissed in the past, this most enjoyable face gives climbing on superb slabby rock, starting at sea-level in some instances. Due to the nature of the face, a wide variety of routes exist, not all of which have been recorded. Obvious descents exist between the areas of crag. The easiest descent from the summit is the north ridge, which leads to the Glen Sligachan track.

A big slabby mass of crags stretches over a wide area of hillside. Innumerable crags of all sizes jostle together for attention. All deserve a visit. In essence, there are two main areas, one about 100 metres from the Bad Step, the Scavaig slabs, and the other, a clean mass of slabs with walls behind, immediately above the point where the River Scavaig flows out of Loch Coruisk. This is Stepping Stone Buttress.

STEPPING STONE BUTTRESS

This is a big sprawling mass of slabs interrupted by overlaps and with a steep right-bounding edge. Behind is a gully that separates the slabs below from the steeper rocks above.

Bee Cee Crack   140m   VS   (1965)
The climb takes the fourth crack from the left on the prominent whale-backed buttress, seen clearly from Loch Coruisk. Start on the lower band of rock separated from the buttress by a grassy promenade.
1. 30m   Climb a crack below and left of an obvious white overhang to a terrace. Move up the terrace to a large overhang.
2. 35m   Go up easy rocks to a stance behind a flake. Then climb left *via* a hand traverse (peg runner) to a belay below a crack.
3, and 4. 75m   Follow the crack, steep at first, to the top of the buttress.

The Happy Wanderer   140m   Mild VS 4c   (1968)
This route provides much easy slab padding separated by strenuous overlaps. Start at the foot of the prominent slabs that rise above the path, taking in an optional little slab to start. Climb the slabs easily to a large overlap. Traverse right to a shattered crack and ascend this, crux, to gain the slabs above. Follow another 60m of pleasant slabs to another overlap. Take this more easily on the right *via* a cracked bulge. Traverse right across the large rolling slab above towards a steepening and the right-hand edge. Climb the slab bordering the edge direct, including the overlap above (avoidable on the left) to easy slabs to finish.

Skye Ride   120m   Very Difficult   (1968)
Cross the gully behind Happy Wanderer on the left. This route takes the curving groove near the middle of the steeper rocks above. Start at a crack, taking either a dirty rake on the left or the better cracked slab to the right; belay on the ledge above. Mount the small overlap, then traverse right to the groove. Climb the groove in two loose pitches, then either climb an easy slab on the left or, better, climb up right over a bulge and continue easily over broken ground to finish.

THE SCAVAIG SLABS

The slabs are a big sheet, falling nearly to the water's edge, about 100 metres from the Bad Step.

Phaeton   120m   Severe *   (1968)

Start at a small spring and climb the short slab above (15m). Step up left over the overhangs at their lowest point and continue for a further 12m to a flake belay. Traverse left and follow a curving groove up a steepening slab, then belay on the heather ledge above. (Escape is possible to the left). The slabs above are roofed by overhangs. Climb the centre of the slabs over a small overlap at 15m and go up boiler-plate slabs. At 25m, traverse right to a broken rib and poor belays. Climb up left of the rib, near the edge of the roofs, to the top.

The Cuillin Outliers

To the east of the main Black Cuillin peaks, in the district of Strathaird, there are several other fine hills. They may also enjoy better weather, being protected from wet westerly winds by the Main Cuillin Ridge. While the climbs on Bla Bheinn and Clach Glas are justly famous, it is less well known and perhaps surprising that good climbing is also available in the Red Cuillin on Marsco, and on a relatively low-lying crag on the north ridge of Garbh-bheinn.

MARSCO
736m   (Map Ref 508 252)

The rough and excellent granophyre of the north-west and south-west faces of Marsco offer climbing of a similar quality to that of the best gabbro. Although the rock is generally sound, care should be taken with loose blocks and on the darker rock, some of which is brittle. Marsco, being lower and isolated from the main Cuillin, often has better weather. The crags lie next to a feature called Fiaclan Dearg at an altitude of around 450m.

The approach follows the path up Glen Sligachan from the hotel for 6km. North-West Buttress faces Sligachan whilst South-West Buttress is seen in profile on the approach.

NORTH-WEST BUTTRESS

Although this buttress looks rather unimpressive on the approach, closer aquaintance gives a better impression. A cave lies in the centre of the crag, just left of the highest point.

The Boojum   115m   HVS *   (1968)
This is an interesting climb with a good top pitch. The initial pitch is a little loose but can be avoided by using the start of Teflon. Start below the highest point of the buttress where an overhang guards the base, with another overhang 10m above.
1. 40m 4c   Climb a shallow groove through the lower overhang to reach a left traverse. Go across this until it is possible to climb straight up to the cave.
2. 40m 4a   Move out of the cave on the right, then step back left onto the lip. Go up slightly left to the base of a clean ribbed buttress.
3. 35m 4a   The buttress gives a fine pitch.

Teflon   125m   HVS   (1976)
First climbed in torrential rain with the leader *in extremis* on the crux
top pitch. "I had to layback on my knees with no adequate protection
and Gwyn with a useless belay". Start below and left of the cave and
scramble 45m to a stance below the buttress left of the cave.
1. 40m 4a   Climb the buttress until it is possible to traverse down and
right into the cave.
2. 25m 4b   Move out of the cave on the right and step back left onto
the lip, then climb straight up to a ledge.
3. 35m 4a   Climb up to the final wall.
4. 25m 4c   Traverse left under an overhang, then climb to the top.

SOUTH-WEST BUTTRESS

This is the attractive buttress seen in profile from Sligachan, named
Fiaclan Dearg on the O.S. 1:25000 Outdoor Leisure map. The promi-
nant skyline buttress is Central Buttress with First and Second
Terraces clearly seen on the approach. Immediately above Second
Terrace is The Shoulder.
   To the left of Central Buttress is a large amphitheatre capped by a
steep headwall which Odell's Route turns on its right at The Shoulder.
To the right of Central Buttress is an area of steep brown rock with a
waterfall. Right again is an area of slabs.
   To descend from the climbs, from Second Terrace it is possible to
scramble up left over The Shoulder and reverse Odell's Route. From
the top of the crag the best descent is to go up and a long way left,
crossing a deep-cut stream, and returning under the amphitheatre.
Do not be tempted to descend the stream, the ascent of which
makes an interesting expedition in a drought.
   The routes are described from left to right.

Odell's Route   180m   Difficult *   (1943)
This is the original route on the crag. Despite being mostly
scrambling, Odell saw the potential of the crag - "Rock of excellent quality (coarse dusty granophyre) and the whole crag seems
to be worthy of further exploration." Start near the centre of the
amphitheatre and follow easy left-slanting slabs for 75m to a
scree patch. From there head for a shoulder which is a long way
off to the right above the Second Terrace of Central Buttress.
From there climb the best part of the route, the steep rock above
for 100m to the top of the crag. Route finding is open to much
variation.

Central Buttress   165m   Very Difficult *   (1953)
This route climbs the corner system which delineates the mass of
Central Buttress from the amphitheatre. Start at the foot of the buttress
to the right of the amphitheatre. Follow a line of corners passing close
to the gangway of The Snark at 40m and First Terrace at 80m.
Scramble up and left to the foot of a more vegetated corner. Climb this
for 50m to the Second Terrace. Scramble onto The Shoulder to join
Odell's Route. Finish up this.

April Fools   130m   VS   (1979)
Rather a hybrid route, with little independent climbing, described as "a
more direct line than Central Buttress to the top wall". Climb Central
Buttress for 80m until it debouches onto easy ground near First Terrace
and below the pedestal of The Snark. Gain the pedestal from the left
and climb pitch 4 of The Snark to the pinnacle (20m 4c). Above, move
right to the arete and go up this until it is possible to move right onto a
wall. Continue up rightwards to the peg runner on Slow Riser and finish
up the short wall above to Second Terrace (30m 4c).

The Snark   230m   VS **   (1968)
This is the classic of the crag and it deserves to become popular. The
rock is superb and it is often dry when the Black Cuillin are wet. Though
a little contrived in line, it takes in the best climbing and starts directly
below the middle of Central Buttress.
1. 25m 4b   Climb a wall and over a small overhang. Traverse left and
go up a small corner to a ledge.
2. 45m 4c   Continue up and slightly left until, at about 20m, an
exposed gangway on the right can be gained. Follow this to a groove
and climb to the first terrace.
3. 25m 4a   Scramble up slabs to a crack right of a pedestal below a
steep smooth wall. Climb the crack and belay on the far side of the
pedestal.
4. 40m 4c   Climb the undercut crack on the left to a groove with a
large detached pinnacle. Move out onto the right wall, then go up to a
crack leading to the second terrace.
5. etc 95m 4a   Scramble up to the shoulder and go straight up to the
final wall. Climb the wall and finish by a prominent V-cleft with two small
overhangs.

Slow Riser   230m   HVS **   (1980)
An excellent route, though a little loose in places, which takes the most
direct line up the crag. Central Buttress is split by an obvious deep
groove. Start directly below the groove, just right of the start to The
Snark.
1. 20m 5a   Climb directly up to the foot of the groove by a faint crack
line. Just left of the foot of the groove are a good stance and belays.
2. 25m 4c   Move into the groove and climb this using the right wall to
gain a ledge and belay on the right.
3. 25m 4b   Step back into the groove and continue to a steepening.
Turn this on the right and continue up the groove, taking another
steepening directly. Belay on easier ground below First Terrace.
4. 15m   Scramble onto First Terrace and belay beneath a steep wall.
5. 40m 5a   A vertical fault splits the steep wall at its centre. Climb the
fault to a sentry box at 5m and a horizontal dyke. Hand traverse left for
10m to an arete. Gain a crack above and climb it for a few metres until
it is possible to move left into a groove. Go up the groove and a wall
past a peg runner to finish on Second Terrace.
Right-Hand Finish: (1995)
5a. 30m 5a   Climb the vertical fault past the sentry box at 5m and
continue up until a diagonal fault leads off to the right. Traverse this
past a hard move to gain a short crack leading to easier ground and a
belay on Second Terrace.
6. etc 105m   Pleasant easy climbing leads to the top. Belay as
required.

Zeke   110m   HVS **   (1995)
This route climbs the steep brown rock between Central Buttress and
the waterfall. Start 10 metres left of the stream.
1. 30m 5a/b   Climb a wall for 8m and ascend diagonally leftwards
over slabs to a niche. On the left is a steep wall. Cross this horizontally
(crux) and move up over a hollow flake. Continue left to a mantelshelf
onto easier ground, then climb directly to a large bay.
2. 25m 4b   Leave the bay at its left end and ascend a deep groove
past a rowan sapling. Step right to a rib and groove and gain a stance
in the main groove on the left.
3. 30m 4c   Ascend the groove for 6m and make a rising traverse
rightwards to gain a wet chimney. Escape from this on the left and
continue up and left to the First Terrace.
4. 25m 4c   Climb the right-hand edge of the steep wall above First
Terrace and belay on Second Terrace. Descend *via* Odell's Route or
continue to the top as for Slow Riser.

Heart but no Sole   130m   Severe   (1995)
Right of the waterfall is an area of slabs starting at a lower level. Start
at the lowest point of the slabs at a cracked slab.
1. 50m   Climb slabs pleasantly to a belay.
2. 30m   Further walls and slabs lead to easier ground. Belay on the
right.
3. 50m   Step right and continue upwards until the angle eases. A
scrambling descent can be made diagonally rightwards finishing under
some low overhangs at about Difficult standard.

BLA BHEINN and CLACH GLAS

The majority of the climbs on Bla Bheinn and Clach Glas are most
easily approached from Loch Slapin, following the course of the Allt
na Dunaiche. The south ridge and western flanks are best approached
from Camasunary. Although an approach from Sligachan is possible,
it is very long.

BLA BHEINN
928m   (Map Ref 530 217)

Bla-bheinn (previously spelt Blaven) is a magnificent mountain, considered by many to be the finest peak in the Cuillin. The twin summits
are less than 300 metres apart, with the south-west top being just lower
than the main summit. The bulk of the mountain is of gabbro with
intruded dolerite sheets, together with north-west to south-east trending basalt dykes. These dykes have often been eroded to create gullies
on opposite sides of the mountain, for example at the dip between the
summit and the south-west top.
    The steepest and most complex section lies at the northern end,
where the east ridge twists down from the summit to form the north
side of Coire Uaigneich. The lower section of this ridge is easy-angled

---

KEY TO MAP OPPOSITE

1   Bla Bheinn, South Buttress
2   Bla Bheinn, North-East Wall of East Ridge
3   Clach Glas, West Face
4   Clach Glas, East Face
5   Sgurr nan Each, Bealach Buttresses
6   Garbh bheinn, Creag Druim Eadar Da Choire

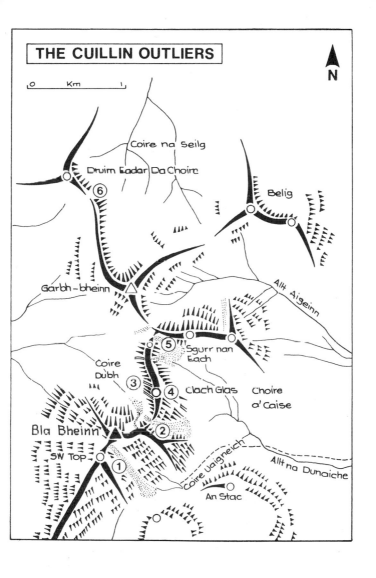

THE CUILLIN OUTLIERS

N

0   Km   1

Coire na Seilg

Druim Eadar Da Choire

Belig

Garbh-bheinn

Allt Aigeinn

⑥

Coire
Dubh

⑤

Sgurr nan
Each

③

④

Clach Glas

Choire
a' Caise

Bla Bheinn

②

SW Top

①

Coire Uaigneich

Allt na Dunaiche

An Stac

on its southern flank and provides the normal route to the summit.

Cars can be parked at the small gravel quarry just south of the bridge over the Allt na Dunaiche, from where a much improved path follows the north bank. After 1km, pass some fine wooded waterfalls and a little further cross the stream and head due west. Cross a tributary just below a rocky gorge and follow the path more steeply south-westwards up Coire Uaigneich. Pass below the triangular area of rock at the foot of the east ridge, which contains C Gully on the left and D Gully on the right. Once in the flatter upper reaches of the corrie, turn right and zigzag up steep grass and rocks on the south flank of the east ridge; the route becomes easier to follow on the scree higher up.

Pass the top of The Great Prow (740m), which juts out from the face on the right, and reach a small top on the shoulder at 800m. From there the ridge narrows and curves first left then right, with easy scrambling, and the angle eases just before the summit.

There is an easy but exhilarating walk southwards along the summit ridge to a col at 896m. The east (left-hand) gully is Great Scree Gully, which gives a quick but unattractive descent to Coire Uaigneich. The south-west top (924m) can be reached after a short scramble out of the col. On a good day this is one of the finest viewpoints in Skye.

An alternative descent is to go south from the south-west top and, after a short distance, descend the broad south-east ridge on the left, taking care not to stray too far left over South Buttress. Continue down to the bealach at the head of Abhainn nan Leac and regain the ascent path.

Another easy route of ascent and descent is the long south ridge. Cars can be left at a small car park 1km south-west of Kirkibost on the road to Elgol. Follow the track for 2km to Am Mam and continue for a further 1km to a hairpin bend. Follow the path which leads straight on at the bend, rather than descending towards Camasunary, then leave the path soon after crossing the Abhainn nan Leac. Strike up the hillside, gaining the crest of the ridge from the right (east) side. Follow the ridge over minor bumps, moving right on occasion to avoid the tops of gullies on the west face. About 90 metres beyond the south-west top, scramble down to the col from which the ridge leads to the summit.

The extensive western flank of the mountain is a great sweep of broken rock overlooking Loch na Creitheach and Srath na Creitheach. It is seamed with gullies, of which the longest was descended by the Willink brothers in 1873. They were stopped by a pitch halfway down, where they traversed out onto the north-western slopes. The broad buttresses on either side of the gully offer easy but reasonably pleasant ascent routes. Willink's Gully corresponds to Great Scree Gully on the opposite side of the mountain.

Pinnacle Ridge lies on the north face, easily identified from Loch an Athain. Much further round, a large stone chute gives a fast descent route from the north face to Srath na Creitheach. Its top is reached by descending the east ridge from the summit to the small saddle at 795m. Descend the chute, taking a dog-leg to the right where it joins another stone chute originating from higher up the face. At its foot it merges with the scree slope on the west side of the Putting Green, some 70m below the bealach.

The Traverse of Clach Glas and Bla Bheinn   Difficult ***

This is a superb expedition which should be compulsory. In thick mist, or if you suffer from dubious route-finding ability, the words of an early guide should be heeded: "Many strangers who tackle the two peaks in thick mist fail to carry out their programme". The turreted north ridge of Clach Glas is the mountain's finest feature and is best approached as for Bla Bheinn initially, but then head up into Choire a' Caise by any dry means. The twin Bealach Buttresses lie to the right of an easy scree chute; right again is another scree chute which marks the western end of the south flank of Sgurr nan Each. To gain the base of the ridge at the bealach at 630m, follow the chute to the left of the Bealach Buttresses, turning a wall of rock easily on the left. The bealach is not a pass, as the western side is Arch Gully. If this bealach has to be reached from the west, it can be gained by ascending to another bealach at 636m, further north between Sgurr nan Each and Garbh-bheinn. From there, traverse south across the western end of Sgurr nan Each for 350 metres. Alternatively, a more direct right-curving line can be taken starting some distance to the north of Arch Gully.

Keeping to the ridge, climb the exposed arete to a crest, then steeply descend leftwards by grooves to a full stop just short of a little col. A feature of this mountain is the seductive lines terminated by vertical drops, in this case turned by another groove on the left. Ahead the ridge broadens, so go up right and traverse slabs to reach a stone chute which ends at an exposed and narrow col. Ahead, a wall of about Mild Severe standard is the most sporting line, but an easier alternative is to take the narrow slanting gully inset into the wall a little further down to the right. This leads over some short pitches and arrives at a ledge. Climb directly up a fine steep wall with excellent holds. In 30m the angle relents and scrambling leads to easier ground. Continue up slabs and broken rocks to the summit of Clach Glas.

Traverse the airy summit and descend the south-east ridge, firstly down a crack in a slab, then by a narrow arete, The Imposter. At the bottom, a little overlap gives an exposed move to reach easy ground on a shattered horizontal crest. Follow this to its end, then descend a little gully leftwards for 15m and return along a ledge to the crest of the ridge. Move left (east) to the Loch Slapin side and descend a shallow gully and a rib to its south in an exposed position. Reach a ledge which leads right to a notch on the ridge. An awkward short tower out of the notch has good holds and leads to a traverse on the left, past the final pinnacle, and so to the small grassy bealach known as the Putting Green. It is possible to escape from there by descending steep scree on the east side of the ridge, but it is necessary to bear south-east or right at the base of the scree to avoid a steep gully.

From the Putting Green (695m), the complex north-east spur rises up to Bla Bheinn. This requires good route-finding. Follow an easy path on the left side of the ridge for 60m, which avoids the initial step, then continue easily up to a small col. Climb the short wall above on good holds. Traverse scree rightwards for about 60 metres, past a steep chimney to a narrow stone chute. Climb this to an enclosed *cul-de-sac* scree platform. Above and to the left lies the prominent Half-Crown Pinnacle, sometimes called The Horn.

From the platform, gain a narrow boulder-filled gully and climb it on perfect gabbro for 20m by its right wall, moving right on superb holds at the top. From the shoulder cross some big stones rightwards and descend slightly to enter the upper section of a large stone chute. Ascend this leftwards to a cairn at a saddle on the east ridge (795m), where the major difficulties cease. There are several other variations which can be taken onto the east ridge, from either side of the col behind Half-Crown Pinnacle. Turn right and follow the upper section of the east ridge to the summit of Bla Bheinn.

There are several descent options, as described above. Either partially retrace steps and descend the normal route on the east ridge, or descend Great Scree Gully from the dip between the two tops. Also possible is a descent of the south-east ridge from the south-west top. All these routes lead to Coire Uaigneich. A nice variation at the end of a hot day is to initially descend the south-east ridge, then to contour grass to the col above Fionna-choire. The lochan will give the over-heated a chance to cool off before rejoining the path into Coire Uaigneich.

Winter: III ***

Though not often in good conditions of consolidated neve, the usual being unconsolidated powder, the traverse in winter is a magnificent expedition which can be very time-consuming. Route-finding is the main difficulty and it is wise to be able to lead Grade IV. It is usual to traverse Clach Glas first, following the summer line and turning difficulties on the right. The slabs on the west face of Clach Glas can be very tricky, as can the descent from the summit under powder. Bla Bheinn is normally more technically straightforward, though the chimney-gully above the *cul-de-sac* scree platform can be awkward.

WINTER BUTTRESS   *(Map Ref 532 213)*

On the south-west side of Coire Uaigneich, below South Buttress, is a buttress which can be clearly seen from the bridge at the head of Loch Slapin. Under the right conditions, a 50m icefall forms to give two excellent routes.

Escape from Colditz   50m   III **   (1994)
This route takes the left-slanting gully left of the icefall, which may be transformed into a tunnel of ice with short, near vertical pitches.

Sailaway   50m   IV **   (1994)
Climb the icefall direct, *via* several vertical steps separated by terraces; ice-screw protection.

SOUTH BUTTRESS   *(Map Ref 529 215)*

This is easily approached *via* Great Scree Gully which lies between the two tops of Bla Bheinn. The crag lies in Coire Uaigneich, close under the south top. The most obvious feature of the buttress is a sweeping pillar of pale-coloured slabs on its left-hand side. To the south (left) of the main buttress is a deep gully, followed by a smaller slabby buttress, which is separated from a prominent conical tower on the extreme south by yet another scree-filled gully. The crag gives pleasant middle grade climbs on mostly sound rock that gets the morning sun.

The descent from the main buttress is by a diagonal ledge which starts about 30m up the slope above the top of the climbs, then slopes down across the north wall to join Great Scree Gully on the right.

1   Belinda   90m   Very Difficult   (1968)
This climb lies on the smaller buttress to the south of the main crag. Start centrally at an arrow.
1. 25m   Climb to a spike belay situated amidst blocks.

2. 30m   Climb up for 10m, then traverse right to cross an overlap and continue left to a ledge and chock belay.
3. 35m   Continue to a grassy terrace where an arrow on the right indicates a pleasant finish (crux).

The following climbs lie on the main crag:

2   Central Pillar   195m   Severe *   (1968)
This is the prominent light-coloured pillar on the left of the face. Start from the base or from a chimney on its right. Climb up the right-hand side of the pillar to belays (45m). Climb a steeper corner up a scoop (15m). Continue up the left edge and climb to an open scree ledge. Climb the corner above to gain the left edge of the pillar, then ascend the corner on the right of the wall and exit left at the top. Scramble to finish.

3   Birthday Groove   195m   Very Difficult **   (1968)
A good line which follows the deep groove to the right of Central Pillar. Climb the groove for 120m to a large grassy ledge, the terrace. Above lie two big corner chimney lines; climb directly to the top by the left-hand chimney.
Winter: IV,5   (1996)
Follow the summer line by good mixed climbing.

4   Virgo   195m   Difficult *   (1968)
About 5 metres right of Birthday Groove lies another groove line. Climb the groove all the way, finishing by the right-hand of the two corner-chimneys.
Winter: IV,5   (1995)
Excellent mixed climbing following the summer line.

5   Judas   195m   Severe   (1968)
Start 12 metres right of Virgo below a large but shallow slabby corner which is guarded by a bulge. Climb the crux bulge on the left, then follow the line of corners to the terrace. Follow a line of thin cracks up the great slab above, starting a few metres to the right of the chimney of Virgo, and finish by a small corner.

6   Rosie's Stash   195m   VS *   (1986)
A good line, probably easier if dry. Start to the left of Escalator. Climb cracks, then a narrow right-slanting ramp (above and parallel to Escalator), to a ledge. Move left and climb a bulge using a large block (4c). Continue up to the terrace, then climb the arete between Birthday Groove and Virgo, with a move right to avoid a bulge.

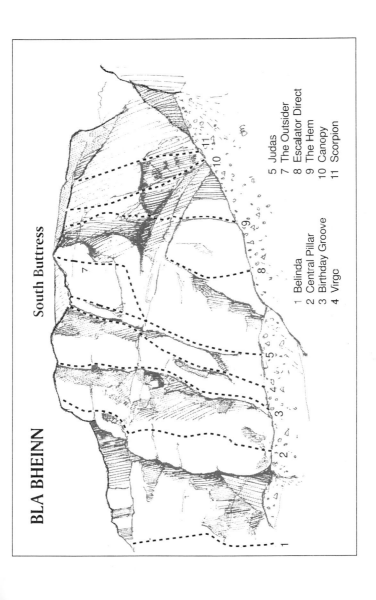

BLA BHEINN

South Buttress

1 Belinda
2 Central Pillar
3 Birthday Groove
4 Virgo
5 Judas
7 The Outsider
8 Escalator Direct
9 The Hem
10 Canopy
11 Scorpion

7   The Outsider   65m   Very Difficult **   (1968)
A superb and exhilarating route up the outside edge of the great slab.
Start from the terrace below the chimney of Virgo and go easily up right
to a steepening in the slab. Now follow a line of right-trending cracks
to a grass ledge and belay below a large flake. Climb a short scoop on
the left, then move diagonally up the slab to the top of the flake. Finish
up the arete above.

8   Escalator Direct   115m   Severe   (1968)
Start 10 metres right of Judas at a prominent groove. Follow a line of
grooves to finish at the terrace below the crux pitch of The Hem. Either
finish up this (4c), or by one of the easier routes to the left.

9   The Hem   180m   VS **   (1968)
A very good route with three difficult pitches. Start near the right edge
of the buttress and scramble up to the bifurcation of two groove lines.
Climb the steep left-hand groove to a ledge and belay. Above is another
groove, distinguished by a corner of white rock which is a prominent
landmark from the foot of the buttress. Climb the groove, then continue
more easily to a grass terrace, the right-descending continuation of
the terrace. Climb a bulge to enter a slab corner and follow this, keeping
left, until a short slab on the right leads to a small ledge below an
overhang. Climb the overhang, crux, to another slab, then follow this
up right until another bulge leads to the foot of a glacis (35m, 4c). Follow
the glacis to its end, move back left on a fault and climb up to belay in
a chimney on the right-hand side of a huge flake. Finish up the chimney
and the arete above.

10   Canopy   130m   Severe   (1968)
A good sustained climb. On the north wall of the buttress (facing Great
Scree Gully) is an obvious line of overhanging chimneys. Gain the foot
of the chimney line by a right-slanting groove and follow it, passing
several bulges to a grass ledge. Finally, follow further chimneys on the
left to the top.

11   Scorpion   110m   Severe   (1968)
This route follows another prominent crack line, starting from the the
foot of Canopy.

A face lies above the South Buttress and runs parallel to it. At the
right-hand side of the face is a short steep chimney.

Eventide   60m   Severe   (1983)
Start at a grassy bay below the chimney and about 15m above a large
cave. Climb a wall to the chimney, then go up this and the continuation
crack, which bears left to finish after a bulge.

SOUTH-EAST BUTTRESS

This is the broken crag that lies on the north side of Great Scree Gully.

South-East Buttress   Moderate   (1907)
"This is an indefinite route which lies over easy slabby rocks and up
trap dykes." Such a description should pose no difficulties to true Cuillin
aficionados, where acres of rock could be so described.

K Route   Very Difficult
To the right of the edge of the buttress is a left-slanting chimney line.
Climb the crack into the chimney and follow it to the left skyline.

NORTH-EAST WALL OF THE EAST RIDGE
(Map Ref 534 217)

This is the complex series of buttresses and gullies that lie to the
immediate right (north-east) of the east ridge of Bla Bheinn. It contains
the mountain's most famous feature, The Great Prow. The long east
ridge forms the crest of the crags which rise above the scree gully. The
most prominent features are the jutting buttress of The Great Prow
(740m) and Main Wall, which lies to the right below The Horn (Naismith's Half-Crown Pinnacle). The Horn rises above The Putting Green
col. The crags are riven by deep gullies and chimneys which are usually
wet. Facing north-east, the rocks can be slow to dry with the exception
of the south-east face of The Great Prow. The Great Prow route itself
dries quickly apart from the first pitch.
    All the routes on this face can be reached by following the path up
the Allt na Dunaiche, then struggling up the unpleasant scree slopes
towards the Putting Green at the bealach. A less arduous approach can
be made up the broken rocks of Clach Glas to the immediate right of
the scree, zigzaging up easy rocks. Another approach to The Great
Prow area is to ascend the east ridge and descend Scupper Gully.
    In descent, either follow the east ridge (original way), avoiding the
lower rocks (easily regained from the base of the crags by scrambling
up Scupper Gully or Access Gully), or descend the scree, or reverse

the line of ascent by the broken rocks of Clach Glas. If descending from the bealach (The Putting Green) by the scree, avoid the steep gully at the base of the scree on the Clach Glas side by trending south-east.

The routes are described from left to right.

1   C-D Buttress   Difficult   (1914)
This lies left of the east ridge proper between two prominent gullies, C Gully on the left and D Gully on the right. Climb centrally over glacier-worn rocks to a protruding belt of rock. Keep left up cracks and steep grass and climb a deep narrow chimney. Above, the route crosses the left fork of D Gully to the right and joins the east ridge at the second pinnacle.

2   The East Ridge   Moderate
This is the spur which runs up to the north top of Bla Bheinn. The only difficulties are the ascent of the lower pinnacle and the passage above which leads to the second. The lower pinnacle is most easily climbed by a fault which runs straight to its top.
Winter: II/III *
The lower chimney provides the key to the ridge.

3   Serious Picnic   240m   III   (1995)
This route takes the prominent right-rising ramp line low down on the north wall of the East Ridge of Bla Bheinn. It almost certainly takes the other two arms of the crucifix formation. The route is obvious from the point where the path leaves the Elgol road and it is above a lower ramp. To approach, ascend the snow slope leading up to the Prow area to the point where an easy gully leads up left to a notch on the East Ridge and an obvious pitch leads to the lower end of the ramp line. Easy ground leads to the foot of the pitch. Climb up left, then go back right on turf to gain the ramp line (40m). Climb this for several pitches to a col and continue past a short difficult step to the top.

Thrutcher's Groove   250m   III   (1996)
The precise relationship of this route to others in the area is not clear. Start at the foot of the slabby ramped south-east face below the north peak of Bla Bheinn. The gully system is left of centre on the face and right of the deeper diagonal gully (Serious Picnic). Move up easy ground to below a steep and very narrow chimney. Climb the chimney (crux), then head for well defined gullies higher up. When the first gully banks out, a short traverse leads right to another gully, and so to the top.

4   The Crucifix   200m   II   (1994)
This deep gully lies on the lower east face, well down from The Great
Prow. It runs up left to make a prominent cross with a transverse fault
line. Climb the gully over a short iced chockstone, then turn right into
the fault. The fault splits into three gullies on the upper face and the
route follows the right-hand one, gained by a very tight through-route
behind a chockstone. Two long easy pitches then lead to the top.

5   A1 Gully   300m   II   (1992)
From the tourist path at an altitude of about 400m, as it climbs steeply
left towards the upper corrie, a deep gully runs up right into the broad
cliffs at the base of the East Face. In fact this cleft cuts right through
the cliffs and from a col drops down into the Crucifix gullies on the true
East Face. On the first ascent, the cleft was well filled with snow and
it allowed a simple passage through its deep narrows up to the col.
Above the col on the left, a short fierce wall bars access to easier mixed
ground and the top of the buttress. This was climbed with a nut for aid,
but it almost certainly coincides with the hard part of Serious Picnic,
reached from the other side of the col.

6   Hawse Pipe Chimney   130m   VS   (1969)
This is the prominent chimney on the buttress left of and lower down
from The Great Prow, just left of Access Gully. There is a cave to the
right of its base and a series of caves and overhangs in the chimney
itself. Climb the chimney direct, belaying in the various caves *en route*,
and exit right of the chockstone.

7   Access Gully   100m   Moderate   (1969)
The base of this deeply-cut gully is a short way up scree. A chockstone
high up is a landmark and the gully gives a possible descent route
when dry, or a sporting way up when wet.

The next feature is the The Great Prow, a jutting rib of gabbro that
houses several classic climbs. The best descent is by Scupper Gully,
which lies to the west.

8   Sidewinder   110m   Severe *   (1968)
This good climb follows the left extremity of the big left wall of The Great
Prow, left of the big corner of Jib. Start at a short slabby groove in the
wall left of Jib which leads to a crack in its right wall.
1. 30m   Climb the crack and its right fork to a stance.
2. 15m   Continue up grooves to a ledge.

3. 35m   Continue in the same line for 20m, then follow a fault diagonally right to a pedestal.
4. 30m   Climb the wall to the top.

9   Jib   130m   E1 **   (1969)

This excellent route follows the big corner to the right of Sidewinder. After an intimidating start the climbing eases; protection should be placed at the earliest opportunity. Start 5 metres right of the true chimney-crack below an overhung gangway.
1. 40m 5b   Climb the left-trending gangway, then go up a steep wall to a ledge. Traverse left past the ledge into the main line.
2. 40m 4c   Climb the crack with continuous interest in a fine position.
3. 15m 4c   Climb the chimney above to a stance.
4. 35m 4b   Climb the fine groove on the right to the top.

Direct Chimney Start: E2 5b   (1977)

This rarely climbed variation is more often used as the first pitch of Stairway to Heaven. It may be wet and gives some thrutchy off-width climbing.

10   Stairway to Heaven   120m   E5 ***   (1977)

A great Skye classic, giving some impressive climbing. Start below the main chimney-crack, left of the normal start of Jib.
1. 30m 5b   Climb the groove and chimney through the Jib traverse, then traverse left to a niche.
2. 20m 4c   Follow the crack above to a further niche.
3. 30m 6a   Move up to a fault line and follow this leftwards until it is possible to climb the overhang by a short crack. Traverse right with difficulty to a narrow ledge, then climb diagonally up right to a short crack which leads to a stance and peg belay on a slanting gangway.
4. 40m 5b   Follow the crack, climb an overlap, then move up in a tremendous position to a flake-covered wall which leads to a ledge. Finish up the wall and move right to the top.

11   The Great Prow   105m   VS *   (1968)

Despite its classic status and great position, the climbing could be better. Beware of loose rock in places. Start below an overhanging chimney-corner.
1. 35m 4c   Climb the awkward crack to exit onto a slab, then climb the slab to a belay at its top.
2. 40m 4b   Continue up the crack above to a pedestal ledge.
3. 10m   Move back down from the pedestal, level with an orange slab, then follow a thin diagonal fault up the wall leftwards to the crest.

EAST FACE OF BLA BHEINN

The Great Prow

6 Hawse Pipe Chimney
7 Access Gully
8 Sidewinder
9 Jib
10 Stairway to Heaven
11 The Great Prow
SG Scupper Gully

4. 20m   Continue up a ramp until a crack on the right leads back to the crest and the summit.

Twilight Slab Variation: VS *   (1975)
From the cracks on pitch 2, below the orange slab, traverse left across the prominent slab on the front of the Prow; belay on the edge. Continue up and right to a large block, then go straight up to join the original line for the final pitch.

To the right of Scupper Gully is a narrow subsidiary prow, which gives a rather scrappy climb (Severe).

The next feature is Main Wall, which lies higher up the scree than The Great Prow and is clearly identified at its right end by The Horn. There are two prominent chimney-gullies at the top right end of the wall, just left of The Horn: Clough's Cleft on the left and Chock-a-Block Chimney on the right. The ramp below and left of Clough's Cleft is taken by Ecstasis.

12   Loss Leader   110m   VS *   (1969)
At the head of the screes and to the left of and lower than The Horn is a steep wall. Several diagonal faults lead up left; this route starts across the bottom gangway of the wall. Where the ledge narrows, move down to a lower gangway and go across onto a smooth wall. Gain the chimney which splits the wall from the bottom and ascend this to a central bay (shared with The Creep). Continue directly up the corner to a large ledge. Move 5m left after the exit from the corner and belay under the wall. Move right up the wall, then go up a gangway to a short steep wall. Climb this by a crack, go left on a basalt pavement to cracks on a steep wall, then climb the wall directly to a chimney and the top.

13   Creep   90m   Very Difficult   (1969)
This climb follows the middle of the three dykes to the recessed central bay, shared with Loss Leader. Exit diagonally leftwards across slabs and broken walls to the top.

14   Route One   110m   Hard Severe   (1968)
The climb follows the third dyke, and lies left of Clough's Cleft. Traverse up left to the dyke and large detached flakes. Continue along the fault, passing under a jammed square block, to a sentry box. Continue the traverse to the central bay. Climb the steep chimney above on the right to finish.

BLA BHEINN AND CLACH GLAS

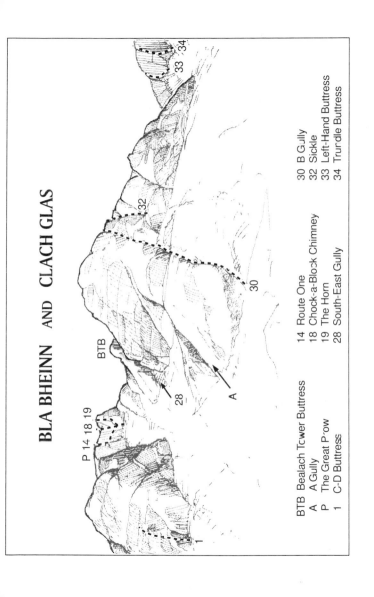

BTB Bealach Tower Buttress
A   A Gully
P   The Great Prow
1   C-D Buttress

14 Route One
18 Chock-a-Block Chimney
19 The Horn
28 South-East Gully

30 B Gully
32 Sickle
33 Left-Hand Buttress
34 Trurdle Buttress

15   Ecstasis   90m   HVS ***
Undoubtedly the route of the wall, similar to Botterill's Slab on Scafell and of the same quality. The second pitch is quite bold. The climb takes the topmost ramp that leads out of Clough's Cleft.
1. 25m 5a   Start up Clough's Cleft, then follow the slabby ramp pleasantly to a stance.
2. 40m 4c   Continue, easily at first, to a spike runner. Then climb poorly protected undercut slabs leftwards to a belay in the bay.
3. 25m 4b   Climb the slab rightwards and finish up a steep crack.

16   Bargain Offer   100m   E1   (1969)
Start near Route One, just left of Clough's Cleft.
1. 40m   From a slanting rake, climb the first crack break to the bottom of the chimney.
2. 20m   Climb the chimney to a good ledge.
3. 20m   Climb the wall above blocks.
4. 20m   Go up a steep wall right of an easy gangway exit.

The following two lines can be seen from the Elgol road at the apex of the scree, left of The Horn.

17   Clough's Cleft   105m   VS   (1968)
This is the left-hand of the two chimney lines left of The Horn. The grade varies in proportion to the amount of seepage, but it is very rarely dry.

18   Chock-a-Block Chimney   105m   Hard Severe   (1961)
The right-hand chimney gives another route whose grade varies directly in proportion to the moisture content. Climb the bed of the gully, breaking out right to below the first overhang (15m). Go up steep rocks right of the chimney proper, then traverse back into the chimney above the first overhang. Just above is a small cave topped by a greasy chockstone (crux), best climbed by back and foot. The boulder bed above recedes into the misty depths; far back, a cave leads to a subterranean chimney. Above the chimney, continue easily up the scree channel to the col.

The Pinnacle lies above the col. There are two short routes to its top; either direct from the col at Hard Severe or by the easiest route on the west face at Very Difficult.

Descending The Imposter just below the summit of Clach Glas

19   The Horn   120m   Severe   (1967)
This is the east face of Naismith's Half-Crown Pinnacle. Start at the toe of the buttress and climb beside Chock-a-Block Chimney for 30m. Traverse right across a steep wall, then continue up the right (north) side of the buttress. Turn the final band of overhangs on the right by a steep and exposed wall above the north face.

20   The Horn Direct   105m   HVS   (1968/77)
Start about 10 metres right of Chock-a-Block Chimney. Climb a rib and a short smooth groove, then move left to a ledge and belays. Climb the wall above and move right up slabs to a bay. Continue more easily by cracks, a corner and broken rocks to belay below the final belt of overhangs. Climb these in the centre, crux, to the top of the pinnacle.

NORTH FACE

This is a complex mass of broken rock which offers one recorded route, a good choice of ascent from the north-west side of the mountain.

21   Pinnacle Ridge   Moderate *   (1905)
This is the most prominent feature of the north face as seen from Loch an Athain. The lower 90m are quite steep and interesting but this is followed by scrambling. Higher up, it reforms into a narrow ridge again.

CLACH GLAS
786m   (Map Ref 535 222)

This is the superb pointed peak some 600 metres north-east of Bla Bheinn. It is possibly the Cuillin's most difficult peak, especially in winter, and despite it being little more than Moderate to reach the top, the almost alpine-like positions can make otherwise bold crag rats quake in their lycra. The mountain is geologically similar to Bla Bheinn, having dolerite sills interspersing the gabbro. As these are inclined to the north-west, there are numerous ledges eroded out on the east face.

The east face consists of broken rock crossed by grassy ledges and is split by two long gullies, A Gully on the left and (yes, you've guessed it) B Gully on the right. These can be identified from Torrin. The easiest way up the face is *via* Sid's Rake, which starts up left from A Gully, then slants right to finish at the top of B Gully near a tower, some distance north of the summit. The west face has more continuous rock and is

Crack of Zawn, Suidhe Biorach (Climber, Bill Kemball)

also cleft by gullies, the two most prominent of which lie on either side of the summit tower. The left-hand one, The Black Cleft, is unattractive and unclimbed and corresponds to B Gully on the east face. The right-hand one is Pilkington's Gully, the line taken by the first ascensionists in 1888. It is only a scramble and leads to the crest of the south ridge just below the summit. Pilkington's party were surprised by a "knife-edge of tremendous steepness" above them, but soon discovered that by crossing round to the right and pulling up a little gully, the 'knife-edge' is merely the arete formed by the edge of a modestly-angled slab. It is quite easy and has since been known as The Imposter.

WEST FACE

This overlooks Coire Dubh and is of fairly continuous rock, much of it slabby. It is split by gullies of which the two most conspicuous lie either side of the summit tower. The routes are described from left to right.

22 Arch Gully   Moderate   (1907)
Below the col between Garbh-bheinn and Clach Glas is a well pronounced deep gully. It has a big chockstone pitch halfway up, a natural arch and a few interesting pitches underneath all these obstacles.

23 Consolation Gully   Moderate   (1907)
This lies left of The Black Cleft; it contains three pitches.

24 Naismith's Route   Difficult *   (1896)
This is a good route on sound and clean rock. Start midway between the lowest rocks and Pilkington's Gully, bear up left towards The Black Cleft, then reach the summit ridge north of the summit.

25 Penelope   70m   Very Difficult   (1958)
To the south of the summit, a chimney cuts vertically through the upper rocks. It can be approached either from the ridge to the south or from Pilkington's Gully. Climb the chimney direct.

26 Penelope Right Wall   70m   Severe
Climb the right wall of the chimney.

It should be possible, given judicious route-finding, to select clean lines up the west face at around Very Difficult standard. Lines are conspicuous by their absence and much of the climbing is on smooth but sound gabbro.

EAST FACE

This lies above Choire a' Caise on the normal approach up the Allt na Dunaiche. The face presents a mass of steep broken rock mixed with grass ledges. The easiest approach is Sid's Rake, as described above. In winter the easiest lines on the face are likely to be around Grade II.

Left of the main mass of Clach Glas and right of The Putting Green lies Bealach Tower Buttress, which is separated from the main east face by a gully. The routes are described from left to right.

27   South-East Route   300m   Difficult   (1914)
The gully right of Bealach Tower Buttress is deeply-cut with a very steep north wall. This route tackles the steep wall, starting just below where the gully emerges on to the screes. Start just left of a deep black chimney and climb up past some grass patches. Now follow a face and a chimney to broken ground some 60m below and south of the summit cairn. A landmark at three-quarters height is a transverse slab.

28   South-East Gully   250m   II   (1994)
This is the gully between Bealach Tower Buttress and Clach Glas. It has one pitch at the top of the right-hand finish.

29   Central Buttress   600m   Difficult   (1915)
This is the discontinuous buttress between A and B gullies, starting anywhere between them and taking the line of choice. "It is likely no two parties will follow the same route on the lower section", to quote the original description. The ascent is by ledges connected by steep walls, "until the angle becomes too severe", where a ledge leads to a 20m chimney near A Gully. Above, the rocks are more broken.

30   B Gully   600m   Severe **   (1920)
This is the deep-cut gully right of A Gully. The initial section gives ten delightful short pitches, the penultimate being the crux. Above, the gully is unfortunately easy and it is best to gain the fine ridge on the right by a subsidiary grass gully. Climb the ridge, bypassing the prominent tower on the left, and reach the summit *via* slabs.
Winter: IV   (1991)
The gully requires the unfortunately uncommon conditions of heavy snowfall and a long freeze, and it is almost certainly harder under thin or powder conditions. Numerous short steps are interspersed by long easy sections. Short excursions out of the true line of the gully may be necessary at two points.

31   The Big Ramp   400m   II   (1995)
This route follows the big snaking ramp on the right-hand side of the face, and finishes 30 metres right of B Gully. From the top, follow a steep but simple snow line leftwards across the top of B Gully and go up ramps to finish at the summit cairn of Clach Glas. This avoids the Imposter, but it needs a good banking of snow.

PINNACLE BUTTRESS

This buttress is right of B Gully. There are several detached pinnacles near the exit of B Gully, most climbed by Naismith and Parker in 1896.

32   Sickle   85m   VS 4c **   (1968)
This fine route lies on the vertical north wall of the first pinnacle of the buttress. It is most easily gained by a slabby glacis that runs from the north and is gained by scrambling. A prominent chimney marks the start.
1. 30m   Climb the chimney to a belay.
2. 15m   The chimney continues above, but the route follows a tempting right-curving gangway to the foot of a steep corner.
3. 20m   Climb the corner with difficulty, then exit onto a ledge on the crest of the buttress below a steep wall.
4. 20m   Climb the wall on small holds at its exposed right edge to reach the summit of the tower. Continue up by easy climbing over another pinnacle, then scrambling leads to the summit ridge.

BEALACH BUTTRESSES   (Map Ref 534 226)

These quite attractive crags lie on the eastern side of the bealach between Clach Glas and Sgurr nan Each. They provide an interesting way of reaching the bealach from the east, prior to a traverse of the Clach Glas-Bla Bheinn ridge.

33   Left-Hand Buttress   135m   Very Difficult   (1968)
Climb pleasant slabs for 60m to a grass ledge below a bulge. Climb the bulge and continue to the top. There is an easier variation to the right.

34   Trundle Buttress   120m   Very Difficult *   (1968)
Start at the left edge of the right-hand buttress and follow the crest. Two steep steps give good climbing, but after 120m only scrambling remains.

ABHAINN NAN LEAC   (Map Ref 530 209)

Immediately south-west of the bealach of Fionna-choire which leads
to Camasunary, is a scrappy, slabby set of ribs. One route has been
done to the right of the ribs, on a fairly continuous mass of rock and
taking a central line (**Mistaken Identity**, 135m Difficult 1994). Winter
potential may be better.

COIRE NA SEILG

Coire na Seilg is enclosed between the north ridges of Garbh-bheinn
and Belig. A large cliff lies astride the north ridge of Garbh-bheinn, and
is probably best approached from the head of Loch Ainort by this ridge
to the col just beyond Pt 489m. Allow 1½ hours.

CREAG DRUIM EADAR DA CHOIRE
(Map Ref 528 242)

The crag is at approximately 500m, faces due north and takes two
days to dry completely. It often has better weather than the main areas
of the Cuillin due to its sheltered position. The cliff presents faces to
both east and north, the eastern being quicker drying. The crag is best
described to the left and right of a pronounced gully line which rises
centrally above a series of heathery rakes. Left of this gully the crag
has a steep wall at the bottom, above which is broken ground and more
walls which are bounded on the left by a fine rib. The lower wall has a
vertical central groove, a little edge on the left, and a pair of vertical
corners on the right. The rib falls steeply into a groove which forms a
slab below half-height.

Right of the gully, a splendid overlapped slab is split by three crack
lines and to their right a steep edge swings north, well seen from the
corrie floor. This vertical north wall gradually diminishes in height
towards the ridge and has two pronounced lines, both impressive, a
deep cracked groove and a shallower banana-shaped one to its right,
with a tapering buttress between. To the right again are vertical cracks
above vegetated ledges before the cliff becomes blocky and low near
the ridge. Some of the rock is blocky and high up on the east face there
are small sections of brittle rock. In descent, keep to the west towards
the north ridge of Garbh-bheinn, descend it to a col, then traverse the
scree slopes below the crag.

The routes are described from left to right, starting on the east face.

1   Far East Buttress   150m   Difficult   (1980)
Left of the recessed slab of Cubs' Corner is a long, easy-angled buttress which gives delightful climbing, taking the line of choice on excellent rock.

2   Cubs' Corner   60m   Severe   (1980)
Left of Skye Ride is the recessed slab. Climb this, then trend left and go up the blocky crack to finish up easy ground.

3   Skye Ride   100m   VS *   (1980)
This climb is worthwhile for the rib pitches.
1. 25m 4c   Climb the artificial, but fun, left-hand edge of the lower wall (cairn) direct to easy blocky ground and a block belay.
2. 25m   Continue to the base of the fine rib, well seen from below.
3. 25m 4c   Climb the rib direct, following a thin crack left of a drainage groove, crux, then pull over onto a slab below an overhanging corner with a tiny stance below it.
4. 10m 4c   Climb the corner on jams, then belay on the ledge above.
5. 15m 4b   Step up to another ledge with flakes and climb a straight crack to big ledges. Scramble another 20m up and right to finish.

4   Cunning Stunts   100m   E1 *   (1988)
A very varied first pitch makes this climb worth doing, though the line is artificial above. Start at the right-hand corner at the right end of the steep lower wall, cairn.
1. 40m 5b   Climb a slab to reach the corner, then traverse right along flakes to a grass patch. Climb a crack right of perched flakes to an overhanging corner. Surmount this using a hidden hold, crux, then exit into a groove. Climb the bold slab on the right in a fine position, trending up left to belays.
2. 25m   Climb pleasant rocks first right then left to belays below a cracked wall which lies right of the rib pitch of Skye Ride.
3. 35m 4b   Climb a gangway slanting left below the vertical crack. Trend up right, then traverse right for a few metres until a scoop can be climbed to a narrow ledge below a steep friable wall. Traverse right to a grassy groove to finish. Scrambling to the top, as for Skye Ride.

5   Seilg Gully   150m   Very Difficult   (1980)
This is the long broken gully that lies left of the big slab. Climb it direct, by interesting pitches, one or two being trickier than they appear.
Winter: III/IV
The gully gives four pitches, but needs a good freeze to come into condition.

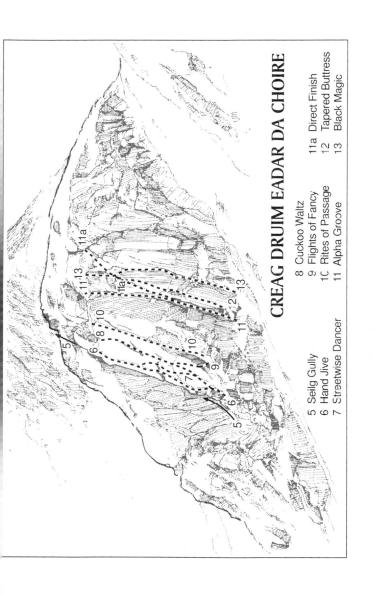

CREAG DRUIM EADAR DA CHOIRE

5 Seilg Gully
6 Hand Jive
7 Streetwise Dancer
8 Cuckoo Waltz
9 Flights of Fancy
1C Rites of Passage
11 Alpha Groove
11a Direct Finish
12 Tapered Buttress
13 Black Magic

The big slab to the right of Seilg Gully is the crag's finest feature. To reach the base, approach either up Seilg Gully then traverse right, or scramble up heathery shelves and rock steps to the same point. A grass ledge lies centrally beneath it and forms a convenient stance and belay for the next three routes.

6   Hand Jive   55m   VS **   (1981)
A good introduction to the crag, taking the left-hand crack.
1. 20m 4b   A lobed crack runs diagonally up left from the stance. Climb up to the lobe, step right onto the slab beneath it, then follow this trending left to a stance and belay overlooking Seilg Gully.
2. 35m 4c   Step right and follow the crack through the overhanging corner. Climb the crack beyond in a fine position to the top.

7   Streetwise Dancer   50m   HVS *   (1981)
Start at the same point as Hand Jive.
1. 25m 4c   Below the centre of the curved overlap is a niche; climb the steep slab directly below this, then follow a right-slanting crack until a line of holds trends up left before stepping back right into the niche itself. A bold, sparsely protected pitch on good rock.
2. 25m 5a   Climb up above the niche to gain the overlap on the right, then pull over this at its highest point, crux. Now trend left along little edges to join Hand Jive to finish. A well protected and nicely airy pitch.

8   Cuckoo Waltz   50m   E1 5b ***   (1980)
An excellent well protected line on excellent rock, which reveals the way only on close inspection. Start at the same point as Hand Jive. Climb Streetwise Dancer initially, aiming for the right end of the overlaps. The right-slanting crack then straightens out and breaks through the upper overlaps *via* a finger crack. Climb this (crux), then continue more easily to the top.

9   Flights of Fancy   50m   E2 5b   (1990)
A bolder start that joins the parent route where the right-trending crack straightens out. Start up and right on a higher ledge, as for Rites of Passage, and step left onto the bald slab. Surmount a little overhang, then trend up left to join the crack.

10   Rites of Passage   50m   E1 5b ***   (1990)
A splendid line that follows the cleaned cracks up the wall left of the bounding arete. After a fiddly start, protection improves with height. Scramble up heather and rock as for the other routes, but go further

right to a commodious ledge and belays. Climb up left to the corner, then follow a diagonal crack right to a thin move which gains the base of the main crack. Follow the crack in a great position to the top, where a step left onto a slab gives a fitting finish. It should be possible to take a belay in the little cave below the upper crack, otherwise the second has to move left from the belays to allow sufficient rope for the leader.

The last four routes all end on a balcony, from which there are easy ways off up grooves either side. At the back is a wall split by a hanging chimney. This chimney gives a 15m Severe pitch, a pleasant finish to the lines on the slab.

The North Face, to the right of the black arete, is very steep and is characterised by grooves and a banana-shaped corner. It is very slow to dry and could take a week or more. The climbing is completely different in character from the previous routes, being similar to that found in the Lake District.

11   Alpha Groove   60m   VS *   (1981)
A very good first pitch, in the classically strenuous style, provides the meat of the climb. Near the left end of the North Face is a very prominent groove.
1. 20m 4c   Climb the increasingly awkward groove to a tight exit onto a fine eyrie stance.
2. 20m 4c   The continuation groove to the right of the stance is usually wet, so step right to and climb a subsidiary groove. Move back left across the top of the main groove on wet underclings to belay below the upper wide grooves.
3. 20m   Continue to the top.
Direct Finish: 45m   HVS   (1981)
A much drier alternative to the top pitches.
2. 30m 5a   From the stance, step right into and climb the subsidiary groove to a steep and awkward crack which ends at a large stance below the top pitch of Black Magic.
3. 15m   Climb the cracks splitting the right wall. Finish by scrambling easily up a narrow gully with a bridged chockstone.

12   Tapered Buttress   60m   E1 **   (1981)
The fine tapered buttress between Alpha Groove and Black Magic. Start directly below the banana-shaped groove of Black Magic.
1. 30m 5b   Climb the steep buttress direct.
2. 30m 5b   Continue in the same line to the top.

13   Black Magic   75m   E2 **   (1990)
This route takes the obvious banana-shaped groove which is often wet.
An excellent middle pitch makes the route worthwhile. Small wires
protect where it matters.
1. 25m   Climb either the vegetated groove below the main line or the
Hanging Gardens by a line of choice further right. Either way gains a
meadow, a delightful oasis of wild flowers. Belay below the main
groove.
2. 30m 5c   Climb the groove, initially stepping left, then go back right
to a small ledge. Climb the steep and sustained groove in a fine position
to a precariously wedged block by a wet seep. Stand above the block
(without using it), then traverse left to a rib and crack (the top few moves
of Alpha Grooves Direct Finish) to avoid the very wet final few metres
up the groove. Belay on the large stance above.
3. 20m 5b   Finally, climb the artificial but increasingly difficult corner
direct. Numerous escapes are possible, but unsporting.

The Cioch, Skye

Skye Outwith The Cuillin

There is a lot of climbing on Skye away from the Cuillin and Red Hills. Many routes have been put up over recent years on the sea-cliffs in particular, and there are now plentiful alternatives for the climber when mist and rain shroud the Cuillin. Indeed, there are now over three hundred climbs in parts of Skye beyond the Cuillin, and developments continue.

The coastline of Skye is very convoluted, being more than 570 kilometres in length. Although the island has many spectacular sea-cliffs, some over 300m high near Duirinish Head for example, most of them consist of crumbly basalt which is too unreliable to give enjoyable climbing. Most of the best routes are on sills of better quality dolerite, which occur in the far north and west. The majority of the lines required prior cleaning to remove loose flakes and blocks. The resulting climbs are generally quite sound, but many of them have had few if any repeat ascents, so the rock and the grades should be treated with caution. Note also that the star system has only been partially implemented. Many routes not given stars may deserve them. Although the routes are rarely more than one rope length, they offer pleasant and varied climbing in some of the most delightful corners of the island.

The several peninsulas which offer climbing are now described, starting in the south and going clockwise around the island.

SLEAT

There are only crags of minor interest to the climber in Sleat. Short sea-cliffs of Torridonian sandstone on either side of Ob Gauscavaig near Tokavaig offer some bouldering opportunities. A number of routes of Severe and VS standard have also been done on a 16m high crag of metamorphic rock near Point of Sleat, just below a hillock of spot height 74m. These routes are only likely to be of interest to climbers reaching Skye by the Armadale Ferry. They are best tackled outwith the nesting season.

STRATHAIRD

Around the southern end of the Strathaird peninsula there are short sea-cliffs of Jurassic sandstone, which offer a rather different style of climbing to anywhere else on Skye. This is one of the driest parts of the island, and the rock dries quickly after rain.

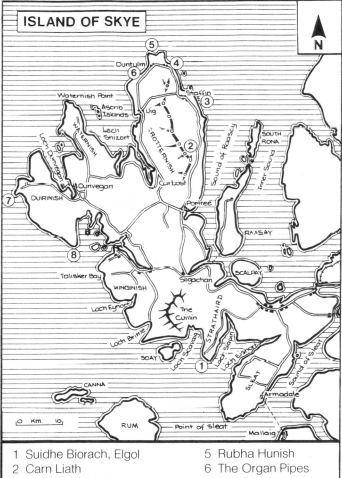

ISLAND OF SKYE

N

Duntulm
Staffin
Waternish Point
Ascrib Islands
Uig
Loch Snizort
TROTTERNISH
WATERNISH
Loch Dunvegan
Dunvegan
DUIRINISH
Curbost
Portree
Sound of Raasay
SOUTH RONA
Inner Sound
RAASAY
Talisker Bay
MINGINISH
Loch Eynort
Sligachan
The Cuillin
STRATHAIRD
SCALPAY
Loch Brittle
SOAY
Loch Scavaig
Loch Slapin
Loch Eishort
SLEAT
Sound of Sleat
Armadale
CANNA
Km.
RUM
Point of Sleat
Mallaig

1 Suidhe Biorach, Elgol
2 Carn Liath
3 Staffin and Kilt Rock
4 Flodigarry
5 Rubha Hunish
6 The Organ Pipes
7 Neist
8 Macleod's Maidens

To reach Strathaird, turn off the A850 at Broadford and follow the B8083 around the head of Loch Slapin and across to Elgol on the western side of the peninsula. Park in the ample carpark well above the shore, rather than at the Port na Cullaidh road end, which is used for turning.

SCHOOLHOUSE BUTTRESS

This crag is very accessible, being situated 100 metres north of the school at Elgol. It lies west of a longer line of crag behind the ruined house. Despite some suspect honeycombed rock lower down, the sandstone is generally sound, and gives good protection. The routes are described from left to right, starting on the north-west face.

Schoolhouse Rock   18m   VS 4c *   16.6.98. Led ī Simon   (1992)
There is an obvious slanting corner on the left-hand side of the north-western face. Climb up overhanging shelves to gain the corner, and follow this to exit left.

Wafer Wall   18m   VS 4b   16.6.98. Led ī Simon   (1992)
Climb the overhanging wafers right of Schoolhouse Rock to reach a short corner right of a slab. Climb up left and exit as for the previous route.

Apiary Arete   20m   Hard Severe   18.8.78 Led ī John M   (1994)
The vertical south-eastern face is split centrally by a crack high up. This route climbs the arete further left. Either climb the arete directly (VS 4c), or start further right and climb a flake crack before moving left to gain the arete (4b).

Schoolhouse Buttress   20m   VS 4c **   16.6.98. Led ī Simon   (1987)
The first and best route on the crag finishes up the central crack on the south-east face. Climb the lower wall, and step left to a flake. Follow this to gain the central crack which is climbed to the top.

The west-facing wall which runs behind the main buttress has two routes.

Bee Keeper's Bother   E1 5b **   18.8.98. Led ī John M.   (1994)
On the left of the crag is a prominent square-cut corner. Climb the arete to the left of this on large holds, and then swing round left onto a small ledge. Continue directly up the crux groove to the top.

'Orrible Crack   Mild Severe   (1994)
To the right of the square-cut corner is a large crack. Climb this
unpleasantly to the top.

SUIDHE BIORACH

There is good climbing on the coast about 1km south of Elgol. Most of
the routes are concentrated on a buttress named Suidhe Biorach
(sharp seat) on OS maps. It is approached by a faint path along the
cliff top. The rock is a quartz sandstone, and although the upper section
is rather lichenous, it gives well protected, strenuous climbing.

A few hundred metres before the point of Suidhe Biorach is reached,
there is a large sea-stack called Suidhe nan Eun *(seat of the birds)*.
With two 50m ropes tied together, it is possible to anchor both ends
on the mainland in such a way that the centre of the rope is draped
over the stack's grassy summit. An entertaining Tyrolean traverse can
then be made from either side to gain the summit. Good training for
Handa!

Just after this there is a prominent canyon formed by a landslip.
Some 200 metres beyond this is the flat rocky top of Suidhe Biorach
itself. Here a massive cracked block, shaped like India, juts out from
the cliff top. Immediately west of this is the obvious corner of Jamie
Jampot, which gives the most convenient abseil approach to the
routes. Just below the cliff top immediately to the west of this corner is
a sheltered, sun-kissed ledge known as Paradise Ledge.

The routes can also be reached by scrambling in from either end of
the crag at low tide. The western approach involves descending near
a cave and crossing a geo. The routes are described from left to right,
when facing the crag.

1   **Transept**   20m   E3 5c **   (1993)
This route climbs the bulging wall just right of the cave. Ascend to the
overhang and step rightwards across it. Climb directly up the wall
above, then move left across the top bulge to finish up easy slabs.

2   **The Fringe**   20m   E1 5b *   (1993)
Takes the narrow, right-facing groove-ramp to the right of the cave,
crossing a crucial bulge at half-height. Avoid the overhang at its
left-hand end. Finish easily up slabs.

3   The Golden Fleece   25m   E2 5b **   (1993)
Bridge up a left-facing overhanging corner to an overhang at 15m.
Surmount this and finish up a prominent right-facing corner.

4   Right Fright   25m   E2 5b   (1993)
Climb directly up into the hanging corner immediately right of the
previous route, and layback up it strenuously. Swing right at the top.
Finish less pleasantly by climbing a crack line up and rightwards to
finish on Paradise Ledge.

5   Hairy Beast   25m   E1 5b *   (1993)
Climb a crack line to a prominent roof. Swing through this (crux) to a
ledge. Step left and follow a lichenous crack line rightwards to finish
on Paradise Ledge as for the previous route.

6   Veritas Splendour   25m   E3 **   (1993)
At the right-hand end of the western wall there is an arete. A 10m
section at the bottom has fallen away leaving a left-curving crack
tucked under an overhang.
1. 12m 5c   Climb the crack and pull strenuously onto the left wall of
the arete. Move up and back right more easily to a belay.
2. 13m 5c   Climb directly up the arete with a hard move to finish. Belay
on Paradise Ledge.

7   Crack of Zawn   25m   E1 5b **   (1992)
This route climbs the intermittent crack line in the centre of the face
left of Jamie Jampot. Climb the initial crack line until it fades. Step left
(crux) to the base of the ramp. Move up and right to reach the upper
crack line and follow this to finish on Paradise Ledge.

8   Jamie Jampot   25m   VS 4c ***   (1992)
The prominent central corner gives a fine sustained route. Belay on
spikes and a thread well back from the top.

9   Digitalis   25m   E3 5c ***   (1993)
This climb takes the wall right of Jamie Jampot. Start on the left side
of the undercut arete and climb this boldly to the base of a short
hanging crack. Climb this, then move left to some suspect flakes.
Continue directly to the top passing a crucial one-finger pocket.

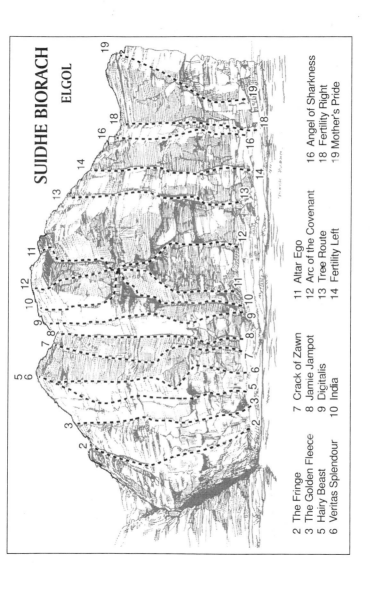

SUIDHE BIORACH
ELGOL

2 The Fringe
3 The Golden Fleece
5 Hairy Beast
6 Veritas Splendour

7 Crack of Zawn
8 Jamie Jampot
9 Digitalis
10 India

11 Altar Ego
12 Arc of the Covenant
13 Tree Route
14 Fertility Left

16 Angel of Sharkness
18 Fertility Right
19 Mother's Pride

10   India   30m   E3 ***   (1993)
This fine route starts up a prominent corner just right of the previous route. It is strenuous, but well protected. The lower pitch can be damp.
1. 5c   Climb the corner through the stepped roofs and gain an airy stance and belay across on the right.
2. 5c   Move back left along the lip of a roof to gain a short crack. Climb the overhang above and finish up the prominent jamming crack in a superb position.

11   Altar Ego   30m   E1 **   (1992)
This route starts immediately right of the corner of India, and finishes up the right-hand side of a big roof.
1. 5b   Climb the left side of a pillar on large holds. Continue up the blanker wall above (crux), moving right at the top to the stance on India.
2. 4b   Move up right into a corner and climb to the roof. Undercut rightwards in an exposed position and finish more easily up a deep cleft.

12   Arc of the Covenant   30m   E3 **   (1994)
This route forms a counter-diagonal to Altar Ego. Start some 5 metres right of that route beneath a curving roof.
1. 6a   Climb easily up a crack and through an overhang to a ledge below the roof. Fight leftwards under the roof and make a hard move to attain a standing position in the groove at the lip. Continue up this more easily to the stance on India.
2. 5c   Climb the groove left of the deep corner to the big roof. Undercut left to gain a small ledge on the arete. Swing round this and finish up a short crack.

13   Tree Route   30m   E2 5b **
Follows a steep crack line up the wall to the right of the big roof. There is a prominent left-facing corner a short distance further right. Climb the very steep crack to an overhang, then surmount this (crux) and continue past a small tree to the top.

14   Fertility Left   25m   VS 4c *   (1987)
Gain the prominent left-facing corner from the left and climb it directly.

The next three routes are on the left wall of another prominent left-facing corner a little further to the right.

15 Rum Doodle 25m E3 5c (1995)
On the left side of the wall the rock begins to overhang. Climb a short corner leading to an overhang. Use a pocket above this to reach right, then continue by cracks to the top.

16 Angel of Sharkness 25m E1 5b ** (1994)
This route follows a thin crack in the centre of the wall. Climb the crucial upper wall direct on good pockets.

17 Pick Pocket 25m HVS 5a * (1995)
Climb the right-hand side of the pockoted wall 3 metres to the right of the previous route, avoiding the corner.

18 Fertility Right 25m Severe ** (1987)
A pleasant climb taking the prominent left-facing corner at the right-hand end of the crag.

19 Mother's Pride 25m E4 *** (1994)
The main line gives outrageous climbing up the seriously overhanging prow at the right-hand end of the face.
1. 5c Climb the crack leading to a roof. Swing up through this to land on a ledge.
2a. 5c Climb the groove above the ledge. Swing right (crux) onto the face, then continue directly up the crack line on wilting arms.
Variation Finish: 5a
Swing left around the arete to gain the more reasonably angled wall and finish up this trending rightwards. This reduces the overall grade to E3.

East of the main crag is a cave-archway. Left of this is a crack leading to a corner which gives the line of the next route.

Green Green Green 25m HVS 4c (1995)
Climb the wall left of the crack, then follow the crack over a bulge to reach the corner. Climb the left edge of the corner and finish up the wall just right of the upper corner.

The next three routes climb the wall on the eastern side of the cave-archway.

Fault Finding   25m   E1 5a *   (1995)
Start below the overhang left of the obvious scoop. Climb up to an overlap and surmount this left of centre. Continue direct to the overhang and the first good runner. Step right and climb the scoop trending rightwards.

Plenty of Onomatopoeia   25m   HVS 4c   (1995)
This route climbs the rock between the previous route and the right-hand end of the wall. Surmount the low overhang at two flake holds, then take the line of least resistance.

Rusty Old Wire   25m   VS 4b   (1995)
Climb the corner which is right of the right edge.

Further east is a 15m high east-facing cliff. The right-facing corner is Very Difficult. The wall just right gives a poorly protected HVS 4c.

A minor road leads from Elgol to the eastern side of the peninsula. Here lies the small community of Glasnakille and its famous Spar Cave. The cave is well worth a visit with a head torch. It lies at the back of a deep cleft formed by an eroded basalt dyke, and is only accessible for a short time at low tide. Some climbing has also been done on the small calcareous sandstone cliffs along this stretch of coast.

MINGINISH

The straggly peninsula of Minginish is dominated by the magnificent Cuillin. The sea-cliff climbs here are only of minor interest.

EILEAN REAMHAR

The islet of Eilean Reamhar lies just over 1km south of the Coruisk Hut on the west side of Loch Scavaig. It is accessible at low tide. The following routes are on south-east facing gabbro sea-cliffs and are described from left to right as approached from the mainland. The first route is on a barrel-shaped buttress.

No Gain Without Pain   E2 6a   (1990)
Start centrally and follow a line of very small sharp holds. Go up to a corner, move left and follow a basalt intrusion leftwards through a bulge. Unprotected.

Slabsville   VS 4b   (1990)
This route takes a slab right of the previous route. Start at low tide 6m
from the right arete in a small corner with a square block. Climb the
slab on the left to a horizontal crack. Move left slightly, then go straight
up the white streak in the slab above, passing two pockets. Unprotected.

There are two Severes further right. The first climbs the slab and the
second goes up the right arete on a hanging ramp, then over a bulge
and roof to finish up the headwall centrally.

Half Crack   Hard Severe   (1990)
This route is on the east face of the crag, taking the top half of a
prominent crack. Start centrally and climb the wall on good holds to a
big ledge. Go up and left, then ascend the superb crack to a block.
Move left and follow the slab to the top.

The next crag is a 30m slab with overhangs at the bottom left and
top right.

Nettie   Difficult   (1990)
Climb the left edge of the slab.

Sealsville   VS 4c   (1990)
Start at a large spike at the bottom of the slabs. Go up to a V-notch.
Pull through this rightwards, then move left a few feet and follow the
left-hand of two thin cracks. Move leftwards to belay on a grass ledge
just below the top.

Short Spurt   E2 5b   (1990)
There is an obvious protruding block 10m up and just right of the
previous route. The route goes through the overhang to the right of
this. The rope can be flicked over the block as a runner. Bridge up a
short corner on the right and surmount the roof by a good hold on its
lip. Easier climbing leads to the top.

RUBH' AN DUNAIN

There are short routes on the basalt sea-cliffs around Rubh' an Dunain, the headland on the south side of Loch Brittle. They are approached from the camp site in Glen Brittle. The first cliffs, which overlook Loch Brittle, are reached after 3km. Numerous possibilities exist. Lengthy traverses can be strung together, their general seriousness varying with the state of the tide.

Several features of historic and archaeological interest can be found some 5km from the camp site around Loch na h-Airde. Further climbs can be found on sea-cliffs to the south-east of this loch, beneath the Dun marked on OS maps. The main feature here is a tower with clefts on either side. Only a selection of routes is described.

Chimney Route   12m   Difficult
Climb the largest chimney on the wall to the west of the tower.

Clovis Grooves   15m   Severe
The wall and groove line on the west side of the tower, starting directly through a bulge.

Overnight Sensation   12m   VS 4c
The crack line on the east side of the tower, finishing up a ramp.

Wild Thing   15m   HVS 5a
Climb the obvious left-facing corner on the main section of wall to the east of the tower. Move out onto the left wall at the top (crux).

Victoria   20m   E1 5c
The arete right of the previous route. Climb the groove to the overhangs. Traverse left along the break to finish up the vertical crack in the right wall of Wild Thing.

NA HURANAN

A minor road leads west from near Carbost to Talisker Bay. On the north side of this road is a long basalt escarpment called Na Huranan. Two routes are described, but many other lines have undoubtedly been done here. Both routes climb the west wall of the most solid-looking buttress in the middle of the escarpment.

Krishando   20m   VS 4c   (1995)
Climb the lower wall to a ledge below a flake. Ascend the flake until it is possible to step right onto the arete. Gain a second ledge and traverse out to the far arete which is followed to the top.

Freezer   20m   HVS 5b   (1995)
Climb the lower wall to a ledge below an overhanging crack, then climb the sustained crack over three bulges.

TALISKER POINT

There are two basalt sea-stacks at Talisker Point, which can be reached by a walk of just over 1½km from a carpark near Talisker Farm. They are situated on a platform which is easily accessible at low tide.

The Lesser Stack   20m   HVS 4c   (1993)
Climb the seaward ridge, moving right at the top to surmount a short steep wall. Finish along a rickety ridge. Descend by abseiling the south face, having first fixed a rope at the base of the north face.

The Greater Stack, called Stac an Fhucadair (*Fuller's Stack*), is characterised by a grassy north face. The original route (**The Corkscrew**, Very Difficult) spirals up leftwards from the south-west face and finishes up the north face. The following route is more direct, but finishes on unreliable rock.

West Ridge   40m   HVS 5a   (1971)
Scramble easily to the large platform. Climb the rib at the west end of the stack to below an undercut slab on the right. Go up the slab with difficulty to a ledge. Continue up a shallow corner to a stance on a terrace. Climb the edge above on very loose blocks to the level summit ridge. A large sling around the summit rubble enables the top pitch to be down-climbed. Then abseil down the south face from the terrace, peg belays permitting.

To the south of Talisker overlooking Sleadale, there are two crag-fringed summits called Preshal Beg and Preshal More. Their south-western faces are particularly impressive and might possibly repay a visit.

FISCAVAIG

The rambling crofting township of Fiscavaig is approached by road from Carbost *via* Portnalong. The following route girdles a north-east facing basalt cliff on the headland called Gob na h-Oa. Please respect the crofters' wishes by not climbing here on Sundays.

The Struan Face   150m   VS   (1971)
Drive to the road end (Map Ref 321 340). Start at the foot of the cliffs below the croft. Climb a black wall by a right-rising traverse to a large ledge (30m). Continue traversing to the end of the ledge (75m). Descend an awkward chimney a short distance, and traverse the wall to a second ledge (30m). Climb a steep crack to finish (15m).

DUIRINISH

There are many spectacular cliffs around the coast of Duirinish, but most are composed of unsound basalt. The best climbing is concentrated at Neist near Waterstein on the most westerly tip of the island.

MACLEOD'S MAIDENS

At the southern end of Duirinish by Idrigill Point lie three sea-stacks known as Macleod's Maidens, approached by turning off the road to Dunvegan. Cars can be taken as far as the north side of Loch Bharcasaig. A walk of 8km, much of it through forest plantations, then leads to the cliff top overlooking the stacks. An exciting abseil of 75m must be made on the south side of the headland to reach the shore.

The Old Lady   65m   VS 4b   (1959)
The largest of the stacks can be reached from the shore over boulders at low tide. Climb to a ledge on the left, then go up right to a grassy patch and belay (15m). Climb up left along a gangway to a groove, then continue to a terrace at the foot of a wall (20m). Climb the wall, passing a big flake, to a ledge. Traverse left and climb a crack continuing up to the shoulder (20m). Go along the ridge and climb a loose wall (crux) to the summit block (10m). Descend by abseil from the point where the ridge is first reached.

The two outer stacks, also known as The Daughters, are reached by a 50m swim from the fi stack. The Middle Maiden is the squattest

of the three and sits on a commodious platform. It can be climbed by
a variety of lines at about Very Difficult standard.

The Outer Maiden   30m   E2 5b   (1992)
This slender finger is climbed initially by a line of cracks up the arete
on the landward face. Move left to gain the prominent final corner.
Climb this steeply to a very loose finish and pull out right at the top.
Abseil down the seaward face from a huge sling around the summit.

WATERSTEIN HEAD

The district of Waterstein is reached *via* Glendale along the single-
track B884 which starts just south of Dunvegan. The striking arete of
Waterstein Head (296m) dominates Moonen Bay.

Waterstein Arete   300m   Hard Severe   (1980)
This is the longest basalt climb on the island. It is situated in a fine
position, but the rock is little better here than elsewhere. The arete lies
at an average angle of almost 50°. Approach by crossing the stream
which flows from Loch Mor, then contour southwards. Start from a
grassy terrace some 60m above the sea. Follow the arete easily for
60m to where the rock changes and the angle steepens. Climb 6m
direct and traverse a ledge line round on the left side of the arete. Trend
back right to the crest and climb a groove just right of this to gain two
successive difficult steps which are climbed exactly on the arete.
Continue more easily to a further steepening. Climb this starting on
the right and finishing either up a shallow groove in the centre or by
the left edge. The final steepening is the crux. Ascend until directly
beneath the very steep wall, then traverse right on an airy ledge until
it is possible to climb up into a scoop. Exit right from this and go up a
short crack to a ledge 5m from the top. Move slightly right and climb a
groove to the trig point.

NEIST

The road to Waterstein ends at a small car-park on the cliff top
overlooking the promontory of Neist. This is a delightful section of
coastline to visit and explore. The area is built of shales, but intruded
into the sedimentary strata are two parallel sills of dolerite, which form
crags totalling 4km in length. The lower crag rises directly from the sea
and is generally about 30m high, although in the vicinity of An

t-Aigeach it rears up to over 90m in height. The upper crag is also about 30m high, and it is set well back from the sea except at its south-east end where it merges with the lower sill near sea-level.

From the carpark a good path slants down through the upper crag by steps and continues around the impressive hump of An t-Aigeach to the lighthouse. A keeper has not been in residence there since 1989 when the lighthouse was automated. The redundant buildings are now let out on a self-catering basis to visitors.

There are climbs of all grades at Neist, and scope exists for plenty more. The rock is generally good, though not always so. Stakes are required for belays at the tops of many routes, and it is worth checking these out in advance.

THE UPPER CRAG

Although most of the early developments at Neist were on the lower tier, some fine pitches have been discovered on the upper crag in recent years. The routes are described from north to south. A flat stretch of moorland called Mointeach nan Tarbh extends northwards from the carpark towards Oisgill Bay. On the highest part of the cliff top, some 500 metres from the carpark, are the remains of a coast-guard lookout. A further 400 metres past this is a prominent lochan. Apart from the descent path to the lighthouse, the only easy way down through the upper crag is by a grassy gully 75 metres due north of the lochan. The first routes are best reached by descending this gully.

A prominent pinnacle is soon reached from the foot of the descent gully. This was the first route recorded at Neist. Two main variations are possible, but they both finish up the south edge.

The Green Lady   30m   Hard Severe   (1961)
South-West Start:
Either climb up the crest of the subsidiary arete, or squeeze strenuously up the 15m slit which separates it from the main pinnacle, and so reach a jammed chockstone. Traverse 4m right by a thin ledge, then climb straight up to gain lodgement on the south edge. Surmount a bulge on unexpected holds, and so reach the grassy summit.
South-East Start:
Climb a weakness in the south-east face and at half-height traverse left to reach the south edge. Finish as for the original route. There is no satisfactory abseil anchor, and descent is best arranged by fixing a rope at the base of the stack, and draping it over the summit.

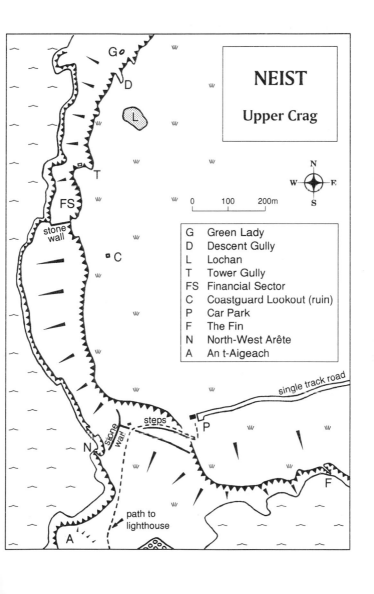

NEIST

Upper Crag

G	Green Lady
D	Descent Gully
L	Lochan
T	Tower Gully
FS	Financial Sector
C	Coastguard Lookout (ruin)
P	Car Park
F	The Fin
N	North-West Arête
A	An t-Aigeach

0   100   200m

stone wall

Stone wall

steps

single track road

path to lighthouse

South-west of The Green Lady there is a smaller pinnacle which gives a pleasant scramble. The next route lies on the crag behind The Green Lady, reached by turning right at the foot of the descent gully.

New Order   25m   E1 5c   (1981)
Start on top of a blocky pinnacle and climb a short wall to gain a crack in a groove. Follow this, move left to a slab and climb a thin crack in a bulge to a ledge. Finish up the wall or traverse right.

The next five routes are very close to each other and have a common finish. They lie on the very first section of crag reached by turning left at the bottom of the descent gully. Here a detached pinnacle on the left forms a wide crack line with a smooth, steep pillar. To the right of the pillar is a short clean-cut corner.

Seagulls   30m   VS 4c   (1983)
Climb the crack line to a ledge. Move round the edge onto a slab and climb this to a short groove on the right, which leads to the top.

The next three routes are on the smooth pillar.

Myopic   30m   E2 5c *   (1992)
Start just right of Seagulls and climb straight up the arete to a bulge. Go up the finger crack above, then continue up the arete finishing as for Seagulls.

Panorama   30m   E2 5c **   (1992)
Start as for the previous route, but move right onto the middle of the pillar as soon as possible. Go straight up to the top, finishing as for Seagulls.

Primeline   30m   E2 5b **   (1992)
Climb the right-hand arete of the pillar, finishing as for Seagulls.

Temptation   25m   E1 5b *   (1983)
Climb to a broad ledge to the right of the pillar. Follow the obvious corner to join Seagulls below the short groove.

The next three routes are also reached by turning left at the bottom of the descent gully.

Gruinard Mutant   35m   E1 5b *   (1992)
Start some 15 metres further right of the smooth pillar, just left of a vegetated chimney-crack. Climb cracks in an obvious slabby arete and finish up a prominent crack.

Monkey Hanger   30m   HVS 5a **   (1990)
This and the next route lie on a fine wall to the right of the vegetated chimney-crack. Follow a crack in a shallow corner in the middle of the wall to a dark recess. Pull out rightwards and climb straight up to a block belay on a big ledge. Abseil off rather than climb the dirty groove above.

Route With a View   35m   E3 6a ***   (1992)
Start about 5 metres right of the previous route, immediately right of a dark streak (often wet). Go straight up, moving slightly left at 8m, then step sharp right to good holds. Climb directly to an inverted-V slot. Gain this (crux) and pull through the roof rightwards. Finish straight up.

Some 250 metres north of the old lookout is a chossy gully called Tower Gully, overlooked on its south side by a prominent tower.

Blockbuster   25m   HVS 5b **   (1996)
This route climbs the tower by an obvious ragged crack line on the left-hand side of the face directly opposite the main cliff. Abseil from stakes down into the gap between the face and the tower, then continue down the loose gully on the seaward side. There is a good stance at the foot of the crack, with a peg belay high on the wall. Climb the obvious crack with a difficult move rightwards early on. There is a good ledge at half-height, where the difficulties ease slightly. Continue directly up the tower. There is some crumbly rock just below the top. Belay on top of the tower. Leap back onto the main cliff to finish.

FINANCIAL SECTOR

About 120 metres north-west of the ruined lookout, a stone wall runs from the base of the upper crag to the top of the lower crag. A short distance north of this wall there is a broad recess with a prominent dyke running through its northern half. The recess is a suntrap in the afternoon and evening. The routes here can be reached most conveniently by abseiling from iron stakes on the cliff top. They can also be reached by descending Tower Gully, then traversing southwards along scary sheep tracks. The first route climbs a prominent groove on the more northerly of two ribs situated in the centre of the recess.

Terminal Bonus   30m   HVS 5b **   (1996)
Climb a short wall and trend left up the slab above. Step left onto a
juniper bush and move back right to the foot of a steep groove. Climb
the groove and gain the slab above with difficulty (crux). Move up and
left to enter the delectable groove, then follow it to the top.

The next two routes lie on the more southerly of the two central ribs.
There is a heather terrace up and right from its foot.

Insider Dealing   30m   HVS 5a **   (1995)
This route finishes up a prominent groove on the left-hand side of the
rib crest. Start by ascending the left side of a small alcove. Continue
up and right to a slight recess. Pull over a bulge, then step up left onto
a slab ramp. A short distance above move hard right to gain the main
groove-crack line. Climb this past a roof at half-height. Finish more
easily.

Shocks and Stares   25m   VS 4b ** *17.7.01, E Simon* (1995)
Start on the right-hand side of the rib and bridge up by boulders until
it is possible to step left onto the buttress proper. Continue leftwards
to gain a prominent crack splitting the crest of the rib. Climb the crack
which widens and becomes harder to protect as height is gained.

Bridging Interest   30m   E1 5b*** *17.7.01 E Simon L* (1996)
This route is up a prominent groove on the left side of a buttress a little
to the south of the previous rib, and north of a pinnacle close in at the
foot of the face. Make some difficult moves to get established on the
wall at the start, then climb the surprisingly sustained and thought-
provoking groove.

Security Risk   30m   E1 5a/b ***   (1996)
A delightful climb up the crest of the buttress immediately right of the
previous route, with scant protection once the main difficulties begin.
Start on the right-hand side of a steep section of the wall. Protection
can be arranged in a groove further right. Climb up leftwards to a good
side hold and pull straight up to better holds. Step left to an obvious
crack-flake line trending up left. Continue up on good holds at first until
the rock steepens slightly. Move right at one stage, then go back left.
Place protection under a giant flake on the left-hand side of the crest
before making some exciting moves up on chicken heads. Continue to
a big ledge and finish more easily.

Powerbroker   30m   E1 5b ***   (1996)
This route requires a couple of days to dry after heavy rain. Start as
for the previous route, but where it moves left continue straight up.
When the rock steepens make some hard moves to get established in
the left-hand bifurcation of a crack. Ascend this until forced to step left
onto the wall. Make some awkward moves up the wall before returning
to the crack and following this with further interest to the top.

Venture Capital   30m   E1 5b ***   (1995)
Towards the southern end of the recess there is a pinnacle close in at
the foot of the face. This route climbs an obvious cracked weakness
immediately right of the pinnacle. Start just left of the prominent crack
and climb small ledges until it is possible to move right to the crack.
Climb the crack past a jammed block and a rock spike until the wall
steepens slightly. Make some hard moves to reach a good foot ledge
on the left. Step right and climb steeply to a small roof. Pull around this
strenuously and finish on better holds.

A Fist Full of Dollarite   25m   E1 5b *   (1996)
This route follows an obvious right-facing corner a short distance right
of the previous route. Climb pleasantly to a large ledge and continue
directly to the top of a big flake. Jam precariously up the corner to a
ledge, place protection in the groove on the right, then continue with
difficulty until it is possible to back and foot across a chimney. Finish
more securely up the chimney.

A prominent stone wall abuts against a projecting section of crag,
where the next three routes are found. The easiest approach is to
descend the steps from the carpark, turn right at the first stone wall
and head northwards along sheep tracks for about 600 metres. Cross
the lower end of the second stone wall before heading up to the crag,
thereby avoiding the worst of the huge boulders below the face.
Alternatively abseil from the cliff top into the broad recess to the north
as for the previous routes.

Wall Street   30m   E2 5c ***   (1995)
A short distance north of the stone wall there is a recessed wall capped
by a roof, with a pinnacle leaning against the face a little further left.
Climb the cracked wall left of centre until forced to trend rightwards.
Reach a ledge where the wall steepens and the main difficulties begin.
Continue by a crack and somewhat friable excrescences on the wall

to its left. Make a hard move to gain a foot ledge. Climb to just below the roof, then step left across a slab to a right-facing corner. Swing out left to pass the roof and continue very strenuously to the top.

Wish You Were Here   30m   E1 5b ***   (1990)
A short distance south of the stone wall there is a shallow recess set into the steep face high up. This route climbs a striking crack forming the right-hand side of the recess, turning a roof at the top on the right. Start at a shallow sentry-box.

Brass Monkeys   35m   E1 *   (1990)
Immediately right of the previous route there is a deep chimney before the crag turns a corner.
1. 25m 5b   Bridge up the outside of the chimney until moves on the right wall allow a ledge to be gained. Step left across the void to a smaller ledge and climb straight up to a small slab. Follow the rounded hanging crack to a big ledge on top of a pillar.
2. 10m 5a   Move right and follow a groove with a big spike to beneath a roof. Move left and finish rightwards.

The crag now turns a corner. On the south face which rises uphill, there are four prominent cracks.

Gritstone Reminiscence   25m   HVS 5a *   (1990)
Climb the rightmost crack with a block in it. After about 15m move left and follow a continuation crack in an interesting position to the top. Finish up a short wall.

Nothing Special   15m   HVS 4c   (1990)
There is a slabby tier of rock a short distance further right. Climb the slab centrally *via* a thin crack. Trend left below a small bulge at the top. Finish on a heather terrace well below the cliff top.

There are several routes on the more scrappy section of upper crag between the lookout and the carpark. They are hard to locate, because they lack conspicuous features, and a fence referred to in some of the original descriptions no longer exists. The first route lies about 240 metres north of the stone wall at the bottom of the descent path from the car-park and a short distance north of a small south-facing headland on the lower crag.

First ascent of Two Step, Neist Point (Climber, Mike Geddes)

Temgesic   15m   E1 5b   (1989)
This route climbs the left-hand side of a small north-west facing slab
with left-slanting ribs at its base. It lies about 35 metres north of a lone
iron fence post. Climb to a V-notch and pull over using the left edge,
then move sharp right to a small foot ledge. Go back left using the flake
in the middle of the wall to a hole and horizontal slot. Move up the crack,
then hand traverse left. Climb the wall and arete to finish on rounded
holds. The crack on the right of the slab is **Pumper** (Very Difficult).

The best reference point for the next two routes is a distinctive rock
spike with several horizontal bands at its top, which forms part of the
lower left wall of a buttress. It is situated about 170 metres north of the
descent path, and about 35 metres south of the lone iron fence post.

Flake Route   25m   HVS 5a   (1989)
Start at a detached flake about 6 metres left of the rock spike. Move
up to a corner crack, then climb it and the wall above. Finish up the
obvious crack in the right wall.

Karen   25m   VS 4c *   (1989)
Start at the distinctive rock spike. Climb the slab on the right to a loose
block under the overhang. Move rightwards, then make a few moves
up a gully until it is possible to pull onto the slab above the roof.

Abrakebabra   25m   E1 5a   (1989)
This route lies about 130 metres north of the descent path. Follow a
black groove, then go rightwards along a heathery terrace to a spike.
Move left from the spike across a black slabby wall to a loose block in
a layback crack. Go up slightly, then follow a line of pockets to better
holds. Climb to a corner under a small bulge. Turn this on the left and
follow the crack in the steep headwall above.

Hanging Groove   25m   VS 4c   (1989)
Start just right of the previous route. Climb through the break on a
slabby wall, then go right and finish up the corner crack.

Bost   40m   Severe   (1989)
This route climbs an arete formed where the crag changes direction
about 100 metres north of the descent path. Finish by a corner crack.

The Blade, Carn Liath (Climbers, Andrew Holden and Mark Hudson)

The remaining routes on the upper crag are situated south of the carpark. The first two routes are approached by going only part way down the path from the carpark and then ducking under the railing and heading hard left. Cross a stone wall, and continue along the crag to a faint rib marked by a triangular roof just left of the crest at one-third height. This gives a pleasant route, all the better for being so accessible.

Baywatch   25m   Hard Severe 4b *   (1994)
Climb a groove in the crest of the rib, and at the top step right to a ledge. Move up to a steeper groove above. Either climb this groove directly, or avoid it by a short hand traverse left. Continue with further interest to the top.

Sonamara   25m   VS 4c *   (1995)
A little further right there is a more prominent rib with a recess on its right-hand side. Climb an obvious groove on the left side of the rib. A worthy companion.

East-south-east of the carpark, where the base of the upper crag meets the sea, a narrow rock ridge known as The Fin forms the south-west wall of an oppressive chasm (Map Ref 136 476). Approach by slanting downhill from the carpark.

Heavenley's Pleasure   45m   E5 6b ***   (1992)
This superb route climbs a crack on the south-west face of The Fin. Harder for those of short stature.

The next three routes are on the north-east wall of the chasm opposite The Fin. Stakes are required for abseiling into the chasm and for belaying at the top of the routes. These may not be in place.

California Dreaming   35m   E1 5b **   (1981)
Climb a prominent crack line towards the back of the chasm, which can quite often be wet.

Breakfast in America   40m   E3 6a **   (1981)
A steep open groove lies 10 metres right of the previous route. Climb easily to below the groove, then follow a very thin crack in its right wall to reach ledges. Ascend a short easy corner to the top.

Sheep Tick   40m   HVS 5a   (1992)
A short distance further right is a chimney-corner crack in the back of
a groove. Start 10m up from the base of the wall on a big ledge. Climb
the groove to a big ledge and finish up the layback crack above.

No routes have yet been recorded on the remainder of the wall which
extends for some distance to the right.

THE LOWER CRAG

All the routes on the lower crag are approached by descending the
steps from the carpark. They are described starting from the north. The
majority of routes start at sea-level and so are affected by tides. To
reach the first group of routes, turn right at the end of the stone wall,
and head north along the cliff top. Some 60 metres beyond the end of
the stone wall a narrow gully cuts down through the crag in a north-
westerly direction. Scramble carefully down the gully. The first three
routes lie on the right wall of the gully.

Patricia   17m   HVS 5a *   (1987)
Start a short distance after the steep section of the descent gully. Climb
the slightly overhanging wall on mantels and make awkward moves to
gain a grooved pod. Climb twin cracks to reach the top.

Warmer Cleaner Better   17m   E3 6a **   (1994)
Just left of Patricia is a crack starting at a niche. Climb the crack.

Bernard's Dilemma   17m   E1 5a   (1987)
Start just left of the previous route at the bottom of the descent gully.
Climb the obvious overhanging crack to reach the dubious flake (poorly
protected). Further awkward moves lead to easier ground.

Turn right at the bottom of the descent gully and walk north for about
50 metres to reach the next route.

Sore Phalanges   18m   E2 5c ***   (1990)
The route lies on a thinly-cracked slab. Climb the slab centrally, moving
left at half-height to place protection in a niche.

There is a Difficult chimney immediately right of the slab. The next
route is reached by turning left at the bottom of the descent gully.

Smeg   17m   VS 4c ✓ *ɛ̄ Coᵧↄ Ǥᵤₜₕᵢᵢᵢ .   ৴*   (1990)
On the first section of wall a rockfall has left an obvious recess. Climb to a ledge and follow the right-hand corner of the recess by a sharp-edged crack.

The obvious narrow ridge opposite the end of the stone wall by the descent path has been ascended (**North-West Arete**, Hard Severe). The crux is towards the top where the rock is slightly suspect. There is a small zawn directly below the end of the stone wall, to the north of North-West Arete, which gives the following rather devious route. Scope exists for more direct lines here.

Gene Therapy   45m   E3   (1996)
Approach at low tide by scrambling down steep grass in a southerly direction, starting a short distance north of the stone wall.
1. 30m 5c   Start 3 metres right of a huge chimney below a large block ledge at about 15m. Climb to the block, veering slightly right then left. Hand traverse left to a groove, then step down and stretch left to attain an exposed bridge above the chimney. Make a commiting layback to a jug, then step left to belay on a glacis.
2. 15m 5a   Climb the groove above trending left to the arete and finish up this. There is no obvious belay at the top.

Just to the south of North-West Arete there is a south-west facing section of crag. This has been climbed centrally by a right-trending line, but the route finished on very loose shale. The remaining routes on the lower crag all lie on the headland of Neist itself.

AN T-AIGEACH

The impressive hump of An t-Aigeach (*the stallion*) is clearly seen from the descent path. It forms the highest section of crag at Neist. Access with dry feet from the north-east is only possible when low spring tides coincide with calm seas. Abseil or scramble round into the obvious bay and cross two inlets to reach a large platform at the foot of the face. Otherwise make an exciting 90m abseil down the line of Supercharger from the cliff edge at the highest point of the headland. Fix a rope well back for a belay.

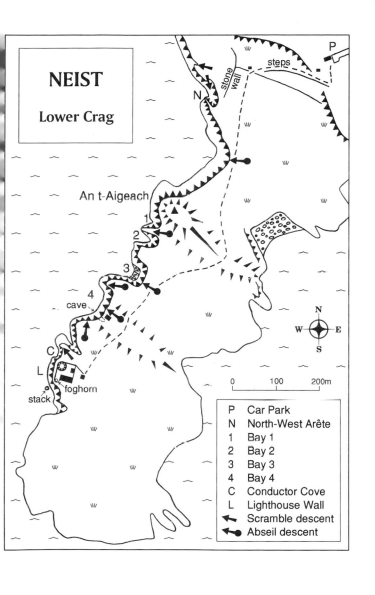

Joint Experience   105m   Severe   (1984)
This route climbs the rather vegetated northern face of An t-Aigeach.
Start about 15 metres left of the platform at the foot of Supercharger
and follow an obvious line of grooves and ramps which slant up left
across the face.

Death Pirate   85m   E6   (1987)
A serious route, with a controversial history, which starts part way up
the face and climbs the spectacular arete left of Supercharger. A lower
pitch up a chimney has been partially cleaned but not climbed. Gain a
belay at the foot of the arete by abseiling from the cliff top.
1. 6b   Climb thin cracks until it is possible to move onto a thankgod
hold on the arete. Move boldly back left to gain a ledge. Ascend the
short wall above until a belay is reached at the base of an overhung
corner. A poorly protected pitch.
2. 6b   Climb the corner, then the arete itself, to a ledge and belay at
the top.
3. 5b   Finish more easily up rock and grass.

Supercharger   110m   E2 **   (1981)
This classic route takes an impressive line up the centre of the cliff at
its highest point. The rock is rathe• suspect in places. The large platform
at the foot of the route is above high tide level. Start at the top left-hand
end of the platform below a crack.
1. 25m 5b   Climb the crack and short groove above. Pull over a small
roof, and continue up the groove above. Climb a short corner to a
stance and peg belays on the left.
2. 25m 5a   Move up left onto a ledge, then move right to a steep
corner. Ascend this and pull out at the top into an easy groove on the
right. Follow the groove and traverse right to a large stance.
3. 35m 5c   Ascend a steep crack to gain a flake line line leading up
left to a corner below a big stepped roof. From the top of the flake make
a fingery move out right onto the face. Climb right and up, with little
protection, to the right-hand end of the big roof. Follow cracks up the
overhanging wall, swing past the roof and pull strenuously into the
leaning groove on the left. Continue to an airy stance on the left.
4. 25m 5a   From the left side of the ledge climb an awkward crack to
easier climbing up a broken arete and grass which leads to the summit
of An t-Aigeach.

Perfectly   105m   E5   (1995)
Start 10 metres right of Supercharger at a groove.
1. 15m 5b   Climb into the groove and follow it to a ledge and belay.
2. 30m 5c   Continue directly to the roof and surmount this *via* a projecting fang. Finish up a crack to the Supercharger stance.
3. 35m 6a   Climb the wall 6 metres right of Supercharger, taking care with hollow flakes, to gain an obvious short groove. Climb this, crux, then step left and continue to the next Supercharger stance.
4. 25m 5a   Finish up the top pitch of Supercharger.

The remaining coastline from An t-Aigeach to the lighthouse is divided into a number of small bays, which are reached by following the path around the back of An t-Aigeach. The bays are now described from north to south. The south-western side of An t-Aigeach is marked by a prominent ridge which ends in a 'see-through' crack and pillar. The first two bays lie either side of this ridge. They are reached by abseiling down the ridge from stakes, then making a further abseil down the flank of the ridge to ledges which are free of water at low tide. It is also possible to traverse in from the north-east at very low tide.

BAY 1

This is a tiny bay just south-west of the Supercharger platform. Both routes lie on the north-eastern flank of the prominent ridge.

Cool Breeze   35m   E4 6a ***   (1983)
Climb the obvious corner to the left of the pillar.

Hot Blast   35m   E3 5c ***   (1983)
Climb the obvious 'see-through' hand crack at the right-hand end of the ridge.

BAY 2

The next four routes lie on the south-western side of the ridge, which forms the north-east side of Bay 2.

Freeze Dried   35m   E2 5c **   (1983)
Climb the obvious crack and flared chimney formed where the pillar abuts the ridge, on the opposite side from Hot Blast.

Cold Comfort Corner   35m   E1 5b   (1982)
About 10 metres right of the pillar is an obvious corner with a large
overhang at 15m. Climb the corner to the overhang. Traverse right a
short distance and pull up into another corner crack. Follow this to the
top.

Golden Mile   30m   E3 5c **   (1988)
This route climbs a fine arete of golden rock immediately left of the
prominent V-groove taken by the next route. Start up a crack a short
distance left of the arete. Climb the crack to a ledge and continue
steeply up a groove until the arete can be gained. Follow the arete and
thin cracks on its left to the top.

Frigid Air   30m   E1 5b   (1982)
Start some 15 metres right of the pillar at a prominent V-groove. Climb
this passing an awkward small overhang at 15m.

BAY 3

The third bay has a distinctive square-cut shape and is backed by a
boulder beach. The routes are reached by a straightforward abseil off
stakes at low to medium tide. The first three routes lie on the headland
between Bays 2 and 3. Scramble round from the north-east side of the
bay at low tide.

Two Step   35m   Hard Severe 4b *   (1977)
Climb the prominent left-trending slabby ramp line furthest round from
Bay 3. There are two short steep sections, the first being the crux.
Finish up steep rock on good holds.

Sunken Howker   25m   E2 5c **   (1995)
Start right of the previous route and climb to a bulge below a crack.
Ascend the crack and the continuing corner crack.

Agfa   30m   HVS 5b *   (1994)
Start near the right-hand end of the headland below a left-facing corner
crack. Climb the corner crack, then step left and climb the right-slanting
crack to the top.

The next few routes are on the wall on the north-east side of Bay 3.

Trilobite Groove   20m   HVS 5a   (1993)
Start on a high ledge at the left-hand end of the face. Climb the
left-facing corner, step left before it finishes and climb a groove just
right of the arete. Finish up a crack.

The Ratagan Strangler   25m   VS 4c   (1993)
Start down and right from the previous route. Go up easy cracks to
reach the right side of a ledge of loose stones. Finish up the short
corner crack just right of Trilobite Groove.

Tinderbox   30m   HVS 5a *   (1992)
Climb the face right of the previous route to gain a crack which finishes
up steep rock left of a square nose.

Side Step   30m   VS 4c **   (1977)
Climb faint grooves trending slightly leftwards to reach the right-hand
end of the square nose. Continue up the right side of the nose, or
traverse left below it to finish more strenuously as for Tinderbox.

Luscious   30m   Hard Severe 4b *   (1992)
Climb the obvious left-facing corner crack just right of Side Step.

Disturbing the Wildlife   30m   HVS 5a *   (1992)
The wide crack further right. Either start directly up the chimney or
move up right from the start of Luscious. The crack leads to a slab,
then a short wall.

Solar Furnace   30m   VS 4b *   (1992)
Start up a shallow corner right of the previous route. Step left and
continue up cracks to the slab and short wall.

Tourist Attraction   25m   HVS 5a **   (1994)
Start just right of the previous route. Climb the crack on the left side of
the clean pillar which trends right to finish at the top of the pillar.

Cameras Clicking   25m   Severe   (1994)
The shallow chimney on the right side of the clean pillar.

Camera Obscura   25m   VS 4c   (1995)
Climb the corner crack 6 metres right of the previous route towards the
right-hand end of the wall.

The next routes lie on the steep wall forming the south-west side of
Bay 3.

Ice Diamond   35m   E1 5b   (1981)
This route takes the most prominent crack line on the left side of the
wall, avoiding the lower part which is often wet. Climb a short wall and
a rib to the left of the crack for 12m, then step right and follow the crack
to the top.

Wind and Wuthering   35m   HVS 5a **   (1981)
Start up the less prominent crack 7 metres right of the previous route
and pass a large wedged block to reach a ledge on the right. Follow
the groove and crack line above to an easier finishing crack.

Cold Turkey   35m   HVS 5a **   (1981)
Start 6 metres right of the previous route from a platform at a slightly
higher level. Climb a chimney-crack to a ledge, then continue up
jamming cracks to finish up an open left-facing corner.

An E4 has also been reported on this wall, but it could not be located
from its description.
The next four routes are on the headland between Bays 3 and 4.
Approach either by abseiling into Bay 3 and scrambling round to a
platform at low tide, or by abseiling off blocks at the south-western
corner of the headland.

The Murray Mint   25m   E3 6a *   (1983)
On the left-hand side of the headland, just right of a corner and left of
an arete, is a thin crack which widens higher up. Climb a thin crack in
the wall to ledges. Move up to gain the thin crack, and continue up this
as it widens to the top.

Grooveless Bodily Harm   35m   E4 6a ***   (1983)
This strenuous route takes the left-hand of two obvious groove lines
in the centre of the headland. Start right of the arete. Climb boldly up
the groove and continue through a stepped bulge. Ascend the wall by
a shallow groove and crack, then move up right to finish.

The Cruiser   25m   E1 5b   (1989)
This climb takes the right-hand crack-groove line. From the initial crack
gain a right-slanting groove which leads to a wider crack and the top.

Fisherman's Friend   25m   HVS 5a/b   (1983)
Climb the obvious stepped corner system more or less in the arete
where the headland turns a corner into Bay 4.

BAY 4

There is a small white building on the highest point of the cliff above
the back of this broad bay. The first route is on the north-east of the bay.

Neist an' Easy   20m   E1 5a *   (1988)
This route lies between the left arete and a large chimney-rift on the
right. From the start of Fisherman's Friend traverse an easy shelf
rightwards to a corner. The corner below the shelf is climbable, but is
only accessible at low tide. Climb the distinct corner groove and
continue directly up the wall by a groove and cracks. An easier variation
(VS 4c) moves right above the corner to gain the top of a pedestal,
then moves back left to finish.

The next route lies on the back wall of the bay, to the right of the
large chimney-rift mentioned for the previous route. Abseil directly to
good ledges below the obvious right-curving corner groove.

Inanimate Objects Fight Back   E4 6a **   (1995)
Climb the right-curving groove to a huge jammed block and the top.
Good sustained climbing.

There is a prominent pillar in the back wall of Bay 4 with a through-
route at its base best seen from the south side of the bay. The next two
routes are reached by abseiling off fence posts on the north side of
the white building and running the ropes down the northern side of a
small promontory which ends in the pillar.

Fat Man's Folly   35m   HVS 5a *   (1983)
An atmospheric route which follows the chimney-crack formed by the
south side of the pillar. Climb up inside the chimney until further
progress is barred. Squeeze out to regain the outside world and
continue up the corner crack to the top.

Bay City Roller   35m   E3 6a   (1983)
This route lies below the white building and climbs the obvious corner
and wall just right of the previous route and just left of the mouth of a
deep cave.

The next five routes lie on the clean section of rock at the seaward
end of the south wall of the bay. There is a prominent unclimbed corner
towards the landward side. Approach by abseiling from a large boulder
well back from the cliff edge.

Sealy Dan   25m   HVS 5a *   (1983)
A line up the wall just left of the large corner. Start on a ledge on the
left side of a rock fin. Pull round right into a groove which leads to the
top of the fin. Move up the thin crack above, then finish rightwards.

Starfish Enterprise   25m   E4 6b ***   (1983)
Gain and climb the prominent V-groove immediately right of the large
corner to finish over a small roof and up the thin crack above.

Jellyfish Roll   25m   E2 5c **   (1983)
Start from a ledge 3m up and just right of the previous route. Climb the
left-hand of the obvious cracks.

Sea Enemy   25m   E1 5b *   (1983)
Climb the crack just right of Jellyfish Roll, starting from the same ledge.

Prawn Broker   25m   E2 5b **   (1983)
Climb the obvious crack right of the previous route.

CONDUCTOR COVE

Just beyond Bay 4 there is a deep narrow inlet. Conductor Cove is
approached from the end of the point on the south-western side of this
narrow inlet by a blocky scramble which broadly follows the half-buried
lightning conductor of the lighthouse. Towards the end of the point, turn
left and descend a short chimney to reach the tiny cove just below the
lighthouse. Most of the lines are quite short, but enjoyable and on
excellent rock. Immediately left of the descent chimney (looking up) is
a short wall which gives a good 5c boulder problem on small finger
ledges.

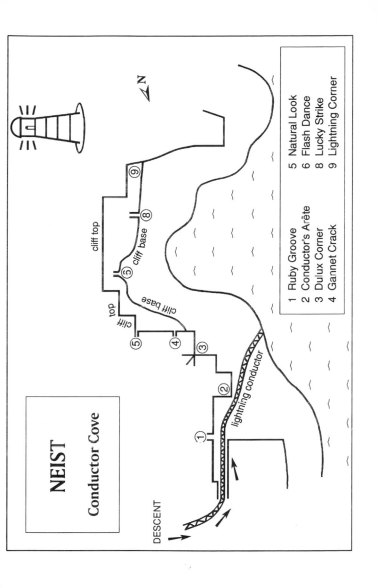

NEIST
Conductor Cove

DESCENT

cliff top
cliff base
cliff top
cliff base

lightning conductor

N

1 Ruby Groove
2 Conductor's Arête
3 Dulux Corner
4 Gannet Crack
5 Natural Look
6 Flash Dance
8 Lucky Strike
9 Lightning Corner

1   Ruby Groove   8m   VS 4c   (1990)
Climb the first steep chimney-groove level with the descent chimney, starting from the lightning conductor.

2   Conductor's Arete   8m   Very Difficult   (1990)
The blocky arete 3 metres right of the previous route, again starting from the lightning conductor.

3   Dulux Corner   12m   Hard Severe 4b   (1990)
To the right again is a jamming crack in a smooth-walled corner with a choice of three finishes.

4   Gannet Crack   12m   Severe 4a   (1990)
Turn the corner to reach an expanse of south-facing wall. Climb the first crack in the otherwise smooth wall.

5   Natural Look   15m   Severe 4a   (1990)
Climb a blocky crack 5 metres further right, approached direct by a crack or better *via* the lower wall.

6   Flash Dance   20m   VS 4b   (1990)
Further right the back wall of the cove faces west. Start up the obvious wide chimney and move right at its top. Move up again before finishing back left above the chimney.

Lottery Winner   20m   E1 5c*   (1996)
The corner left of Flash Dance.

7   The Umpire Strikes Back   20m   VS 4c *   (1996)
Climb the crack a little further right, followed by a bulge at twin square overhangs.

8   Lucky Strike   20m   Severe 4a   (1980s)
Start 5 metres right of Flash Dance. Climb the prominent narrow chimney which splits the base of the wall; not recommended for the stout! Continue up the wall directly above.

9   Lightning Corner   25m   HVS 5a **   (1981)
Start at the far right-hand end of the wall where it turns seawards again.
Climb a chimney-crack to a platform, then move right and climb a
groove over a small overhang to the top.

LIGHTHOUSE WALL

The remaining routes lie on the steep face directly below the lighthouse. They are very difficult to identify from above. The first few routes
are approached by abseiling from metal fence posts at the north end
of the wall around the lighthouse. There is a foghorn at the southern
end of this wall. The routes are described from north to south.

All Quiet in the Western Front   25m   HVS 5a**   (1996)
Climb the left-hand of three corners beneath the abseil.

How the West Was Won   25m   VS 4c**   (1996)
Climb the middle corner. The right-hand corner bends left to join it half
way up.

Neisty Beisty   25m   E3 5c   (1983)
Climb a crack and groove system left of the obvious crack of the next
route. The groove is characterised by undercut blocks and flakes.

Westagain   25m   HVS 5a   (1900)
Climb a prominent chimney-crack line.

Westcoastin'   25m   E2 5b   (1983)
Follow the next chimney-groove to the right with a sustained crux
section.

Wild West   25m   E2 5c   (1983)
Climb a corner-groove right of Westcoastin'.

Horny Corner   20m   VS 4c *   (1991)
Climb the corner beneath the foghorn that faces a rocky island with a
squat sea-stack.

TROTTERNISH

There is much climbing on the most northerly finger of Skye, known as Trotternish. The region is dominated by the longest continuous ridge on the island, which extents for some 30km from Portree in the south to Kilmaluag in the north, and has its high point on The Storr (719m). The ridge is the crest of an east-facing escarpment built of basalt lava flows, which dip gently westwards. Numerous spectacular landslips have taken place in an easterly direction from the face of the escarpment, the lavas having slipped on underlying sedimentary rocks.

Some climbing has been done on various basalt pinnacles dotted along the escarpment, notably the Old Man of Storr, but the basalt is intrinsically loose, and the climbs are not popular.

The only significant outcrop of sound rock discovered on the escarpment lies 2km north of The Storr at Carn Liath, where many routes have been put up in recent years.

Away from the Trotternish Ridge, numerous sills of dolerite exposed around the coast give some of the best climbing outside the Cuillin. The routes are now described from south to north – the normal direction of approach.

THE BRAES

Just to the south of Portree, before Trotternish proper, a short section of dolerite sea-cliff offers some diversion. It is accessed from the B883 road to The Braes. Park near Lower Ollach at Map Ref 515 365 and follow the Ollach River down to the sea, then turn north to reach a natural arch. Some enjoyable sea-level traversing can be done as well as superb bouldering. Short pitches up to 5c have also been climbed.

THE STORR

The long Trotternish Ridge which starts north of Portree has some spectacular cliffs on its eastern side, but most of them are unsuitable for rock climbing.

The following winter routes lie on the cliffs to the east of The Storr. The first one is situated about 500 metres north-east of Bealach Beag at Map Ref 497 533. The cliffs here start from a slightly lower level than the Old Man of Storr, which stands just to the north.

Aperitif   100m   III/IV   (1995)
This route takes a drainage line left of the steeper north section of the cliff. Easy snow leads to the first pitch, a conspicuous icefall.
1. 50m   Climb the icefall to a belay below the upper gully.
2. 50m   Climb the corner or shallow gully over several steepenings to the top.

   The line of cliffs due east of The Storr and directly behind the Old Man is split by several gullies.

The Main Course   100m   V   (1995)
The left-hand gully gives an exciting climb up a natural drainage line. Easy snow leads into the depths of the gully and the first pitch.
1. 50m   On the first ascent, an ice umbrella choked the gully at 20m and gave a challenging obstacle, above which further steep ground leads to a belay beneath icicles on the right wall.
2. 50m   Traverse up and right across the icicles to gain an ice ramp leading back left to more steep ground and the top.

Blue Moon Gully   170m   II   (1995)
The next gully to the north is much easier and gives the easiest way up the Storr cliffs, primarily on steep snow.

Deeply Digestible Gully   150m   V **   (1995)
Further right is a very impressive buttress directly behind the Old Man. Its right-hand side is bounded by a very deep gully.
1. 40m   Climb the left-hand start which curls around rightwards to join the main gully at about 50m.
2. 50m   Snow leads to several steep awkward steps in the depths of the gully and a belay below a vertical section capped by an icicle fringe.
3. 30m   Chimney up the corner above and continue over a variety of interesting obstacles to easier ground.
4. 30m   Climb easily to the top.

THE OLD MAN OF STORR

The remnants of landslipped masses below The Storr have been eroded into numerous impressive pinnacles, the most dramatic of which is 50m high and called the Old Man of Storr. This has been climbed by three lines. Follow a path on the north side of a forest plantation and continue more steeply to the foot of the pinnacle which sits amidst tumultuous terrain. The base overhangs all round. The Old Man is very rarely climbed and the grades given for the first two climbs are only best guesses. The routes are described from south to north.

The Portree Face   60m   E2   (1967)
At the foot of the south face is a 6m pillar, which is climbed easily from the left. The overhanging wall above was originally climbed with two points of aid to reach a belay in a cave. Traverse right into a steep groove and climb this to a peg belay below an overhang. Step left to the foot of a steep crack and climb this a short distance, before making a hard move right (peg runner). Go up to an obvious traverse line left and go round the arete to a peg belay in the final crack. Climb the crack to the top. In descent, the top pitch was reversed before abseiling.

The Original Route   65m   E4   (1955)
A route which still retains its reputation. Start from the neck on the uphill side of the Old Man. The lower part of the north-west face is climbed by a diagonal line from right to left. The route has a fiercesome start, which several E5 leaders have failed to climb free.
1. 25m 6a   Start at a block which takes a long sling and go up about 6m to a circular hole where a dubious peg was originally used. Make very strenuous moves left to gain the top of a prominent nose in the centre of the face (crux). Climb to a grassy cave directly above, then move left again to a ledge of shattered blocks on the left edge of the pinnacle.
2. 40m   The rest of the climb is easier. Move right above the cave and continue diagonally for about 30m. Climb a corner chimney, then trend leftwards to the small exposed summit. Descend by two abseils, the first to the block ledge.

The Staffin Face   65m   E3   (1988)
Poor protection and dubious rock make this another horror show. Start at the crest on the northern side.
1. 25m 5c   A deceptively hard pitch. Climb diagonally leftwards to some holes at 6m. Move left and up to a dubious block (a peg runner was placed while hanging from this). Gain a slight groove above (peg runner) and trend rightwards to the arete. Follow this for 5m to a good stance common with the original route.
2. 40m 5b   Climb straight up above the collapsing thread of the belay (peg runner), then follow the right-hand side of the arete, regaining it at about 20m *via* a large dubious block. Easier ground leads to the top.

The Old Boy   Severe
Immediately beside the Old Man on its uphill side is another pinnacle which has also been climbed. Start from the neck beside the Old Man. Spiral leftwards round the back of the pinnacle, and from an inadequate belay finish up a steeper section opposite the Old Man.

The Cathedral   55m   E1   (1960)
This pinnacle is situated some 60 metres north of the Old Man. It has windows left by fallen blocks, and is sometimes called (less appropriately) Needle Rock. The rock is unnerving, and the route is not recommended. Scramble for 30m to a stance and belay on the arete opposite the Old Man. Steep climbing leads up the arete in three short pitches. Reverse the top pitch before abseiling.

Some winter climbing has been done just north of The Storr in Coire Scamadal. Several small streams which fall over the north-east facing rock band in the corrie occasionally freeze up.

CARN LIATH   (Map Ref 496 559)

The best climbing on the Trotternish Ridge is concentrated some 2km north of The Storr on Carn Liath. The main cliff is particularly impressive, being steep and 60m high. It is hard to account for the crag's neglect until recently, even though it is inclined to attract mist because of its altitude. Several fine climbs are now to be found here. There are also some smaller buttresses at a slightly lower level in the immediate vicinity of the main cliff, which offer a great variety of routes. The rock is a rough sound dolerite with good frictional properties, quite unlike the rotten basalt which forms the remainder of the Trotternish escarpment. However, the routes tend to have fairly sparse protection.

At the foot of the crags is a hidden valley leading northwards which is floored by a jumble of gigantic blocks. There is also an extraordinary tongue of rock debris, 260 metres wide and 500 metres long. It descends from 400m to 260m in a north-north-west direction, and is thought to have originated as a rock avalanche in post glacial times. The whole scene presents an awesome spectacle - more chaotic than in An Garbh-choire in the Cuillin. The bouldering potential is immense.

The approach takes just under 40 minutes. Park some 13km north of Portree beside the A855 where the Rigg Burn goes under the road (Map Ref 512 561). Walk due west up a grassy spur between two streams. After the first rise the top of the crag can be seen directly ahead in profile on the skyline. The gentlest approach is to aim for a low notch in the distant hillside slightly north of the cliff. Cross moorland to a stile over a diagonal fence, mount a low green bank and continue across further moorland to where the hillside steepens. Go diagonally rightwards to the notch. Contour round the grassy hillside and continue round until the main cliff comes into view. The hidden valley is reached suddenly and this soon leads up to the prominent arete of Thief Buttress which is situated well below the main cliff.

THIEF BUTTRESS

The first climbs lie on the north wall of the buttress, well seen in approach. The routes are described from left to right.

1   Bad Man Zone   25m   Hard Severe 4b   (1992)
Start at a corner on the left of the face. Follow a diagonal line rightwards past creaking blocks to a ledge shared by the next route. Take the corner above, and break leftwards through the overlaps.

2   Thief   25m   VS 4c *   (1992)
This climb takes the vertical crack system in the middle of the wall, finishing up the left-hand corner of the upper recess. Gain a diagonal grassy break at 5m before pulling onto the deceptively steep wall (crux). Sustained moves lead to a spike at 15m. Take a direct line above.

The crag now turns a corner and slants uphill. There is a large block at the foot of the arete which gives the next short route.

3   K.I.P.   8m   VS 4c   (1992)
Climb a diagonal crack on the south face of the block to a roof. Bold moves on good holds lead to a ledge. Finish delicately.

4   Bengal Lancer   40m   E2 ***   (1994)
This fine route climbs the prominent arete of Thief Buttress. There are abundant runners on the thought-provoking first pitch, but sparser protection on the second.
1. 25m 5b   Follow grooves and cracks immediately right of the toe of the buttress to reach the true arete at 10m. Gain a higher foot ledge (crux) before making an exhilarating swing rightwards into a bottomless groove. Exit up the hand crack above to a ledge and belay.

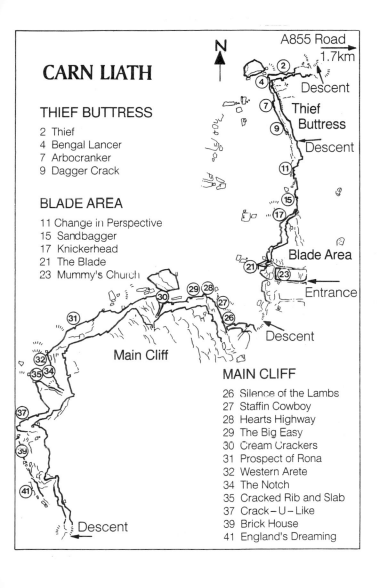

CARN LIATH

THIEF BUTTRESS

2 Thief
4 Bengal Lancer
7 Arbocranker
9 Dagger Crack

BLADE AREA

11 Change in Perspective
15 Sandbagger
17 Knickerhead
21 The Blade
23 Mummy's Church

N

A855 Road
1.7km
Descent
Thief Buttress
Descent
Blade Area
Entrance
Descent

Main Cliff

MAIN CLIFF

26 Silence of the Lambs
27 Staffin Cowboy
28 Hearts Highway
29 The Big Easy
30 Cream Crackers
31 Prospect of Rona
32 Western Arete
34 The Notch
35 Cracked Rib and Slab
37 Crack–U–Like
39 Brick House
41 England's Dreaming

Descent

2. 15m 5b   Make a couple of airy steps rightwards up the arete to pegs on a shelf round on the west face. Further wild and committing moves lead up the arete in a sensational position to the top.

The next section of crag faces west.

5   The Judge   30m   HVS 5a **   (1993)
Climb the impressive crack system 2 metres right of the arete, taking in the obvious inverted beak at half-height. Strenuous, but well protected.

6   The Negatron   30m   E1 5b *   (1993)
A bold line which finishes up the right arete of a massive hanging block. Start 2 metres right of The Judge at a prominent left-facing corner. Climb the poorly protected corner for 12m to a large ledge. Continue up the crack line above for 5m, then traverse left on foot ledges and attain a bridging position across the corner (crux) using a foothold on the right arete of the large hanging block. Swing onto the arete and climb up the overhanging face of the block on well spaced holds to a ledge. Step left to finish up The Judge.

7   Arbocranker   30m   E2 5b **   (1993)
A more direct line up a striking overhanging crack, starting at the same place as The Negatron. Climb the poorly protected right arete of The Negatron corner for 12m to ledges. Continue up the steep and sustained, but well protected crack directly with the crux moves high up.

8   The Forty Nine Steps   30m   E1 5a   (1994)
This route takes the wall right of Arbocranker with sparse protection; RPs essential. Start in the middle of the wall directly below its highest point. Climb easily to a ledge, then move up and right on good holds before making a harder move to reach a second ledge. Traverse 2 metres left to a spike and climb the wall directly above to where the angle lessens. Move delicately up the top wall to finish on better holds.

9   Dagger Crack   25m   VS 4c   (1993)
This route is up the right-hand of three cracks. Only the central section warrants the grade. Climb the straightforward corner to a ledge and continue by an off-width crack. The upper section is wide enough to admit a body, but is best climbed on the outside.

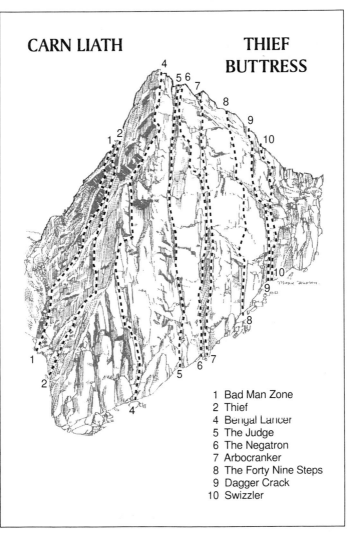

CARN LIATH

THIEF BUTTRESS

1 Bad Man Zone
2 Thief
4 Bengal Lancer
5 The Judge
6 The Negatron
7 Arbocranker
8 The Forty Nine Steps
9 Dagger Crack
10 Swizzler

10   Swizzler   25m   Severe 4b   (1993)
Climb to the ledge as for Dagger Crack, then move right to a big flake.
Ascend this, then finish up the blank-looking wall. Better than it looks.

Thief Buttress now gives way to more broken ground which allows
a steep scramble descent at about Moderate grade.

THE BLADE AREA

Further south up the valley the west-facing wall forms several short
buttresses, culminating in a distinctive feature called The Blade. The
first of these buttresses has two lines.

11   Change in Perspective   20m   VS 5a   (1994)
Scramble up the broken corner on the left edge of the wall (or climb
the harder right-hand corner at 4b) to reach a spacious ledge. Follow
the obvious twin cracks until a dynamic stretch allows the prominent
protruding block to be passed. Finish direct. Well protected.

12   Jenga   20m   Very Difficult   (1994)
Gain the ledge as for the previous route. Follow the recessed corner
until it is blocked by the roof, then swing out right and continue direct.
Pleasant climbing on blocky holds.

13   Dirtsman   12m   Hard Severe 4b   (1992)
Climb a hidden left-facing corner 3 metres right of the previous route.
Layback the crack past a foot ledge at half-height.

14   Donkey   15m   VS 4c *   (1995)
The arete immediately right of the Dirtsman offers steady climbing with
sparse protection.

15   Sandbagger   15m   VS 4c   (1994)
The wide crack on the right-hand side of the buttress. Start in a recess
and climb easily to the roof. Surmount the overhang and continue up
the widening crack. Very large Hexentrics will be a big comfort in the
upper section.

16   Perce Strings   15m   VS 4c   (1994)
The obvious crack 5 metres right of Sandbagger. Bridge up to the
protruding block. Climb over this and continue up the crack and corner
above.

CARN LIATH
MAIN CLIFF

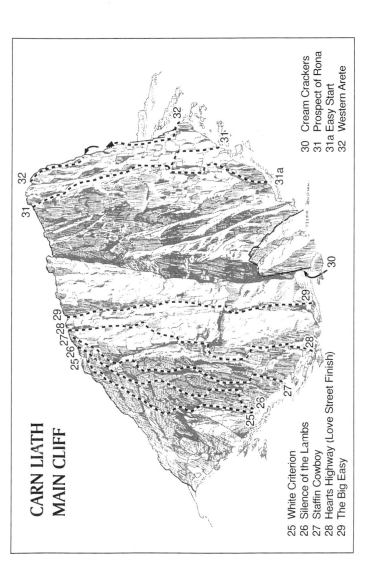

25 White Criterion
26 Silence of the Lambs
27 Staffin Cowboy
28 Hearts Highway (Love Street Finish)
29 The Big Easy

30 Cream Crackers
31 Prospect of Rona
31a Easy Start
32 Western Arete

Some 10 metres further south up the block-strewn valley, a well defined rake runs diagonally leftwards across the wall. The next route climbs the wall beneath the rake.

17   Knickerhead   20m   E1 5b *   (1995)
Step across the crevasse onto the wall and follow the groove direct to the small overhang. Gain this and follow the left-trending ramp to a large block below the overhanging band. Mantel up, stretch high for the horizontal break and continue direct to the last moves of the rake.

18   Rogue's Rake   25m   Very Difficult   (1992)
Follow the rake leading left past an airy move at 15m.

19   Fifties Special   20m   VS 4c   (1994)
Start 2 metres right of Rogue's Rake. Climb the vertical V-groove and the overhanging crack above.

Right again is the prominent pinnacle called The Blade. This notable landmark has a church-shaped appearance when seen from the road.

20   Sixties Special   20m   Severe 4a *   (1990)
This route takes the gently overhanging chimney-crack which forms the corner left of The Blade. Scramble to the foot of the chimney and thrutch up, finishing either inside, or better outside, the massive jammed block at the top. A variation finish climbs the wall left of the chimney by a diagonal crack at the same grade.

21   The Blade   25m   HVS 4c ***   (1991)
A serious and exposed route up the western edge of The Blade. Start below the edge on its right-hand side. Move up the gully over a protruding lip until moves leftwards up the wall gain shattered ledges. Mantelshelf onto a smaller sloping ledge which leads onto The Blade. The last protection for 10m can be arranged here. Gain the knife-edged arete (crux), then climb it past a prominent notch to the top.

22   Marking Time   15m   VS 4b   (1993)
Some 5 metres right of The Blade is a less obvious square-topped buttress with a V-chimney on its right-hand side. Climb the wall right of the chimney until a move right can be made to reach a ramp which leads rightwards to a big ledge. Finish by stepping right and climbing the front face of a little pinnacle. Other variations are possible.

There is a grassy depression on the eastern flank of The Blade buttress, where three narrow 'catacomb' entrances can be found leading westwards into the hillside. These can be reached by staying left of Thief Buttress on the normal approach by the hidden valley, or by taking a more direct line from the road. Two novel climbs start from the central of the three entrances. The first half of each expedition is underground, so a head torch will prove useful.

23 Mummy's Church 25m Very Difficult * (1990)
Enter the narrow central cleft and follow the passage as it deepens. Turn right at the end and drop down into an earth-floored chamber 12m underground, below a skylight. The climbing begins at the northern end of the chamber. Bridge up past a lateral shaft of light, and emerge onto ledges. Gain the pinnacle above directly by further bridging and chimneying, or by the columns on either side.

24 One in Thirteen 25m Severe 4b (1992)
A second, slightly more sustained subterranean climb, which follows a crack in the west wall of the chamber. Start in the chamber as for the previous route, but 3 metres further south. Back and foot up the well protected crack line to a constricted exit between boulders. The leaning corner above provides a reachy finish to the top of 'the church'.

THE MAIN CLIFF

The main cliff of Carn Liath is an impressive crag, although it can be a sombre place because of its north-facing aspect. The best time to climb on the central face is late on a summer's afternoon, when it catches the sun. Some of the routes have quite a serious air about them. Although the crag can be approached up the hidden valley past Thief Buttress, it can also be reached more or less directly from the road. A short easy descent a little to the south of The Blade leads to the foot of the face at its eastern end. The centre of the crag is marked by a repellent line of seepage known as Snoozing Crack. The routes are described from left to right.

25 White Criterion 40m VS 4c (1991)
Start at the extreme eastern end of the main cliff by an obvious corner-chimney. This forms the left-hand end of an east-facing section of crag. Climb the corner-chimney to an awkward exit at 15m (possible belay and escape). Continue up the wall above, moving onto the left wall via a large sloping hold. Small holds and scant protection lead to

grass ledges at 30m. Ascend the undercut wall and ledges to block belays, and a stake 2 metres back from the edge.

26   Silence of the Lambs   50m   E1 5b **   (1994)
An intricate and sustained line up the big east wall. Start just right of White Criterion, climb the wall for 3m using diagonal edges, then traverse 3m right before moving up to a small flake. Ascend the shallow groove above for about 6m, until it is possible to traverse left into another groove system in the centre of the wall. Climb this until it peters out, then make a delicate rising traverse back right to a niche. Layback the steep wall above (crux) and use good holds on the left to gain a ledge. Finish up the easier ledges above to the stake and block belays used by White Criterion.

27   Staffin Cowboy   50m   HVS 5a *   (1991)
This climb follows a shattered corner-chimney high up on the right-hand side of the east wall. Start up grooves some 5 metres left of the arete, then transfer to another groove on the left. Reach a spike on the right at 20m and carry on up the shattered corner past two bulging sections, the second being the crux. From its top, swing right onto the arete and go up a ramp to a grass ledge. Continue rightwards up the wall to reach the stake belay.

28   Heart's Highway   60m   E1 ***   (1992/1993)
Start up grooves in the eastern arete. The best combination takes the Love Street Finish and gives a superb climb with two contrasting pitches. Begin on a pedestal at the toe of the arete.
1. 30m 5b   Strenuous, but well protected. Climb grooves until a step left can be made onto a small shelf at 12m. Continue left and up a shattered chimney before stepping delicately back right. Make a rising traverse until some overlaps can be surmounted with difficulty at their right-hand end. Follow the groove above to a stance on a small ledge.
2. 30m 5b   The Love Street Finish. Bold and airy. Head diagonally rightwards, making delicate and committing moves to gain the vague bulging nose. Reach and climb the crack-line above by further enigmatic moves.
Original Finish: 30m 4b
This reduces the overall grade to HVS 5b **. Climb the crack behind the stance and move delicately right to a rising ramp. Finish up a wall on the arete to the stake belay.

29   The Big Easy   65m   HVS *   (1993)
The prominent vertical crack system splitting the main face between
the left-hand arete and Snoozing Crack is often wet, and it requires a
long spell of dry weather to bring it into condition.
1. 25m 5b   Climb past tricky but well protected moves at 5m to gain
easier ground leading up to the overhang. Surmount the crucial
overhang by a wide crack to reach the more pleasantly angled wall
above. Stance with peg belay some 3m higher.
2. 40m 4c   Follow the crack system to the top. A good sustained pitch
despite appearances.

The huge fallen block below Snoozing Crack has several pleasant
lines on its gentler face, as well as the following gem on its vertical face
opposite the main cliff.

30   Cream Crackers   12m   VS 4c   (1993)
A variety of starts at the left-hand end of the block lead to a move right
to the foot of a groove. Interest is maintained to the top.

31   Prospect of Rona   65m   E1 ***   (1991)
This excellent route takes the line of least resistance up the big face
on the right-hand side of the crag. The direct start gives a more
consistent climb, although the hard section on the second pitch is
much more difficult than the rest of the route. The left-trending traverse
of the undercut headwall is surprisingly reasonable, but in a stupendous position. The compelling direct finish is unclimbed. Reach the two
possible starts by slanting up scree to the right of Snoozing Crack.
1. 25m 4b   Start at the toe of a subsidiary buttress which slants
slightly right. Climb easy initial rocks to a swing left at 15m. A groove
above leads to ledges.
2. 40m 5b   Move left up the wall to the obvious weakness in the
overhangs. Pull over into a niche (crux) and traverse left onto a curious
pocketed wall. Move up to a traverse left on foot ledges, heading for a
large notch on the skyline in a very exposed position. Climb the corner
5m before the notch, and continue over a roof to a final overhanging
layback.
Variation: The Direct Start   12m 5a
This is the better option. Start at a vertical crack some distance up and
further right of the normal start. Climb the crack by a bouldery and
poorly protected start, and finish by a precarious layaway onto a ledge.

32   Western Arete   40m   VS **   (1991)
Slant up scree at the right-hand end of the main face to reach the foot of the arete.
1. 20m 4c   Traverse in leftwards to an obvious jutting block. Zigzag up the wall above, passing a small diamond overlap (crux) to reach a ledge. A poorly protected pitch.
2. 20m 4b   Climb the right-hand of two grooves past a roof, then move into the left-hand groove in a fine open position. Move back right to finish up the vertical blocky arete.

The next two routes start from a ledge above and right of the jutting block that marks the start of Western Arete.

33   Another Notch   40m   Hard Severe 4b   (1993)
Scramble to the ledge from broken ground right of the arete. Climb cracks in the slabby wall and move slightly left to easier rock above. Stay just right of, and parallel to, the groove and roof on the second pitch of Western Arete. Finish up a tough little crack with a small notch immediately right of the main arete.

34   The Notch   35m   Hard Severe 4b   (1991)
Scramble to the ledge as for the previous route and climb a crack system through steep initial bulges. Head slightly right for the obvious chimney-notch on the skyline. Avoid grassy sections and climb a bulging jam crack (crux) to finish up the easier overhanging notch. An easier finish traverses right below the jam crack and climbs a broken gully with a precarious exit.

The remaining routes are on more broken ground right of the main crag.

35   Cracked Rib and Slab   35m   Difficult   (1992)
The untidy rib to the right of a gully. Start 6 metres right of the jutting block on Western Arete. Climb the rib taking care with loose rock to a large stance. Continue up the slab above, trending first left then right to finish directly by its right edge.

The next rib further up the scree has three crack lines. Each gives 15m of climbing followed by a scramble to the top of the cliff.

36   Captain Cacky and Commander Energy   20m
Hard Severe 4a   (1993)
Climb the left-hand of three cracks in a gentle S-shape.

37   Crack-U-Like   20m   VS 4c   (1993)
The middle corner crack of the trio gives a well protected layback.

38   Rocks-R-Us   20m   VS 4b   (1993)
The right-hand crack separates a spur from the parent rib and gives
12m of offwidth jamming.

39   Brick House   30m   HVS 5b   (1995)
Start 5m uphill from the previous route and follow a north-facing corner
to a criss-crossed overhanging wall. Climb this at a central weakness,
then follow the easy rib above. Reach a large triangular jug in the final
wall from the right. Disproportionally hard in the middle.

Further right up the slope to the south a spiky mace-like boss of rock
can be seen against the skyline.

40   The Mace   30m   VS 4c   (1995)
A series of disconnected walls leads to a ledge and belay below a small
square roof. Pass this on the left, then step up before moving right to
finish up the central groove.

41   England's Dreaming   30m   Severe 4a   (1993)
This pleasant route takes the slabs immediately right of The Mace.
Follow the prominent S-shaped crack for 10m, then cross higher slabs.
Climb the wall above by a poorly protected mantelshelf and finish on
the very highest point of the whole cliff.

SGURR A' MHADAIDH RUAIDH

Some 3km further north along the Trotternish escarpment lies the
distinctive peak of Sgurr a' Mhadaidh Ruaidh (*peak of the red fox*). This
can be approached from Lealt along a rough track which ends by Loch
Cuithir. The huge buttresses on its north-west flank are best avoided,
but hidden away at the foot of a gully due west of the peak (Map Ref
470 584) is a basalt dyke, which has eroded to form a miniature version
of the Inaccessible Pinnacle. This offers some mild entertainment - its

long southern ridge is Moderate, and its short but steep northern ridge is Very Difficult.

THE QUIRAING

Towards the northern end of the Trotternish Ridge lies a spectacular section of landslipped terrain which includes the Quiraing. This scenic feature is well worth a visit, although its climbing interest is minimal. It is approached from the Staffin to Uig road. A distinctive pinnacle called The Needle, which points the way up to The Table inside The Quiraing, has been climbed.

The Needle   55m   E2
Start up the east face and finish on the north. The entire climb is on loose, rotten and dangerous rock. Four abseil slings were left around the mound of grass and broken rock which constitutes the top. Recorded more as a warning rather than as a recommendation.

Due west of Loch Langaig near Flodigarry there are several assorted pinnacles situated immediately below the escarpment (Map Ref 453 708). These offer agreeable scrambles as well as some meatier problems.

The remaining routes in Trotternish lie on dolerite sills which are exposed around the coast. The crags are described in an anti-clockwise direction starting on the east side of the peninsula.

STAFFIN

Dolerite sills are intruded into the sedimentary rocks of Trotternish from Portree northwards, but the first outcrops to yield good climbing so far lie on the coast to the east of Staffin. Some of the most southerly routes on the famous Kilt Rock can be seen at a distance from the viewpoint by Loch Mealt. The cliffs can be approached from the viewpoint carpark, but it is easier to park at a small layby with a phone box on the left a little further north and walk along the road for 250 metres to a gate on the right. Go through the gate, and with a fence on the left at first, head north-east for 400 metres. Reach a fence along the cliff top, and cross this where a gully cuts back into the cliff edge. This gully is named Cadha an Tuill (*narrow pass of the cavity*) and it gives a straightforward scramble descent immediately west of Kilt Rock.

Grey Panther, Kilt Rock   (Climber, Noel Williams)

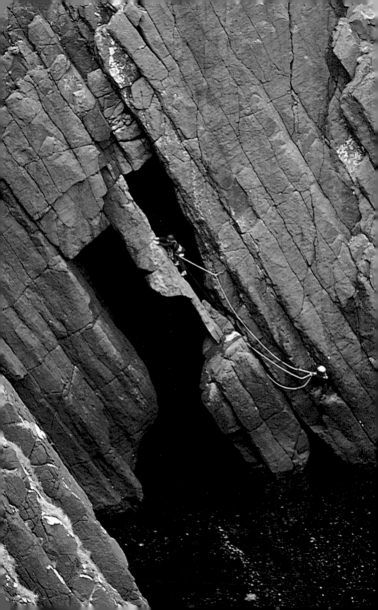

There are few natural belays on the cliff top, so a number of iron stakes have been placed at the tops of routes. The cliff top soil is quite thin in places so it is not advisable to rely on single stakes. In most cases it is best to arrange a belay with a separate rope before climbing.

ELLISHADDER WALL

The right-hand wall of the descent gully and its continuation south-wards is known as Ellishadder Wall. The routes are described as they are approached from the gully, from north to south. The wall can be viewed from the top of Kilt Rock. There are some short problems on the upper section of the descent gully.

Cak 10m VS 4b (1991)
Climb the crack right of a pinnacle with a loose block at the top.

Marmelada 10m Difficult (1990)
Chimney up the left side of a pinnacle to gain its top. Finish up a short crack.

Confiture 10m Very Difficult (1990)
Ascend twin cracks left of the Marmelada pinnacle.

Jammy Dodger 25m VS 5a * (1983)
Start about halfway down the gully and climb the right-hand of two groove-cracks. Gain a ledge with difficulty, then move right and climb the obvious corner to the top.

Jamboree 25m VS 4c * (1983)
Climb the longer left-hand groove just left of the previous route. Cross rightwards and finish up another crack.

The View 30m HVS 5a * (1990)
A pleasant, well protected route up the groove up the left side of a pillar just left of the previous two routes and right of a deep gully. Climb the groove to a grassy ledge at the top of the pillar. Move up then left into a wide crack and climb this to the top.

Spantastic, South Tunnel Buttress (Climbers, Noel Williams and Anne Scoular)

Ragged Robin   25m   Severe   (1989)
The deep gully chimney left of The View gives a through route of
interest to ornithologists and botanists. This is possibly the 'cavity'
referred to in the name Cadha an Tuill.

A Haggis Called Wanda   40m   E2 5b **   (1995)
Climb twin cracks just left of the gully where the wall becomes higher
and more continuous. There is a small triangular roof towards the top.

Fancy Free   40m   E2 5b **   (1983)
Climb a prominent groove-crack just left of the previous route. High up,
move left and climb a rust-coloured shield of rock to gain a square-cut
recess just below the top.

Y Bilidowcar   40m   E4 6a **   (1992)
This route takes a striking finger crack in the wall opposite the main
part of Kilt Rock to finish in the same recess as Fancy Free. Climb a
groove below a small butterfly overhang for 3m, then move up and right
to gain the crack. Follow this all the way to the recess at the top.

The descent gully now ends and the remaining routes are reached
by traversing out on grassy ledges below roofs on the wall high up.
There is a conspicuous mass of ivy growing on the bottom section of
the wall at the low point of the traverse. The start of the next route is
reached by climbing up a short distance just past the ivy.

1   Received with Thanks   40m   E2 5b *   (1984)
Start some 6 metres right of a small pedestal and climb up and slightly
right to a groove which goes to the left of a roof high up. Follow the
groove past a lighter-coloured patch of smoother rock at half-height.

2   Drop the Pilot   40m   E4 6a **   (1984)
Start just right of a small pedestal and move right and up to gain a
crack just right of a vague prow. Climb the crack, passing jammed
blocks with difficulty near the top.

3   Black Crow King   40m   E3 6a   (1987)
Start beneath the right-hand end of the prominent stepped overhangs
high up, about 6 metres left of Drop the Pilot. Climb a groove for 3m,
then step right to a crack and follow it to the roof. Use a flake on the
right at first, then layback round the right-hand side of the roof and go
up the crack to finish.

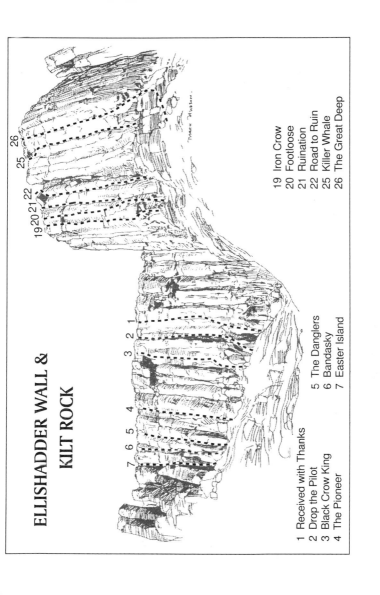

ELLISHADDER WALL & KILT ROCK

1 Received with Thanks
2 Drop the Pilot
3 Black Crow King
4 The Pioneer

5 The Danglers
6 Bandasky
7 Easter Island

19 Iron Crow
20 Footloose
21 Ruination
22 Road to Ruin
25 Killer Whale
26 The Great Deep

4   The Pioneer   35m   E1 5a/b **   (1983)
Climb a prominent crack in a left-facing corner not far left of the stepped overhangs. The crack is very wide near the top.

5   The Danglers   30m   E1 5a *   (1989)
Left of The Pioneer is a corner crack which fades out at two-thirds height. This route climbs the corner crack immediately left again.

6   Bandasky   30m   E1 5a **   (1990)
Climb the front of the small pillar just left of The Danglers, then follow twin cracks above, making more use of the better defined left-hand crack. Sustained.

7   Easter Island   30m   HVS 5a *   (1994)
Climb the corner crack left of Bandasky to the top of the statue. Finish up the corner crack above.

8   Pinnacle Chimney   15m   Very Difficult   (1983)
Ascend steep grass at the left end of the wall to reach the neck behind the prominent pinnacle. Follow chockstones up the wall and finish by chimneying up behind a smaller pinnacle to the cliff top.

9   Ellishadder Pinnacle   15m   VS
From the neck behind the pinnacle traverse round right to climb a crack on the south side to the summit.

10   Entrevennes   30m   E1 5b **   (1991)
Just south of Ellishadder Pinnacle are three corner lines. This route climbs the left-hand corner which faces the pinnacle, and finishes as a crack in the wall.

KILT ROCK

There are some good and varied routes on the left wall of the descent gully before it swings round onto the dramatic front face of Kilt Rock itself. The unnervingly steep grass and loose shale forming the lower half of the cliff makes it preferable to access the routes here by abseil. The well developed columnar jointing in the sill has produced many parallel grooves and cracks which can be difficult to distinguish from above. For this reason it is worth inspecting the front face from the cliff top to the south in order to help identify the routes. Most of the climbs on the front face involve a full rope length of very steep and sustained jamming.

The routes are described from the gully round onto the front face.

Romper   10m   Severe   (1983)
Climb a small recess near the top of the gully, moving left at the top.

Sporran   20m   HVS 5b *   (1983)
A little further down the gully there is a J-shaped recess. Gain this and bridge up to holds on the left. Reach a projecting block and climb onto it with difficulty. Continue more easily to the top.

Pied Piper   25m   E1 5b   (1983)
The obvious weakness right of Sporran. Move straight up to the left side of a giant flake-pedestal. Make hard moves right and climb up to better holds and a ledge. Continue up the front of a large flake and a crack on the left to the top.

The Electric Bagpipe   35m   HVS 5a ***   (1983)
This delightful climb starts at a short left-facing corner just over halfway down the gully. Climb the corner and continue up the front and/or the left-hand side of the giant flake above. From the top of the flake, layback up the crack on the right. Step left onto the wall and climb to a ledge. Move up and right to finish. Low in the grade.

Clandestine   40m   VS 4c ***   (1983)
A pleasant route which slants rightwards across the lower gully wall, with exposure increasing as height is gained. Climb the short left-facing corner (crux) as for the previous route, then move right and go up to a triangular recess. Step right again to another recess and climb the left-hand of two parallel cracks. Climb the left side of a pedestal to the top.

Brazen   35m   E2 5c *   (1983)
Start just down from the short corner of the previous two routes. Gain the small overhung recess from the right with difficulty, then make a hard move up to better holds. Continue to the triangular recess as for Clandestine, then climb straight up the obvious crack to the top.

11   Secret Service   40m   HVS 5a *   (1983)
Near the bottom of the gully a ledge runs horizontally right across the wall. Traverse out along the ledge, then move up to a platform above. Slant up leftwards to a corner. Make some poorly protected moves to gain a left-slanting crack (crux), then follow this more pleasantly to the second recess on Clandestine. Climb the right-hand of two parallel cracks and finish up the right side of the pedestal.

The next three routes all finish on a prominent slab near the top of the wall. They are reached by turning left at the bottom of the descent gully, and all of them offer a good introduction to the more exposed routes on the front face.

12   Tartan Terror   40m   E1 5b **   (1983)
Start just round the corner at the bottom of the descent gully, and climb a broken groove to the platform on Secret Service. Step right and climb the steep crack to the slab. Finish easily up a short wall.

13   Skyeman   40m   E2 5b ***   (1983)
Climb the crack immediately right of Tartan Terror to finish in the middle of the slab. Sustained.

14   Wide Eyed   40m   E2 5b **   (1983)
An unpleasant traverse over broken ground leads to the corner right of Skyeman. Climb the chimney crack with an off-width crux to finish at the right-hand end of the slab. There is a worryingly deep crevice at the back of the slab.

Most of the remaining routes on Kilt Rock have hanging belays or poor stances at the start, and are best approached by abseil. It is prudent to tie a big knot in the end of the abseil rope.

15   Edge of Beyond   45m   E2 5c ***   (1983)
There is a large boulder at the top of this route. Climb the next groove right of Wide Eyed, with an excursion onto the left-bounding arete at half-height.

16   Mystery Cat   45m   E3 6a   (1987)
The thin crack line just right of the previous route. Start up Edge of Beyond for some 12m, then move out right under a small overlap onto the pillar. Climb the crack line to finish up the left arete.

KILT ROCK

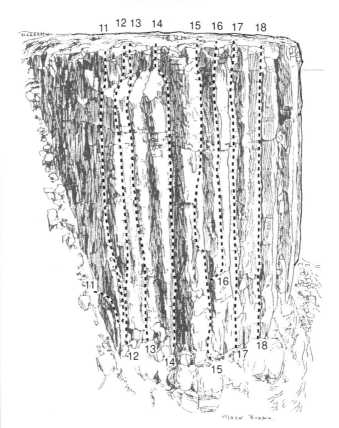

11 Secret Service
12 Tartan Terror
13 Skyeman
14 Wide Eyed

15 Edge of Beyond
16 Mystery Cat
17 Grey Panther
18 Internationale

17   Grey Panther   45m   E1 5b ***   (1983)
A popular route, which is sustained but not quite as thuggish as most of its neighbours. It climbs a fairly prominent recess with angled walls immediately right of the previous route. Ascend twin cracks in the back of the recess by jamming and elegant bridging.

18   Internationale   45m   E3 5c ***   (1983)
A very sustained and photogenic route up the centre of Kilt Rock. Climb the conspicuous jamming crack right of Grey Panther to a horizontal break. Continue directly and move right to finish. It is difficult to carry enough large protection devices.

19   Iron Crow   45m   E3 6a **   (1987)
This route follows a thin crack line right of Internationale. From a good grass stance climb the right-hand crack to a roof. Pull left round the roof and go up the crack to the top of a big flake. Finish by the crack.

20   Footloose   45m   E3 5c *   (1983)
Start right of Iron Crow in a slight recess. Climb up to reach a left-slanting lichenous crack. Follow this and its vertical continuation which includes 20m of unprotected off-width.

21   Ruination   45m   E3 5c *   (1983)
Start up Footloose for 6m, and where that route moves left continue straight up. Make a hard pull up onto the girdle ledge. Continue by slightly easier climbing to the final awkward moves on inferior rock.

22   Road to Ruin   45m   E2 5b ***   (1983)
Climb a prominent jamming crack left of a wide chossy gully. Near the top move right onto the left wall of the gully for a few moves.

23   F.B.C.   45m   HVS 5a   (1991)
Start up Road to Ruin, step right and climb the appalling chimney gully.

24   Brightside Crossing   100m   E2 **   (1987)
An increasingly exposed left to right girdle of Kilt Rock along an obvious break some 30m up the face. Very spectacular. Rope drag is a problem.
1. 45m 5b   Start in the descent gully by a little shelf at the top. Traverse rightwards with an awkward move before Secret Service. Continue with feet in the break below the finishing slab of Skyeman and belay in the corner of Wide Eyed.

2. 45m 5b   Continue traversing with feet and then hands in the break to reach the prominent crack of Internationale. Climb 3m up this before swinging around the lichenous arete on large holds. Follow a line of holds until a mantelshelf can be made onto a ledge in the chossy gully.
3. 10m   Finish up Road to Ruin.

25   Killer Whale   45m   E4 6a **   (1983)
This is the prominent crack line up the great open corner groove right of the chossy gully. Start above the limestone band on a small ledge. Climb the right-hand crack for 40m, then move into the left-hand crack for 3m before moving left and up to finish.

26   The Great Deep   45m   E3   (1987)
The crack line just right of Killer Whale. Start on a grass ledge with a peg belay directly under that route and below the limestone band.
1. 10m 5b   Traverse right along the ledge and climb onto a crumbling block at its right side. Climb straight up the bulging wall with two peg runners on the left, and pull up left onto the dolerite. A groove leads to small belay ledges and the base of the crack line.
2. 35m 5c   Climb the crack to the top, and belay at the exit of a nearby chimney.

TEMPEST BUTTRESS AREA

The next few routes are reached by descending an easy south-trending gully from the cliff top 150 metres to the north of Kilt Rock. The buttress to the east of the descent gully is known as Tempest Buttress.

Fe Fi Fo Fum   45m   E3 5c **   (1987)
Descend the gully and head south towards Kilt Rock to reach a buttress with an obvious block roof high up on its left-hand side. Start 10 metres or so right of this, below a crack just right of an arete. Climb the crack to finish right over blocks. A fine jamming pitch.

Frisky after Whisky   45m   E3 5c ***   (1993)
This enjoyable route can be seen clearly by heading north along the cliff edge from Kilt Rock. It starts a little to the south of the previous route, and climbs twin cracks in a recess immediately left of the obvious large block roof. The latter looks like an 'Indian's Nose' when viewed in profile from the cliff top. The right-hand crack is a finger crack and the left-hand crack is a chimney/off-width.

The next two routes are on Tempest Buttress.

Stormwatch   30m   Mild VS 4b   (1987)
Start halfway down the descent gully on its left-hand side at a left-facing corner. Climb the corner-groove to a ledge on the right. Move up and left to gain another ledge and finish directly.

The Tempest   45m   E3 6a **   (1984)
From the bottom of the descent gully continue round the front of Tempest Buttress to gain its south-east face, or abseil directly to the start. The route follows a prominent crack right of a hanging column. Move up from a ledge at the start, then go right *via* a flake handhold to a thin crack. Climb this (crux) to a wider crack, enter a niche and at the top climb directly up an awkward little off-width.

Ill Wind   75m   E5   (1987)
This route lies some 200 metres north of Tempest Buttress. Descend the gully as for Tempest Buttress and walk northwards, either at sea-level, or at higher tides along a sheep track just below the limestone band. About 30 metres before a distinctive pinnacle called The Chimney Stack is reached, there is a large groove leading to a hexagonal roof. Rising from the left-hand side of the roof is a straight finger crack, and to its right is a groove. Start on the grass below this groove.
1. 35m 6a   Zigzag up grass and soft limestone with care to gain the base of the groove (Hex7 and RP2). Climb the groove with continuous interest to belay 3m below the roof.
2. 10m 6b   Continue to the roof and cheval into the crack on the left. Climb this strenuously to ledges on the left.
3. 30m 6a   Climb the crack above, passing a small roof with difficulty, until a crack leads diagonally left around the arete to the top. Three superb pitches.

THE CHIMNEY STACK

A few hundred metres north of Tempest Buttress, an amazingly slender pinnacle lies close in by the cliff top. The stack has been climbed by two routes. The top of the stack was originally reached by means of a grappling-iron. Two bolts have been placed on the summit for a belay. It is possible to reach the foot of the stack by a precarious descent down a steep gully immediately to the north. Otherwise abseil into the gap behind the stack. Descent from the summit is by abseil.

Sheer Sear   30m   E5 6a ***   (1987)
This route climbs a shallow groove, split by a finger crack and capped by a small roof, on the south face. Follow the crack with a hard move at 10m to a good rest. Continue with interest past a further hard section at a steepening in the groove to gain better holds near the left arete. The final section is deceptive and the ledges prove awkward to gain. Climb up a short flake crack with a sharp final pull onto the top.

Over the Rainbow   40m   E5 6b ***   (1985)
The groove on the east face may need further cleaning; take plenty of small nuts. Move right and climb the bulging crack. Continue, very sustained, over two overlaps (the second being the crux) to reach a peg runner. Pass this to gain a good resting ledge and a further peg runner. Step left into a little corner, then go straight up to the top.

FALLEN PILLARS AREA

Some 450 metres north of The Chimney Stack, two much less spectacular stacks of similar height lie close in near the cliff top. The southern and larger one is known as Bob Bob Stack, and this marks a possible descent to the next few routes. Climb down steeply onto a jammed boulder in the gap beside Bob Bob Stack. The heather-covered summit can be gained by a short ascent of Moderate grade. Turn left and follow easy grass ledges to reach the gap behind the northern stack. Go over the crest and duck beneath a small jammed boulder on the other side. Careful scrambling leads down to bouldery terrain and a section of cliff with tottering columns known as the Fallen Pillars. Alternative approaches from the north are described in the next section on the Staffin Buttresses. The routes are described heading north from the Bob Bob Stack descent.

Blasphog   35m   E2 6a   (1987)
Near the foot of the descent from the Bob Bob Stack is an obvious nose of reddish rock. This route starts just left of the nose and takes a crack line leading up over a small roof at 10m. Start up on the right and swing in left to gain the crack line. The roof is the crux and a good belay can be taken just below the top.

Actually Hyperbole   35m   E3 5c   (1987)
The central of three grooves in the wall further right. Move into the groove from the left and climb it to exit left. An extra rope is needed to belay on the fence post 15 metres further back.

The remaining routes are best described in relation to the Fallen Pillars. A slumped and fractured pillar is conspicuous in an alcove. To its right there are two hanging pillars facing a slender outward leaning pinnacle. Below and left of the fractured pillar is a shorter pillar leaning against the wall. Immediately left again are a group of much longer more upright pillars. To the left of all the pillars is a slot line capped by a roof. Left again are twin parallel cracks.

Demon Lover   40m   E5 6a   (1987)
Just round to the left of the twin cracks is a corner developing into a deep chimney. This route takes the fine finger crack in the groove immediately left. Protection is perfect, but the climbing is very sustained. Belay near the top.

High Noon   40m   E2 5b   (1987)
Climb the twin parallel cracks right of the corner-chimney for 12m, then move out left up a flake. Climb the obvious hand crack; a rotten flake at the top needs trundling.

Toll Dubh   50m   HVS 4c   (1987)
A remarkable hidden shaft lies up the back of the leftmost of the slumped pillars. Enter a cave on the left side of the first pillar, or climb a 5b crack on the outside (less rope-drag). Climb the shaft up the back of the pillars to emerge in a chimney. Continue the through route under a boulder to the top of the pillars. The easiest finish is by a small hanging corner on the right (loose).

Fish Tail Cracks   50m   E1 5b   (1987)
On the right side of the leftmost pillar are three parallel cracks. Start up twin cracks, then follow the right-hand pair. Continue up the central crack which develops into a chimney (also climbed by Toll Dubh). Finish direct up a blunt rib, or by a loose corner on the right as for the previous route.

Bocan Mor   45m   E2 5c   (1987)
To the right of the fractured pillar in the alcove are two hanging pillars. This route takes the crack line on the right side of the right-hand pillar. Clamber over big boulders to reach the start. Climb a thin crack and traverse out right under the roof to gain the crack. The exit from the crack is dirty.

Mushroom Billy   40m   E2 5b **   (1984)
This route follows a prominent disjointed crack in the wall to the right
of the Fallen Pillars. Climb the crack, then move leftwards across the
large flake to reach the continuation of the crack. Follow this to the top.
Sustained.

THE STAFFIN BUTTRESSES

A little to the north of the Fallen Pillars the cliff turns seaward for a short
distance to form a south-east facing crag which marks the start of the
Staffin Buttresses. Some distance further north the crags start to peter
out and the cliff top slants down as a broad grassy ramp towards Staffin
slipway. The Staffin Slip crags lie north and west of this ramp.

Staffin Buttress is divided into two main sections, north and south,
by a steep gully/alcove. On the cliff top above the northern buttress
there is a large hexagonal block near a short section of seaward-
trending fence. Immediately north of the fence is a high point on the
cliff top. A prominent rock near here is an obvious feature seen on the
skyline from Staffin slipway.

The buttresses are best approached from the north. Turn right on a
bend in the main road just north of Staffin and follow a narrow road all
the way to Staffin slipway. When parking at the road end take care not
to obstruct access to the concrete slipway. The small bay here is called
Ob nan Ròn (*bay of the seals*). There is a sandy beach at low tide on
the point opposite Staffin Island, about 500 metres before the road
end. Access to the beach is *via* a large car park immediately to the
south; worth knowing about for family outings. From the slipway a
pleasant walk south-east along the shore on grassy ground eventually
leads to a rock platform immediately above the sea. Stay on this
platform for as long as possible, tide permitting, until it peters out a
little over 1km from the slipway. Slant up slightly left over sedimentary
strata and big boulders to reach the foot of the southern buttress. This
is marked centrally by a group of hanging columns. The Bob Bob Stack
and the Fallen Pillars should be visible further left. The ground below
and right of the northern buttress is very difficult to negotiate, consist-
ing of massive jumbled boulders and birch jungle with high
leg-breaking potential. A right traverse from below the southern buttress probably gives the most pleasant approach from below to the
routes on the northern crag.

An alternative approach, which is certainly preferrable for pre-fixing
belays at the tops of routes, starts across boggy ground behind the

boathouse at Staffin slipway and follows a short section of old path to the west of the Staffin Slip Buttresses. (This path was contructed in 1846 at the time of the potato famine.) When the path finishes, head south-east more or less along a ridge crest above the Staffin Slip Buttresses. Eventually drop down slightly and cross a fence to reach the distinctive hexagonal block near the fence on the cliff top above the northern buttress. It is worth detouring further south to the Bob Bob Stack to get a view of the routes.

The climbs are described from south to north.

The first two routes lie on the south-east facing wall of the southern buttress, round and well left from the hanging columns, and just left of a triangular roof high up. They are clearly seen from the Bob Bob Stack and both start on a ledge about 10m up from the base of the crag. The most convenient approach is to abseil directly to the ledge at the start of the routes.

Dustbin Jimmy   45m   E3 5c *   (1984)
Climb a very prominent groove directly with a threatening flake at about one-quarter height.

Sailin' Shoes   45m   E3 6a **   (1985)
The fine crack immediately right of the previous route. From the ledge move right and up across a big flake to gain the crack. Follow the crack with the crux where it narrows at one-third height.

The next two routes lie on the northern buttress directly below the hexagonal block on the cliff top. They both have exceptionally long pitches of 50m. A further 3m of steep grass and rock leads to the cliff top and it is then a further 3m to the hexagonal block belay. It is best therefore to secure an extra rope on the block and ensure that it hangs over the vertical rock at the top of the climbs. This rope can also be used as an anchor for a 50m abseil to the start of the climbs.

A great pillar stands slightly proud from the cliff on the left-hand side of the buttress. Both routes lie immediately south of this pillar.

Prometheus   55m   E2 5c   (1994)
This route takes a groove immediately left of the crack on the left side of the pillar. Climb broken blocks, apparently sound, to gain a crack in the groove. Follow it with sustained interest, passing a roof near the top on the left.

Heracles   55m   E2 5b ***   (1994)
A compelling line which climbs the prominent crack on the left side of
the pillar. The crack starts some 7m up as a thin finger crack and
gradually widens to slim body size near the top of the pinnacle. Very
large and exotic camming devices such as No.9 CADs are required for
protection, since much of the crack is wider than a Friend 4. Start at
the same place as the previous route, and climb up broken blocks as
for that route. Reach a recess at about 7m and traverse right to reach
the base of the thin finger crack. Climb the widening crack with
continuous interest. Veer diagonally left near the top to join the
corner-groove on the left at the end of the vertical section.

The next two buttresses are south of the road end at Staffin slipway.

STAFFIN SLIP SOUTH

This is the large left-hand crag visible from the road end by the slipway.
It offers a similar sort of climbing to that on Kilt Rock, but without the
access problems. However the crag is rather lichenous and being
north-facing it does not catch the sun. Many of the routes have had
few repeat ascents and may need further cleaning. The lines should
improve if they become more popular. The rock is generally very sound,
and the climbing is almost invariably strenuous and sustained.

The ground under the crag is an extraordinary jumble of giant blocks
and dwarf birchwood. The best approach from below involves staying
on the lower grassy ground until in full view of the crag, then weaving
a way up sheep tracks at first to emerge eventually below the right-
hand end of the crag. An alternative approach is to take the old
pathway, then slant up left to reach the top of Sgeir Bhan. Go along
the top of that crag, then descend an easy grassy gully at the western
end of Staffin Slip South.

There is a prominent fractured column leaning against the face on
the left-hand half of the crag. In the centre there are two pinnacles
close in against the face. Descent from the top of the crag is by the
grassy gully at its western end. The right-hand end of the crag is quite
short, but further left its height increases to nearly a full rope length.
The routes are described from right to left.

1   Lateral Thinking   15m   E1 5b **   (1990)
Just left of the first wide crack at the right-hand end of the buttress are
twin cracks. Climb the strenuous right-hand one. A good route to warm
up on.

2   Hand Jive   17m   E2 5c **   (1994)
Climb the left-hand crack, with a vicious jam for its crux. Finish just left of a tiny roof.

3   Lat up a Drainpipe   17m   HVS 5a **   (1988)
Just round to the left of the previous routes is a corner recess with twin cracks above a solitary rowan tree. This pumpy route climbs the twin cracks.

4   The Avon Man   18m   E2 5c **   (1990)
This route climbs the crack immediately to the left of the previous route. There is a section missing from the base of the column on its right, and a small roof high up.

5   Swillington Common   20m   E2 5c **   (1989)
Climb the crack immediately left again. The prow to its left has a small roof at one-third height. The main difficulties are at about half-height.

6   Dial Card   25m   E1 5b *   (1988)
This and the next two routes lie in another slight recess. Climb twin cracks in the right-hand corner of the recess, just left of the prow separating it from the previous route. Not as sustained as its two partners.

7   Silly Pollack Two   25m   E3 6a *   (1988)
The thin crack in the back wall of the recess just left of centre gives sustained climbing.

8   Captain Patience   30m   E2 5c **   (1988)
Climb the left-hand corner-groove with a thorny plant at 6m.

9   The Latvian   35m   E2 5c **   (1988)
This route starts a little further left directly above a heather topped pedestal, with three tumbled blocks immediately to its right. Start up twin cracks which merge to a single crack at one-third height.

10   Lats in Space   40m   E1 5b *   (1988)
Climb a deep crack in a V-groove immediately left of a sharp prow just left of the previous route. There is a lichenous wall to the left.

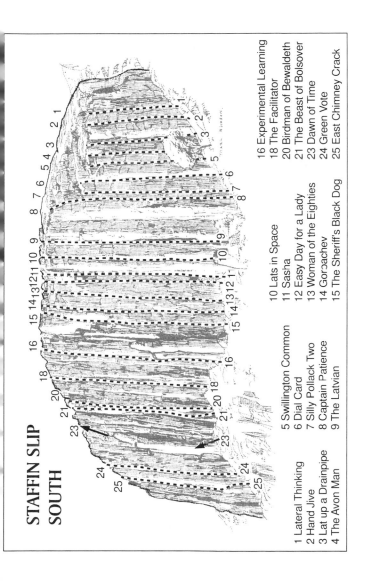

STAFFIN SLIP SOUTH

1 Lateral Thinking
2 Hand Jive
3 Lat up a Drainpipe
4 The Avon Man
5 Swillington Common
6 Dial Card
7 Silly Pollack Two
8 Captain Patience
9 The Latvian
10 Lats in Space
11 Sasha
12 Easy Day for a Lady
13 Woman of the Eighties
14 Goroachev
15 The Sheriff's Black Dog
16 Experimental Learning
18 The Facilitator
20 Birdman of Bewaldeth
21 The Beast of Bolsover
23 Dawn of Time
24 Green Vote
25 East Chimney Crack

11   Sasha   40m   E3 5c ***   (1990)

There is an obvious groove with twin cracks leading to stepped black roofs at the left-hand end of the lichenous wall. Reach a sentry box at the start and climb the groove above to a resting place below the roofs. Surmount the roofs by rather brutish but spectacular climbing, and finish up a short crack.

12   Easy Day for a Lady   40m   HVS 5a **   (1989)

The prominent V-groove left of Sasha offers more genteel climbing.

13   Woman of the Eighties   45m   E3 5c ***   (1988)

The second crack in the wall left of the previous route offers strenuous and sustained finger jamming with a flake at 12m.

14   Gorbachev   45m   E2 5b ***   (1988)

This fine route climbs twin cracks and a groove left of the previous route. The cracks are rather ragged for the first 12m. Well protected and a good introduction to the crag.

15   The Sheriff's Black Dog   45m   E2 5b *   (1988)

Start immediately left of a slight prow with a moss-covered boulder beneath it, and just to the right of the two pillars (about 20m high) which stand clear of the crag at its centre. Climb the thin crack to a roof high up, and pass this on the right with difficulty.

16   Experimental Learning   45m   E3 6a ***   (1988)

This route starts just to the left of the two pillars in the centre of the crag. Climb a smooth white-walled groove containing a finger crack. Pass a roof at the very top on the right. An impressive line; high in the grade but well protected.

17   Living Hell   45m   E2 5b   (1988)

A little to the left of the two pillars is a scruffy recess. Further left again is a deep crack at the back of a prominent groove. This route climbs a thin crack on a buff coloured wall 2 metres to the right of the deep crack. It requires further cleaning.

18   The Facilitator   45m   E3 5c   (1988)

Climb the deep crack with black walls at the back of the lichen-covered groove, marred by a loose finish.

19   Silly Pollack   45m   E2 5b **   (1988)
Climb twin cracks in a recess just left of the previous route. Move into the left-hand crack to avoid a series of stepped roofs high up.

20   Birdman of Bewaldeth   45m   E3 6a ***   (1989)
The right-hand crack in a slight recess just left of the previous route leads to a small triangular roof at 6m. Gain and climb the crack above, passing right of a nose high up.

21   The Beast of Bolsover   45m   E2 5b **   (1988)
The left-hand crack in the recess leads *via* an undercling left to a steep but easier crack above. The crack runs up the crest of a slight prow and finishes left of a nose high up.

22   Lusting after Glenys Kinnock   40m   E2 5b **   (1989)
This route climbs a thin crack just round left from the previous route, and right of a vegetated groove. It passes to the left of a long narrow roof at half-height.

23   Dawn of Time   40m   VS 4b   (1987)
The obvious leaning and fractured pillar gives an unusual climb. Chimney up behind the pillar, finishing up its left side. A short chimney leads to the top.

The next two routes are reached by descending slightly immediately after the leaning pillar.

24   Green Vote   45m   E3 5c ***   (1988)
An interesting and varied route; one of the best on the crag. Climb an obvious crack with an awkward start on the white wall right of the next route, passing a tiny rowan with care at two-thirds height.

25   East Chimney Crack   40m   HVS 5a *   (1988)
Ascend the prominent chimney at the left-hand end of the crag, just before it turns a corner.

Two recently (1996) reported routes on Staffin Slip South are **Jugs of Deception**, 18m E4 6a**, which climbs the pillar to the left of Hand Jive using thin cracks, and **Glorious Five Year Plan**, 35m E2 5c**, which is the corner right of The Latvian.

SGEIR BHAN - STAFFIN SLIP NORTH

The right-hand of the two Staffin Slip crags can be approached directly from the slipway, or more easily by following the old pathway to the first bend, then traversing left. The majority of the routes are concentrated on its cleaner north face, but there are also two routes at the southern end of the less attractive north-east face. The latter is covered in light coloured lichen, which probably accounts for the crag's gaelic name, Sgeir Bhan (*white rock*). To approach these two climbs, walk along the crest of the crag towards the descent gully leading down to South Crag. Before this wide gully is a short steep chimney-gully which gives a scramble descent. The routes are on the right (looking down) and are described from right to left (facing in).

Tremour   12m   E2 5c **   (1992)
The wall just south of the chimney-gully with a grass ramp at its foot gives a fine well protected route. Climb the groove, surmount the overhang and climb the upper wall strenuously (crux).

Earthquake   20m   VS 4c   (1992)
Left of Tremour is a perilous flake. Climb the crack on its left to a ledge and a small tree. Exit up the rather wobbly chimney.

The most striking feature of the north face of the crag is the soaring crack in the arete between the two main faces. The routes on the north face are described from right to left.

1   Staffin Follies   20m   E2 5b   (1990)
At the right-hand end of the face is a short wide chimney. Left of this are two wide cracks. Start by climbing to a grass ledge with a rowan tree, then follow the right-hand chimney-crack.

2   Post Marital Blues   25m   E2 5b   (1992)
Climb the left-hand crack.

3   The Swelling   30m   E1 5b **   (1992)
This enjoyable route climbs a crack just right of a faint arete in the centre of the north face. Immediately to its right is a grassy groove capped by a small roof.

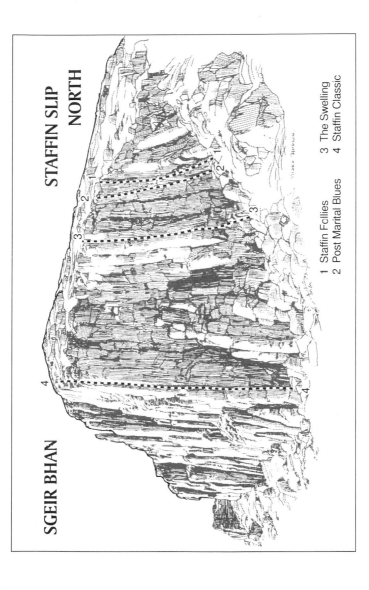

STAFFIN SLIP
NORTH

SGEIR BHAN

1 Staffin Follies
2 Post Marital Blues
3 The Swelling
4 Staffin Classic

4   Staffin Classic   40m   HVS 5a **   (1987)
This fine route follows the steep chimney crack on the right-hand side
of a large tapering pillar marking the arete between the north and
north-east faces. Climb the widening crack with considerable interest.
Protection in the upper section is surprisingly good, thanks to numerous small cracks in the right wall. Take a stance on top of the pillar with
belays behind.

FLODIGARRY

Some 6km north of Staffin lies the tiny settlement of Flodigarry. The
road hereabouts is rather uneven because of the instability of the
landslipped ground. The second steep turning on the right leads down
to the Flodigarry Hotel, where meals and refreshments are served in
the bar - a handy venue for 'après climb'.

A further kilometre north along the coast are some sea-cliffs which
offer numerous routes for the lower grade climber. They are situated
on columnar dolerite which is tilted back at slab angle. There are some
varied and enjoyable routes here, which may appeal to those who
struggle on the jamming routes at Staffin. The routes are approached
by parking just off the verge on the left of the road 1km north of the
turn–off to the Flodigarry Hotel. Do not obstruct access for the crofters
who cut peat near here. Head north-east parallel to a faint escarpment
to reach the cliff top, then turn right and follow the cliff edge. There are
two possible routes down through the steep upper cliffs. Both follow
grassy ramps descending in a south-south-east direction. Incidentally,
some distance to the south of the descent ramps and just east of the
high point (116m) on Druim nan Slochd (*ridge of the pits or hollows*),
there are some spectacular crevasses in the cliff top. An ideal place
for hiding a body!

The northern ramp gives a more convenient approach to the climbs.
Cross two wire fences with care, and with a crag on the right, soon
reach a lower section of cliff top on the south side of a small bay.
Looking east, a wire fence runs out leftwards to the tops of the two
main crags. To the right the fence runs round the rim of a small bay
with a broad sea-stack, then cuts across the back of a small promontory. The descent to the first two climbs lies on the south side of this
right-hand promontory. The routes are described from south to north.

Scramble down steep grass with an awkward step at half-height
to reach the shore. The large crag immediately to the south,

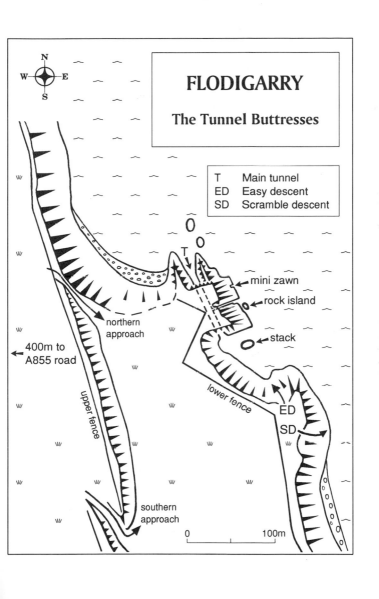

Creag na h-Eiginn, is impressive but unclimbed. Its most prominent feature is a huge hanging chimney. Instead turn north to reach the start of the first line (**Captain Nemo**,VS 4c). This is a rather scruffy affair which climbs up the first section of rock at the bottom of the descent. An awkward start from the bottom left-hand corner leads to easier climbing on inferior rock. A much better route lies a little further north above a platform. It may not be readily accessible at high tide.

Buoy Racer   50m   VS **   (1989)
This route climbs a prominent rib just right of a grassy gully.
1. 25m   Climb easily up the rib at first, and eventually make a slightly harder move up a grassy crack to gain a good stance with poor belays.
2. 25m 4c   Continue up the slightly steeper rib above to a stake belay at the top of the promontory.

The next route is reached by an easy grassy scramble down into the bay on the north side of the promontory.

Newspaper Taxis   40m   Severe *   (1990)
The start is not accessible at high tide. Climb a prominent broad rib of clean rock in the back wall of the bay opposite the stumpy sea-stack. There is a stake belay on the grass slope above. A pleasant route.

Immediately north of the stumpy sea-stack are two neighbouring buttresses with slabby seaward faces. A large tunnel runs right through the back of both buttresses, and several narrower crevices lead off this at right angles on the seaward side. Canoeists have paddled through the tunnel at high tide. A remarkable pillar spans both walls of the tunnel at its southern end. The tops of the buttresses are accessed by crossing a wire fence at a corner. Numerous stakes have been placed at the tops of both buttresses, although some of the shorter stakes may be hard to find when the grass is fully grown. A belay should be arranged at the tops of the routes before climbing. Most of the climbs are approached by abseil.

SOUTH TUNNEL BUTTRESS

The first three routes lie on the south wall of the buttress which forms the north side of the small bay with the stumpy sea-stack.

Head in the Clouds   40m   VS 4c *   (1990)
This route finds a way up the wall just left of the tunnel. Approach as
for the previous route by descending easy grass on the south side of
the bay. Walk across rounded boulders on the shore at low tide to reach
the start. From a small platform climb grooves trending rightwards to
an overlap formed by the base of two columns. Reach a crack to the
right of the overlap. Continue up this, then move rightwards up ledges
to finish.

Spantastic   40m   HVS **   *July 2000 ? Paul Colemon .*   (1990)
This memorable route climbs the astonishing pillar spanning the
southern entrance to the tunnel. The pillar has a narrow base which
may not support it for much longer. This is perhaps the only route in
the country which attracts a weight limit. The climb can be started from
boulders on the shore at lowest tide (Severe), but it is more atmospheric and slightly more reassuring to make an ascent at high tide
when the sea can help cushion a fall. Abseil down to a leaning niche
just below the base of the pillar.
1. 20m 4c   Fix a high runner before setting off up the pillar. The
technical grade assumes a complete lack of imagination. Continue up
the recess above, then break right to a good stance.
2. 20m 4c   Continue up ledges trending right. Where the ledges lead
horizontally right, make a steep move up the wall and climb slightly
leftwards past the left end of a horizontal roof. Finish more easily.

Lucy in the Sky   40m   HVS 5a ***   (1990)
This very agreeable route climbs the obvious thin crack line in the wall
to the right of Spantastic. It is more sustained than its neighbour, but
not as worrying. Start in the leaning niche as for Spantastic. Traverse
very delicately right until it is possible to pull up onto a small ledge.
Continue more easily slightly leftwards to gain the main crack. Climb
this with increasing interest and at the top go up the left side of a
leaning pedestal. Join Spantastic on top of the pedestal, then move up
the wall and slant left past the roof as for that route.

The slabby seaward face of the buttress is undercut at its southern
end, and has a flat rock island below its northern end. Unlike the
northern buttress it is not possible to traverse easily along its base.

Floating Voter   35m   Severe   (1990)
This route lies just to the right (north) of the left-bounding arete.
Position the rope carefully before abseiling. Start on a narrow foot
ledge a few metres above the bottom of the fiercely undercut slab. After
an easy start, protection becomes more difficult to find as the climbing
gets harder towards the top.

Swingometer   40m   Mild VS 4b *   (1990)
This route starts from a square-cut niche with steep walls immediately
left of a deep cleft. Abseil as for the previous route, then carefully drop
down a few more metres into the niche, taking care not to swing into
the cleft on the right which connects with the main tunnel through the
back of the buttress. Escape from the niche by climbing up its right-
hand side (crux). Move up slightly right and bridge up the cleft which
soon becomes sealed. Circumvent a huge block on the right, and
continue by the line of least resistance to the top.

Lipstick   40m   VS 4c *   (1991)
This route starts some way right of the cleft. Abseil down the middle
of the slab past a boss of rock at half-height. The base of the crag is
not undercut here, and a narrow foot ledge slanting left from the rock
island has a stance at its top end which lies above high water. Traverse
hard left along the lip of the obvious overlap, then climb up delicately
to a small roof. Continue more easily for some distance. Slightly more
devious route finding leads to the top.

One Armed Bandit   40m   Severe   (1990)
Start from the same stance as the previous route and climb up slightly
leftwards to a tapering recess. Ascend this, pull over the small roof at
the top and continue directly past the left side of the boss of rock at
half-height.

Slab and Tickle   40m   Very Difficult   (1989)
Abseil from the southern end of a shrub-filled depression. Start
opposite the south end of the rock island on a narrow foot ledge. Climb
up and slightly left to reach the top of the boss of rock in the centre of
the slab. Continue rightwards to the top by an awkward final move.

Election Chimney 40m Hard Severe 4b * (1990)
This route ascends a prominent chimney opposite the rock island on
the right-hand half of the crag. Start from a ledge by the left wall of the
chimney above high water mark. Ascend the chimney (crux), step out
left at the top and continue by the easiest line, finishing as for Slab and
Tickle.

Rock Island Line 40m Severe *** (1989)
A good climb on immaculate black rock to the right of Election Chimney.
Abseil from the centre of the shrub-filled depression to a ledge
opposite the rock island. (At low tide it is possible to step onto the
island.) At high tide start from a tiny triangular foot niche a few metres
higher. Climb up very slightly rightwards at first and continue directly.

NORTH TUNNEL BUTTRESS

This buttress is reached by continuing left along a grassy ridge from
the southern buttress. The line taken for the abseil approach to the
routes is not so critical on this buttress, because it is possible to
traverse along its base at about Difficult grade. The most awkward
section involves crossing a mini geo in the centre of the crag. The
southern half of the traverse is above high water, but the northern half
of the traverse is awash at high tide.
    The south face of the crag has no routes at present. The first route
starts from a deep chimney at the southern end of the slabby front
face.

Reach for the Sky 40m E1 5b * (1994)
A bold and gymnastic start leads to easier climbing just right of the
left-bounding arete. Start from a pedestal at the base of the deep
chimney. Gain the left wall and pull boldly round the arete to get
established on the front face. Continue pleasantly, with some further
interest at an overlap near the top.

No No Hervo 40m HVS 5a * (1990)
The obvious deep chimney near the left-hand end of the face gives
wide bridging to the crucial bulge, above which the climbing eases.

Black Beauty   40m   Hard Severe 4b **   (1990)
Starting a short distance right of the previous route, either climb a right-slanting crack, or go up the yellow slab to its right starting from a slightly higher level. Continue pleasantly up the narrow section of black slab above and finish more or less directly.

Stalking Horse   40m   Very Difficult *   (1990)
Start on a huge block jammed in a rift to the right of the previous route. From the top of the block climb up the slab on the left of the rift, then trend slightly right above where the rift seals and continue to a good ledge. Step right and finish directly.

Men in Suits   40m   Hard Severe 4b **   (1994)
Start in the same rift as the previous route. Climb the right edge of the rift for a short distance, then traverse right and continue up the rib directly, joining the previous route near the top. A fiercer direct start (5b) begins a little further right from an overhung recess immediately left of the tiny geo in the centre of the crag.

Gutter Politics   40m   VS 4c *   (1994)
This route climbs the obvious weakness in the centre of the crag. Start immediately right of the mini geo and climb up to a deep recess. Continue directly with an overlap giving the crux.

Trespassers Will Be Prosecuted   40m   HVS *   (1989)
1. 15m 5a   Start just right of the mini geo and climb a tapering narrow slab up leftwards to join the previous route in a deep recess.
2. 25m 4b   Move up to a ledge on the right. Pull over a bulge and finish directly.

House of Horrors   40m   E1 5b *   (1990)
Start beside the previous route and climb twin cracks up a bulging wall and the slab above. Trend rightwards up ochre streaked rocks, then finish directly.

Councillor Dubh   40m   E2 5b/c **   (1990)
Start from a large platform below overhanging rock a short distance right of the previous route. The platform becomes awash at high tide. Climb the obvious overhanging crack to gain the recess above. Move up and left and continue boldly up a narrow steep slab and rib. Finish directly by the upper section of the previous route.

At this point the crag turns a corner and the remaining routes all finish on a narrow ridge extending northwards. The main cliff top can only be reached by climbing a tricky wall (5b) at the top (southern end) of this ridge. If an abseil rope is left down the next route it is possible to enjoy the easier lines here and return to the base of the crag without climbing this wall. Take care not to let the end of the abseil rope drop into the deep chimney where it can jam.

Karl Marx's Lament   40m   HVS 5b **   (1989)
1. 30m 4c   Climb the crack and deeper chimney to a platform. Continue up the steep corner above to a shallow recess, then climb the shallow right-slanting groove to the ridge.
2. 10m 5b   From the top end of the ridge make an improbable move left across a steep wall to a ledge. Move left for 3m and climb a right-slanting groove. (The more direct finish going slightly right up the steep wall from the ridge is no easier and disconcertingly loose.)

The pitch lengths give for the next three routes are only for the climbing up to the ridge.

Rightward Drift   25m   VS 4c   (1989)
Start just right of the previous route and climb a shallow slabby groove to a ledge by a short right-facing corner. Gain a higher ledge on the left, then step right to enter the bottom of a groove. Follow the groove to the crest of the ridge. Now go along the ridge and either finish by pitch 2 of the previous route or abseil back to the foot of the crag and escape by an easier route.

A little further right the crag turns another corner. The next two routes lie either side of a columnar rib.

Castaway   25m   Hard Severe 4b   (1994)
Start a few metres right of the corner and climb the groove on the left side of the rib to a small ledge. Step left, continue up a neighbouring groove, then trend left to finish above the corner and below a step in the ridge. Climb the surprisingly awkward step and finish as for the previous route.

Brinkmanship   25m   Hard Severe 4b   (1994)
Climb straight up the groove on the right-hand side of the rib to reach the ridge crest. Go up the narrow ridge and finish as for the previous route.

KILMALUAG

The district of Kilmaluag lies at the northern end of Trotternish. There are numerous small sea-stacks dotted around this section of coast as well as some spectacular cliffs overlooking Loch Hunish on the most northern tip of the island.

The first few climbs are all approached from a small turning area at Map Ref 448 738 (about 150 metres beyond an old building at the roadside where a track twists up to a viewpoint).

STACAN GOBHLACH

These twin stacks lie 2km north-west along the coast from the Tunnel Buttresses near Flodigarry. Approach by descending the cliff a little to the south of the stacks. A short swim is necessay at low tide. The south ridges of both stacks have been climbed, (15m Difficult).

STAC BUIDHE

This distinctive stack lies some 300 metres further north-west along the coast on a large platform which is well clear of the sea at low to mid-tide. It is approached by a 50m vertical abseil from the cliff top opposite. Cross a narrow channel easily to reach the platform. Be sure to shake hands with the resident on the summit. Descent is by abseil.

North Ridge   25m   Hard Severe 4b   (1991)
Traverse round the left side of the stack to a ledge below a groove. Climb columnar ribs and the well protected groove above to an unstable exit.

Original Route   25m   VS 4c   (1990)
Starting from a big ledge forming a toe to the stack, climb the western face by an obvious groove with horizontal columns. Make a delicate traverse out left on suspect rock at the top (crux) to gain the ridge which soon leads to the summit block.

South-west Face   30m   HVS 5a *   (1995)
Start on the same big ledge as the previous route and traverse 5 metres right to the prominent groove. Climb this, taking care with the dubious block at its finish, then move right up the ramp before finishing up easier ground.

There is a small bay just over 100 metres north-west of Stac Buidhe. The next section of sea-cliff to offer climbing is a little further north of it.

SGEIR NAN EATHAR BANA

The next two routes lie on an east-facing section of cliff which has a prominent left-facing corner rising from the sea at its northern end. A platform slopes gently up leftwards from the bottom of this corner. The upper part of the platform generally remains above high water mark. A prominent band of friable rock runs across the face and marks the start of the much steeper upper section of cliff. Immediately to the north, the cliff has a broad apron of easier-angled rock at mid-height, which makes it less attractive for climbing. Abseil down a steep and slightly loose chimney to reach this apron, then continue abseiling further south near the left-facing corner, or abseil directly down the line of the routes. The cliff hereabouts is marked Sgeir nan Eathar Bana *(rock of the white boats)* on OS maps. The two routes described are widely separated at the start, but finish close together. The top pitches of both routes give quite strenuous climbing.

Minnie the Moocher   50m   E1 *   (1991)
1. 20m 5a   Starting from the upper left-hand end of the sloping platform, climb a left-slanting groove-crack line. Continue up and then right, before moving left to belay in a corner.
2. 10m 4b   Traverse well right and climb up at a small niche to reach a prominent ledge running horizontally across the face. Go easily right to a belay below a short left-facing groove capped by a small triangular overhang.
3. 20m 5b   Climb up into the groove, then move left and go up to a pedestal. Continue up and move slightly right past a small chockstone. Finish directly.

Goofus Band   55m   HVS *   (1990)
1. 35m 5a   Start towards the bottom end of the sloping platform a few metres left of the prominent left-facing corner. Climb a groove until it is possible to traverse right onto the crest of a vague buttress. Continue up the buttress staying left of the corner to the prominent horizontal break. Traverse left to a peg belay.
2. 20m 5a   Move a little further left and climb up to a small ledge at 2m, which is just right of Minnie the Moocher. Climb straight up, then slant leftwards and break right to finish.

There is a small sea-stack hidden in a little inlet 200 metres further north. This sports a summit cairn, but no route has been claimed on it. The next recorded route lies on a stack the other side of Kilmaluag Bay.

STAC LACHLAINN

Walk out along the north shore of Kilmaluag Bay to reach this rather squat stack, passing an intriguing inlet called Slochd a' Mhadaidh *en route*. The stack is only possible at low tide.

Double Dragon   25m   HVS 5a   (1981)
This route climbs the south-west face. Start on a large ledge below a short wall between two grooves. Climb the wall and continue up until forced to traverse left into an obvious groove. Follow the loose groove for 5m, then traverse on good holds to a belay.

RUBHA HUNISH

The northerly tip of Skye is one of the most picturesque corners of the island. Being more than 2km from the nearest road, it is a wonderfully wild and peaceful spot offering fine views across the Minch to the Outer Isles including the Shiants. Closer at hand are the islands of Trodday and Fladda-chuain. The headland is reached by leaving the road at Duntulm either on a bend by a phone box (Map Ref 422 742), or a little further west at a former coastguard station by Loch Cleat. The latter option offers slightly easier walking along the shore of Duntulm Bay. Head for a trench-like depression in the distance which leads to a surprisingly easy descent through the sheer cliffs overlooking Loch Hunish. A delightful walk past old lazy beds leads out to the low headland of Hunish itself, which is built from a single sill intrusion. The name Hunish is of Norse origin and is thought to mean headland of the ravine, which possibly refers to the trench-like feature which gives access to the headland.

There are a number of 30m sea-stacks hidden from view on the north-east side of the headland leading out to Rubha Hunish. These offer some entertaining climbs.

SOUTH STACK

The first stack encountered on the north-east side of the headland is approached by swimming across a narrow channel. The easiest descent is to down-climb the south ridge.

Willie Hunish   25m   VS   (1986)
Ascend the stack by its mainland face.

Maol Groove   30m   VS 4c   (1993)
Climb a left-facing groove on the seaward face.

MIDDLE STACK

This was originally reached by means of a grappling hook from the headland. Alternatively abseil down the cliffs north of a prominent corner to a small platform, then swim 20m.

Original Route   30m   Mild VS   (1987)
Climb the mainland face *via* the central groove until near the top, then traverse left and go up and back right to finish.

Eilean Groove   35m   E1 5b   (1992)
A sustained climb up the well defined north-facing corner. The rock is a little loose.

SPLIT STACK

This stack lies 30 metres south of North Stack. It lies close in by the cliff top and is split in two by a narrow gap. It is reached at low tide by an easy scramble down a gully to its south.

Trodday Wall   30m   Hard Severe 4b   (1993)
Traverse round onto the seaward face. Follow a line of holds just left of centre to reach the south summit.

NORTH STACK

An involved and committing outing by either route. Approach by swimming from the north-west corner of Split Stack to gain a small platform on the south-east corner. At low tide with calm seas the stack can be reached by boulder hopping with a tricky channel to finish, but this does not allow very long for an ascent and return.

Original Route   25m   E1 5b   (1987)
Left of the landward face is a chimney-rift which closes near the top and effectively divides the stack into two disproportionate legs. Climb the rift, then continue on easier ground, first left then right, to the top.

Shiant Corner   30m   HVS 5a   (1993)
Climb the prominent left-facing corner on the north-east face. Pull through bulges to reach easier ground and the top.

The remaining routes are on the big cliffs on either side of the descent path. The cliffs are of great interest to geologists, being built from a single 90m thick sill of unusually complex character. The upper section of the sill is the most attractive for climbing and consists of non-columnar dolerite. The middle section is built of more basic picrodolerite, which is dark green and rather friable in places. It is also generally well jointed. The lower section also consists of dolerite.

MEALL TUATH

There is former coastguard look out by the summit of this, the northern hill, which lies on the north-east side of the trench-like depression. The first few routes all lie on an impressive crag immediately to the east of the descent path below Meall Tuath. The routes are described from left to right when facing the crag.

1   The Red Barron Flies   HVS 4c   (1989)
This climb starts up a corner crack just left of the arete at the left-hand end of the crag. The rock should be treated with caution. Climb the crack, then turn the overhang by stepping right to reach a good stance and belay. Continue in the same line towards a notch in the skyline.

2   Opening Gambit   85m   E1   (1987)
This route takes a fairly obvious line of weakness on the left-hand end of the front face, where the dark coloured rock has a pocketed and rather crumbly appearance. An adventurous climb. Start at a groove containing a small pillar.
1. 25m   Move up and then right, and follow a groove with increasing difficulty to gain a good ledge.
2. 25m   From the right end of the ledge climb a steep corner-groove using the ribbon flake (apparently sound). Gain a ledge where the nature of the rock changes. Continue moving up, then trend left over easier ground to a good ledge.
3. 35m 5b   Make an exposed traverse right using the obvious hand break to gain a groove. Climb the chimney-groove until easier cracks can be gained. Step right into the corner, then go back left up a short crack until an easy ramp slants rightwards to finish.

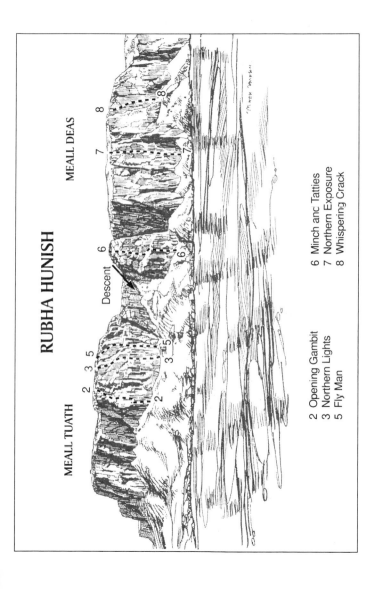

RUBHA HUNISH

MEALL TUATH

MEALL DEAS

Descent

2 Opening Gambit
3 Northern Lights
5 Fly Man

6 Minch anc Tatties
7 Northern Exposure
8 Whispering Crack

The next three routes lie parallel to each other on the right-hand half of the crag. They all start up steep corner grooves and finish up leftward-trending crack systems.

3   Northern Lights   70m   E2 ***   (1991)
This route starts up an obvious groove system just right of centre. On the face to its left at one third height is a long narrow roof. Start at a diamond-shaped block.
1. 15m 3c   Move up, then climb diagonally left across a grassy bay. Step left and move up to gain a groove and stance on the left side of a pinnacle. A rather loose and grassy approach pitch to the groove line proper.
2. 35m 5a   Move up onto the pinnacle and climb the crack-groove system above to the top of a large pinnacle. Continue up and step left awkwardly to exit the groove about 4m below a roof. Move up, then step right before climbing to the roof. Gain a handhold on a flat-topped block just below and right of the roof. Pull right into a corner-groove and ascend this for 3m until an exit left can be made. Continue up the groove directly above the overhang and pull over blocks onto a heathery ledge. Step up and left to a perfect eagle's nest stance and peg belay.
3. 20m 5c   Follow the leaning and tapering corner groove-ramp, which leads steeply leftwards to the top. A superb pitch.

4   Friends in the North   80m   E2 **   (1996)
This route lies right of the previous one, and finishes up the central of the three leftward-leaning crack systems. Fine climbing with plenty of exposure. Start at a diamond-shaped block as for Northern Lights.
1. 20 4a   Climb up to a rightward trending grassy ramp. Follow this to belay by a small pinnacle boss at the base of the corner crack proper.
2. 35m 5b   Climb the corner crack on excellent sandpaper rough rock. The fist jam crux at 15m may prove harder for those with smaller hands. Step right at the overlap and continue up the corner crack in the dark reddish rock, which terminates in a pinnacle column abutting the headwall. Step up and left to gain a ledge. Move left to belay on small friends in a short corner groove.
3. 10m 5a   Climb the short groove to gain a leftward traverse. Follow this easily to friend belays in a steep crack.
4. 15m 5b   Step left to gain the thin parallel cracks. Follow these up the wall past a heathery niche to finish up a short groove formed by a large block.

5   Fly Man   70m   E3   (1989)
This route completes the trio. It takes the prominent corner and
left-leaning flake-groove on the right-hand side of the crag. This is the
first significant line seen on the right from the descent path.
1. 40m 5b   Climb the initial corner and go past roofs on the right to
reach a stance at the foot of the flake.
2. 30m 5c   Continue strenuously up the flake to easier ground. A
serious pitch.

MEALL DEAS

The remaining routes lie to the south-west of the descent path, below
the rounded summit of the southern hill. The first route is reached by
leaving the descent path early on. Head downhill, then go round left
for a short distance to the base of a distinctive rock bastion.

6   Minch and Tatties   65m   E1 *   (1994)
A prominent left-facing corner is capped by a long roof, with a steeper
face above. Scramble and bridge up the grassy corner for 10m to a
stance by a big flake with a wide crack on its left side.
1. 20m 4b   Climb up trending right to reach a ledge just beyond the
right-hand end of the roof. Teeter right to reach a stance. After fixing a
belay on the wall, it is more comfortable to step down to a lower ledge.
2. 10m 4b   Traverse delicately back left above the lip of the roof and
continue left with the help of an amazing banister rail. Climb up to a
slanting shelf and belay by an obvious crack at the base of a steep
wall. These first two pitches can be run together if runners are clipped
carefully to avoid rope drag on the roof.
3. 35m 5b   Climb the crack, and where it splits slant left and up (crux)
to gain a small ledge. Continue more or less directly up flakes and
cracks and eventually slant right and back left to finish left of a roof. A
fine pitch in a superb position.

7   Northern Exposure   90m   E2 ***   (1993)
This excellent climb ascends the longest and most continuous section
of rock at Rubha Hunish. It lies over 100 metres south-west of the
previous route, and is reached by scrambling over boulders and grass
at the base of the cliff. There is a rib of rock a short distance to the right
of the start, after which the wall becomes noticeably reduced in height.
Start at the bottom of a great crack-groove line soaring up through a
sizeable double roof.

1. 30m 5a   Climb the discontinuous crack within a groove to a small overhang and foot ledge.

2. 50m 5b   A big pitch in every sense. Above the small overhang the crack becomes continuous and rises to an overlap guarding the deep hanging corner. This in turn rises to a double stepped roof. From the belay move into the crack and climb it with lots of determination. Some hard moves allow a little roof to be gained beneath the corner. Surmount this and follow the corner to the first stepped roof. Move over this to the top roof which extends 3m out from the face. Move out left across this and pull out strenuously and continue up to a great chockstone. Belay on top of this.

3. 10m 4c   Climb the wide crack directly above to a stake belay.

8   Whispering Crack   55m   E3 ***   (1989)
This route starts some distance right of Northern Exposure and climbs a prominent left-curving crack on a clean section of wall set at a higher level than the rest of the cliff. It is one of the most stunning lines on the island, and gives a remarkably sustained climb. The ground below the face is inaccessible to sheep and consequently flowers grow in profusion there in the warmer months. It is best to arrange a belay at the very the top of the route before climbing, using stakes well back from the cliff edge.

1. 10m 4b   Start on the left and climb up trending right to join the crack where it becomes better defined. Go up to a small ledge and take a semi-hanging belay on *in situ* pegs backed up with nuts.

2. 45m 5c   Climb the crack and gain a pod with difficulty (crux). The crack gives continuous interest above. Eventually reach a flake-ledge on the right wall, which proves surprisingly difficult to make good use of. Move left and continue with very little respite until the top is gained.

The remaining routes lie on the west side of the Trotternish peninsula.

BORNESKETAIG

The first few routes lie on the coast north of Bornesketaig, about 5km south-west of Duntulm. They are reached by turning off the road some 7km north of Uig. Follow signs for Camus More at first, then take the first turn on the right just before a cattle grid. Park at the end of the road.

THE ORGAN PIPES

Go down the field to the cliff top. On the left a pillar can be seen forming a natural arch with the main cliff. A sea-stack lies 100 metres further west. An easy descent can be made 50 metres further west again. The crags are rather vegetated and the only climbing done so far has been on the two features mentioned.

The Mitre   25m   Severe   (1984)
Climb cracks on the east face of the sea-stack. Keep to the left side of the face.

Mitre Groove   30m   E2 5b   (1992)
There is a prominent square-cut corner on the north corner of the stack. Gain it from the right and climb to its top. Move right onto a ledge and continue up the crack above to the rickety summit.

King Canute   50m   E2/3   (1984)
This takes the seaward face of the pillar that forms a natural arch.
1. 35m 5c   Climb the slender face to a peg runner. Move up awkwardly, then go round the right arete to a flake foothold. Climb up to good jugs.
2. 15m 4b   Climb the crack line to the top.

STACK OF SKUDIBURGH

This sea-stack lies just over 1km north-west of Uig. It can be reached easily from the shore below Dun Skudiburgh at virtually all states of the tide. Approach by skirting the southern flank of Creag Liath, then slant north-westwards down to the beach. The top section of the stack is rather loose.

Landward Face   25m   VS 4b   (1995)
Start at a prominent flat-topped boulder. A series of cracks lead slightly left to a loose finishing groove.

Seaward Face   20m   VS 4c   (1995)
Start at the foot of a left-facing corner where a pillar abuts the main stack. Follow jamming cracks to a loose finish.

Index of Routes

Note: Entries refer only to the pages on which route descriptions are given